THE NEW CANADA

Preston Manning

Macmillan Canada
Toronto, Ontario, Canada

Canadian Cataloguing in Publication Data

Manning, Preston, 1942.
The new Canada

Includes index.
ISBN 0-7715-9150-0

1. Manning, Preston, 1942-   . 2. Reform Party of
Canada.   3. Canada -
Politics and government - 1984-   .* I. Title.

JL197.R4M3 1992   324.271′0983   C91-095492-5

Excerpts from *Home Game* by Ken Dryden and
Roy MacGregor are used by permission of the
Canadian Publishers, McClelland & Stewart, Toronto.

Macmillan Canada
A Division of Canada Publishing Corporation
Toronto, Ontario, Canada

1 2 3 4 5 JD 95 94 93 92 91

Printed and bound in Canada by John Deyell Company

Contents

To the REFORMERS
Past, Present, and Future

AUTHOR'S PREFACE

The spring of 1987 was a time when new political forces—forces which would eventually end the Cold War, dismantle the Berlin Wall, and reorganize the Soviet Union—were stirring across eastern Europe and western Asia under the banner of Reform.

During that same spring, on the weekend of May 21-23, I was one of three hundred people from across western Canada who met at a conference in Vancouver to discuss a "reform program" for Canada.

The common issue that brought us together was a feeling of being left out of our own country. We felt that the West's constitutional concerns were never given the same priority by the national government as those of Quebec. Nor were the West's economic aspirations ever given the same priority as those of southern Ontario. We believed that the solution lay not in mere protest or threats of separation, but in developing a short list of constructive changes, that is, reforms, to the Canadian federal system and finding an appropriate political vehicle to promote that list in the federal political arena.

As a result of the discussions of that weekend, a convention was held in Winnipeg from October 30 to November 1, 1987. The purpose of that convention was to found a new federal political party called the Reform Party of Canada. The new party began with a membership list of less than three thousand. I was elected its first leader. Our motto was "The West Wants In."

The fledgling party grew. It participated in the 1988 federal election, finishing second in nine ridings. In 1989 the Reform Party elected two representatives to Parliament—MP Deborah Grey in a by-election in the federal constituency of Beaver River, and Canada's first democratically selected senator, Stan Waters. In 1990, the party experienced dramatic increases in membership and financial support, mainly in western Canada.

As more and more Canadians became aware of the new party's existence, its proposals for constitutional, fiscal, and parliamentary reform began to resonate across the country. Western Canadians had no monopoly on "feeling left out" of major aspects of Canadian life. Many Atlantic Canadians, northern Canadians, and people in northern and rural Ontario and Quebec also feel left out.

Aboriginals and other Canadians of neither English nor French extraction feel left out of a country whose politicians insist on defining it as an equal partnership of the English and the French. Meech Lake made many Canadians feel left out of the remaking of their own constitution.

And then there are the Canadians who feel "driven out." These include investors, entrepreneurs, professionals, workers, and shoppers who feel that Canada's spending and taxation levels are so high that they have to go to the United States.

Add to these the Canadians, mainly sovereigntists in Quebec, who "want out," because in their hearts they have already left Canada or were never really in it.

Whether "left out," "driven out," or "wanting out," Canadians are alienated from the life, politics, economy, and decision making of their own country, and Reformers began to see this as the one common characteristic shared by their compatriots from sea to sea. On the other hand, if there is a common aspiration with a potential for linking Canadians together in a new way, it is this: Canadians who are still committed to Canada "want in"—into the life, economy, culture, politics, and decision making of our own country.

In May 1991, a referendum was held among the fifty-five thousand members of the Reform Party in western Canada to determine whether the Party should expand from its original base to become a truly national party. Ninety-six percent of the votes cast in that referendum favoured expansion. In April 1991, for the first time, the Reform Party of Canada registered a higher level of public support in a national public opinion poll than the governing Progressive Conservatives.

As the party expanded, many Canadians realized that the Reform Party was likely to be a key player in federal politics in the 1990s and began to ask for information about the party platform, its origins, and myself as its leader. This book is a response to that demand.

The autobiographical section, Part One, was written somewhat reluctantly, as I am by nature a private person, uncomfortable with talking or writing about myself and my family. I understand all too well, however, that the great missing ingredient in federal politics today is trust and that

Canadians cannot be expected to have confidence in politicians they do not know.

People who take federal politics and the Reform Party seriously have asked, "Who are you and where are you coming from? What perspectives and experiences do you and your associates bring to the treatment of national issues? Why did you choose to create a new party rather than work within a traditional party? What has drawn you into federal politics at this time? What are your most deeply held values? Do you have a hidden agenda? Is there anything more to you and the Reform Party than the politics of protest?" These are appropriate questions, and in the first part of this book I have tried to answer them.

As membership in the Reform Party has grown to more than one hundred thousand, I have also felt an increasing obligation to provide more personal information to those who have joined us. There are thousands of people who, with very little knowledge of who I am or where I am coming from, have volunteered to work with me and for me to achieve political reform in Canada. I greatly value this support, but do not want such people to work under any illusions, or to be disappointed in the end because they had some misconceptions about my strengths and weaknesses. Part One may give such people a more realistic basis on which to assess my leadership capacities.

The sceptics, of course, will say that any political autobiography is self-serving and therefore not to be relied upon. An increasing number of books and articles, however, are being written on the Reform Party and myself from an unsympathetic and critical standpoint. Taken together with this book, which contains much information unavailable to others, the reader should be able to get a realistic perspective.

Part Two describes the history and growth of the Reform Party from its inception to the present, and the people who have put it together. Many of the names mentioned in this part will not be familiar to the media or the reader, just as the names of many of the people who are building the democratic reform movements in other countries are not as familiar as those of the politicians of the old political order. If the Reform Party succeeds in making a useful contribution to Canadian federal politics, it will be largely as a result of the efforts of these people, and their story deserves to be recorded. Since the Reform Party is still being built, especially in regions outside western Canada, Part Two will help those involved to learn from the mistakes, successes, and experiences of the people who contributed to the party's earliest development.

Part Two also records the evolution of the Reform Party's vision of a New Canada. Like Lord Durham long ago, we take as our starting point the perception that Canada is composed of two nations warring in the bosom of a single state. The "two nations" we see, however, are not French Canada and English Canada, but an Old Canada that is dying, and a New Canada that is struggling to be born.

The leaders of Canada's traditional federal parties continue to think of our country as "an equal partnership between two founding races, the English and the French"—a federation of founding peoples and ethnic groups distinguished by official bilingualism, government-supported multiculturalism, and government enterprise. Their approach to national unity is to grant special status to those Canadians who feel constitutionally or otherwise disadvantaged. This is Old Canada—and it has become "a house divided against itself."

Reformers seek a New Canada—a Canada which may be defined as "a balanced, democratic federation of provinces, distinguished by the sustainability of its environment, the viability of its economy, the acceptance of its social responsibilities, and the recognition of the equality and uniqueness of all its citizens and provinces." New Canada must include a new deal for aboriginal peoples and a new Senate to address the problem of regional alienation. New Canada must be workable without Quebec, but it must be open and attractive enough to include a New Quebec.

Part Three focuses on the roads to New Canada, in particular the steps required to get Canada's constitutional, fiscal, and parliamentary houses in order in the 1990s.

I make no apologies for the narrowness of the focus of Part Three. The items on which various interest groups want action by the national government are numerous and diverse—everything from greater environmental protection, to social concerns, to support for the arts and sciences, to a new role for Canada internationally. But as I have told audiences from one end of the country to the other, as long as our country is seriously divided, and divided by its own constitution; as long as the federal government and the economy are financially crippled by deficits, debt, interest payments, and excessive taxation; and as long as Parliament fails to adequately represent majority opinion on major issues, the federal government will be an ineffective instrument to address all the other demands we place on it. We seek, as Carl Sandburg once wrote of reformers during an especially turbulent period in American politics, "to link the tangled past to the uncertain future, by proposing only that which is workable in the immediate present."

Part Three concludes with an appeal to you, the reader, to make a decision. Do you and your children want to live in the Old Canada represented by the traditional federal parties? Or are you prepared to join with Reformers on the road to New Canada?

According to public opinion polls conducted in the fall of 1991, about 19 percent of the committed federal vote outside Quebec would go to Reform Party candidates in a federal election. If this support level remains constant or improves, the Reform Party could elect forty or more members to the next Parliament and become a major player in federal politics during the crucial decade of the 1990s.

The Reform Party, and myself as its leader, have an obligation to inform Canadians on how such a bloc of Reform members would use its influence in the next Parliament.

Finally, a word on the way this book has been written. As a management consultant for twenty years, my previous writing has been directed primarily to technical audiences and decision makers. In a business where you can be sued for errors in fact and misguided advice, there is a tendency to overqualify even the simplest statements. I have tried to resist this tendency, but it is difficult to break old communication habits, and parts of this book may contain more detailed backup material than readers are used to seeing in political writings.

Some of my friends and advisers have suggested that this book should be aimed primarily at the opinion leaders, pundits, and commentators who are the principal reviewers and critics of political ideas in Canada. My own inclination, however, has been to speak to the type of person who has taken the trouble to attend the hundreds of Reform meetings that have been held across the country over the past four years. These are rank-and-file, common-sense Canadians who are worried about their country. They want the assurance that political communicators like myself have consulted expert opinion on the major issues of the day. But they want the results reduced to short summaries of fact and proposals for action, and they want to hear anecdotes and illustrations relevant to their own experience.

I also want to assure the reader that, unlike many contemporary books by politicians, this one has not been ghost-written by someone else. Although I often rely on others for researching and editing background material, I believe it is important that the words and phrases chosen to express my positions be my own. I personally do not trust politicians whose communications are always crafted by others.

I specifically want to thank the following people for their encouragement and support in bringing this project to fruition:

- My wife Sandra, our children, my parents, and Sandra's parents for
  their inspiration and encouragement, and for reviewing the autobiographical section.
- Dr. John Redekop of Wilfrid Laurier University for his review of the
  section on the interface between faith and politics.
- Past and present members of the Reform Party's Executive Council—in
  particular, Diane Ablonczy, Gordon Shaw, Cliff Fryers, Neil Weir, and
  Elwin Hermanson—for their political and personal support and for
  reviewing the sections on the development of the party.
- Reform Party advisers and members of head office staff who assembled
  information or provided advice on key points, especially Bob Muir, Vic
  Burstall, Mel Smith, Ken Warenko, Ron Wood, and Virgil Anderson.
- Dale and Ginny Assmus for reviewing the material on the Yellowhead
  campaign, Deborah Grey for reviewing the material on the Beaver
  River by-election campaign, and the late Stan Waters for reviewing the
  material on the Alberta Senate campaign.
- Dr. Tom Flanagan, the Reform Party's Director of Policy, Strategy, and
  Communications, and Stephen Harper, the Reform Party's Policy
  Chief, especially for their help with Part Three.
- Jack and Daphne Pirie, Guil and Lillian Brett, Jack and Sheila Mackenzie, and the Political Science Department of the University of Calgary
  for providing me with "safe houses" where I could escape from the
  phones and the media to work on this project.
- Ron Besse and Denise Schon of Macmillan, and Philippa Campsie for
  her editorial skills.
- Jeanie Clemenger, my executive secretary for the past fifteen years, for
  her coordination of the background research and for typing and
  proofing the text.
- Others helped provide information, including David Berger, David
  Salmon, Bert Brown, Perry Kirkham, Reg Gosse, and Dennis Young.

Lastly, my sincerest thanks to the more than one hundred thousand
Canadians who have decided to become Reformers, without whom I
would still be a voice crying in the political wilderness of the Canadian
prairies.

Preston Manning
October 1991
Calgary, Alberta

PROLOGUE

Tributaries

High in the Rocky Mountains, east of Lake Louise, there is an olive-coloured lake from which flows a small stream.

That stream is so small you can easily wade across it, but it is moving, and therein lies its potential for growth and for influence.

Further along, that stream is joined by other streams and creeks. By the time it reaches the foothills, it has become a small river.

That small river cuts across the prairie—terrain very different from the mountain setting where the original stream had its beginnings. The small river joins another river, which in turn is joined by another.

Still further along, the larger river, now strong and powerful, cuts into the Canadian Shield. A tiny portion of it courses through great turbines generating electricity for Manitoba and the United States before it plunges into Hudson Bay to join the great northern ocean.

The political life of Canada may be likened to any one of our country's great river systems—the St. Lawrence, the Nelson, the Saskatchewan, the Fraser, the Mackenzie. And the political life and experiences of an individual or a party may be likened to that small lake and stream high in the Rockies which contribute their portion to the whole. The waters from a thousand different sources, many of them small and apparently insignificant—combine through an intricate network of streams and tributaries to form immense waterways that are capable of dividing, uniting, or otherwise shaping the landscape through which they move.

In Canada, the political landscape has been shaped by such traditional political forces as conservatism, liberalism, and socialism. It is also being significantly rearranged by other rivers of thought and action: nationalism, protectionism, regionalism, internationalism, trade liberalization, consumerism, environmentalism, and feminism.

The story of the birth and development of the Reform Party of Canada is linked to powerful forces—some new, some old—which will further shape the political topography of Canada in the 1990s. My own personal political story is just one tiny tributary of that larger stream.

If these stories will help you understand the origins and objectives of the Reform movement in Canada and encourage you to make your own unique contribution to federal politics in the 1990s, then the telling will have been well worth the effort.

In relating such stories, I hope to demonstrate that there are many people in this country whose viewpoints and perspectives on national issues differ from the conventional wisdom. These perspectives deserve a hearing, but they have had difficulty finding expression in the federal political arena through the traditional party structures. They are more likely to be voiced through a new political movement which is not hide-bound by conventional wisdom or fossilized ideologies, and which insists that bottom-up consultation with the rank and file of Canadians should be the starting point for improving public policy and establishing new directions for Canada.

My personal perspective on life and politics has been significantly influenced by a number of factors. These include my father's twenty-five-year involvement in politics as premier of Alberta, a personal decision at an early age to follow Christ, twenty years of adventures in the marketplace as a management consultant, primarily in the energy industry, and the practical demands and personal satisfactions of life at home with my wife Sandra and our five children.

My personal political convictions are rooted in the populist political traditions of western Canada. This tradition has produced a variety of new political movements over the last century, including the Progressive Party of Canada, the Social Credit Movement, and the Canadian Commonwealth Federation (CCF), which later became the New Democratic Party of Canada. It is a tradition characterized by the politics of regional alienation and concerted efforts to secure fundamental changes in the economic and political system by operating outside traditional political party structures and appealing to the common sense of the common people. It is also a tradition characterized by frequent attempts (with mixed results) to inject certain moral and spiritual values into the political arena.

In the West's historic search for fairness and equality within confederation, and the proposals for systemic change engendered by that search, there is something that should appeal to all Canadians who feel the need for greater fairness and balance in the actions and policies of the federal government.

In the West's attempts to balance the need for moral and spiritual values in the political arena with the need to safeguard majorities against the moral imperatives of religious and secular minorities, there are also lessons and strategies which should prove helpful to all Canadians as we prepare for the twenty-first century.

During my twenty years as a management consultant, I dealt with marketplace mechanisms for allocating scarce resources and developed alternative strategies for reconciling conflicting interests. I am convinced that on the national political level, such mechanisms and strategies could be used to help the next Parliament cope more effectively with the demands of fiscal responsibility, international competitiveness, and national reconciliation.

During periods of national stress Quebec and the West have had a historic propensity to generate new political movements—movements with populist dimensions, dedicated to systemic change, and operating outside the traditional party structures. In the current crisis, I see an opportunity emerging. It is an opportunity for you—whoever you are and wherever you live—to participate in the creation of a new political movement for Canada, through which your personal experience, your values, and your aspirations can be impressed upon the structures and actions of your national government in a new way.

I hope that this book may serve to open up your thinking to that possibility—a Reform movement for Canada, leading the way to a New Canada. In certain respects, that Reform movement will be like the democratic reform movements that have irreversibly altered East-West relations on the global scale and toppled parties whose insensitivity to the will of the people had become intolerable. At the same time, a Canadian Reform movement, rooted in more than a century of political experience in a free country tolerant of diversity, should have greater prospects for long-term success, and the potential to provide leadership to those for whom genuine democracy is still a distant ideal.

Part One

Personal Perspectives

CHAPTER ONE

Prairie Populism

In April 1935, in the midst of the Great Depression, thousands of Albertans—dirt-poor farmers, bankrupt businessmen, unemployed workers—joined together to launch a new provincial political party. By mid-May, they had established constituency associations in all sixty-three provincial ridings, and by the end of May had selected candidates to run in the next provincial election under the name "Social Credit." My father, Ernest C. Manning, aged twenty-six, was one of those candidates.

On August 22, 1935, the Alberta voters went to the polls. When the smoke cleared, the new party had elected fifty-six members. Every government-party candidate, including the premier and all his cabinet ministers, had been defeated.

This political phenomenon—illustrated by the rise of the Progressive and Social Credit movements in the 1920s and 1930s—is the political equivalent of a prairie fire. Its generic name is "democratic populism," and faith in its potential lies at the heart of my own political life and the formation of the Reform Party of Canada. From the day I was born to the day I left home to attend university, I lived in an environment shaped by the consequences of that political explosion on August 22, 1935.

As I grew up, I learned that the "prairie populism" with which I was familiar—the Social Credit movement in Alberta—was not an isolated political aberration, but part of a much broader political tradition.[1] That

1. People often ask me for a short list of books describing the western populist tradition and the emergence of alternative parties in Canada. References that I have found helpful are: C. C. Lingard, *Territorial Government in Canada* (Toronto: University of Toronto Press, 1946); W. L. Morton, *The Progressive Party in Canada* (Toronto: University of Toronto Press, 1950); John A. Irving, *The Social Credit Movement in Alberta* (Toronto: University of Toronto Press, 1959); S. M. Lipset, *Agrarian Socialism: The Cooperative Commonwealth Federation in Saskatchewan* (Berkeley, California: University of California Press, 1971); and Maurice Pinard, *The Rise of a Third Party: A Study in Crisis Politics* (Montreal: McGill-Queen's University Press, 1975).

tradition is as western as wheat, oil, forests, prairies, rivers, and mountains. But it also has its counterparts in the older regions of Canada, especially in Quebec, and in many other countries throughout the world.

Years later, I developed a more objective view of populism, including a healthy fear of its darker side and a more realistic assessment of its potential as an agent for political change. I compiled summaries for future reference of "lessons to be learned" from previous populist movements in western Canada, thinking they might come in handy should the phenomenon ever manifest itself again.

Somewhere along the line I also came to the conclusion that if I was ever to be personally involved in politics, I wanted to be involved in a genuine populist movement rather than a traditional political party. I also decided that, rather than getting in on the tail end of the populist movements produced on the Canadian prairies during the Depression, I would wait for the next one.

By 1986, there were signs that another populist movement was in the making in western Canada. When these signs were confirmed through consultations with others across the West, a number of us undertook to provide a new political vehicle through which that movement could express itself in the federal arena. That is how the Reform Party of Canada was born.

Because the Reform Party's roots are in the populist reform movements of western Canada, it is impossible to understand the party and my role in it without looking at the significance of those movements. In my particular case, this means reflecting on my father's experiences in politics and government.[2]

Born in 1908 in Carnduff, Saskatchewan, my father, Ernest Manning, was raised on a homestead near Rosetown, eighty-five miles southwest of Saskatoon. One Christmas, he and his brother Bill assembled a three-tube radio set they had ordered through a mail-order catalogue. Listening to that radio, my father became acquainted with the religious radio ministry of William Aberhart, a high school principal and Christian layman in Calgary, Alberta. Aberhart was a pioneer in the use of radio to communicate Christian teaching. His broadcasts were heard across western Canada in the 1920s and 1930s.

---

2. I cannot review here in any detail my father's political, legislative, and administrative adventures as premier of Alberta from 1943 to 1968. At present, no adequate reference book on this subject exists. For those interested in my father's recollections, the University of Alberta Archives has tape recordings and transcripts of interviews covering the period 1935-68.

As a result of listening to Aberhart, my father decided to leave the farm in 1927 to study at the Calgary Prophetic Bible Institute, Aberhart's training school. He was the school's first graduate and became Aberhart's assistant. Aberhart had an analytical mind and a genius for organization. My father also had an analytical mind and an administrative talent, which no doubt drew him to Aberhart's attention.

Moved by the deplorable economic and social conditions on the prairies during the Depression, Aberhart began to study the monetary reform proposals of Major C.H. Douglas, whose social credit theory was attracting some attention in Alberta. According to Douglas, poverty in the midst of plenty was caused by an inadequate supply and distribution of purchasing power in the hands of workers and consumers. He proposed that this inadequacy could be remedied by reforming financial institutions to finance consumption as well as production, and by expanding the money supply through the direct payment of "social dividends" to the people.

Before long, Aberhart was discussing social credit on his weekly radio broadcasts and his listeners began to be convinced that the idea would work. Eventually this led to the formation of more than 1,600 economic study groups across the West, primarily in Alberta.

These study groups formed constituency associations and ran candidates in the 1935 Alberta provincial election under the Social Credit banner. The provincial government of the day (the United Farmers of Alberta), weakened by scandal and the impossible task of coping with a 60 percent drop[3] in provincial income, was ripe for replacement.

And it was replaced. Every member of the government was defeated and fifty-six members of the new Social Credit group were elected, none of whom had ever sat in a legislature before. Among these new members was my father, who at twenty-six became the youngest cabinet minister (his portfolio was Trade and Industry) in the British Commonwealth since Pitt the Younger.

In 1936 my father married Muriel Preston. She had once worked as a legal secretary in Calgary in the office building where R.B. Bennett, not yet prime minister of Canada, had his law offices. She was an accomplished musician and played the piano on Aberhart's radio program. Through her involvement in church work in southern Alberta she had seen the ravages of the Depression first hand, visiting homes where

---

3. In 1928-29 the average-per-capita income in Alberta was $548. By 1933, it had declined to $212, a decrease of 61 percent. Source: *Report of the Royal Commission on Dominion-Provincial Relations: Canada, 1867-1939* (1940), Book I, p. 150.

"gopher stew" was on the menu and mothers made clothes for their children from flour sacks.

Her mother, Mary Hutchison, had come west from Ontario and married a musician named William Preston. She left him when my mother was very young, and took on schoolteaching assignments in various communities across the West during the 1920s to support herself and her daughter. My mother did not travel with her, but was raised at Catholic convents in Prince Albert and Calgary. It was the sisters at the Sacred Heart Convent in Calgary who taught her to play the piano. By the time she was sixteen she had achieved the proficiency of a concert pianist, with a degree from the Royal Academy of London.

My grandmother started to attend Westbourne Baptist Church in Calgary in 1923, where William Aberhart served as a lay teacher. She continued to go to his Bible classes when he established the Calgary Prophetic Bible Institute in 1927. Aberhart encouraged my mother's interest in sacred music and musical ministry, and recruited her as the pianist and musical director for his radio broadcast work. In certain respects, Aberhart took the place of her own father, and she probably knew him better—both his strengths and his weaknesses—than my father did. It was William Aberhart who "gave her away" at her wedding.

It has always surprised me that none of the journalists or academics who have written about William Aberhart ever interviewed my mother in depth concerning him. She has met and observed more provincial and federal politicians than most people are ever likely to meet, and she is a shrewd judge of character. I once asked her, for example, about Aberhart's legendary indifference to criticism. In the rough and tumble of Depression-era politics, he had been branded by his political opponents (especially the Liberals) and by the media as everything from a fascist rabble rouser to a religious fanatic on a par with Rasputin. But Aberhart could give as good as he got. He particularly loathed the Southam Press because the editorialists (although not the street reporters) of the big dailies in Calgary and Edmonton sided with the political and business elites against the common people during the Depression. He considered this an indelible stain on their journalistic record, which no amount of editorial hand washing after the fact could ever erase.

My mother confirmed that Aberhart had "the hide of a rhinoceros" when it came to absorbing and deflecting criticism. But there was one occasion when that hide was pierced by an unlikely dart hurled from an unexpected quarter.

Aberhart always considered himself an educator first and a politician second. So when the Alberta government faced bankruptcy in the late 1930s, and some of the province's MLAs wanted to reduce funding for the University of Alberta (most of whose faculty were hostile to the new "peasant" government), Aberhart beat them down with characteristic vigour. Gradually the university administration began to realize that in Aberhart they had a friend of higher education, and this made for a great improvement in relations between the university and the government.

In 1941, the president of the University of Alberta, Dr. W.A.R. Kerr, told Aberhart that the university would like to offer him an honorary degree and that he would be invited to give the spring convocation address that year. According to my mother, no honour—including that of being sworn in as Alberta's seventh premier—touched Aberhart as deeply. He even prepared his acceptance speech well in advance of the convocation date, a departure from his usual practice.

But Aberhart's honorary degree was never conferred. The university Senate, which had to approve the granting of honorary degrees and which usually simply ratified the recommendations of its committee on honorary degrees, refused to give the go-ahead. Liberal members of the Senate, still smarting from their electoral defeats at Aberhart's hands, could not bring themselves to be magnanimous toward their old foe.[4]

President Kerr resigned in disgust over the incident, which the *Edmonton Bulletin* described as a "despicable trick" and a "tactless fiasco" rooted in the "mean machinations of little men." Aberhart pretended to shrug it off, but my mother knew him well enough to understand that this was one barb that really did get through.

Years later she showed me the copy of his undelivered convocation address, which she had somehow acquired and kept. I was attending the University of Alberta at the time and vowed that some day, if I had any influence with my alma mater, I would try to persuade it to award the degree posthumously and hang it on the wall under Aberhart's portrait in the Legislature Building across the river.

After all, it is a Canadian custom first to vilify unique political actors (such as Riel and Haultain), and then to rehabilitate them about seventy-five years after their death. In about twenty-five more years, Aberhart's transformation from rabble rouser to statesman will no doubt begin, and the posthumous awarding of his degree would be a good start.

---

4. Source: Walter H. Johns, *A History of the University of Alberta from 1908 to 1969* (Edmonton: University of Alberta Press, 1981), pp. 162-70.

In 1943, William Aberhart died in office and my father succeeded him as premier, a post he was to hold for the next twenty-five years. Altogether, my father held a seat in the provincial legislature for thirty-three years, until his retirement in 1968.

During his long tenure in public office, my father held a variety of cabinet posts besides that of premier. These included provincial secretary, minister of trade and industry, minister of mines and minerals (Alberta's petroleum ministry), provincial treasurer, and attorney general. He later served in the Canadian Senate from 1970 to 1983.

My father gained experience in governmental responsibility in a variety of economic and social climates, including the Depression, the period of wartime restraint, the postwar resource boom that began with the discovery of the Leduc oilfields in 1947, and the broadening of Alberta's social, cultural, economic, and population base during the 1950s and 1960s. During his time in office, he saw the budget of the government of Alberta go from an annual expenditure of $17 million in 1935 ($9 million of it consisting of debt-service charges), to almost $700 million in 1968-69. He also became personally acquainted with all the Canadian prime ministers from Arthur Meighen to Joe Clark, and had extensive dealings in the area of federal-provincial relations with the King, St. Laurent, Diefenbaker, and Pearson administrations.

I was born on June 10, 1942, in Edmonton, so for all of my childhood and until I was twenty-six, my father headed the provincial government and led the Social Credit Party of Alberta. As I was growing up, I got some unique insights into the inner workings of a provincial government, its relations with the federal government, and the trials and triumphs of a populist political movement born out of western frustration and alienation.

My father—the premier who always carried at least one other cabinet portfolio, the Christian layman, the radio preacher, and the farmer—was always working. His idea of recreation was to change from one type of work to another. From him I inherited my own inclination and ability to work long and hard.

Our relationship during my childhood was distant but harmonious. I greatly admired his speaking ability, and even as a youngster used to take notes of his political speeches and sermons. We spent more time together and got to know each other better after he retired from provincial politics and we were able to work together on various consulting projects.

The home my parents lived in when I was born was a small white bungalow on the corner of 82nd Street and 112th Avenue in Edmonton.

I remember nothing about it except that we had a large St. Bernard dog there, named Monty. When I was six, we moved to a green and white two-storey house on 112th Street just across from the University Hospital in Edmonton's Garneau district. Our neighbours were Mr. and Mrs. Wensel and their family on the one side, and Mr. and Mrs. Fry (Mr. Fry was then mayor of Edmonton) on the other.

When I reached school age, I went to Garneau Public School, just across the North Saskatchewan River from the Legislature Building at the south end of the High Level Bridge. Midway through grade six, we moved to a farm a few miles east of the city along the river, but my father took me into town with him every day for the rest of the year, so I could finish my grade at Garneau. Whenever possible, I would walk across the bridge to have lunch with him. After school, I would sometimes read or do homework in a small side office next to his while I waited for him to drive home.

In those days, most of the cabinet had lunch in a small room off the main cafeteria in what was then called the Administration Building (now the Haultain Building). I was shy, but gradually came to know some of the ministers—Gordon Taylor, the highways minister who knew every trail and pothole in Alberta; Bob Jorgeson, the welfare minister who supervised the building of fifty senior citizens' homes across Alberta for the Jubilee year of 1955; Harry Strom, the agriculture (and later municipal affairs) minister who would one day succeed my father as premier; Anders Aalborg, the provincial treasurer; and Dr. W. W. Cross, the minister of health.

Dr. Cross especially intrigued me because I knew he had been minister of health and welfare during the Depression, and I had heard many stories about how he had attempted to cope with the overwhelming demands of that tragedy at a time when the government could not even afford to pay its own secretarial staff. The minister himself was often directly involved in dispensing aid, but to take a "handout" from the government was considered the ultimate in humiliation by many of Alberta's ruggedly independent farmers. Doc Cross's task was to provide help without adding to that humiliation.

On one occasion when a desperate farmer, hat in hand, came to see him, Doc told him he had his nerve coming for help when so many of his neighbours were in far worse shape. The farmer bristled, his listless eyes sparkling with anger. He told Doc he wouldn't take a dollar from him if he was the last source of help on earth, and he stomped out of the office. Doc watched him go, then sent his deputy scurrying after the farmer to give him the help he needed. The farmer got his assistance, but did not "lose face" in the process. The next time they met, he was still able to look Doc in the eye.

Dr. Cross had practised medicine in the Hanna district of east-central Alberta, one of the areas most seriously hit by the drought and crop failures of the 1930s. Few of his patients could afford to pay him, but he continued to serve them anyway. When he was elected to the Legislature in 1935, it was said that he simply destroyed his account books and went on to serve his people as an MLA and cabinet minister. For months after he moved to Edmonton, however, baskets containing baked goods or eggs or chickens would occasionally be found outside his office door, as former patients attempted to repay their doctor in kind.

When I was twelve we moved to a ranch-style house that my parents had designed themselves on our farm east of Edmonton along the banks of the North Saskatchewan River. I attended a rural high school, Horse Hills High School, and lived and worked on the farm (we milked seventy head of dairy cows) until I completed university. My father was known in the community as "the Mr. Manning who runs the dairy farm in the valley, and goes into town to run the government during the week."

Like Louis St. Laurent, my father kept his public life completely separate from his family life. Home was a place where he and my mother escaped from the public and the media, and the public and the media were never invited in.

This is not to suggest that my parents insulated themselves from the public; far from it. After William Aberhart's death, my parents continued his radio broadcast, and in connection with his government, political, and religious work, my father carried on a correspondence of 50 to 250 letters a week for fifty-five years (from 1935 to 1990). He also attended innumerable public and private meetings and gave hundreds of speeches.

During all his years in public life, my father's name and home phone number were always listed in the telephone directory. And people used it! My mother often said that if she had kept a journal of the phone calls received at home, especially some of the peculiar ones, she could have written a bestseller.

My father held two beliefs that made him extremely open, even vulnerable, to the public. One was his view that he had an obligation as premier to listen to any Albertan who wanted access to the government. This sometimes exasperated my mother, who would say, "Ernest, why are you spending time listening to that person?" My father would most often respond mildly, "But Muriel, he (or she) is a resident of Alberta." The second belief that reinforced this openness was his Christian conviction that every human being, no matter how flawed or unattractive, was a creature made in the image of God. You couldn't write anyone off, because God hadn't written anyone off.

The greatest sorrow our family faced during my growing-up years had to do with the health of my older brother Keith. At birth, he had been the victim of oxygen deprivation, which had destroyed part of his brain. He suffered from epileptic seizures, coordination problems, and arrested mental development all his life until his death in 1986 at the age of forty-seven. Keith was unable to attend school, but my grandmother Preston, the former schoolteacher, who lived near us for a number of years in Edmonton, carefully and painstakingly taught him to read. This proved to be a great source of enjoyment to him throughout his life.

My parents did everything possible to discover some medical advance that would help him. They consulted Dr. Wilder Penfield of the Montreal Neurological Institute, who was then doing some of his pioneer mapping of the human brain. Penfield was able to suggest a drug therapy to help control Keith's seizures. Dr. Walter Mackenzie, dean of medicine at the University of Alberta, recommended a special school in upstate New York which Keith attended for a number of years.

Progress in drug and educational therapy later made it possible for Keith to function more normally and he returned to Alberta and lived for many years at the special school for disabled adults known as the Red Deer School Hospital. Still later, he lived in a group home in Edmonton and participated in a sheltered workshop program operated by the Western Industrial Research Centre.

In the early 1980s he moved to the McGugan nursing home in Edmonton, where he met Marilyn Brownell, who was also a resident of the home. They decided to marry, and their three years together before he died of a brain tumour were the most contented of his life.

Besides his reading, the other thing in Keith's life was his faith in God. In many respects his faith was childlike, yet it somehow gave a meaning and a purpose to his existence which nothing else could do. Most of the friends he had—his real friends—were people he had met at church. It was they who took him to dinner, invited him to their homes, remembered his birthdays, attended his wedding, and genuinely grieved at his funeral. Anyone who feels that faith has no role to play in the treatment of the seriously ill and the permanently handicapped—in giving hope and meaning in situations where rationality alone is unable to give hope and meaning—should have met my brother Keith.

As a child, I did not really understand the emotional and financial strain that Keith's handicap put on my parents. The most my father ever received in pay as premier of Alberta was $18,000 a year, plus the sessional indemnity of $7,000 per year that was paid to each MLA. Keith's special care, particularly at the residential school in New York, stretched the family budget to the limit.

I also suffered from the fear when we were out together that Keith would have a seizure. This happened frequently enough to make me apprehensive on every occasion that we went somewhere as a family. When I was younger, I also resented the fact that Keith could not play ball or hockey when I wanted someone to play with. He too resented the fact that he was not physically able to participate in the games and activities in which I took part so easily.

As we both grew older and his condition improved under drug therapy and other treatment, our relationship became less strained. But when people speak to me about the special problems and challenges of living with and caring for the handicapped, I know exactly what they mean. Recognizing that there is still much to be done, I also cannot help but marvel at the enormous progress that has been made since the 1950s and 1960s in recognizing the needs and potential of physically and mentally disabled persons.

All in all, my parents' home provided me with both the security and the freedom necessary to make my way in life. My parents, who are in their eighties now, have always been my staunchest supporters in everything I've done, including the decision to participate in the creation of the Reform Party of Canada.

In the 1950s and 1960s, the media generally respected a politician's desire to keep his public life and family life separate. As long as the politician did not try to exploit his family for political purposes (here is my attractive wife, vote for me; here is my lovely family, vote for me; here is our devoted family dog, vote for me), the media left the family alone. As a result, the fact that my father was premier of Alberta and heavily involved in politics (nine provincial general elections, numerous by-elections, and various federal elections) had little direct impact on my childhood or adolescence.

At school, the subject of my father's occupation hardly ever came up, except perhaps immediately after the opening of the Legislature. In those days, the opening of the new legislative session was followed by a reception featuring copious quantities of very small and delicate

sandwiches. During the week after the opening I took leftovers of those
sandwiches to school in my lunch bag. It was always a source of
wonderment to my friends at school why anyone would go to the trouble
of hacking up perfectly good sandwiches into such small pieces.

My father's work as premier had both an administrative and a political
side. My exposure to the political side came through Orvis Kennedy, who
was the president of the Alberta Social Credit League and a family friend.
Orvis was a master of grassroots political organization and promotion,
but it was his personal integrity that made him such an invaluable asset to
my father.

The people of Alberta have never been told how much they owe Orvis
Kennedy—not so much for what his political work accomplished, but for
what his personal integrity prevented. Very few North American political
parties that have been in power during an oil boom have managed to
avoid the corruption that comes so easily with such a sudden explosion of
wealth and power. It was the honesty of Orvis Kennedy—and hundreds of
others like him in official capacities in the governing political party and
the civil service—that prevented Alberta from experiencing the types of
scandals that plagued the early days of the oil industry in Texas, Okla-
homa, and Louisiana. For the most part, Kennedy and his contemporaries
had entered politics and government in the Depression, out of a concern
for public service rather than financial gain, and it was this motivation
that tended to inoculate them against the many temptations that later
accompanied the resource boom.

Although I was familiar with the political side of my father's job, it was
the government side in which I showed more personal interest and into
which I was given opportunities to gain some insight.

The Alberta premier's office has been renovated and rearranged numerous times over the last three decades. But in the late 1950s, you
entered the premier's office through a reception area separated from the
waiting area by a wooden railing and a gate. Behind the railing and gate
were my father's two secretaries, Dorothy Hope and Jessie Pirie, who
were sometimes referred to as "the dragons at the gate." To one side of
the waiting area was another office occupied by his executive secretary,
Peter Elliot, and later by Russ Shepherd.

Inside the premier's office itself, there were a few chairs and a couch
and a large desk at the east end of the room. To the right of the desk (to
the visitor's left), there was a large built-in safe with a walk-in door, and
two lights above it, a red one and a green one. To the right of the safe was
the door to a small side office sometimes used by extra secretarial help or
for special projects.

To a child, the safe was intriguing, as it was to most visitors. If you entered it, you were supposed to put on the red light, and when you left you were supposed to put on the green light, to prevent someone from being entombed. At first I believed that this was where the government kept the "oil money," and I was disappointed to learn that it was only used to store papers and old recordings from Aberhart's radio broadcasts.

In those days, the premier and cabinet would meet personally with every major provincial association and interest group before the spring session. Whenever I could persuade my father to "take me to the office," I would do my homework in the little side office to the right of the safe. I would sometimes leave the door slightly ajar and listen in on some of these meetings between small groups and the premier. My father tolerated this up to a point, but prepared me with those words: "These are good people. They have many interesting things to say, and they will say them well. But if you will listen closely, you will always hear the distinctive sound of 'the grinding of an axe.'"

Years later, I became much more familiar with interest-group politics and have come to regard the representation and reconciliation of conflicting interests as the chief function of the contemporary politician. My first exposure to this phenomenon, however, was as a schoolboy, sitting in that side office straining to hear "the grinding of an axe."

During this same period I got my first exposure to law. Although my father was not a lawyer, for some time he handled the portfolio of attorney general. He tended to have a somewhat different view of law from that of lawyers, and it wasn't until many years later that I understood the nature of this difference. My father's view of law was first and foremost that of a legislator—someone who makes law—and secondly that of a public executive and administrator—someone who implements legislation.

While he was premier, Alberta did not have a Hansard to record the speeches in the Legislature. It was his view that the product of the Legislature was not speeches, but laws. If you wanted to find out what the Alberta Legislature had done last year, it was all there in one volume, namely the Statutes of Alberta for that year.

At a fairly early age, therefore, I received some exposure to the law—but from the legislator's perspective. I somehow acquired my own sets of the *Revised Statutes of Alberta* and the *Revised Statutes of Canada,* and during my last years in high school and first years in university, I "read law."

While this may strike some readers as bizarre—what could be duller and drier than reading statute books, particularly if you have no intention of becoming either a politician or a lawyer—to me it was not. From my father's perspective, a statute was not a dead, dry piece of paper.

Behind every statute there was a story—of real people, tangled interests, political pressures, administrative adventures—of which the statute was the end product and paper record. It was the business of legislators in a democratic system to know those stories, to ask certain questions which the legislative draughtsman or solicitor or administrator may never ask, and to learn to distinguish between a good law and a bad law.

For example, I once came across the Gas Export Act (full title: "An Act to Permit the Temporary Export of Gas to Montana for Essential Defence Production," 1951)—not exactly a scintillating piece of literature. I was about seventeen at the time, and asked what this was all about. From my father, the legislator, came the story.

One day during the Korean conflict, he had received a telephone call from C.D. Howe, the legendary federal minister of trade and commerce who had played such a prominent role in organizing the production side of Canada's contribution to World War II. (Howe and my father knew each other fairly well, Howe sometimes addressing him as "Brother Manning," a gentle dig at my father's religious convictions and activities as a lay preacher.) Howe was calling to ask the Alberta government to rush a bill through the Legislature to permit the construction of a natural gas pipeline from Alberta to a copper mine in Montana. Howe had been advised by his counterpart in the American government that the output of the copper mine was needed to support the war effort in Korea, and to hear Howe tell it, the future of the free world depended on that bill getting through the Alberta Legislature immediately.

Howe's request created some difficulties for the Alberta government. It had been criticized for allowing pipelines to be built helter-skelter in the pioneer days of Alberta's oil and gas industry, and was in the process of establishing regulatory mechanisms to impose order and discipline on the process. But Howe wanted the pipeline approved now, and the only way to do so was by special statute.

Reluctantly, my father agreed to see what he could do. The Gas Export Act was subsequently drafted, debated, and passed, but not without generating justifiable political flak, even from government MLAs who objected to bypassing, with unseemly haste, the government's own regulatory system.

After citing the urgency of the war effort as the reason for rushing the bill through, the government then suffered considerable embarrassment when the pipe lay beside the ditch for months because of unforeseen delays in approvals by United States regulatory authorities. By the time the pipeline was completed, the war was over.

In retrospect, the interesting thing to me in all of this was that the Gas Export Act case was a preview of the great Canadian pipeline debate, which rocked the Canadian Parliament a few years later and contributed directly to the defeat of the St. Laurent government. Once again, C.D. Howe—the man who got things done—was in a hurry, this time to build the huge Trans-Canada Pipeline to carry western gas to central Canada and the United States. But this time, the attempt to move precipitately created enough political flak to topple a government.

By listening to the stories behind the bills going through the Alberta Legislature and assimilating the lessons to be learned from them, I developed my own list of questions that a legislator in a democratic society should be expected to ask.

These included: What is the story behind this bill? Who really wants it? Who is affected, and how? Should the legislature or the parliament even be considering this bill—that is, is there someone else who could or should be doing what this legislation calls upon the state to do? Does the legislature or parliament have the constitutional authority to pass this legislation? Does this bill clearly express the will of the legislature or parliament? (If not, the legislature or parliament is surrendering power to the courts who will be called upon to interpret it.) Is this legislation administratively feasible? What are the economic and social ramifications of this legislation? What is the likely environmental impact? (This question wasn't added to my list until 1970.) Is this bill fair? That is, what are its moral and ethical implications, if any? What is the regional distribution of costs and benefits? What are the political implications? What will this legislation cost, and who pays? Can we afford it? What is the view of expert opinion on this legislation? What is the view of my constituents and the electorate at large on this legislation? How could this legislation be improved? How should I vote with respect to this legislation?

All of these questions, and the establishment of a legislative system for ensuring that they are systematically asked and answered, are vitally important if you believe—as most populists do—that the elected representatives of the people ought to have a direct and meaningful role in making laws.

In Canada, unfortunately, the assumption of the law-making function by the executive, bureaucratic, and judicial arms of government, combined with the exercise of excessive party discipline in parliament, has reduced the average MP to merely rubber-stamping the legislative proposals of others. One of the principal objectives of the Reform Party is to revitalize the role of the elected member in the legislative process. Suffice it to say here, however, that my personal interest in the art and science of legislating goes back to my youthful days of reading law and listening to the stories that made those laws live.

Through other contacts and associations to which I was exposed through my father's political and governmental work I began to realize that the Social Credit movement in Alberta was part of a wider phenomenon.

I learned, for example, that one of the first acts of the Social Credit government in the 1930s had been to deal with the recommendations of a commission established by the United Farmers' government to look at Métis land claims. These claims had a history that stretched back to the mid-nineteenth century and were directly connected to the populist movement that led to the Riel Rebellion of 1870.

Under the Social Credit government, the Métis Population Betterment Act established a number of Métis colonies throughout the province, and brought the government into regular contact with various Métis leaders. Some of these leaders, such as Adrien Hope of the Kikino Colony, tended to think of Louis Riel as "the first western Reformer"—the man who in 1870, against all odds, organized and led a grassroots uprising of Métis people and had the province of Manitoba created on terms and conditions quite different from those favoured by the federal government and the Liberal and Conservative parties of the day.

They would tell the story of how the Dominion Land Survey crew once attempted to cross the land of Louis Riel's cousin near the Red River Settlement in Manitoba. Louis, backed by a group of younger Métis, reportedly placed his foot on the surveyors' chain and declared, "This is our land"—the first confrontation between the West and the new federal government over resources. Some of my Métis friends jokingly refer to the Reform movement as "the third Riel Rebellion."

Another important populist, who has been neglected by the history books, was Sir Frederick Haultain. While my father was the youngest cabinet minister in the provincial government of 1935, his deputy minister at Trade and Industry, a man named Edward Trowbridge, was the oldest deputy and was nearing retirement after more than thirty years of public service. Trowbridge, who also taught my father to play golf, had known and assessed every premier of Alberta and Saskatchewan from 1905 to 1935 and could remember the days when he had been a clerk in the old North West Territories government when Haultain was president of the executive council (from 1897 to 1905).

Many westerners who lived through the transition from territorial to provincial status considered Haultain to be the greatest statesman the West has ever produced—on a par with Sir John A. Macdonald and Sir Wilfrid Laurier. It was Haultain who led the Autonomy Movement that eventually resulted in the creation of the provinces of Alberta and Saskatchewan. It was also Haultain who argued, unsuccessfully in the end, that if the prairie politicians would conduct themselves as "Big Westerners" rather than "Little Westerners" (narrow provincialists), they would insist on the West remaining "One Big Province" with enough size and weight to achieve equality with the central Canadian provinces of Ontario and Quebec. Although Haultain's memoranda to the federal government on constitutional reforms are among the most eloquent and logical expressions of western demands for equality that have ever been penned, Haultain was later forgotten except by men like Eddie Trowbridge.

Until recently, very little has been written about this remarkable Canadian, and until the mid-1970s all I knew about him was based on political hearsay. I do, however, remember looking at his formal portrait on a fourth-floor wall of the Alberta Legislature Building. What made it stand out from all the other formal portraits of long-gone premiers and speakers in their black robes was the cigarette in his hand. He looked like René Lévesque in a choir gown.

Haultain and the political movement he led represented another important link in the chain of western populist movements, which I was beginning to regard as my political heritage. The next link in that chain was provided by the Progressive Party of Canada. In certain respects, the Progressives have perhaps been the most successful third party to emerge on the Canadian federal scene during this century.

On February 26, 1920, eleven members of the Canadian Parliament, all associated with the agricultural reform movement that had been growing in Canada over the previous decade, met in caucus and formally constituted themselves the National Progressive Party. They were encouraged and supported in this initiative by thousands of Canadians who wanted fundamental reforms in agricultural policy, tariff policy, transportation policy, and the operations of Parliament itself.

On June 27, 1921, the new party won a crushing by-election victory in the federal constituency of Medicine Hat, Alberta, where Robert Gardiner, an unknown farmer candidate, defeated well-known Liberal and Conservative candidates by a margin of 9,765 votes.

In the federal general election later that same year, the new party, not yet two years old, elected sixty-five members to the House of Commons, displacing the federal Conservatives as the second-largest group in the House, and forcing the minority Liberal government to embrace key elements of the Progressive platform.

The United Farmers of Alberta (UFA) was the provincial counterpart to the federal Progressive Party of Canada. The Social Credit movement and the UFA were bitter rivals during the 1935 provincial election, but my father and other Social Credit leaders respected the accomplishments of the United Farmers and the Progressives and the tradition they represented. Although the UFA ceased to be a political party after 1935, we bought farm supplies from the UFA store in North Edmonton, and I was often reminded that "these people used to run the government of Alberta."

Ask any informed Alberta audience, "What one constitutional amendment in the twentieth century has benefited the prairie provinces more than any other?" and after a little murmuring someone will shout out, "The Natural Resources Transfer Agreement of 1930"—a legacy of the Progressives.

This agreement was the constitutional amendment that belatedly transferred the ownership of natural resources, including oil and gas, from the federal government to the prairie provinces. The transfer should have occurred at the time Manitoba, Saskatchewan, and Alberta were created as provinces had they been treated equally with the older provinces of Canada, but did not occur until twenty-five years later. Because of this amendment, the royalties from oil and gas from Leduc and other petroleum reservoirs in Alberta flowed to the Alberta government in Edmonton rather than to the federal government in Ottawa.

While this constitutional amendment was actually negotiated between the King government and the provincial governments of the three prairie provinces, both the federal Liberals and the Conservatives had been forced to declare themselves in support of the measure as a result of unrelenting pressure applied by the Progressives in the federal Parliament and on the hustings during the 1920s.

When my father was provincial treasurer, another portfolio that he held for ten years, he sometimes sat at the kitchen table, checking the budget figures with an adding machine. After Leduc, whenever Alberta treasurers added up the revenue column in the provincial budget, they would murmur a short prayer of thanks for the Natural Resources Transfer Agreement and a generation of Progressive politicians who fought so hard to secure it. Because of the success of new parties like the Progressives in the 1920s (and the CCF-NDP in the 1950s and 1960s) in forcing the traditional federal parties to adopt policies that they would otherwise have rejected, knowledgeable westerners simply do not believe Liberal and Conservative spokesmen when they claim that "a vote for a new party is a wasted vote." Just as Alberta had embraced Social Credit as a new political alternative during the Depression, a few years later Saskatchewan embraced the Canadian Commonwealth Federation (CCF) under Tommy Douglas.

Although the Social Credit Party called for a complete reform of the capitalist system and the CCF originally called for its abolition and replacement by socialism, the one thing the two movements had in common was their populist roots. My father would point out that the very same type of people who brought Social Credit to power in Alberta (farmers, teachers, ministers, the unemployed) had helped bring the CCF to power in Saskatchewan. For this reason, he and Tommy Douglas had more in common with each other than with the Liberal or Conservative leadership in either province.

At this point I should make clear that most of my knowledge of the western populist tradition had been obtained by listening to the stories or reading the first-hand accounts of those who had been deeply involved in these movements. It wasn't until I got through university that I began to examine some of the formal literature on these movements. Some of this, particularly treatises on western populism written by distant academics with no respect for the people involved, had little to do with my own understanding of populism. I began to understand how the Indians and Métis—people with an oral tradition—feel when they read some explanations of their culture, history, and politics, written by people who have never lived what they are describing.

As I grew older, however, I began to evaluate more critically the political parties and movements with which I was generally familiar, and to put them in some sort of perspective. What were their strengths and weaknesses? What were the lessons to be learned that might be of relevance to the future? If one could have been a consultant to Riel, or Haultain, or Woodsworth, or Aberhart, or Douglas—what might one, with the benefit of hindsight, have advised them to do differently?

In starting to think this way I was indirectly assisted by a lawyer in Edmonton named Bill Simpson who handled my father's personal legal affairs. Simpson had known every Alberta premier from Alexander Rutherford (the first one) to Peter Lougheed, and had some shrewd observations to make on their relative strengths and weaknesses.

One year, while I was still in high school, Simpson presented our family with Will and Ariel Durant's ten-volume *Story of Civilization*. My father didn't have the time to read the massive work, but I did, and over the next three years plodded through all ten volumes. As I read, I developed the view that everyone with political interests should be required to examine "the dark side of the moon." By this I mean the negative side (or downside) of whatever political philosophy one finds attractive, whether it be liberalism, conservatism, socialism, nationalism, or populism.

Years later, as a consultant, I would sometimes encounter zealous ideologues of both the right and the left. I would suggest that they temper their enthusiasms by examining how the dark side of their own philosophy could be carried to extremes by unbalanced leaders.

To conservatives I recommended a serious reading of *The Politics of Cultural Despair* by Fritz Stern, a treatise on how conservative ideologues in the 1920s inadvertently prepared the way for Hitler and the rise of fascism. And to over-zealous socialists I recommended Solzhenitsyn's *The Gulag Archipelago,* or stories about the atrocities committed by Pol Pot in the killing fields of Cambodia, to get a feel for socialism run amok.

In the case of Depression-era politics in Alberta, the dark side of populism with which my father had to contend was its potential to be misdirected into racism. Some key people within the Social Credit movement, for example, traced the ills of the Depression not simply to the defects of the system but to the activities of particular ethnic groups (such as the "Jewish financiers") whom they believed to be controlling and manipulating the financial system.

It took my father and others almost twenty years to root anti-semitism out of the Alberta Social Credit movement. Eventually he and his colleagues were largely successful—a fact that was acknowledged by the Israeli government on his visits to that country and by the Canadian Jewish community when he was later awarded the B'nai Brith Humanitarian Award in 1982. But this success was achieved only as a result of considerable effort and diligence over a period of years.

If there is a lesson to be learned from the Social Credit Depression experience, it is that an ounce of prevention is worth ten pounds of cure. If a new political movement can prevent extremism of any kind, particularly racism, from taking root in the first place, it will save itself and members of minority communities an infinite amount of trouble later on.

In October 1990, in an address to Jewish community leaders in Calgary (copies of this address are available from the Reform Party's head office), I elaborated on some of the measures currently employed by the Reform Party to protect itself from racial extremists. These include the adoption of racially neutral policies on the constitution, immigration, and multiculturalism; use of a candidate questionnaire which inquires into the views and past associations of potential candidates on racially sensitive issues; the use of grassroots "moderators" at public meetings to counter-act extreme expressions of opinion; and statements by the party leader-ship to distance it from policy proposals and ideas with a potential for racism.

If a revival of grassroots democratic populism is to be a characteristic of the revitalization of Canadian federal politics in the 1990s, especially in Quebec and the West, it is of primary importance that its leaders be well versed in ways and means of preventing populism from developing racist or other extremist overtones. (This, of course, is also the number-one challenge facing those attempting to lead the reform movements of eastern Europe and the Soviet Union.)

On the positive side, I became convinced that while populist move-ments have a potential for extremism that must be constantly shunned, they also have the potential to moderate ideologues. It is significant that the general population of Alberta and Saskatchewan—the real grass roots—would never permit the ideologues in the Social Credit or CCF movements to implement their theories as much as they would have liked to. Once the Depression was over, Alberta's populace threatened to throw its Social Credit government out of office if it failed to broaden its narrow focus beyond the single issue of monetary reform. Saskatche-wan's CCF government experienced the same kind of redirection. Despite the fact that in most agricultural countries the first plank in the platform of any socialist party is the nationalization of land, the Saskatch-ewan CCF was forced almost immediately to abandon that portion of socialist doctrine if it wanted the continued respect and support of the province's voters.

These lessons from western political history helped me clarify several points that have had a direct bearing on my own political pilgrimage and the creation of the Reform Party of Canada.

First, there is such a thing as a "reform tradition" in Canada. In western Canada it is just as deep and valid a tradition as those represented by the federal Liberal or Conservative parties, and it is even more charged with future possibilities.

Secondly, the strength of this tradition lies in the fact that there is such a thing as "the common sense of the common people," and if a politician, a party or a government can tap into it and harness that power to the formulation and implementation of public policy, there is no more potent political force on the face of the earth.

This power was known to many western politicians: Louis Riel and F.W.G. Haultain; the Progressives like Thomas Crerar and Henry Wise Wood; J.S. Woodsworth, the founder of the CCF; Depression-era politicians like Aberhart, my father, and Tommy Douglas; and others like W.A.C. Bennett and John Diefenbaker. All of them at one time or another in their careers came face to face with the raw power of grassroots western populism, and the experience had a lasting impact on their approach to public life.

Our contemporary federal political leaders and parties appear to have lost any faith they might once have had in the common sense of the common people. This is reflected in their tendency to cling to public policies that simply do not reflect the judgment of the rank and file (for example, the official languages policy) and to impose upon the public constitutional measures (such as the 1982 Constitution and the Meech Lake Accord) for which there is no broad basis of public support.

One of the reasons behind my own decision to become directly involved in federal politics in the 1990s was my personal conviction that there is a need to restore "the common sense of the common people" to a more central position in federal politics. This will involve the promotion and implementation of reforms designed to allow the public to have more say in the development of public policy through direct consultation, constitutional conventions, constituent assemblies, national referenda, and citizens' initiatives.

Canada's reform tradition did not begin in the West. It originated with the early reform parties of Nova Scotia, Upper Canada, and Lower Canada—the parties that fought colonial elites such as the Family Compact and the Château Clique and sought to replace them with more representative and responsible institutions of government. These reform parties prepared the way for Canadian Confederation.

During the present century, the two Canadian regions that have shown a consistent tendency to generate and support reform movements have been Quebec and western Canada.

Quebec has a long tradition of third-party movements outside the traditional parties, namely, the Bloc Populaire Canadien, the Union Nationale, the Ralliement des Créditistes, the Parti Québécois, and the Bloc Québécois. While not all of these movements have been populist, the majority have been so. And in each case, with the exception of the Union Nationale, these movements have been dedicated to radical changes, including fundamental changes in relations between French Canada and the rest of the country.

Given the need for fundamental changes in the Canadian federal system in the 1990s—in particular, major changes in our constitutional, economic, fiscal, and parliamentary systems—it is highly appropriate to challenge Canadians to answer the following question: "Should we revive our own reform traditions and harness them to the task of getting our constitutional, economic, and parliamentary houses in order during the 1990s?"

It is the thousands of people—myself included—who have been answering "Yes" to this question who are largely responsible for the birth and growth of the Reform Party of Canada.

CHAPTER TWO

Transitions

Although I spent my childhood and adolescence in a political house-hold, my brief exposure to the operations of a provincial govern-ment and a populist political party did not constitute a political apprenticeship in any way.

Like most boys growing up on a farm, I was much more preoccupied with other concerns—chores, school, dogs, horses, sports. I simply learned a little about interest groups, legislatures, laws, elections, politi-cians, and civil servants by osmosis and association, just as I learned a little about cows, pigs, chickens, crops, seeding, harvest, machinery, and farmers by being on the farm.

The high school I attended at Horse Hill was a small, friendly place of which I have nothing but fond memories. The teachers there managed to keep some semblance of law and order while imparting an appreciation of learning to those who wanted to learn. I was especially helped by a Mrs. Lepard, who presided over the combined grade seven and eight class when I first arrived; Mr. Nick Kraychy, the principal, who encouraged my interest in science; Mrs. Cardiff, who helped me develop my taste for history and social studies; and Dr. Kirchmeir, who believed that students should learn to think.

Mrs. Cardiff, like many teachers of that period, was of the CCF persuasion, although that didn't seem to bias her teaching or her rela-tions with me. Only once do I remember getting into an awkward situation because of our different political positions. We got into a discussion on whether capitalism should be reformed or replaced and I said indirectly that if such a question came up on an exam I wouldn't know whether to tell her what she wanted to hear or what I really believed. She blushed and became momentarily flustered, something that rarely happened. When I realized later that she was hurt because I had implied that she would mark my answer unfairly, I felt bad for days, all the more so because I valued her so highly as a teacher. She had convinced some of us that history was important for today, and she had got me interested in reading history at an early age when there was time to do so. That in itself was a tribute to her skills and dedication.

Dr. Kirchmeir was an Austrian who we understood had recently come to Canada, and who had to put in a year teaching at a high school to complete his qualifications for more advanced teaching positions. (At least that was what we students thought. The facts may be hazy, since most of what students know about a teacher's background comes from hearsay.)

At any rate, he was a highly educated man who was assigned to teach us grade eleven health, a Mickey Mouse course that interested neither him nor us. So to liven things up he taught us the elements of "symbolic logic"—the basic forms of deductive and inductive reasoning—something I wouldn't encounter again until my second or third year of university.

It was 1959, a provincial election year (our family kept track of time by the provincial elections in which my father participated—1935, 1940, 1944, 1948, 1952, 1955, 1959, 1963, 1967), and Social Credit candidates were in the media every day advancing arguments as to why the government should be re-elected. On our final health exam, Dr. Kirchmeir took one of these arguments and asked us to analyze it using the rules of symbolic logic he had taught us. According to those rules, the argument was fallacious, and if I wanted to get full marks that was the answer I would have to put down.

As soon as I read the question, I suspected it had been designed specifically for my benefit. I looked up from my paper to see Dr. Kirchmeir grinning at me. So I gave him the answer he wanted, but then launched into a convoluted essay on how in democracies, because the public can be illogical, it is sometimes necessary to use illogical arguments to arrive at the right result. I ended with a flourish, reminding the good doctor that it was possible to arrive at true conclusions using false premises (something else Kirchmeir had taught us), citing the example, All dogs are reptiles (false); all reptiles are warm-blooded (false); therefore, all dogs are warm-blooded (true).

I am sure that Dr. Kirchmeir must have roared at my attempt to give him the answer needed to pass the test and still justify the rationale being used by the government in its election campaign. In any event, he gave me a high mark, and, fortunately for my current political career, that essay has been lost. To this day, however, I am still conscious of the need to carefully "test the logic" of political arguments.

On yet another occasion, Dr. Kirchmeir asked me, out of the blue, to define intelligence. I was in the process of giving him some vague answer, when he interrupted by saying emphatically, "Intelligence is the ability to recognize that which is significant." For some reason this definition stuck with me, and has served me well in both the consulting and the political business.

At Horse Hill, we would often choose teams for football, hockey, or baseball by someone calling out "dairy farmers against the pig farmers." This was basically a friendly rivalry, but it did heat up at times. I was also part of a small gang called "The Fearless Five." We often played on the same hockey and football teams, and looked after each other when there were scuffles. Because I was small, membership in the Fearless Five was a great benefit to me. The other members of the gang were North Yoachim, whose family had a farm just down the road from ours; Dave Carmichael, who had a good voice and was generally admired for his imitation of Elvis Presley; and Laverne and Ed Wilkins. Both of the Wilkins boys were excellent athletes, and Ed was my best friend.

Because Horse Hill was a small country school, its library was very limited, and we did not have ready access to the city libraries. From time to time, therefore, when Ed Wilkins or I needed a "quote" from some learned authority in order to complete an essay, we would make up our own and attribute it to "that great Canadian philosopher and historian, George Pepki."

George Pepki was actually a hired man who worked for Ed's uncle on a farm near Bentley, but Mrs. Cardiff did not know this, and for a time she took these quotes from George at face value. Eventually, however, her suspicious were aroused—perhaps when George showed signs of plagiarizing Shakespeare by expressing a Canadian perspective on opportunity in these words: "There is a tide in the affairs of men which taken at the flood leads to sudden death by drowning."

North Yoachim and I each had a horse. His was a grey mare called Amigo and mine was a white wall-eyed gelding that I had named Silver (though our farm foreman called him Crowbait). North and I would ride for hours on the quarter north of our place and east of the Yoachims', along the banks of the North Saskatchewan River, where there was a large area of bush and gravel pits.

Every so often, just around dusk, we would come across a parked car—some couple from town who had come out to the country to be alone together. We would cut boughs off poplar trees, wait until dark, and then come whooping out of the bush on horseback, beating the boughs on the roof and sides of the parked car. We were never really certain what was going on inside those cars, but we sure did flush out some confused and angry people that way.

Every member of our gang was a dedicated football fan and devoted to the Edmonton Eskimos. Those were the years of Jackie Parker, Johnny Bright, Normy Qwong, and (yes) Don Getty, when the Eskimos won three Grey Cups in a row—1954, 1955, and 1956. When the Eskimos lost in overtime of the third game of the western semi-final in 1957, on a bitterly cold night at Clark Stadium, our gang went into mourning and didn't speak to anyone for three days.

The first time the Grey Cup game was played in the West was in 1955, and I went to Vancouver with my father that year to take in the Grey Cup parade and the game.

The Eskimos' opponents that year (as in 1954 and 1956) were the mighty Montreal Alouettes, with Sam "The Rifle" Etcheverry at the helm. Jean Drapeau, the mayor of Montreal, had come out for the game, and so had Jimmy Gardiner, the federal agriculture minister from Saskatchewan. W.A.C. (Wacky) Bennett was there, too, of course, and had actually met us at the plane, although relations between him and my father were generally cool.

Western wheat was not selling well in 1955, and many western farmers were mad at Gardiner. Some Saskatchewan farmers had entered a "float" in the Grey Cup parade that was really just a huge grain truck, loaded with wheat, and two burly fellows in the back carrying scoop shovels. When they got to the officials' stand the truck stopped and the fellows in the back proceeded to dump wheat all over the agriculture minister. Gardiner was furious and Drapeau was astounded, but Wacky and my father, neither of whom had much love for federal Liberals, were cheering for the farmers.

Back on the farm, the most influential person in my life was our farm foreman, Ron Galloway. Although my father came home to the farm at night and sometimes drove the tractor on weekends, he didn't have time to supervise the day-to-day operations. So when I worked on the farm, I took orders from Ron. The Galloways were really more like family, as Ron's wife Esther had been our family housekeeper for years when she was younger.

Before he came to work for us, Ron farmed his own land near Fort Saskatchewan. I came to know the place well in 1952 when my parents went to the Coronation of Queen Elizabeth and my brother and I went to stay at the Galloways'. This was a grand adventure. The Galloways had no electricity, so we got to light and use kerosene lamps. Ron also had an Aberdeen Angus bull at which, under Ron's watchful eye, we were permitted to pitch rocks. When my parents returned from England with stories about Buckingham Palace and Westminster Abbey, we had our own tales of high adventure featuring kerosene lamps and charging bulls.

Ron Galloway was a good mechanic, and the little I know about tools, engines, and farm machinery I learned from him. He was also an excellent herdsman, and under his direction our dairy grew and prospered. With Ron's supervision, I raised a shorthorn calf one year, appropriately named Touchdown, which won the 4-H championship for northern Alberta.

Ron was also wise in the ways of the marketplace. The morning before we sold the calf, he threw a handful of salt in its feed. This made it thirsty enough to drink about twenty-five pounds of water, which at $1.35 a pound added about $34 to the sale price. Ron explained the ethics of this by saying that the buyers deducted 2 percent for shrinkage anyway, so we had to make sure there was something to shrink!

Like most dairy farms of our size, we also had hired men, most of whom were colourful characters and some of whom became good friends. Among them was an Englishman named Eric Baker. One summer, he and I built a barbed-wire fence along the pasture land that bordered the North Saskatchewan River, and it was there that I became interested in the history of World War II—not in a conventional way, of course. When we got tired, we would go down to the river and throw in bottles and cans, which we had already christened, using the actual names of warships that had sailed in the last war. Eric would tell me all about the great sea battles of the war, including the ships and commanders involved. Then we would bomb the cans and bottles to oblivion with rocks. Later that year I got a different view of military history when my parents gave me Winston Churchill's *A History of the English-Speaking Peoples,* and his complete memoirs of the Second World War.

While my mother directed the Manning household, she usually had a housekeeper or nanny to help her, and some of them played an important role in our lives. Esther Walter and her sister Winnie were two who really became part of the family. They cared for my brother and me as if we were their own children. We had other housekeepers, too, some of whom went to rather elaborate lengths to protect us children from the slings and arrows to which a political family may be subject. One, for example, took it upon herself to cut out of the daily newspaper all derogatory references to my father and his government in news articles or editorials, on the theory that such articles would hurt our feelings. By the time she was finished, the newspaper sometimes looked like confetti, especially when the Legislature was in session, and she was finally persuaded to stop.

A description of our home life, especially on the farm, would not be complete without some reference to dogs. We always had dogs, lots of dogs—a spaniel, St. Bernards, collies, litters of collie pups, a keeshond, a boxer, and a handful of mongrels. In many respects, my best friends were dogs. I played with them, chased cats, gophers, and birds with them, and suffered with them when they got into trouble. In fact, my first real exposure to death—and the feelings that accompany the death of a friend—came when a number of our dogs met untimely ends.

One night, the coyotes lured our spaniel outside the circle of illumination that spread from the yard light, and Mickey was no more. On another occasion, a careless hired man operating a hay mower somehow failed to see two collies bounding through the alfalfa. One of them, old Lassie—the only dog I ever knew who could kill a porcupine without getting quilled—lost three legs, and the other lost one. Ron Galloway came running, took one look, and went for his rifle. Lassie had been with him many years. (For a moment I wasn't sure whether it was the dog or the hired man he meant to shoot.)

And then there was the keeshond named Koning (Dutch for "King"). He was the only dog we ever had that probably needed psychiatric treatment. He liked heights. If there was a box sitting out in the yard, he would try to get on top of it. He would chase cats up ladders, scrambling up to the loft of our barn, then sitting there yapping because he could not get down. And if someone parked a car in the yard, he would scramble on top of that, and scratch the paint.

One day Koning followed us to the nearby town of Fort Saskatchewan, where we had taken some equipment to work Ron's land on the other side of the river. When it was time to go home, Koning was nowhere to be found. Two days later he still hadn't turned up, so I retraced the route, inquiring at every farm along the way. Finally when we got to the Fort, I went to the dog pound, where the dog catcher's wife said her husband had gone about an hour ago to shoot the unclaimed dogs he had collected during the week. We rushed down to the spot on the river where he did his work. No dog catcher was to be found, but there was blood all over the snow. Down at heart, we went back to the dog pound to wait for him. When he finally came, he had one dog left in his truck—Koning. "I was going to shoot him too," he said, "but he had that fancy collar, and I figured someone might be looking for him."

For all that I was surrounded by the influences of farm and politics, my parents never led me to believe that I was expected to carry on the farm or go into politics myself. They left me perfectly free to pursue my own interests, science in particular. They helped me equip a small laboratory at one end of our bunk-house building—though it made the hired men uneasy, especially when I managed to acquire some hydrolysis equipment for manufacturing hydrogen.

For some reason (perhaps at the suggestion of my high school princi-pal), I subscribed to a British magazine on nuclear physics. I also made up cards to help me memorize the atomic weights and numbers of all the elements of Mendeleev's Periodic Table, a rather useless enterprise, since we were always allowed to take a copy of the table into chemistry exams anyway. The collective standing of the Fearless Five was enhanced at school, however, when Ed Wilkins would holler out the name of an obscure element and I would rattle off the atomic weight to the fourth decimal place.

I have always had a fascination with matrices, from Mendeleev's Table in chemistry to Wassily Leontief's input-output tables in economics, which I trace back to this period. It struck me as very ingenious that Mendeleev, by taking data on the then-known elements, and rearranging it into the rows and columns of a matrix, was able to predict the existence and properties of unknown elements simply by filling in the blanks.

For my birthday one year I was given a geiger tube, which I put into a hollowed-out broom handle and hooked to a small amplifier. My father obtained some pitchblende samples for me from the Alberta Research Council which I kept in the lab. I would ask someone to hide the pitchblende sample in a room, and then find it using my home-made geiger counter, all the while hinting darkly that I was conducting experiments involving radiation and hydrogen. I had at least one hired man convinced that I was just one step away from manufacturing the Bomb.

By my last year in high school, I had decided that I wanted to go to the University of Alberta and study physics, even though I had very little counselling on the matter and little idea as to what was really involved. I enrolled in the honours physics program at the University of Alberta in fall 1960 and had little time for anything other than studies for the next three years. Because I was totally immersed in physics and maths, I had little contact with the political science, economics, or history departments and their professors at the University of Alberta. My initial studies at university therefore had almost no effect on my political thinking. Once, I acted as a backbencher in the university Model Parliament, but more out of duty to support the Social Credit group on campus than out of any authentic zeal.

At that time the real political movers and shakers on campus were Joe Clark, who was leader of the Progressive Conservative club; Jim Coutts, the leader of the campus Liberals, who later became first secretary to Prime Minister Pierre Trudeau; Grant Notley, leader of the campus New Democrats, who later became the leader of the Alberta New Democrats and was tragically killed in a plane crash in 1984; and my friend Ray Speaker, the Socred leader on campus, who also went on to become an Alberta MLA and a cabinet minister in the Strom and Getty administrations. I enjoyed the political debates among these people, but rarely participated and in no way considered myself a political activist.

By the end of my third year I had become convinced that I should change faculties. My academic interests were broadening, and I found it harder and harder to focus exclusively and successfully on math and physics. This was a rather stressful time for me. I had invested so much time and energy in the physics program, I was loath to give it up. I was also by no means certain as to what future direction I should take.

Dr. Walter Mackenzie, the dean of medicine, tried to talk me into trying the new field of biophysics, but my interests were really starting to shift to the social sciences.

My religious training told me that in times of personal uncertainty one should seek God's direction through personal prayer and study of the Christian scriptures. I set about doing this, and also began reading broadly for the first time in three years. I remember reading John Wesley's *Journals* and envying the fact that he seemed to have found a mission in life that he was able to pursue with absolute certainty and dedication for more than fifty years. Only later, when I read Wesley's biography, did I learn that he didn't really discover his mission until he was over thirty. I was then twenty-one.

Finally, after a helpful talk with Dr. Walter Johns, the president of the University of Alberta at that time, I switched to the arts faculty, and economics.

Another factor that influenced my change in studies was my summer job in 1962. I was coming down the steps of the Legislature Building one day during the academic year when I ran into Sid Blair, then president of Canadian Bechtel. Mr. Blair (the father of Bob Blair, the recently retired CEO of NOVA Corporation) had completed a report for the government leading to the development of the oil sands plant at Fort McMurray, the first commercial one to operate in Canada.

Mr. Blair asked me what I was doing for the summer, and I replied that I would probably be working on the farm, as I had the previous two summers. He then asked whether I would be interested in going to San Francisco to work with Bechtel's newly established research and development division. (It was then experimenting with taking on a few university students as summer employees.)

I jumped at the chance, and consequently spent from May to the end of August in San Francisco. I got a one-room apartment in a building on the corner of Bush and Powell, where the cable car came rattling through, ringing its bell at all hours of the day and night. Most of my time was spent on two projects—doing shielding calculations on a facility that Bechtel was building for W.R. Grace and Company to process spent fuel rods from nuclear reactors, and doing a speculative report on the possible commercial value of maser and laser devices.

While I was there, I had many opportunities to visit the Berkeley campus of the University of California, as well as Stanford University. I also visited the Lawrence radiation labs. Perhaps most important, I began to get a broader picture of the scientific-business-government establishment which was then developing in the United States. At one end of the spectrum were the pure scientists who focused on their specialties. At the other end were the many other important players to whom I had had very little previous exposure—the entrepreneurial and management types, the applications-oriented engineers, the bureaucrats and regulators, and of course the ubiquitous consultants, generalists who knew a little about a lot and played a major role in greasing the wheels of scientific and business projects.

That fall, back in university, I took a full load of economics courses. I also did a lot of reading on the side, and for the first time began to read the academic literature on some of the political movements that I knew about from other sources.

At the end of the university year I knew I would have to make some decisions about whether to do postgraduate studies or something else. One day, as I was sitting in a lecture room listening to a very knowledgeable professor who was a very poor communicator, I began to see my options in a new light. I could conceivably go on and get my M.A. or

Ph.D. like this fellow. Or I could find a business or government client who really needed this fellow's expertise and act as the link between the demand for specialized knowledge and the supply. Could I not "rent" the economist's brain for so much per day, hire him out at a higher rate, and use the difference to cover my cost and fee for service?

This, of course, is the essence of the consulting or knowledge business, and I found it an increasingly attractive option. It gave you exposure to all the knowledge and experience of these specialized people, while allowing you to remain a generalist.

I graduated from the University of Alberta in 1964 with a B.A. in economics, but more than three years passed before I got into the consulting business in earnest. Meanwhile, I worked on various projects that allowed me to help my father in both his religious and his political work.

With Canada's Centennial year approaching, one of the themes my father and others had been promoting through his radio broadcast work was that Canada needed a "national spiritual awakening" like those that had gripped and changed other nations in times past. I studied the Protestant Reformation, the first and second Evangelical Awakenings in Great Britain, and the American revival movements, as well as the theology of "spiritual awakenings" as described in the Christian scriptures. Then my friend Ed Kennedy and I went on an extended cross-Canada speaking tour to churches and youth groups that had an interest in this subject.

1965 was a federal election year, and I was urged by a number of people in the federal Social Credit Party to stand as a candidate in Edmonton East. This seat had once been held by Ambrose Holowach, who was now provincial secretary in my father's cabinet. A realistic assessment of my chances in the riding indicated a very slim chance of winning. But I thought the experience might be worthwhile, so I threw my hat into the ring.

This was the election in which Pearson tried to bolster his standing in Quebec by recruiting "the three wise men" (Pierre Trudeau, Gérard Pelletier, and Jean Marchand), and in which Diefenbaker focused his campaign on charges of corruption and dishonesty in the Pearson administration. I finished a distant second to the Progressive Conservative candidate, Bill Skoreyko, who had first been elected in 1958 and went on to enjoy a further fifteen years as an MP.

The campaign left me with two lasting impressions. The first was that none of the candidates, myself included, had the skills or the knowledge to properly represent the long-suffering people of Edmonton East in the federal Parliament or on the big issues of the day. Our knowledge on any issue (including that of the incumbent) could be exhausted in ten minutes, and our parties had very little to offer in terms of training or advice to make up for our deficiencies. My second impression was a solid appreciation of the great ethnic and cultural diversity of a riding like Edmonton East. Here was the Canadian mosaic in miniature.

During the campaign I got to know a remarkable Latvian named August Osis, who became one of my best friends. August had participated in the Finnish campaign against the Russians in the opening rounds of World War II. When he left home to go to war, his mother tore a page from the Latvian Bible and sewed it into the lining of his tunic. The page contained Psalm 91, which speaks of how God protects those who trust in him against the terrors of evil.

When the Russians invaded Latvia, August's family was dispersed. His young wife and son were sent to the Soviet Union. August survived the war, including internment in a prisoner of war camp, escaped to the West, and immigrated to Canada. He brought with him his faith in God, his training as an engineer, his belief in himself, and the clothes on his back.

August's first job was shovelling gravel for the CNR at fifty cents an hour. By the time I got to know him, however, he had set up his own company, Du-Al Block. Du-Al manufactured a unique building block which substituted treated wood chips for gravel in a concrete aggregate.

August made a point of introducing me to some of the key leaders of the ethnic and religious groups in East Edmonton. He wanted me to get behind the superficialities of token appearances at cultural festivals, and get some real understanding of what these people could contribute to Canada's economy, politics, and social fabric. Through August, I met people who did not share the Anglo-Saxon conception and experience of law—people who had lived under regimes where the law was stacked against them, and obeyed out of fear, not respect. They explained to me how difficult it was to look at the law in any other light, even after coming to Canada.

I attended the meetings of a number of ethnic groups, including ones commemorating the Russian invasions of Estonia, Latvia, and Lithuania. The calibre and depth of the political speeches and discussions at these gatherings made a typical Canadian partisan political meeting appear trivial. I recall a speech given at one of these meetings by a woman (I do not remember her name) on what she described as "the three great commandments of Western culture." These she identified as: Know Thyself, from Socrates and the Greeks; Control Thyself, from Moses, the great Hebrew lawgiver, and the Roman lawmakers like Cato; and Give Thyself, the greatest commandment of Jesus Christ and the Christian tradition. She traced the history of European adherence to and abandonment of these great cultural imperatives, and discussed their relevance to current issues in Canadian politics. Whether one agreed with her or not, the depth and scope of her analysis was impressive, and her delivery was memorable.

A few months later, August and I went to listen to a spokesman for the federal Liberal Party addressing a similar group. This was in the early days of the Liberals' policy on multiculturalism. It manifested itself at the community level in Edmonton East in the belief of local Liberals that the entire Ukrainian vote of that area could be purchased simply by inviting Ukrainian dancers to perform at a Liberal convention and offering a few leaders a grant to form a cultural society or build a cultural centre.

The superficiality of this speaker's remarks and the shallowness of his assumptions about the interests and capacities of the audience were insulting and demeaning. Here was an audience whose political culture and experience were far deeper and broader than the speaker's, yet he talked to them like children, as if his party could obtain their allegiance by throwing them a few baubles.

It was through my father's radio broadcast work and participation in a College and Career class at the Baptist church we attended, that I first met Sandra Beavis. In the spring of 1966 I asked her out to dinner (on a double date with my friend Ed Wilkins), in October we were engaged, and on March 23, 1967, we were married.

Those of us in the management consulting business who are always trying to perfect decision-making mechanisms for our clients and ourselves are usually humbled by the following question. If you ask us how we made the big decisions in our personal lives—where to go to school, what career to pursue, whom to marry, how many children to have, where to live—it is highly unlikely that we used any of the matrix analyses or decision trees or cost-benefit calculations that we are always recommending so highly to our clients. Usually we use our God-given common sense, and the percentage of right decisions seems to be about as high as that obtained by using more sophisticated approaches to decision making.

In my case, I can safely say that the wisest decision I ever made, from the standpoint of my own wellbeing and that of my family—and in terms of my business and political career—was to ask Sandra to be my wife. (This description of my decision and its happy consequences must sound rather perfunctory, but there is a more romantic version, which Sandra is better able to provide.)

Sandra's father, Gordon Beavis, had come to Edmonton in 1952 from Winnipeg. He was a buyer for LePage Lumber and had travelled extensively in the north. His company was the largest creditor of a well-established construction company in Edmonton which got into financial difficulty during the housing slowdown of the 1960s. Rather than putting the firm into receivership, LePage, with the agreement of the Alberta Treasury Branch, appointed Gordon Beavis as a "friendly receiver." He went to the construction company in the official capacity of comptroller. If he had had only LePage's and his own self-interest at heart, he could have held any position he wanted and even ended up as the owner. But his sole purpose was to get the ailing company back on its feet. This, with the cooperation and hard work of the owners and staff of the construction company, he managed to do. Once the company recovered, he stayed on as comptroller until his retirement in 1982.

If you asked the owners and staff of that construction company how best to describe Gordon Beavis, I think they would probably say, "He is a Christian gentleman." The approach he used in reconciling conflicting business interests, in this case those of a debtor and creditors, conform very closely to the New Testament model of reconciliation. By sacrificing his own interests, he brought about a reconciliation which paid the debt and gave the construction company new life.

Sandra's mother, Mary Gibson, is of Scottish ancestry and she is as determined as Gordon is accommodating. They were married in Ottawa in 1942 during the war, when both were in the air force. Sandra was their oldest daughter, followed by three other girls—Lesley, Louise, and Marian.

Gordon was an accomplished tenor soloist, and was therefore in demand to sing at weddings and in church choirs. My mother, who was always on the lookout for good voices for the radio program's male chorus, invited Gordon Beavis to participate. When the Beavises first came to Edmonton, they attended McDougal United Church. Later they began to attend the Baptist church that we attended, and that is where I first met Sandra.

Sandra was an excellent student, and won an entrance scholarship to university, but decided that first she wanted to study the Christian faith in depth. She attended the Prairie Bible Institute, one of several large evangelical Bible schools founded during the 1920s and 1930s in western Canada. Prairie, founded by the saintly and energetic L.E. Maxwell and a businessman named Roger Kirk, had a solid reputation for training and sending Christian missionaries all over the globe. It also had a reputation for being very strait-laced, and Sandra's friends were wagering that she wouldn't last three weeks. She did last, however, graduating with a Christian Education degree (with a music major).

Her original intention was to become a medical missionary, and before I met her, she had worked summers at the Oliver Mental Hospital not far from our farm. In 1965 she enrolled in the University of Alberta nursing program, along with her sister Louise. She was in her first year of nurse's training when I asked her to dinner that first time.

The Beavis household was quite a contrast to the Manning household. We were usually trying to escape from people and find some tranquillity, but the Beavis home was open to everyone, and always full of noise, excitement, and activity. This was a great environment for Sandra, as she is very outgoing. I am the opposite. In many respects Sandra is much better able to deal with people on a personal level because she is genuinely interested in every aspect of their lives.

Sandra and I had very much in common, including our faith and a growing conviction that we were intended for each other. On October 23, 1966, we decided to get married, advised our families, and set the date for June of the following year.

On New Year's Eve 1966, we attended a ceremony at the Legislature grounds where my father and other dignitaries lit an "eternal flame" to initiate Alberta's celebration of the Canadian Centennial. (The next day some university students doused the flame just to prove that no flame, especially one fed by natural gas and lit by politicians, is eternal.) The theme of all the Centennial speeches that night was "planning for the next hundred years." After all the ceremonies were over, Sandra and I did some more planning of our own, and moved our wedding date up to March 23, 1967.

Because Sandra was still at nursing school, and she could only get a four-day leave, we had a very brief honeymoon in Vancouver before settling into our first apartment, a basement suite near the university that we rented for $85 a month. We lived in several different apartments during the early years of our married life, and moved to our first house in the Londonderry district of northeast Edmonton in 1969.

One of the side benefits of participating in the federal election of 1965 was that it brought me into contact with one David Wilson. David had done some high-level fundraising and strategic planning for the Social Credit Party, and that year had just become director of an organization called the National Public Affairs Research Foundation.

This foundation was a small public-policy research group organized by a number of businesspeople, including Bob Brown of Home Oil, the largest independent oil company in Canada. Brown and his associates were interested in developing policy ideas that might be useful to both the Alberta Social Credit Party and the federal Progressive Conservative Party, which was about to enter a period of instability. I was hired as a policy researcher under Dave Wilson's direction.

While employed by the foundation, I worked on three major projects which provided me with insights and experiences that would later prove useful in helping to organize the Reform Party of Canada. The first was the development of a White Paper on Human Resources Development for the Alberta government. The second was an examination of the feasibility of rolling the Alberta Social Credit Party and the provincial Progressive Conservative Party together into a new provincial party. The third project involved research for a book by my father entitled *Political Realignment,* a challenge to the federal Progressive Conservative Party to reform itself from within.

By 1967, my father had made up his mind to retire from provincial politics before the next provincial election. Before doing so, however, he wanted to do some policy work that might provide some new directions and fresh materials for his successors. The Alberta government's White Paper on Human Resources Development was an attempt to address some of the social issues of the 1960s, in particular the causes of poverty and underdevelopment in certain parts of the province, and the need for improved delivery of social services.

The paper was essentially put together by Erick Schmidt, who was executive assistant to the cabinet, myself, and a number of outside researchers and resource people. The senior civil service was not much involved in this project, which later made implementation very difficult.

Our starting point was the premise that Alberta, because of its horrific experience during the Depression, had a fixation on survival economics and physical resources development. The time had come, we argued, to shift public- and private-sector attention to "the other side of the house," namely social and human resources development. At the same time, we wanted to address the issues of poverty and underdevelopment, not from the perspective of the liberal/socialistic thinking which was then guiding the development of the welfare state, but from that of small-c conservative principles tempered by populism.

Like many younger people in the 1960s I was not at all comfortable with the left-right dichotomy of traditional politics. This split was based on the conventional wisdom that if you were interested in wealth creation, freedom of enterprise, and economy in government, you were supposed to belong to a right-wing or conservative party. But if you were interested in the distribution of wealth, people problems like underdevelopment and discrimination, and governmental delivery of social services, you were supposed to belong to a left-wing, liberal, or socialist party.

Many of us were searching for a synthesis of these two perspectives— one that would provide a political home for people with "hard heads and soft hearts," as distinct from the "hard head, hard heart" option offered by conservatism, and the "soft head, soft heart" option offered by liberalism or democratic socialism.

The NDP's economic philosophy made it antagonistic to private enterprise. But, ironically, if the NDP formed a provincial government, it would immediately find itself trying to promote the growth of a provincial economy in which most of the wealth and jobs were created by private enterprise.

It struck us as equally ironic that the philosophy of many Conservatives had very little to say about social responsibility or how to provide social services. Yet once in charge of a provincial government, more than 60 percent of a Conservative administration's budget would be committed to these areas.

The Alberta government's White Paper on Human Resources Development was tabled in the Alberta Legislature in the spring of 1967. Our concept of human resources development focused on achieving certain levels of physical and mental health by requiring the public and private sectors to perform specific functions: development/prevention, rehabilitation/adjustment, and maintenance. The White Paper was accompanied by seven case studies analyzing poverty and underdevelopment problems in various parts of the province, and an inventory of public and private resources available to cope with those problems. It provided for the establishment of a Human Resources Development Authority to bring the resources of the big social-service departments (education, health, social assistance) to bear on particular needs (such as those of native communities) in a coordinated fashion. It also provided for the creation of a Human Resources Research Council.

The White Paper received a lukewarm response from the Legislature, the civil service, and the public, and it did not prove to be of much practical use to the Strom administration. (Harry Strom succeeded my father as premier in 1968.) The recommended initiatives that were implemented were later abandoned by the Lougheed administration when it was elected in 1971. (Interestingly enough, when Peter Lougheed decided to retire in 1985, he too attempted to provide his successors with some new policy material pertaining particularly to diversification of the Alberta economy. It suffered a fate similar to the Social Credit government's White Paper on Human Resources Development.)

From a personal standpoint, however, the White Paper project provided me with my first formal opportunity to study the reconciliation of small-c conservative economics with those social concerns and priorities that were very much a part of prairie populism on both the left and the right.

It also provided me with the opportunity to meet and work with some very talented people. These included George Kupfer and Ike Glick, social scientists who went on to do a number of socio-economic impact assessments on resource projects in Alberta; Owen Anderson, who went on to become a senior official with Indian Affairs; Don Hamilton, the director of the Alberta Youth Corps, who later went into business; Gerry Bigham and Neil Gilliat, who set up the human resources program in the Slave Lake region of north central Alberta; Jack Oberholtzer, a veteran deputy minister who became the first director of the Human Resources Development Authority; Bruce Rawson, a solicitor with the Alberta Attorney General's department, who was assigned to the Community Health and Social Development department and became so involved in its work that he went on to become a senior deputy minister in Alberta and then in Ottawa; and Erick Schmidt, the project director, who went on to get his Ph.D. in sociology, founded a high-tech laser manufacturing company (General Systems Research), and now heads an environmental products and services company.

When Bruce Rawson was eventually appointed deputy minister of Alberta's Community Health and Social Development Department, several of us who had been involved in the White Paper project wrote the following poem in his honour. It summarized one of the main lessons from the project.

> Humpty Dumpty sat on a wall,
> Humpty Dumpty had a great fall,
> All the King's horses, and all the King's men
> Couldn't put Humpty together again.

> And what is the moral to this little rhyme?
> A moral with meaning for men in our time.
> The moral is this, and its lesson is true,
> There are certain things that the state cannot do!

If all the King's horses and all the King's men,
Cannot put an egg together again,
Is it not a false hope, an illusion, a sin,
To ask civil servants to reconstruct men?

Erick Schmidt and I not only became good friends, but his insights into the nature and workings of bureaucracy were a major influence on my own approach to this subject.

Erick has one of the most fertile and agile minds I know. When he was younger, and came to work as the first executive assistant to the Alberta cabinet, my father would have to sit him down in the morning and say, "Erick, I know that before breakfast you had at least a hundred new ideas; and on the way to work you had a hundred more. But today we can work only on the following matters ... ."

Erick's doctoral thesis was entitled "The Morphology of Bureaucratic Knowledge."[1] It drew upon much of the classical literature on bureaucracy, insights based on modern "systems analysis" and cybernetic theory, and Erick's practical experience with the Alberta government bureaucracy. It analyzed bureaucratic organizations, with their layers and layers of "boxes," each reporting to the box above it, as information systems. These systems transmitted information on people, resources, and situations upwards to decision makers, and transmitted decisions, orders, and policy guidelines downwards to workers.

Erick's contention was that these bureaucratic structures transmitted certain types of information accurately, for example, concrete information on things that could be measured and quantified, such as how many barrels of oil were produced per day by a well in the Redwater field. But these same structures could not transmit other types of data accurately at all—for example, subjective data pertaining to values, feelings, emotions—precisely the information you needed to provide services to people, especially people with special needs like the very young, the old, the poor, or the sick.

According to Erick's thesis, not only do bureaucratic information systems have trouble transmitting to decision makers and workers the information they need to care humanely and efficiently for people with special needs, but those systems actually filter out much of the required information and substitute other less relevant information only because it

---

1. Erick Schmidt, "The Morphology of Bureaucratic Knowledge." vols. 1 and 2 (Edmonton: University of Alberta, 1975).

can be quantified and objectified. This is why caring systems, organized in a bureaucratic fashion, tend to reduce people to files and numbers. In the extreme, such systems can even become so anti-human in their functioning that they become a menace rather than a help to the very people they are supposed to serve.

Erick then went on to predict specific people-damaging incidents that might occur in the 1970s to Albertans being served by Alberta's health, education, child-welfare, penal, and social-welfare bureaucracies— incidents that would occur, not because of any lack of professionalism or dedication on the part of Alberta's civil servants, but because of the nature of bureaucracy itself and its inherent inability to handle people with care. In the 1970s a journalist with the *Edmonton Journal*, Wendy Konig, distinguished herself with a series of reports on precisely the type of incidents that Erick had predicted years before.

Erick's thesis got him into all sorts of trouble with some of the ministers in the Strom government. It was a great help to me, however, when I was thinking through both the potential of and the limits to bureaucratic delivery systems in caring for people, especially vulnerable people with special needs.

Erick's conclusions on the destructive potential of bureaucracies as systems for caring for people were arrived at through scientific analysis and the application of modern systems thinking to the bureaucratic phenomenon. It struck me as significant that the great Russian writer Leo Tolstoy had arrived at exactly the same conclusion a century earlier by artistic and religious intuition. Prince Nekhlyudov, the hero of Tolstoy's novel, *Resurrection,* after seeing the inhuman treatment of political prisoners, concluded:

> All this comes from the fact that all these people—governors, inspectors, police-officers, and policemen—consider that there are circumstances when human relations are not necessary between human beings. All these men... thought not of men and their duty towards them but only of the office they themselves filled, and considered the obligations of that office to be above human relations. ... All these people were evidently invulnerable and impermeable to the simplest feelings of compassion only because they held offices. ... It is only necessary that these people should be governors, inspectors, policemen; that they should be fully convinced that there is a kind of business, called government service, which allows men to treat other men as things without

having human brotherly relations with them; and that they should be so linked together by this government service that the responsibility for the results of their deeds should not fall on any one of them individually. Without these conditions the terrible acts I witnessed today would be impossible in our times. It all lies in the fact that men think there are circumstances when one may deal with human beings without love.[2]

If I had gone on to do doctoral studies myself in economics I probably would have done some work on analyzing market economies and command economies as communications systems—in particular, analyzing their efficiency and effectiveness in transmitting economic and other signals to decision makers and workers.

The second project in which I became involved while working with the National Public Affairs Research Foundation was more political. It was an investigation of the possibility of putting together the aging Social Credit Party of Alberta (which had then been in office for more than thirty years) with the up-and-coming Progressive Conservative Party of Alberta under its new leader, Peter Lougheed.

There was never any wild enthusiasm for this study on the part of my father's ministers, most of whom regarded it as a hare-brained scheme being promoted by a few young Turks. Nor were the new and ambitious group of younger politicians who surrounded Peter Lougheed very enthusiastic about it. But my father and Peter Lougheed gave the project a guarded go-ahead, subject to the proviso that they could kill it at any time.

The government party (Social Credit) was represented in this study by Erick Schmidt and me. Mr. Lougheed's group was represented by Joe Clark, who was then one of Lougheed's executive assistants, and Merv Leitch, who was later to become attorney general and minister of energy in the Lougheed administration.

Our "gang of four" met on a number of occasions in quiet and confidential meetings, which Joe took great care in arranging. The main product of our efforts was a draft plan for merging the Alberta Social Credit movement and the Lougheed Conservatives into a new provincial party. Our suggested name was the Social Conservative Party. The plan included a formal statement entitled "Basis of Union," a statement of principles to which the new party would commit itself, which Erick and I wrote and were most concerned about. It attempted to synthesize the

---

2. Leo Tolstoy, *Resurrection* (Moscow: Progress Publishers, 1972), pp. 456-61.

best of the Social Credit outlook (its commitment to freedom of enterprise, its populist roots and social concerns) with some of the newer ideas
and emphases (new blood and new directions, urban priorities, environmental conservation) being championed by the Lougheed group.

The draft plan also included a section entitled "procedure"—a detailed
blueprint of how the two parties would actually be put together. It
included appropriate names, party colours, provisions for honouring old
memberships and providing for a new membership, joint nominating
meetings in preparation for the next provincial election, and so on. This
was the part that Joe and Merv were especially interested in.

As a result of our different interests, our group's joint meetings took on
a rather false sense of progress. As Erick and I reviewed the section on
principles, Joe and Merv would nod in agreement, mainly because they
considered it largely academic and were in a hurry to get on to the
political aspects. As we went through the section on procedure, Erick
and I would nod in agreement, mainly because we considered it quite
secondary. If the scheme came off, what we would really be creating was
a new government, not just a new party, and the nature of the new
government would be determined more by its policy commitments than
by its organizational procedures.

In a relatively short time, therefore, we were able to present my father,
Peter Lougheed, and their respective advisers with a draft plan. Needless
to say, it was not greeted positively by either side. My father's ministers
were not convinced that the Social Credit Party needed any infusion of
new blood, especially if the donor was to be the upstart Lougheed group.
And the Lougheed group were beginning to believe that they would
probably form the next government of Alberta anyway. The only question
was whether the scheme would advance the date, although some of Mr.
Lougheed's advisers were convinced that the whole effort was just a
diversionary tactic to knock them off their game plan.

And so my first involvement in political synthesis at the practical (as
distinct from the philosophical) level also came to naught. In the process,
however, I gained a few insights into Joe Clark's values and priorities
which would be of later use, and the whole exercise was a source of
excitement and stimulation for those of us who participated in it.

In my third project for the National Public Affairs Research Foundation, I researched a book that my father published in 1967.

With the downfall of the Diefenbaker administration in 1963, and the
initiation of a process within the federal Progressive Conservative Party to
replace John Diefenbaker with a new leader, some Conservative

supporters saw a major opportunity to change the party from within. A number of western and Ontario Conservatives approached my father to see whether he was interested in entering federal politics. He told them that he was not, but that he did have some views on how federal politics might be realigned. These were set out in his book *Political Realignment: A Challenge to Thoughtful Canadians.*

More than 30,000 copies of *Political Realignment* were sold (bulk orders were purchased by Ontario and Alberta Conservatives for distribution before the Conservative leadership convention in September 1967).

The central thesis of the book was that Canadians deserved some real choices in federal politics, and that these were not offered by the current alignment of parties. My father then outlined a philosophical position, described as the "social conservative position," which was a synthesis of marketplace economics and some of the social concerns of humanitarian socialism. He used the term "synthesis" rather than "compromise," to distinguish the position of social conservatives from that of the "Red Tories," who were just then beginning to emerge within the Progressive Conservative ranks.

He challenged the federal Conservatives to realign themselves along this axis, asserting that if they did so, the realigned Progressive Conservative Party could prove to be an attractive home for supporters of the federal Social Credit Party and federal Liberals who were uneasy about the leftward drift of their party. His candid analysis of the limited future of the federal Social Credit Party hastened its demise, which was already impending, and paved the way for the federal Social Credit leader Robert Thompson to align himself with the Conservatives.

My father concluded his assessment of the federal political scene with a paragraph headed "Consideration of One Remaining Alternative":

Anyone who speaks or writes on the subject of political realignment is open to the common misinterpretation that he is advocating the formation of another political party altogether apart from those presently in existence. I wish to make it very clear that this is not what I am advocating in this thesis. I do not believe that the formation of an entirely new political party is the best way to meet the serious national political needs of the present hour. Nevertheless, having regard to the prevailing mood of the Canadian people, present national party leaders and federal politicians, especially those affiliated with the Progressive Conservative Party of Canada, should take cognizance of the following fact: if the Canadian political situation continues to

degenerate, and if the cause of conservatism continues to suffer
and decline, not for lack of merit or a willingness on the part of
the Canadian people to support modern conservative principles or
policies, but rather because of unnecessary dissension among
politicians and parties, the idea of establishing a wholly new
political party committed to the social conservative position will
find an ever increasing number of advocates and supporters
among a concerned and aroused Canadian public.[3]

In the final analysis, the election of the cautious Robert Stanfield as
leader of the Progressive Conservatives and the emergence of Pierre
Elliott Trudeau as the dominant figure in Canadian federal politics in the
1970s meant that there was no real market for the political realignment
idea at the time it was promoted. The political realignment project did,
however, give me an opportunity to meet a number of the dissident
elements in the federal Progressive Conservative Party in the late 1960s.
It also gave me a reason to think through the issue of attempting to
reform a traditional party from within and without, versus attempting to
create a new party.

One last thing I learned from my family's involvement with the
grassroots political traditions of the West was that populist movements
are more "human" than the traditional parties. They do not go on
forever. They have a lifespan—just like a human being. They fulfil a
purpose (sometimes well, sometimes not so well). They beget offspring
(the Progressives gave birth to both the CCF and the Social Credit), and
then they die, sometimes with the satisfaction of seeing their progeny
carry on.

Traditional political parties may also cease to live as vital democratic
institutions. Their initial idealism, commitment to principle, reason for
being, and grassroots support shrivel with the passage of time. During
Trudeau's time, as the Liberal administration progressively alienated more
and more Canadians, the western base of the Liberal Party was virtually
destroyed until all that was left after the 1984 election was Lloyd Axworthy's
lonely outpost in Winnipeg-Fort Garry (now Winnipeg South Centre) and
John Turner's in Vancouver Quadra. Under Mulroney, the western base of
the Progressive Conservative Party is now dying from a similar disease.

But the traditional federal parties, especially if they are, or have
prospects of becoming, the governing party, usually have access to

---

3. Ernest C. Manning, *Political Realignment* (Toronto: McClelland and Stewart, 1967),
   p. 86.

"life-support systems"—financial and manpower support based on the promise or prospect of patronage, and not directly dependent on widespread public support. A traditional political party may therefore "die" in terms of democratic support, but this does not mean that the corpse cannot be trotted out at election time, dressed up in its election finery, displayed in lifelike poses on television, and presented to the electorate as a vital and living being.

In contrast, when a genuine populist political party is dead, even if it is a governing party, it is really dead and ought to be buried. By the end of the 1960s I could tell that the Social Credit movement in Alberta was entering its death throes, and that the other remaining Depression-era party, the CCF, was undergoing a transformation that could eventually sever it from its prairie roots.

Rather than identify with a traditional federal party—and I had some good contacts in both the federal Liberal and Conservative parties—I resolved not to become personally involved in politics until the next expression of the western reform tradition came along. This is not to say that I did not attempt to participate in efforts to sustain the Social Credit movement in Alberta or to support those attempting to change the traditional federal parties from within. But I could not bring myself to participate wholeheartedly in these efforts.

I hoped that the next time the West produced a populist reform movement it would have the potential to become a truly national party that had its historic roots and deepest commitments in the hinterland regions of the country (the West, the North, Atlantic Canada, and the northern and rural regions of Quebec and Ontario), just as the Liberals and Conservatives are national parties with their historic roots and deepest commitments in southern Ontario and southern Quebec. I also hoped that next time the West might benefit more from its previous attempts to change the federal system through political innovation, and perhaps act more wisely as a result of lessons learned, especially from the Progressive and Depression-era party experiences.

When my father announced in 1968 that he would retire at the end of the year, a number of cabinet ministers expressed interest in succeeding him. Harry Strom, by then the municipal affairs minister and one of the most decent and unselfish politicians I have ever met, was the leading contender. He had no burning personal ambition to be premier, but others thought he was the best qualified to guide the transition to a new era, and he was willing to serve. Several days before he was to make his formal announcement that he would seek the leadership of the Alberta

Social Credit Party, he invited me to come to his office. He wanted to know whether any of the younger people associated with the party and the government wanted to take a run at the leadership. If so, he said, he was more than willing to help them get the support of the older generation of Social Credit MLAs and organizers. I have not known any politician other than Harry, who was one step away from the leadership of his party and the premier's office, to pause, look around, and sincerely inquire whether he could help someone of the younger generation occupy that spot.

I told him that I thought none of the younger crowd was ready, and Harry went on to win the leadership and occupy the premier's office. For a year afterwards, I worked one day a week to help smooth the transition. At the same time, I began to develop a private consulting practice that would allow me to keep in contact with various western economic interests, to broaden my understanding of the non-governmental sector, and to study various political issues that would be relevant to the future.

CHAPTER THREE

Adventures in the Marketplace

On December 16, 1968, my father and I set up a management consulting firm named M and M Systems Research Ltd. (No matter what we called it, others kept referring to the company as "Mannings'" so we later changed the name to Manning Consultants Limited.)

It was only at this time, when my father had retired from public life at the age of sixty, that he was able to increase his earnings significantly. Besides being appointed to the Senate, he was elected a director of a number of national companies (he had long been an advocate of better regional representation on the boards of national and multinational companies and was pleased to provide such representation himself in later life). Also, by 1970 my parents sold our family farm, which by then had appreciated in value because of the discovery of gravel underneath it and its proximity to Edmonton.

Because of his Senate and board positions, my father was occupied full time, so I took the position of president and general manager of the firm and was responsible for its development and management.

There was still considerable media speculation that my father would try to manage the Alberta government from behind the scenes, so we did not want to market our services to the Alberta government or its agencies. Also, because the energy industry and the provincial government are so closely related, we did not particularly want to work for the big oil companies.

My first official consulting job, therefore, was for a scrap metal dealer (he resented the term "junk dealer") in east Edmonton named Benny Shugarman. Benny wanted to know how many used car bodies there were in northern Alberta, and whether the Stelco steel mill would pay him a high enough price for scrap steel to justify the purchase of a large machine for crushing the old car bodies into bales.

I hired a number of high school students to help us search every back alley and junkyard in northern Alberta for car bodies, and to mark our findings on a huge map. I also examined and priced the crusher Benny wanted to buy, and calculated the price he needed from Stelco to sustain a profitable operation. Benny and I then went to see Bill Grundy, the manager of Stelco, but the price Bill offered was not enough. My recommendation to Benny was to proceed no further. But that was not what Benny wanted to hear; he had his heart set on buying that crusher. Thus I was confronted on my very first job with the dilemma that faces every consultant, and in a certain sense, every politician. Do you tell 'em what they wanna hear, or do you tell 'em what they oughta hear? I found that telling 'em what they oughta hear is not usually as well received, at least in the short run, as telling 'em what they wanna hear.

At the outset, if our firm had any specialty, it was in applying systems analysis techniques to business problems and planning. How we got into systems analysis requires some explanation.

As I was finishing my last year at the University of Alberta, I developed an interest in systems analysis as a planning and management tool, just at the time that this perspective was beginning to be applied in the United States defence and aerospace industries. According to the systems perspective, any organizational unit—from a cell in biology, to a firm or industry in economics, to a government service or social program, to a community—can be viewed as a system. It produces certain outputs (products) which can be defined and measured. It requires certain inputs (resources) to function. Its parts or components are so arranged as to perform various functions that ultimately convert the inputs into outputs. The operations of the system are also subject to certain external and internal constraints.

By analyzing and managing complex organizations as systems you can identify and solve certain types of operational problems and improve the productivity of the organization. By taking output information and feeding it back to the organization as an information input, you can sometimes make the operation more self-directed or automated.

When Erick Schmidt and I were working on the Alberta government's White Paper on Human Resources Development we had used a crude form of systems analysis to analyze the problem of human underdevelopment. While this attracted little or no interest in Alberta, it did catch the attention of an American aerospace firm named TRW Systems of Redondo Beach, California.

TRW was founded by an engineer named Cy Ramo and a physicist named Woolridge who had worked for Hughes Aircraft in the 1950s. When the United States government went looking for a contractor to manage the development of the Minuteman missile program, Ramo and Woolridge submitted a proposal based on the application of systems management principles. They were awarded the contract, and with capital supplied by the Thompson auto products group, established TRW.

By the late 1960s, TRW was heavily involved in systems development for the United States defence and aerospace programs, but they wanted to diversify their base, and were exploring the relevance of their systems analysis techniques to so-called "civil systems" such as health care, education, and municipal government. They set up a health systems group which did some conceptual work for the Alberta government on what was later to become the Walter Mackenzie Research Hospital in Edmonton. While working on this project, the members of that group saw a copy of the White Paper on Human Resources Development and sent a copy to Ramo.

Some months later, Ramo invited my father, Dave Wilson, and me to dinner at his Los Angeles home. He had also invited a number of his political and industry friends to attend, and interspersed the dinner with "readings" from the White Paper (especially the parts that commended systems analysis as a public policy-making tool). After dinner, my father gave a short talk and answered questions, and Ramo expressed an interest in following up on the "systems approach" to human resources development discussed in the White Paper.

In fall 1967, I was given a leave of absence by the National Public Affairs Research Foundation to move to Redondo Beach, California, to work on a short-term research contract with TRW. My specific task was to contribute to a "human resources development model" using systems analysis techniques. (This contract meant that Sandra had to take a leave of absence from her nursing, and she never did get back to it. In retrospect, this was probably not the wisest decision, but at that stage we were as optimistic about the future and our capacities to handle it as it was possible to be.)

The principal benefit to me of my time at TRW was the exposure I gained to the American aerospace effort and the organizational devices used to harness the resources of both the public and private sectors to a single national objective. I was particularly intrigued by the "Requests for Proposals" (RFPs), which contracting agencies like the National

Aeronautics and Space Administration (NASA) used to harness the abilities and resources of hundreds of firms and government agencies to the task of attaining the national goal of getting a man on the moon by 1970.

In Canada, of course, if we had adopted "getting to the moon" as a national objective under the 1960s Liberal administration, we would have established the Get to the Moon Department of the federal government, with a deputy minister and half a dozen assistant deputy ministers. The underlying assumption would be that national objectives must be pursued primarily by instruments of government, and if the private sector was to be involved at all, it would be told exactly what to do and how to do it. No doubt we would also have had a national debate on whether the first astronaut should be a francophone or an anglophone.

The genius of the RFP technique as practised by NASA in the early days was that the United States government focused on defining the goal to be achieved and the constraints (temporal, financial, technical) to which the effort would be subject. But they left it largely up to the contractors to propose how the goal should be achieved and how the resources should be assembled and managed.

It occurred to me that this same Request for Proposals technique, under the guidance of government contracting agencies, might be used to link public and private resources to more down-to-earth objectives like improvements in regional development, health care, or educational services. It would also provide a mechanism for striking an appropriate division of labour between the public and private sectors in relation to particular tasks—a division of labour based not on ideology (only governments should do this, or only private enterprise should do that), but on the more practical criterion of "Who can do the best job in the most cost-effective way?"

After my father and I set up M and M Systems Research, I wrote a promotional booklet entitled "Requests for Proposals and Social Contracts." We marketed the concept through the firm, and became involved in a number of interesting experiments involving the contracting of public and private resources to attain socio-economic objectives. These objectives included providing support and rehabilitation services to single transient men through a hostel operation in Calgary, operating a pioneer "home care" program for Halton County in Ontario, and involving native people in a bitumen trucking operation for Gulf Oil.

Once when I was visiting Washington, D.C., a friend of mine who knew of my interest in innovative procurement mechanisms took me to see a special exhibit at the Smithsonian Institution. There on the wall was an enlarged copy of a two-page RFP issued by the United States Signal Corps in 1908 inviting proposals for the construction and delivery of "One Heavier-Than-Air Flying Machine." And there on the wall next to it was a response submitted by Orville and Wilbur Wright.

By contemporary contracting and tendering standards, the Signal Corps' RFP was simplistic and incomplete. The issuers didn't really know what they wanted other than "one heavier-than-air flying machine." They couldn't tell the contractor how to build it because they didn't know themselves. All they could do, besides stating the objective, was to list a few guidelines, some of which appear quaint in retrospect (such as the requirement that the flying machine should have some device to permit a safe descent in the event of an accident to the propelling machinery). And yet it was that simple RFP that helped lift the aeroplane out of the bicycle shop of two eccentric inventors into the realm of organized production to meet a real need. I couldn't help but wonder what the equivalent social RFP might look like—perhaps one calling for "one innovative child care centre" or "one innovative industrial training centre," and who might issue it or respond to it.

To this day, I believe that many public-policy objectives (such as the establishment of a modern and cost-effective rail passenger service for Canada) might be better achieved by more innovative and inexpensive means than those currently being used. But this would require some government to ask the question, "Is there someone else out there with an innovative idea who could achieve this objective more effectively than we can ourselves?" and then to use the appropriate RFP and contract-management techniques to harness the right mix of public and private resources to attaining that goal.

I should also mention two other events that came out of my second working experience in California. The first was a visit to southeast Asia in 1968 during the Vietnam War; the second was an investigation into interdisciplinary research. The controversy over United States involvement in Vietnam was raging in southern California at that time, and Sandra and I had listened to all the arguments pro and con. We then decided to use the savings we had accumulated from my time at TRW to visit southeast Asia ourselves. We particularly wanted to visit Cambodia before that country was closed to Westerners.

In Cambodia we visited the ancient temple ruins at Siam Reap in the north, a town sometimes used as a rest and relief centre by North Vietnamese regulars. Our guide, who spoke French, engaged a few officers in conversation. He asked precisely what they were fighting for, and their answer was surprisingly nonpolitical. They were professional soldiers, they said. Their fathers had fought the Japanese and the French, and they were fighting the Americans. Their children would probably fight somebody else.

The tragedy that later befell Cambodia is one of the unimaginable horrors of the twentieth century, on the same scale as the Holocaust. What action or policy might have prevented it, I do not know, but even at the time of our visit, the people we encountered had a sense of deep foreboding.

In Japan we were impressed by the cleanliness, the small dimensions of everything (people, roads, machines, houses), the strong anti-war sentiment, the vicious left-right political antagonisms, the high degree of urbanization and industrialization, and the strong role of the private sector in providing social security for workers.

In my work at TRW I became more fascinated than ever with matrices. (The word *matrix* is the Latin word for womb—the place where life begins—and it is in the investigation of new possibilities that matrices are especially helpful.) The marketing people at TRW were always trying to predict the future so that they could spot and exploit a technological opportunity before their competitors. To help them make predictions, I wrote a short paper proposing what I called an Interdisciplinary Matrix of the Sciences. It was to be constructed by simply taking the United States Labor Department's classification of scientific manpower (a list of about a thousand scientific disciplines and sub-disciplines) and organizing it into a matrix. I then proposed to shade in the cells of the matrix based on the extent to which there was a large or small body of literature examining the inter-disciplinary possibilities defined by each cell. For example, the cell defined by the intersection of some well-known branch of mathematics with some well-known branch of physics would be darkly shaded, whereas the cell defined by the intersection of, say, astronomy with linguistics would be lightly shaded.

My thesis then was that a systematic investigation of the interdisciplinary potential of the lighter cells might lead to some innovative discoveries. To my knowledge, this idea was never seriously pursued by TRW, but it did provoke some lively lunch-time discussions as we tried to guess what undiscovered possibilities might lurk at the intersection of paleontology and sociology. Typical of our different national temperaments, my American friends were more intrigued by the lightly shaded cells, whereas my Canadian friends felt that an investment of investigative effort in the darker cells would be a safer bet.

Early in the 1970s, our consulting firm became involved in another line of consulting work in community economic development.

The case studies conducted in conjunction with the Alberta government's White Paper on Human Resources Development had identified the south shore of Lesser Slave Lake, 150 miles north of Edmonton, as one of the most underdeveloped parts of the province. By the late 1960s the Strom administration had launched a major community development effort there, the federal government had designated the region as a Special Area under its Regional Economic Development legislation, and most importantly, the oil industry had become interested in the petroleum potential of the region.

One day, a group of five people came to ask my father and me to join with them in forming a "community development company" for the Slave Lake Region. The group included Leo Boisvert, the mayor of the town of Slave Lake and owner of the local grocery store; Mel Zachary, a town councillor and owner of a small regional air service; Neil Gilliat, the provincial human resources development coordinator and a former forestry man; Walter Twinn (now Senator Twinn), chief of the Sawridge Indian Band; and Jim Ergil, an industrial engineer with the Alberta Research Council whom I had known for some time and who was always promoting "innovative schemes." Stan Kendall, a vice-president of Pacific Western Securities, was also involved.

The members of this group felt that north central Alberta—to which the town of Slave Lake was the gateway—had enormous economic and human potential. They believed that the federal and provincial governments, through their respective development programs, were planning to build badly needed infrastructure and make available millions of dollars in incentive grants to outside developers. What the group wanted to create was a local community development vehicle through which local people could participate directly as investors and project initiators in the social and economic development of their region.

The group had already gone ahead and incorporated a private company called Slave Lake Developments Limited, which had two stated objectives: "to undertake projects which would contribute to the social and economic development of the Slave Lake Region" and "to earn a fair and reasonable return for its shareholders on the capital invested in those projects."

When the group asked my father and me to act as consultants to help develop the company and its initial projects, we were very interested. First of all, we liked the initiative they had taken in putting the company together and seeking us out. There were many underdeveloped communities in Alberta at that time and we were familiar with most of them, but most of them tended to sit back and wait for the government to come to their rescue.

Second, the dual objectives of Slave Lake Developments (SLD) represented an attempt to synthesize social and economic objectives within a corporate vehicle. This was a challenge with which we could readily identify.

We therefore agreed to work with them. We would charge a consulting fee, but defer its collection until the company was able to pay. Several other resource people, including SLD's first solicitor, Andy Andrekson (now an Alberta Queen's Bench Justice in Edmonton), did the same.

On our advice, the company was reincorporated as a public company to allow a larger number of local shareholders to participate. An associate company, Slave Lake Developments Associates Ltd., was incorporated, through which we hoped to encourage some of the oil companies to participate with us in joint ventures.

We identified our first venture as a housing project to be called Woodland Place—two apartment buildings and forty-six townhouse units—in an oil-field service town (Slave Lake) with virtually no rental accommodation. The project satisfied a socio-economic need, and the rental structure allowed it to earn a reasonable rate of return. A long-term mortgage was negotiated with Central Mortgage and Housing Corporation. A prospectus was drawn up seeking authorization to sell SLD common shares, mainly in the Slave Lake region, for $1 per share. An expanded board of directors was chosen, with Leo Boisvert serving as chairman and myself as president.

Although I was an officer of SLD, I really acted more as a consultant and representative of the company to the oil companies and the governments. But for the next twenty years, I travelled at least once a month to Slave Lake for meetings with SLD's board and management people.

Almost everything I know about the people and special challenges of resource-industry service towns—and there are literally thousands of these in Canada—I owe to the people of Slave Lake, my fellow directors on the board of Slave Lake Developments, and our community development adventures in north central Alberta.

Eventually, most of SLD's common shares came to be held by about three hundred families and small businesses, 75 percent of which were in the Slave Lake Region. No one shareholder held more than 10 percent of the shares, which allowed SLD truly to represent itself as a community company. While several shareholders—the Sawridge Band or the Bois-verts, for example—could easily have owned and controlled the entire company, they limited their holdings in order to achieve a broader community base for the company's operations.

My first major assignment for the company was to try to find some joint-venture partners for our Woodland Place Housing Project. We identified six oil companies operating in the area whose workers needed rental accommodation, and went after the companies for a "social investment" of $25,000 each. In the case of Imperial Oil, for example, I started with their field representative in Slave Lake, and worked my way up to a senior official in Calgary. My father, meanwhile, would put in a word for us with someone higher up.

One morning, much to my surprise, I got a phone call from Bill Twaits, the president of Imperial Oil, asking, rather bluntly, "What's all this about you trying to get a $25,000 'social investment' out of Imperial?" I hurriedly explained the concept—that we had a group of people in Slave Lake who wanted to develop their community through private enter-prise, that they had raised some capital through local share sales, that they needed some joint-venture partners to capitalize a project to house oilfield workers, and that they hoped to buy out their joint-venture partners in a short while if the project was a success.

"Why don't you go to our charity people?" asked Twaits.

"Because," I explained, "these people don't want charity or a govern-ment grant. They want investment capital on which their project will pay a return."

"Then why don't you go to our real estate people?" asked Twaits.

"Because" (I could tell he was getting impatient) "I know what kind of return your real estate people will be looking for, and this project can't deliver it. We want you to take a portion of your return in the form of a social benefit—better housing for your field people in Slave Lake and some community good will. That's why we call it a 'social investment.' "

"Imperial doesn't have a policy on 'social investments,' " said Twaits. "I'd have to discuss it with my board. Good-bye." And he hung up.

I could hardly imagine the president of Imperial Oil in Toronto asking his board of directors to discuss an agenda item headed "$25,000 social investment in Slave Lake." Several days later, however, he called back and said, "I discussed this with my people. We are going to give you your $25,000. I know that you are now going to run around Alberta saying you got a $25,000 'social investment' out of Imperial Oil. But I want you to know," his voice was rising, "that as far as I'm concerned, IT'S CHARITY!"

To make a long story short, we got another "social investment" from Rainbow Pipeline (a joint venture between Imperial, Mobil, and Aquitaine). The Woodland Place project was successfully completed and made money from day one. Within three years, Slave Lake Developments was in a position to buy out its joint-venture partners and stand on its own feet.

To celebrate this achievement, we put on a little luncheon in Calgary. The SLD Directors came down from Slave Lake, as did my father and I from Edmonton. Our special guests were Walt Dingle, representing Imperial, and Ed Bredin of Mobil, representing Rainbow. After a nice lunch and a little speechifying, Leo Boisvert handed Imperial's cheque for $25,000 to Walt Dingle. He then handed Walt another cheque representing the 6 percent return we had promised. Leo handed a similar set of cheques to Ed Bredin.

After it was all over, Ed Bredin came to me and said, "Look, none of us expected to get this back, and we've already written it off. Could you find some charitable project up there we could donate this money to?" After a huddle with the Slave Lake directors, we advised him that the Slave Lake seniors were raising money to build a Senior Citizens' Drop-In Centre and that they would welcome a contribution. And so that "social investment" went back to Slave Lake.

Some day, an economic historian will do a thorough case study of the economic and social development of north central Alberta, paying attention to the relative contributions of the federal and provincial governments, the private sector (in particular, the oil and forestry companies), and the local players (in particular, the municipal governments, the Indian bands, and the local entrepreneurs and businesses). The anecdotes and lessons on grassroots economic development contained in the minute books and files of Slave Lake Developments would be a valuable contribution to such a study. At the corporate level, there would be the story of knocking on the doors of thirty-five mortgage companies before obtaining the first commercial mortgage money for an office building in Slave Lake. At the community level, there would be the story of the fire in townhouse no. 37 (total value of the fire/smoke damage, $500; damage caused by the antics of the Volunteer Fire Department, $5,000). There would also be the story of SLD's one serious business failure, an unsuccessful attempt to rescue the local GM dealership during the crash after the National Energy Program, and all the personal heartache these types of failures entail in small towns.

I eventually resigned from the board of SLD in 1987 to pursue my political activities with the Reform Party. I was succeeded by my friend and associate, Doug Victoor, a financial consultant, who is ably assisted by SLD's general manager, Dave Lebsack.

In the year I resigned, the market value of the company's assets was more than $10 million, and SLD had paid common share dividends every year since 1975. The real dividend for me, however, was twenty years of association with the people of Slave Lake and twenty years of experience with the trials and rewards of community economic development.

Despite my personal interest in the economic and financial side of the petroleum business, our consulting firm's involvement with the energy industry was usually on the "softer issues"—community relations, environmental relations, relations with native peoples, regulatory relations, and political relations.

One day in 1978 I got a call from Frank Spragins, the president of Syncrude, asking me to attend a meeting. I had met Frank before, in a small office at Syncrude's research station in Sherwood Park, when the Syncrude proposal to extract oil (and several other minerals) from the Athabasca tar sands was still just a gleam in the developer's eye. In 1973 the project had begun, but Frank now had a special concern he wanted to discuss.

The original Syncrude agreement had included a specific commitment to involve native workers and native businesses in the construction and operations of the plant. However, acting on these commitments was proving to be difficult. Syncrude would invest considerable time and energy in training a small group of natives as heavy equipment operators, for example, only to have some crusty old foreman chew out one of the native crew members his very first day on the job. Then all the native crew members would quit and it was back to square one.

What Frank proposed was that a group of individuals with a number of the larger oil companies should set up an informal discussion group. The group would meet at least once a quarter to exchange information on ways and means of increasing native employment and native business activity in the energy sector. Frank wanted me to coordinate this group, and I readily agreed to do so.

Some of the original members of this Economic Development Discussion Group (EDDG) included representatives of Syncrude, Esso Resources, Shell Canada, NOVA Corporation, TransAlta Utilities, and the provincial government's Native Secretariat. Most of these people were involved firstly because they had a personal interest in establishing better relations between native people and the energy industry, and secondly because their companies supported such an objective.

Over the nine years I was involved with the EDDG, its membership expanded to include, at various times, Husky Oil, Dome, Gulf Canada,

Suncor, Bank of Montreal, Union Oil, BANAC (Business Assistance to Native Albertans Corporation), Peace Hills Trust, Alberta Power, and Indian Affairs.

David Berger originally joined the EDDG as a representative of the provincial government's Native Secretariat. In 1982 he left the secretariat and came to work with Manning Consultants full time, primarily in native relations, government relations, and socio-economic development.

David came from a Jewish family, grew up in Montreal, and studied political science at the University of Alberta. His background and work experience made him very sensitive and sensible in dealing with development challenges complicated by racial animosities and cross-cultural communications problems. David had good writing skills and a general interest in politics and the many other subject areas in which our firm maintained an interest. He also had a wicked sense of humour. (When the provincial Conservatives were having their leadership convention to choose a successor to Peter Lougheed, David produced and distributed a poster promoting Sheik Yamani as the next Premier of Alberta. His campaign slogan was "Yamani or your life.") When I had to give up the EDDG as a result of my increasing political involvements in 1987, David took over the coordination of the EDDG, a position he still holds at the time of writing.

One project the EDDG undertook in 1981 was to organize a Native Business Development Conference in Edmonton. It was designed to bring together owners and operators of native businesses with oil company executives and managers in a position to buy the products and services of those businesses.

Members of the EDDG tended to draw a sharp distinction between "native politicians" who *talked* a great deal about economic development, and genuine "native businesspeople" who actually *practised* entrepreneurship in the marketplace. The 1981 conference was intended to bring real native business operators together with potential customers in a nonpolitical atmosphere.

The conference was attended by 150 native businesspeople representing more than eighty native business enterprises. These included thirty women and some fifteen husbands and wives involved in the same business. Of the native businesspeople who preregistered and paid their own registration fee, only five did not show up. On the other hand, there were sixteen no-shows from among those native delegates who were preregistered but whose registration fee had been prepaid by a band council, native association, or government. Seventy-three industry people representing thirty-three different companies, and twenty-seven political and government people (both native and non-native) also attended.

By far the most important consequence of the conference was the cautious but positive interaction in the halls and at the meals between native businesspeople and industry people. At one point, an oil company vice-president, wanting to break the ice at his table, asked Sam Sinclair of the Métis Association, "Exactly when did 'the Métis nation' begin in western Canada?"

"About nine months after the white man got to the West," Sam replied.

At the end of the dinner and entertainment of the second night, many of the delegates were looking for fun as well as for business. Bob Stuffco, a highly skilled construction worker (who was tragically killed a few years later in an industrial accident), and his brother Phil (a lawyer and my brother-in-law) got hold of the microphones and began to do their imitation of a chainsaw gang operating in the bush. The sound was so realistic that I had to do some explaining to the hotel manager, who had received a frantic call from his staff saying that "those Indians and oilmen have a chainsaw in the main ballroom and are sawing up the furniture!"

Many of the native enterprises represented at the Edmonton conference were new and struggling. One good contract or one good order could spell the difference between survival and collapse. All the same, optimism prevailed in 1981. No one at the conference envisioned the impending downturn in the industry brought on by the National Energy Program and the collapse of world energy prices—a downturn that would wipe out many of the frail and struggling native business ventures in Alberta and result in a severe reduction of the socio-economic development activities of most of the oil companies.

Through the EDDG I had a good opportunity to assess various industry and government efforts to increase native employment in the energy industry and the work done by native enterprises. One company, NOVA, adopted and vigorously pursued a voluntary policy of ensuring that the percentage of natives in its workforce matched or exceeded the percentage of natives in the general population. In my judgment, this approach was more successful and better accepted at the field level than the affirmative action approach (government-imposed quotas).

EDDG members and companies supported an Alberta Native Business Directory, the Business Assistance to Native Albertans Corporation, and a Native Venture Capital Fund. Many of the EDDG members also helped persuade their companies to hold formal workshops and seminars—

for field people as well as executives—on native relations and cross-cultural communications. Our own firm sponsored or participated in several cross-cultural communications seminars in which resource people (such as anthropologist Edward Van Dyke, and cross-cultural communications expert Dan Kelly) used anthropological data and simple communications models to discuss ways and means of communicating effectively across cultural boundaries.

At one of these sessions, for example, we analyzed a memorandum on economic development written by a consultant employed by the Department of Indian Affairs to the Frog Lake Indian Band. The analysis indicated that 45 percent of the words and concepts used in the memo were not even in the vocabulary of the people for whom it was ostensibly prepared.

I found myself beginning to use a "communications planning checklist" derived from a simple Source-Message-Receiver (S-M-R) communications model, in planning my own communications activities (letters, brochures, advertisements, reports) and those of some of our other clients.

This model suggests that in planning any major communications exercise, you should ask and answer such questions as the following:

1. Who is the target of your communications?
2. What do you know about this target that will assist you in communicating effectively with it?
3. What is the general context in which the communications will occur?
4. To what competing messages and "noise" is this target subject?
5. What is the most appropriate medium for communicating with this target?
6. What is the primary response which you desire from this target as a result of your communications? That is, what is your communications objective?
7. What is the net impression you want to leave with this target?
8. What are the key messages to be communicated to this target? Express each message in one sentence or less.
9. What should be the overall "tone" of the messages and the communications effort?
10. Can you identify any useful anecdotes, analogies, illustrations, "pictures," which may be used to effectively illustrate or carry the messages? What analogies or illustrations might the target use in attempting to communicate your message to someone else?

11. Who will be the source (spokesperson) for your communications?
12. How is "feedback" from this target to be received and interpreted?
13. Can you identify any strategic guidelines which would be useful in directing this communications effort?

I noticed that some of my management and engineering friends in the energy industry seemed to take the task of improving their communications more seriously when it was presented in terms of a "systems model" grounded in a scientific explanation of communications. (One of their frequent complaints about the traditional communications and public relations people in their own firms or in advertising agencies was that they always seemed to be "flying by the seat of their pants" with no strategic sense or scientific discipline behind them.) I also noticed that it was getting easier to communicate certain types of information and planning processes to management and engineering people through their personal computers than it was by other means.

I therefore took our cross-cultural communications planning framework (the S-M-R model and checklist) and, with the help of two talented computer people (Ray Wong and Lily Hoy of Compu-Ware Ltd.), incorporated it into a computer software program called COMMUNICATE 500. I then set up a Communications Planning Centre in our consulting offices where this software could be used to develop communications plans. We used it to prepare plans for our consulting clients for presentations, reports, press releases, speeches, and advertising programs.

A client, preferably accompanied by his or her communications people, could come to our Planning Centre with a particular communications task in mind. We would sit around our planning table, in front of computer monitors which popped up from the table, and the operator would call up COMMUNICATE 500. I would lead the planning session, guided by the model, with questions, prompts, and background information appearing on the screens. The operator would capture the essence of our discussions and decisions with a word processing program. And at the end of the session, the client could walk out with a printed communications plan for achieving the objective.

Of course, the process did not always work this smoothly. But its productivity was very high, and COMMUNICATE 500 could be made "smarter" each time it was used. We were able to produce high-quality plans very quickly, and therefore to charge a significantly higher billing rate.

I wanted to expand our Planning Centre capability to conduct other computer-aided planning functions—such as feasibility analyses, preparation of financial and business plans, and even legislative analyses. For example, I drew up a specification for a program called LEGISLATE 500, using my old list of questions for distinguishing a bad piece of legislation from a good one, which could be used to conduct second-reading analyses of bills that were before a legislature or parliament.

All these intentions had to be put on hold when I closed down the consulting practice to work full-time on the development on the Reform Party in 1987. But if I were not in the political business, I would probably be operating and expanding a computer-aided planning centre—a high-tech delivery system for consulting services—along these lines. Even now, I still use COMMUNICATE 500 in planning and preparing my political speeches, and some day I may yet have an opportunity to develop and use LEGISLATE 500.

Two other consequences flowed from my long-time involvement with the Economic Development Discussion Group (EDDG): one was my participation in the socio-economic impact assessment of the huge heavy-oil extraction plant proposed by Esso Resources at Cold Lake in 1979; the other was an opportunity to meet and work with a remarkable Indian woman named Ernestine Gibot.

In 1979, Esso Resources proposed to build a massive heavy oil extraction plant near Cold Lake in northeastern Alberta. To get the necessary regulatory approvals, Esso had to file an impact assessment with the province's Energy Resources Conservation Board, including an assessment of how the plant would affect the seven Indian reserves in the area.

Several false starts had already been made—a preliminary study was considered incomplete, and a study conducted by the area Tribal Council did not fulfil all the regulatory requirements. By the time we got involved, Esso's field people and the bands themselves were getting sick and tired of consultants, meetings, questionnaires, and a seemingly endless process of data collection.

Eventually we got the job done, and our seven impact assessments, along with a huge pile of other material, were filed with the ERCB a few hours before the final deadline. (It has been observed that if Canada ever runs out of oil, we can just start to burn the studies and transcripts that have been generated by regulatory hearings, and that ought to provide enough fuel for another fifty years.)

From my standpoint, the impact assessment of the Cold Lake Project was not only informative, but also fortuitous. The entire impact area lay within what was to become the federal constituency of Beaver River, the site of the Reform Party's first electoral victory when Deborah Grey was elected in a by-election in March of 1989.

The seven bands involved in the assessment were the Saddle Lake Band, the Kehewin Band, the Heart Lake Band, the Whitefish Band, the Beaver Lake Band, the Frog Lake Band, and the Cold Lake Band. The Saddle Lake reserve was the largest of the seven: the band there had some petroleum revenues and a strong, aggressive administration. Saddle Lake was also the home of the famous Steinhauers.

Henry Bird Steinhauer, an Ojibwa Indian who had come west from Upper Canada in 1840, was instrumental in getting the Saddle Lake band to take up agriculture. There is a story told of how he bought the band's first breaking plough. When other members asked what was going to pull the plough, since they had no suitable horses, Henry harnessed himself and others to it.

At the other end of the spectrum was the Frog Lake reserve, a divided reserve with many internal problems and one of the most underdeveloped communities in western Canada. At the south boundary of the reserve, which was the site of the famous Frog Lake massacre during the second Riel Rebellion, there was a small store, with an Esso sign shot full of bullet holes. Rob Fricker, the Esso study coordinator, and I had our picture taken under the sign, and sent it to Calgary with the suggestion that perhaps we should be receiving "hazard pay." In reality, however, the people at Frog Lake were very hospitable to us, and I only wish that we could have proposed some real solutions to their oppressive problems.

The reserve closest to the proposed plant was that of the Cold Lake Band. While the other six bands in the area were composed largely of Crees, the Cold Lake Band was primarily Chipewyan. For historical reasons, the Crees and the Chipewyans did not always get along. I personally knew far less about the Chipewyan people than I did about the Crees, and therefore began to search for a native contact who could bring me up to speed.

One day, a consultant friend of mine, Geneva Ensign, who was involved in evaluating a government-sponsored Native Women Employment Training Program, came to my office. She brought with her a Chipewyan woman named Ernestine Gibot, who eventually taught me at least half of what I know about Indian people and the social welfare system. I asked Ernestine to meet with me for one hour per week to talk about these subjects, and I offered to pay her $20 an hour. With great misgivings, she agreed. We initially met for about twenty-five weeks.

At first Ernestine was shy, and especially reluctant to talk about the spiritual aspects of Indian life. She was afraid that I would not understand or, worse yet, laugh. She referred to people with jobs, especially office jobs or government positions, as "high people," and she referred to the language of bureaucrats and consultants as "high words." Eventually, as she began to feel more at ease, she would talk more about the world of "the spirit"—the Holy Spirit of the Trinity, as defined by her Catholic background; and the spirit of the wolf, the bear, and of Lake Athabasca, as defined by her Indian background. To Ernestine, this spirit world was as real as that of streets, houses, offices, cars, money, and paper.

I learned that she had been born in 1925 in Fort Chipewyan in northern Alberta. Her father, Joseph Fortin, was a trapper and hunter, part Chipewyan and part French-Canadian. Her mother, the former Angèle Ber Reze, was Chipewyan also, from Reindeer Lake, Saskatchewan. Of the fifteen children born to Ernestine's parents, only four survived to adulthood.

When Ernestine was five years old, she was taken from her family to attend the Catholic residential school in Fort Chipewyan. After completing grades one to four, learning French and English in the process, she returned home. But when she got there she did not recognize her mother, sister, and brother, and the ways of the bush had become foreign to her.

At the age of sixteen, Ernestine married a Cree trapper named François Gibot, a man twice her age, who had been married before and had five children. For the next thirty-three years, until 1974, Ernestine lived with her husband, primarily in the bush, hunting and trapping. Ernestine described this period as her "time of suffering"—living most of the time in tents and winter shacks, nineteen pregnancies, fourteen live births, three early deaths, poverty, drinking, physical abuse, sickness, hopelessness. Three things sustained her spirit and will to live during this long period—the rugged beauty of the Lake Athabasca country, the company and comfort of her children and a few friends, and her deep and personal faith in God.

When Ernestine was twenty-six years old her parents died. They had lived and worked together as hunters and trappers for forty-two years and died within eighteen days of each other at the hospital in Fort Smith. Her parents had strongly impressed upon Ernestine two predictions and a promise, which were to have a profound impact on her future. The first prediction was that she would experience much suffering, the second was that she would endure if she remained faithful to God and the things they had taught her, and the promise was that one day she would help others (including whites) to understand Indian ways and the lessons that suffering teaches.

In 1974, Ernestine's health collapsed. She was taken from Fort Chip to a hospital in Edmonton. Before leaving, she was able to get her children into foster homes where she felt they would be safe. Both her doctor and her priest advised her that if she returned to her husband and her old life, she would die. At the age of forty-nine, with little formal education, no money, no friends at hand, no experience of city living or employment, and a drinking problem, Ernestine decided to start over in a strange city.

This is not the place to tell Ernestine's remarkable story.[1] Suffice it to say that after I got to know Ernestine, I retraced her steps from the time she got to Edmonton in 1974, until the time seven years later when she got her first genuine, full-time employment at a wage sufficient to sustain her. The path she followed took her to such agencies and destinations as the Charles Camsel Hospital, Poundmaker Lodge (an alcoholism treatment centre), provincial and city welfare offices, the Department of Indian Affairs, Hilltop House (a residence for Indian women), numerous bars, hotels, and liquor stores, the Court House, the city jail, several Catholic churches, the Edmonton Housing Authority, the Native Friendship Centre, the Alberta Native Communications Society, the Native Women Employment Training Program, the Native Counselling Service, and the Alberta Vocational College.

I noted that this complex network of "helping systems" delivered certain services effectively—health care, financial support, accommodation, and training. At the same time this network failed to provide guidance at critical times or to offer encouragement, incentive, and employment. Although the people who really helped Ernestine during this period were often individuals she would not have met had she not been "in the system," in order to truly help Ernestine, these individuals often had to step outside their professional roles and act on their own initiative, rendering services above and beyond those called for in their job descriptions and sometimes in violation of the system's rules.

This was the case, for example, with the doctor and the priest who said, "We shouldn't really be saying this, but you should leave the north and leave your husband if you want to live." It was also the case with the two workers at Poundmaker Lodge and Hilltop House who treated Ernestine as a friend rather than simply as a client. And it was the case with the staff at the Native Communications Society and the consultant who introduced Ernestine to me—individuals who went beyond the call of duty to bolster and encourage Ernestine's self-esteem.

I also found it significant that Ernestine's first impression of the potential helpfulness of a government agency or program was not based

---

1. Bob Collins, a former editor of the *Imperial Oil Review* and currently a features writer for *Reader's Digest,* has done this in a full-length story in the October 1984 edition of the *Digest* entitled "The Long Hard Road of Ernestine Gibot."

on its literature or the credentials of its personnel but simply on the attitude and friendliness of the secretary or receptionist guarding the door or answering the phone. These were always the first people Ernestine encountered when she went for help, and their response determined whether she persevered or not. (Her positive assessment of Manning Consultants, for example, was originally based not on my interview with her but on the friendly reception she got from our secretary and researcher Jeanie Clemenger.)

While I learned a great deal from Ernestine that was helpful to me in assessing the impact of the Esso heavy oil plant on the Indian bands of northeastern Alberta, I also learned that Ernestine desperately wanted a job—a real job. It became a personal and corporate challenge for me. Here we were, discussing various native employment schemes with a dozen companies on a regular basis. Surely we could help one forty-nine-year-old woman find one decent job—and do so not by pulling strings with employers we knew, but by equipping and encouraging Ernestine to find and hold that job herself.

At the end of one of our sessions, I asked Ernestine precisely how she spent her time during the day. She said she spent much of it visiting native people in the city who were sick in the hospital and needed comforting and counsel. Besides English and French, Ernestine spoke Cree, Chipewyan, and some Slavey, so she could be useful in interpreting the needs of Indian patients to hospital staff.

I told Ernestine that when some white people get fired or can't find a job, they do not go around saying they are unemployed. Instead they get little cards printed up that say they are a "consultant." They then spend their time appearing to be very busy and handing out these cards. After a while, someone actually gives them a job. Ernestine thought this sounded like a scheme that would only work for "high people," but she agreed to give it a try. We had some cards printed up introducing "Ernestine's Counselling Services" and I told her to give my name as a reference, since she had "counselled" me.

Ernestine continued to visit the hospitals. She handed out the cards. Soon I got some calls from the hospital administration asking what all this was about. The welfare people wanted to know if I was paying Ernestine something on the side. One thing led to another. Someone referred Ernestine to the Native Studies Program of the Edmonton Separate School Board. She got an interview. The board was short of funding but referred her to the Native Studies Program of the Edmonton Public School Board. Another interview was arranged. All of Ernestine's friends supplied references and we awaited the results with bated breath.

On September 12, 1980, I came into my office to find a message on my desk from Jeanie Clemenger written in big red letters. The message was "Ernestine has a Job!" She had been offered a position as a native liaison worker with the school board and was soon promoted to teacher's aide. It had taken seven years from the day Ernestine had decided to start a new life until the day she got a full-time job that paid a working wage.

I wrote up my experiences with Ernestine Gibot into a presentation entitled "A Job for Ernestine," and one morning offered it as a case study in "native employment" to our Economic Development Discussion Group. We sat around a boardroom table and discussed the maze through which this one courageous woman had travelled to get her first job. What could governments and oil companies do to shorten that path? I decided myself that the really important question was what are individuals (Indian and white) immersed in those systems prepared to do to shorten the path for the Ernestines of the future?

At the end of the session Ernestine dropped by to say a few words. We never applaud presentations at the EDDG, but that morning there was a departure from that rule.

This was not the end of the Ernestine story. There were to be many more heartaches (sickness, violent deaths in the family) as well as triumphs (the write-up in *Reader's Digest,* which inspired other native women to follow in Ernestine's footsteps). One of the problems with my current political work is that there is no time for this type of project or association anymore, and no opportunity to establish real contacts with people like Ernestine. Although politics broadens one's associations with people, it also trivializes most of them. Ernestine would say, however, that her parents' prophecy has come true. She has helped others (myself especially) "to understand Indian ways and the lessons that suffering teaches."

Another important area of my business consulting practice during the 1970s and 1980s was in regulated industries, particularly the utility industry.

Alberta, unlike most of the other provinces, does not have a single provincially owned electric utility. Instead, most of the province's electricity is provided by two investor-owned utilities—TransAlta Utilities (formerly Calgary Power) and Alberta Power—and one municipally owned generating utility, Edmonton Power.

For a number of years I served as an outside consultant on long-range planning assignments, mainly for TransAlta Utilities. Much of my knowledge of corporate planning, finance, and administration has come from my utility associations, especially my experiences with TransAlta, and I am deeply indebted to the executives, managers, and workers of Alberta's utilities for much of my business education. As Canada's largest investor-owned electric utility, TransAlta was always conscious of the need to ensure that its corporate activities served the long-range interests of Alberta, so as not to give provincial politicians looking for an election issue an excuse to nationalize it.

Because all our utility clients were "regulated enterprises" it was only natural that I should develop an interest in the whole regulatory process. In Alberta, the Energy Resources Conservation Board was responsible for approving and regulating the construction of generation and transmission facilities, while the Alberta Public Utilities Board was responsible for regulating electricity rates.

In the 1970s, the greatest concerns of all the interests dealing with energy regulatory tribunals across the country were "regulatory lag" and "regulatory burden"—the enormous time and cost requirements of regulatory hearings in a period when utility rates were rising sharply.

In 1975-76, I organized and carried out a major study (one of the largest and most expensive our firm ever coordinated) of the rate regulation practices of the National Energy Board, the Ontario Energy Board, and the Alberta Public Utilities Board. TransCanada Pipelines, whose first rate case before the National Energy Board required four years to complete, was one of the principal sponsors. Other sponsors included the three big gas-distribution utilities in Ontario at that time (Consumers Gas, Union Gas, and Northern and Central Gas), two Alberta-based utilities (TransAlta Utilities and Alberta Gas Trunk Line), and the Canadian Gas Association. While this may strike the average citizen as a rather boring subject, it is not so boring when you discover the high cost of regulatory delays, which affects both investors and consumers.

With the help of a number of economic, legal, and regulatory experts, our team produced a three-volume study on reducing regulatory lag—the time between the utility's first filing with a regulatory tribunal for a change in rates and the handing down of the actual rate decision—in the federal, Ontario, and Alberta jurisdictions.

This study gave me an opportunity to meet many of the key players in the regulated energy sector in Canada. It also gave me a number of fresh insights into the extent to which regulation can be used to direct private enterprise toward public policy objectives, and the point at which regulation becomes counterproductive.

In the course of my work, I also conducted a number of interviews in the United States, which has hundreds of investor-owned gas and electric utilities regulated by quasi-judicial regulatory tribunals. In Washington, D.C., I had a long session with a lawyer who had spent most of his career working with the Federal Power Commission. He suggested to me that if I wanted a quick way to find out what utility and interest-group executives, regulators, and legislators thought about regulation in the economy, I should simply ask them, "What is your understanding of the public interest?" Although the concept of "private property vested with a public interest" is much more highly developed in the United States than it is in Canada, I found that lawyer's advice useful, and it has helped to guide my own thinking on ways and means of reconciling conflicting private interests with public-policy objectives.

Some time later I attended a session of the Centre for the Study of Regulated Industries in Montreal under the direction of Dr. Roy Morrison. The centre brought together utility executives, interest-group representatives, regulators, academics, and consultants to compare notes on regulatory practices in Canada.

This particular dinner meeting was at the McGill University Faculty Club and I found myself sitting beside Clarence Powell, the former chairman of the Newfoundland Public Utilities Board. In keeping with the advice of the FPC lawyer, I asked him what he understood "the public interest" to be. He looked at me for a moment, took out his pen, and began drawing on the napkin. After a few moments he looked up and said, "The public interest is a vector sum." He then proceeded to explain.

To the regulator, "the world is a ball of tangled interests." These interests come in all sorts of guises, sizes, and colours, but they have two important characteristics. First, every interest possesses "direction" in relation to the issue or application at hand. Thus the regulator seeks to be sure that he understands the direction in which an interest is pushing or pulling. Second, every interest possesses a "magnitude," a weight which theoretically could or should be assigned to it relative to the decision or issue at hand. An entity which possesses both direction and magnitude may be represented by a "vector," as you may vaguely recall from those early courses in algebra or mathematics.

The regulatory arena thus becomes a place where vectors meet, a "field" where a number of these competing or cooperating interests are brought together in relation to some particular project or issue. The regulatory arena is more than a meeting place, for it provides a frame of reference by which the assembled interests may be identified, examined, weighed, and balanced. The role of the regulator within this frame of reference is to either approve or disapprove a proposed course of action, or to approve it subject to certain conditions. The determination of a course of action "in the public interest" is not a matter of choosing in favour of one particular interest or another. Rather, it is a matter of determining the alternative that best reconciles conflicting interests and rights, and also satisfies other important criteria.

I recount this incident to introduce one of the basic tools I continue to use in attempting to sort out and reconcile conflicting private and public interests in the political arena. Whenever I am approached by an interest group (and I believe interest groups play an essential role in our system of government), I try to assess the "direction" in which that group is pulling or pushing in relation to the issue at hand—the approval or rejection of a development project, for example, or the modification of some public policy. I assign a weight to this interest, taking into account its relative influence with the public and other factors. Invariably I find myself discounting the weight that the interest group itself assigns to its position, because it has been my experience that most interest groups tend to exaggerate their own influence and representativeness. (I know a number of politicians whose working definition of an interest group is "a group which places its own interest ahead of everyone else's.")

When an issue or public policy debate brings together a number of competing and cooperating interests, I usually search for a course of action that will reconcile them to the greatest extent possible while still satisfying other important criteria such as fairness and cost-effectiveness.

I am not suggesting that dealing with interest groups in the political arena can be reduced to some form of mathematical calculation. But if you are an interest-group representative—and I applaud you for feeling strongly enough about some public issue to organize with other like-minded people in that way—and you come to me with your brief, and you see me doodling with axes and arrows on my note pad, you should know that I am trying to weight and position your interest in relation to those of others and to "the public interest as a vector sum."

The nationalization of utilities interested me and I studied the takeover of enterprises such as Quebec's Shawinigan Light and Power, Nova Scotia Light and Power, and B.C. Electric by their respective provincial governments. In these cases those governments believed (rightly or wrongly) that their policy objectives could not be achieved as long as those utilities were in nongovernmental hands.

From 1972 to 1975 I monitored the effects of threats by the Barrett government in British Columbia to take over three investor-owned utilities in that province—threats which succeeded in driving away millions of dollars of potential investment capital from British Columbia.

(Alberta usually benefited economically from the election of NDP governments in the other western provinces, as nervous entrepreneurs moved capital and jobs to a friendlier economic environment.)

I also provided some consulting services to one of the utility companies that Barrett had threatened to expropriate, drawing upon our accumulated materials on "how to avoid being taken over by your provincial government." The chief executive officer of this company was a Maritimer who was intimately familiar with Herman Melville's famous sea story of Captain Ahab and Moby Dick. (Captain Ahab was the deranged captain of a whaling ship named the *Pequod*, who ultimately brought about the destruction of himself, his ship, and its crew through his fanatical pursuit of the great white whale, Moby Dick.)

Partly for security reasons, and partly because I find communication by analogy both amusing and effective, we would carry on a discussion of the Barrett government's pursuit of his company in terms of Captain Ahab and Moby Dick. Dave Barrett was Captain Ahab, the British Columbia government was the *Pequod*, the NDP cabinet and MLAs were the crew of the *Pequod*, and the company in question was Moby Dick. To make a long story short, Captain Ahab never got the great white whale. And when the *Pequod* finally capsized in the seas of electoral defeat in 1975, I sent a telegram to our client saying, "Captain Ahab is no more; long live Moby Dick!"

As an alternative to public ownership of public utilities, I had also thoroughly studied the model provided by the Alberta Gas Trunk Line—the forerunner of the present multinational energy and petrochemical company NOVA Corporation—and the case of an investor-owned company with a legislated public purpose.

In the early 1950s in Alberta a debate had raged on how to organize a single gas-gathering system, or "trunk line," for the province that could supply both the provincial gas distribution utilities and the export market. The socialists represented by the CCF argued that a provincially owned trunk line company was the only way to go, the petroleum industry argued for unfettered free enterprise, and my father's government ultimately opted for the creation of "a private-enterprise company with a public purpose."

In March 1954 my father rose in the legislature to introduce "The Alberta Gas Trunk Line Company Act." It created by statute an Alberta company whose prime purpose was to transport natural gas from the growing number of gas fields in the province and deliver it at the provincial boundaries to companies operating national and international pipeline facilities for the export of gas to eastern Canada and the United States. Most export companies would have preferred to build their own gathering lines within the province as an integral part of their national or international pipeline systems, which would have made the entire system subject only to the regulatory powers of the federal government under the federal Pipelines Act. The province opposed this arrangement for two reasons. First, it wanted to retain jurisdiction over the gas transmission facilities within the province in order to regulate or even terminate the delivery of gas to export companies' transmission lines should such a step ever become necessary in order to protect the interests of Alberta gas users. Second, it wanted to be in a position to ensure that the internal gas-gathering system was designed and operated to serve the interests of Alberta gas utility companies as well as gas exporters.

The Alberta Gas Trunk Line Company Act met both of these requirements. Gas producing companies, gas export companies, and gas utility companies within the province were empowered under the act to elect their own representatives on the company's board of directors. The act further provided for the government to appoint additional directors to represent the interests of the people of Alberta. Capital to finance the company's operations was raised by a stock offering, and while the shares carried no voting privileges and were offered exclusively to citizens of Alberta, the issue was vastly oversubscribed.

Because AGTL was not a provincial Crown corporation, it had greater political and constitutional freedom to do business outside the province. The potential existed for the owners of AGTL to develop a Canadian-based multinational energy company from a stable energy-utility base. Years later this is precisely what was done when the Lougheed government significantly altered the structure of AGTL, and, under Bob Blair, it was transformed into NOVA Corporation of Alberta. The concept of developing internationally competitive, Canadian-based multinational corporations from a utility base is now widely accepted (and practised) and shows exciting potential as an economic development strategy for Canada, as witnessed by companies like Canadian Pacific Ltd., Bell Canada Enterprises, and Norcen Energy Resources. The fact that the seeds for such a strategy existed in the original AGTL concept in the 1950s is a tribute to the foresight of those who conceived it.

Finally, I monitored the effects of massive federal government intervention in the energy market through the National Energy Program. This intervention affected virtually all our clients—energy company operations, megaprojects, and socio-economic activities; regulatory agencies, by completely changing the magnitude and direction of energy price regulation; service companies like Slave Lake Developments, whose markets contracted; and western political interests, who saw in the NEP a symbol of the institutional imbalance of the Canadian federal system. I will have more to say later on the contribution of the NEP to western alienation and the formation of the Reform Party of Canada.

During the twenty years that Manning Consultants Limited was a going concern, we undertook a variety of other projects and studies which gave me practical exposure to a wide spectrum of the Canadian community.

For example, when Charlie Hay, the former president of Gulf Canada, took on the job of organizing Hockey Canada before the first Canada-Soviet Union hockey series in 1972, he asked me to work with Chris Lang and others on Hockey Canada's long-range planning and organizational development. Like many other Canadians who are hockey fans, I remember exactly where I was (at Qualicum Beach on Vancouver Island with my family on a holiday) at the time Paul Henderson scored the winning goal with thirty-four seconds remaining in the eighth game in Moscow to win the series for Canada. All of us who had worked on the organizational development side of Hockey Canada had an exaggerated sense of our importance that day.

I have also had some exposure to the difficult task of encouraging scientific and technological innovation in Canada—a climate generally considered cool to such innovation. One of our earliest clients, for example, was a small company named Advanced Systems. It had been started by a retired American military man, who was attempting to adapt one of the earliest computer-operated supervisory control systems developed by the American space industry to monitoring pipeline and storage battery operations in the western Canadian oil patch. This particular system, which is still being marketed today, has gone through at least half a dozen hands since it was first brought to Canada, with each successive owner making some progress in refining and marketing the product before running out of capital and either going bankrupt or being forced to sell off the technology to a new owner with greater resources.

In 1970 the Senate Special Committee on Science Policy, chaired by Maurice Lamontagne, produced a three-volume report called "A Science Policy for Canada," recommending that the Canadian scientific community set more specific goals in its research and development efforts. After the report appeared, we tried to get some work helping scientific research teams make their funding applications to the federal government more goal-oriented. We soon found that it was a mistake to attempt to force basic scientists into goal-oriented research. I concluded that the only non-technical condition that governments should attach to funding such research should be the request that a greater and more focused effort be made to communicate the results of such research as broadly as possible and in a form that applications-oriented scientists and entrepreneurs might more readily digest.

In 1979, I got a call from David Mitchell, chief executive officer of Alberta Energy Company, saying that he and some other businesspeople wanted to establish a foundation to provide significant cash awards to Canadian innovators, and asking me to help with the organizational design and procedures. I took the job on and did considerable background research on the early detection of innovators. My father and I also took a trip to Norway and Sweden, where we met with representatives of the Nobel Prize Foundation and its selection committees to discuss their organizational, financing, and selection procedures. What my father didn't know at the time was that Mitchell and his colleagues intended to name their foundation the E.C. Manning Awards Foundation. (The foundation was subsequently established and currently awards a grand prize of $100,000, two prizes of $25,000 each, and another two prizes of $5,000 each to Canadian innovators each year.) My father has received more genuine satisfaction from this project than from many of the other honours he has received over the years.

A number of our projects had political ramifications. One of these was a major effort to secure the entrenchment of property rights in the Canadian Charter of Rights and Freedoms; another was development of "The Deal Model of Confederation," a model for predicting the outcome of federal-provincial negotiations and conferences. I also made presentations from time to time concerning our interpretations of various political events in the light of western Canadian history and political experience and addressed small study groups (some of our own creation) interested in such issues and interpretations. Very little of this work ever got into the public eye, although I still draw upon some of it in my current capacity as leader of the Reform Party of Canada.

In fall 1977, I wrote a memorandum on prospective constitutional changes for one of our utility clients, noting that the federal government's priority seemed to be entrenching language and cultural rights in a prospective charter, but no one seemed to be giving equal attention to the constitutional treatment of economic and property rights. This particular executive was connected with the newly formed Business Council on

National Issues, which subsequently made available some research funds that allowed our firm to draft and promote a property rights protection clause for possible inclusion in the Canadian constitution. The intention was to provide greater protection against confiscation of private property by governments than that provided by the common law, or the Diefenbaker Bill of Rights, or the draft Charter of Rights contained in the 1971 Victoria Charter.

I made arrangements with Professor Gerry Gall at the University of Alberta Law School to do some of the research and drafting. This was incorporated into a brief for presentation to various provincial governments, to whom Section 92 of the British North America Act assigned responsibility for "property and civil rights."

In our brief we argued that if the federal and provincial governments were going to consider entrenching any rights in a new constitution, then economic rights should be included. By "economic rights" or "economic civil liberties" we meant freedom of contract, the right to just and favourable conditions of work and fair wage compensation, certain consumer rights, and the right to the use and enjoyment of property. We wanted the Charter of Rights to include a provision that "in Canada no person shall be deprived, directly or indirectly, by any law of parliament or of a provincial legislature, of the use or enjoyment of property, unless that law provides for just compensation." This clause did not attempt to prevent governments from expropriating private property where this was necessary for public purposes, but if the government did take property for such purposes it should be required by the constitution to "pay fair."

Once the drafting was completed, the fun began. The challenge was to convince some provincial government to carry this clause, or one similar to it, into any federal-provincial discussion dealing with the Canadian constitution.

I drafted letters to the premiers and appropriate ministers of all ten provincial governments, asking them to consider our brief. I also met with representatives of the four western provincial governments, while some of our eastern colleagues went to see Premier Bill Davis of Ontario. Our communications with the governments of Quebec and the Atlantic provinces were primarily through correspondence.

At that point, I had grave reservations about the principle of entrenching rights in the constitution. But our argument was that if this was going to be done, conservative provincial governments should ensure that the list of rights went beyond Trudeau's, to include economic and other rights of particular importance to their electors and constituents.

In writing to premiers like René Lévesque of the Parti Québécois in Quebec and NDP Allan Blakeney of Saskatchewan—leaders of governments that could not be expected to be wildly enthusiastic about protecting property rights—my argument was that if you extended the definition of property to include "property held by the Crown in the right of the provinces," you would have constitutional protection against the expropriation of provincial resources (like oil, gas, and hydroelectric power) by the federal government through confiscatory taxation or price regulation.

In the end, we were not able to persuade even one of the provincial governments to champion the entrenchment of property rights in the Charter, despite the fact that six of the ten provincial governments at that time were of a professedly "conservative" persuasion.

In certain provincial administrations, we ran into the difference between a professed belief in conservative principles and administrative practices and preferences. One minister I talked to looked at our draft property rights protection clause and exclaimed, "But if this were in place, it could be more difficult for us to expropriate property or to depress property values through regulation prior to expropriation!"

"You're right, Mr. Minister," was my cheerful reply.

If we had received a warm reception from the conservative provincial governments but objections from the others, I would have advanced the idea that, from a practical political standpoint, no government could afford to promote property rights protection without seriously considering the protection of other economic rights as well.

My suggestion would have been to assemble a small group of labour, business, and consumer representatives and their lawyers, and lock them up in a hotel for a week. If they could come up with a list of economic rights on which they could all agree—something for everyone, with the price of anyone's getting his or her priorities included being that person's willingness to include someone else's priorities—this would provide a draft list of economic rights that a provincial government could safely promote.

Years later, once it became evident to everyone that the Charter of Rights and Freedoms was going to be adopted as part of the Constitution Act of 1982, there was belated criticism from the Conservative opposition in Parliament and several provincial governments concerning the Charter's heavy emphasis on cultural and linguistic rights and its perfunctory treatment of economic rights. In 1983, the British Columbia legislature even passed a property rights entrenchment resolution that received the official support of the New Brunswick legislature and also garnered support in Ontario, though no resolution was passed.

But attempting to correct the deficiencies in the Charter by amendment is an even more formidable task than securing agreement for the
original Charter. If more of the provincial politicians—especially the
Conservative ones—had been looking ahead in the early 1970s the way
Trudeau was looking ahead, there would have been an opportunity for a
constructive trade-off. If at least some of the premiers had made their
support of the cultural and linguistic sections of the Charter conditional
on stronger protection of economic rights (including stronger protection
of property held for the Crown by the provinces), everyone would have
been better off.

With the emergence of the federal-provincial conference as one of the
principal forums for dealing with national unity issues and the reconciliation of national and regional interests, our firm was sometimes asked by
clients to comment on the dynamics and consequences of such
conferences.

We were in an advantageous position to do this in that my father had
attended every major first ministers' conference since Mackenzie King
reinstituted them after World War II. Although he was a practitioner
rather than a theoretician of federal-provincial relations, my father
supported my desire to build a simple theoretical model, informed by his
experiences and those of other participants, for analyzing such conferences and attempting to predict their outcomes.

In 1975 we therefore drew up a proposal for the development and
application of the "Deal Model of Confederation." The inelegant but
common-sense premise behind this model was that confederation could
be viewed as an ever-evolving "deal" among differing interests represented by the federal and provincial governments. Each party to the deal
could be envisioned as coming to the federal-provincial bargaining table
with a list of concerns and aspirations—a wish list of the things that
government hoped to get out of the federal-provincial conference,
ranked in order of importance. We proposed to organize these lists of
concerns and aspirations into a national unity matrix.

By working through the cells of this matrix it was possible to see the
various trade-offs that the participants might be prepared to make in
order to secure agreement and action on their particular concerns. Thus
Quebec was willing in 1867 to give up equal representation with Upper
Canada (Ontario) in Canada's Parliament for equal representation in the
new Senate of Canada and greater provincial control over its own affairs.
Likewise, British Columbia was willing to agree to the terms and conditions of Confederation, provided a transcontinental railway was built to

link it to the rest of Canada. The price of a particular provincial government getting a portion of its concerns and aspirations dealt with was its willingness to cooperate to ensure that at least some of the concerns and aspirations of the other players were also dealt with.

The federal government's role could be analyzed from two perspectives—its role as a player representing various federal interests, and its role as a facilitator of the deal-making process among the other participants. The national interest would rarely be synonymous with either the federal interest or a particular provincial interest, but would be the vector sum of various federal and provincial interests. The federal government had a special role in ensuring that the deal was maintained, and that in the long run every participant was a net beneficiary of the deal-making process.

What made the deal making feasible and so rich in possibilities was Canada's diversity and the variety of interests represented at the table. Each party was after different things, and attached different weights to the items on its list at different times.

The Deal Model was not intended to generate a "Vision of Canada," although any transcendent vision of the country would have to accommodate the particular elements in the national unity matrix. Rather, the Deal Model represented how (in the view of my father and other practitioners) federal-provincial conferences actually work.

We wrote up a short proposal describing the Deal Model and a workplan for its further development and application. We proposed to illustrate the model by describing the wish lists and trade-offs involved in the original "confederation deal" of 1867. We further proposed to draw up a description of the wish lists and trade-off possibilities of the various provincial governments and the federal government in the late 1970s. From this contemporary national unity matrix we would suggest federal and provincial courses of action that would maximize the benefits to participants and "maintain the deal" (that is, national unity).

Originally we tried to get financial support for the study from individual private-sector concerns, since we felt that the national unity debate was too important to be left to the politicians. We were unsuccessful, however, in generating enough interest or support. The fear of Quebec separatism was beginning to subside, and for many companies it was "business as usual." I recall the vice-president of one Canadian manufacturing company (which manufactured toilet paper dispensers, among other things) with whom we discussed our proposal. His only comment was, "Even if the country breaks up, people will still need to use toilet paper. Perhaps they will even use more. National unity is the politicians' problem, not ours."

Meeting with little success in getting direct corporate interest in our Deal Model study, we presented a scaled-down version of our proposal to the Canada West Foundation. The Canada West Foundation is an independent, nonpolitical, nonprofit think tank established by the Mannix family in 1970 to conduct research programs concerning the economic and social characteristics and potentialities of western Canada and to present information programs to encourage appreciation of the Canadian heritage and stimulate awareness of future possibilities throughout western Canada. After 1970, the foundation's support was broadened to include several provincial governments and the private sector. My father had known Fred Mannix, Sr., for a long time and had supported the Canada West Foundation from its inception. He also served as a member of its governing council for a number of years.

In 1976, the president of the Canada West Foundation was Stan Roberts, a former Liberal MLA, provincial Liberal leader from Manitoba, and former vice-president of Simon Fraser University. The Canada West Council at that time included my father; Walt Dingle; Dr. J. Clayton Gilson, vice-president of the University of Manitoba; Dr. Harry Gunning, president of the University of Alberta; Jo Anne Hillier from Atomic Energy of Canada; Frederick Mannix of the Mannix Group; Senator Duff Roblin; Mel Smith, deputy minister of constitutional affairs for the government of British Columbia; and Dr. Francis Winspear, president of Winham Investments in Edmonton. Francis Winspear, Stan Roberts, and Jo Hillier were later to play key roles in the formation of the Reform Party of Canada.

Stan Roberts and a number of members of the Canada West Council felt that the Deal Model study was worth supporting, and we secured the authorization and funding to proceed with the first phase.

Some councillors, of course, had other priorities, and at least one councillor from British Columbia raised a rather chilling and revealing objection (one which continued to trouble me long after the study had been completed). This gentleman (a veteran of many federal-provincial conferences) maintained that if you actually spelled out with stark precision (as our national unity matrix would do) exactly what each provincial government wanted to get from the confederation deal, and if you laid out all the trade-off possibilities in such a way as to distinguish the real ones from the imaginary ones, and if you threw into that mix a federal government with a headstrong leader and its own distinctive wants and trade-off list, you would succeed in demonstrating graphically that Canada is an unworkable federation. Canada, in this man's judgment, only survives because enough people believe in the myth of its viability. Too much realism, too much hard-headed analysis, could destroy the myth and with it the country.

To make a long story short, we completed the Deal Model study in 1976. It was published and distributed by Canada West in 1977. This was one study in which I did virtually all the research and writing myself, rather than relying on hired researchers or a consulting team. This involved reading scores of standard and obscure references on the formation and development of Canadian confederation (documented in 485 footnotes), and consultations with our network of "practitioners" past and present.

Although the full development of the Deal Model as envisioned in our original proposal was never completed, I continued to use it over the next decade to analyze various developments in federal-provincial and interprovincial relations that were relevant to our consulting clients.

For example, in the early 1980s our Alberta utility clients were surprised by a request from the Alberta government to give top priority to a western Canada power grid. The government proposed that electricity be transmitted from hydro-electric projects on the lower Nelson River in Manitoba via a high-voltage direct-current line to Saskatchewan and Alberta.

The idea seemed to make little sense from the point of view of a utility company or of an Alberta consumer. But one look at our matrix of provincial concerns and aspirations for the 1980s and the trade-offs that were being made as part of the energy war between Ottawa and Alberta provided a ready explanation for the Alberta government's sudden interest.

The Alberta government was looking for support from other provincial governments (especially in the West) for its efforts to establish that the petroleum-producing provinces were entitled to receive the world price for their oil and gas. Saskatchewan and British Columbia, being petroleum-producing provinces themselves, were naturally supportive, but Manitoba was lukewarm. If Manitoba were to support Alberta on world prices for western oil and gas, what could the Manitoba government ask the Alberta government to do in return?

Premier Sterling Lyon of Manitoba was having political difficulties and facing an election. He urgently needed to stimulate economic development in his province; accelerating the development of the hydro-electric potential of the province was one way to do it. But this would require a new market and additional financial backing (possibly from the Alberta Heritage Trust Fund). Hence the Western Canada Power Grid concept and the immediate interest of the Alberta government in considering it.

This example illustrates one of the great drawbacks of basing development decisions and policy positions solely on high-level political trade-offs (trade-offs that the Deal Model makes evident). Fewer and fewer issues, once they get into the realm of federal-provincial or interprovincial relations, are decided on their own merits. They simply become chips in a bigger poker game. The Western Canada Power Grid concept had very little to do with the electricity needs of Manitobans or Albertans (although a case could be made for the grid on these grounds) and everything to do with the higher-level political and economic concerns and aspirations of the Manitoba and Alberta governments and their relations with Ottawa.

Similarly, our Deal Model made it quite easy to predict in 1986 that what would become the Meech Lake round of constitutional discussions would satisfy no one in the end.

The principal constitutional demand for which public support emerged in western Canada in the 1980s was the demand for more effective regional representation in national decision making through Senate reform. When it was proposed at the annual premiers' conference in Edmonton in August 1986 that the first round of new constitutional discussions should be devoted exclusively to "bringing Quebec back into the constitutional family" and to the consideration of Quebec's five constitutional demands, with the constitutional concerns of the other provinces being deferred to a second round, the western premiers should have refused to consider such an arrangement. By agreeing to a first round to satisfy Quebec and the federal government, they were giving up all their bargaining leverage and virtually guaranteeing that there would be no meaningful second round to consider Senate reform or any other constitutional concern of primary interest to the western provinces.

According to the Deal Model, the bargaining position of the western premiers at the very outset of the Edmonton conference or even as late as the weekend at Meech Lake on April 30, 1987, should have been as follows: the price of central Canada and the federal government's getting a major constitutional amendment to accommodate Quebec is a concurrent constitutional amendment (focusing on Senate reform) to accommodate western Canadians' desire for more effective representation in the federal Parliament.

How did the western premiers get snookered into giving up their bargaining leverage so easily? I, of course, did not attend the premiers'

luncheon meeting of August 12, 1986, which produced the so-called
Edmonton Declaration (laying the groundwork for the Meech Lake
Accord), but I know enough about the process to make an educated
guess.

A new premier, Don Getty, hosting his first premiers' conference, is
anxious to appear accommodating and conciliatory. The premiers go to
lunch; no advisers are present. Someone (Bourassa? Hatfield?), having
previously consulted with the federal government, says, "Wouldn't it be
nice if the premiers could announce some progress toward a plan for
bringing Quebec back into the 'constitutional family'?" He brings out a
single piece of paper suggesting that the premiers agree to a constitutional conference to deal first with Quebec's constitutional demands,
and a second round to deal with other important matters like Senate
reform. It is all so simple and candid, everyone agrees. The lunch is over.
Premier Getty steps outside the room. The media are waiting. "Can the
premier report any significant developments?" "Why yes ..." and the
premier reads the so-called Edmonton Declaration. The dynamics of
Meech Lake have been set in motion; back at the hotels the advisers to
some of the western premiers are appalled, but it is too late. The die is
cast.

The dearth of leadership in western Canada on these constitutional
issues in the mid-1980s gave added impetus to my own interest in a new
political voice. And when, as leader of the Reform Party of Canada, I am
called upon to discuss the constitutional development of Canada and
proposals for constitutional change, I still draw to a large extent on
knowledge gained and conclusions reached as a result of fifteen years of
viewing federal and provincial concerns and aspirations using the national unity matrix and the Deal Model of Confederation.

Perhaps it is not inappropriate to quote here from the concluding
comment of our Deal Model study for the Canada West Foundation in
1976:

> From time to time the West has contributed its fair share to the
> stresses which strain Canadian unity. Even today, there are those
> in our midst who, professing to perceive the foundering of
> Confederation, suggest that now is the time to abandon ship.
>
>   Now is not a time for abandoning ship. Instead, it is a time for
> providing new directions to the helmsman, and, if need be, even
> taking a turn at the helm, if the rest of the crew and the
> passengers be agreed.

The West has never been, nor is it now, prepared to accept definitions or conceptualizations of Canadian Confederation which fail to correspond with the historical realities of Western Development, or which fail to provide for the satisfaction of the legitimate aspirations and concerns of our people.

But to withdraw into regionalism, or the contemplation of separatism, at the very moment when the old models and the old formulae are proving inadequate, even to meet the aspirations and needs of Central Canada, would be to mistake the nature of our opportunities.

The presence of the West is required in Confederation today, more urgently than ever before. We are needed, but for once, not only for our lands and resources and economic potential, but to provide a new and realistic perspective as to what this country is and can become.

Now, therefore, is not a time for indifference or pessimism or intransigence. Now is the time for new initiatives toward a new and better federalism.

By 1971 I was no longer heavily involved in the central organization of the Alberta Social Credit Party, but I did participate in the provincial general election of that year at the constituency level, in support of my friend Werner Schmidt in Edmonton Belmont. This was the election that brought Peter Lougheed and the Progressive Conservatives to power in Alberta, ending the thirty-six-year Social Credit era. I found it instructive that the Social Credit Party spent about four times as much money on the 1971 provincial general election campaign (which it lost) as it had on the 1967 campaign (which it won).

In June 1971 I made a personal submission to the Special Joint Committee of the Senate and House of Commons on the Constitution of Canada chaired by Senator Gil Molgat and Liberal MP Mark MacGuigan. My submission consisted of twenty questions concerning secession and how it should be handled by a federal government.

One of these questions was: "If the right to secede were provided for in a revised constitution, and one region of the country exercised this right, but a portion of the seceding region desired to remain in Confederation, would the federal government be obligated to uphold the right of the latter to remain if it recognized the right of the former to secede?"

Needless to say, the committee did not attempt to address any of my questions in its final report, and I was chided by Conservative committee member Marcel Lambert for being an alarmist on the secession issue.

Before the 1972 federal election I met once or twice with Joe Clark and some of his friends to discuss running as a Conservative. Joe had decided to run in the Rocky Mountain constituency, and it had been suggested that I might consider running in Pembina, a large rural riding surrounding Edmonton.

After Joe got the nomination in Rocky Mountain I sent him a letter wishing him well, but adding the following:

> My own plans do not call for pursuing the nomination in Pembina in the near future. This decision is based, in part, on:
> 1. My continued reservations about the present leadership and capacities of the national PC party as a whole.
> 2. The desire to gain more experience in the management of affairs and the operations of government bureaucracies via opportunities currently available through our consulting practice.
> 3. A vague (and perhaps unfounded) premonition that the Canadian political map may be so radically altered in the next four years (primarily by a secession crisis) that the current party set-up could be discredited and open to challenge from without.

The federal Conservatives were successful in the 1972 election in reducing the Trudeau Liberals to a minority government, but the Liberals rebounded in the "wage and price control" election of 1974. Soon the winds of revolt began to blow among the Conservative backbenchers, who were becoming increasingly critical of Robert Stanfield's leadership.

Normally, I did not pay much attention to the internal machinations of the federal Liberal and Conservative parties, being mindful of the old adage made popular by the Progressives that "once elected, Liberals tend to desert their principles, while the Conservatives desert their leaders." On one occasion, however, I was invited to sit in on several meetings of a group of Conservative backbenchers (the two I got to know best were Stan Schumacher from Drumheller, Alberta, and Sean O'Sullivan from Hamilton, Ontario), who were increasingly unhappy with Robert Stanfield's acceptance of the Trudeau model of Canada and the legislation that flowed from it. The group had started to meet separately from the PC caucus, and because they met at the Château Laurier Hotel, the press dubbed them "the Château Cabinet."

Nothing much came of this revolt, mainly because there were no real leaders among the group who could give voice and direction to their concerns, and no resources to sustain their activities. Eventually party discipline was brought to bear, and most fell back into line. The experience did, however, give me some insight into the gaping intellectual and leadership weaknesses of a federal party that still presented itself to the public as a viable alternative to the governing Liberals. I began to wonder whether the Conservatives had been born under an unlucky star, with a congenital inability to govern even themselves, let alone the country.

During these years my father's seat in the Senate provided a good window on all the legislation that was going through Parliament. I sympathized with Paul Hellyer (Action Canada, 1971) and Jim Richardson (One Canada, 1978) in their efforts to initiate movements for political change, even though they were unsuccessful.

In 1977 and 1978, through our consulting firm, I initiated several study groups of my own which we grandly labelled "The Movement for National Political Change." We met once a month or so with small groups of interested friends and acquaintances to discuss the lessons to be learned from the political reform movements of the past and to discuss the knowledge and skill needed to participate in contemporary federal politics.

Occasionally I was invited to give lectures to groups who were interested in forming new provincial political movements in Alberta (such as Tom Sindlinger's short-lived Alberta Reform Movement and Ray Speaker's Representative Party). My theme on these occasions was usually "Lessons to be learned from past attempts to start new political parties in the West." I developed a format that conveyed the necessary information but in such a non-newsworthy way that the media paid scant attention to my presence as a "resource person" at these gatherings.

In February 1982, Gordon Kesler of the Western Canada Concept won a by-election in the Olds-Didsbury riding of central Alberta on a western separatist platform. While I understood and sympathized with the frustrations over the National Energy Program and other federal policies that fuelled the western separatist movement, I did not agree with its tactics or avowed objective. I did not know Kesler, but I did know Howard Thompson, the man who ran the Olds-Didsbury by-election campaign, and was invited by Howard to sit in on a meeting of the WCC leadership in Edmonton soon after Kesler had taken his seat in the Legislature.

As I recall, there were six people at the meeting. I asked them, "Is your advocacy of separatism simply a tactic to draw attention to western grievances, or is it a genuine objective that you intend to pursue as such?" Right away, the great weakness of the WCC manifested itself.

Three of them said separatism was only a tactic to get attention; the other three said it was a real goal to be vigorously pursued. One man summed it up by saying that advocating separatism wasn't much of a tactic unless your opponents thought you meant it.

After that, I had little contact with the WCC, although I am pleased that many of its members, those whose real desire was for a more fair and balanced Canadian confederation rather than a separate western Canada, have since seen fit to join the Reform Party of Canada.

In 1984, my father and I participated in a small one-day seminar sponsored by the Marigold Foundation, a charitable organization established by Jack and Sheila MacKenzie in Calgary. Marigold was engaged in "mentoring"—bringing together students and associates with resource people around a common subject of interest. My father and I made a presentation entitled "An Overview of Selected Political and Economic Issues." In it, we touched on the possibility of the West producing yet another populist party and the lessons to be learned from its predecessors.

Three years later, Jack and Sheila became two of the most active and generous supporters of the Reform Party of Canada. Jack's background and breadth of interests (military service, MBA from Harvard, president and founder of an oil and gas development company, former chairman of the Calgary Public School Board) have made him an invaluable contributor to the cause of political innovation.

Generally speaking, from 1968 to 1986, despite various federal initiatives which fuelled the fires of western alienation, conditions were not right for the emergence of another broadly based western reform movement with the potential for becoming a national force. During this period the build-up of regional alienation in the West was more likely to find expression through increasing support for "the other major federal party"—the Progressive Conservatives, and even the NDP, rather than through any new movement.

After 1986, however, if the federalist Reform Party of Canada had not been started, there would today be a full-blown separatist movement in western Canada analogous to and perhaps working in concert with the Bloc Québécois in Quebec.

All in all, my political activities in the 1970s and 1980s probably consumed 15 to 20 percent of my billable time as a consultant. Because these activities were seldom profitable from a consulting standpoint, they were actually an expense to the firm, although I tended to regard them as investments in my continuing political education. Many of our more profitable consulting projects, however, also had similar political and educational value—for example, our work with requests for proposals and government contracts, community economic development, native economic development, and energy markets and regulation.

With all due respect to my lawyer friends (who recommend a law practice as the ideal political launching pad), if one is not independently wealthy, I would highly recommend to younger people an independent consulting practice as an excellent vehicle for pursuing public policy studies, interacting with that tangled ball of conflicting interests which is the essence of modern politics, and preparing for direct political involvement.

CHAPTER FOUR

The Spiritual Dimension

One of the distinguishing features of the political reform tradition of western Canada, a feature that has often generated suspicion and contempt for that tradition from journalists and academics who comment on western populism, is that four out of the five major western populist movements have had a significant religious or moral dimension.

Many Canadians do not know that even the first one included religious concerns. Louis Riel was not only going to establish the new Métis Nation; he also had elaborate plans for reforming the Roman Catholic Church.

Likewise, the Progressives and the Depression-era parties of the CCF and Social Credit each had a distinctly religious dimension. One of these was the so-called social gospel movement. J. S. Woodsworth, the Methodist-minister-turned-politician who was the first leader of the CCF, was one of its chief proponents.

According to adherents of the social gospel, the primary purpose of the Christian religion is to heal and strengthen relationships between people. Their favourite New Testament passage is the story of the Good Samaritan, the man who "loved his neighbour as himself." The same community and farm leaders who helped put together the Progressive Party on the political front were also heavily involved in both the temperance movement and the founding of the socially oriented United Church of Canada in 1925, Canada's largest Protestant denomination.

Later, the social gospel movement gained renewed impetus from the deplorable social and economic conditions of the Depression. It informed and inspired some of the early leaders of the CCF. Tommy Douglas, for example, and Stanley Knowles were both clergymen who initially entered politics because of their religious convictions. When I was at university I used to tease some of my Marxist acquaintances, who were then in the NDP, by showing them old CCF pamphlets which emphatically described this agrarian socialist party as "a Christian party."

Also during the Depression, what is known as the evangelical movement emerged and grew in western Canada. This movement was partly a reaction to the social gospel movement, but it was also a religious movement in its own right. It too was in part a response to the desperate conditions of the 1930s, when people lost everything and began to seek security in the spiritual rather than the material world.

According to the evangelicals (and William Aberhart was one of the principal leaders and communicators of this perspective), the primary purpose of the Christian faith is to establish right relations between people and God. Their favourite New Testament passage is the third chapter of John's gospel which speaks of the necessity of a spiritual new birth before one can comprehend or work for the kingdom of God.

If the Christian faith is appropriately represented by the symbol of the cross, with its vertical (God-directed) and horizontal (person-directed) dimensions, the social gospel people were carrying around the cross-bar and the evangelicals were carrying around the vertical shaft. The maturing of these two traditions in more recent times has meant a search for a personal relationship with God by social gospel people, and a working out of the social implications of their faith by evangelicals.

The significant thing about these perspectives is that "reconciliation" is the principal concern of both religious professions. For evangelicals, the main focus is on reconciliation between people and God, or personal salvation. For the social gospel people, the main focus is on reconciliation among people, or social justice.

During his long political career, my father was always very active in communicating the Christian gospel from the evangelical perspective. From 1943 to 1989 he directed Canada's National Bible Hour, the radio broadcast started by William Aberhart in 1925. The broadcast consisted of a sermon and Christian commentary on current events delivered by my father, interspersed with sacred music selections performed by a musical cast directed by my mother.

For many years, the one-hour broadcast was produced live from an Edmonton theatre with an audience in attendance. In later years, it was shortened to a half hour and was produced in a radio studio. The program, which was carried weekly by anywhere from fifty to a hundred radio stations across Canada, was financed through contributions from the radio audience. It was a voluntary ministry and none of the directors or participants received any remuneration. The program continues today under the auspices of Global Outreach Mission of St. Catharines, Ontario.

I was therefore raised, as a child and adolescent, in the evangelical Christian tradition. During my late teens and university years I went through a period of trying to decide what I believed for myself as distinguished from the convictions passed on to me by my family and local church. I was considerably helped during this period by reading the writings of the pragmatist William James (in particular, his *Varieties of Religious Experience* and his essay on "The Right to Believe"). Although James was not a "believer," he argued that faith was intellectually defensible. I do not like to use traditional labels to categorize people's religious beliefs, and I would today simply describe myself as a practising Christian.[1]

As a practising Christian I engage in such disciplines as studying the Christian scriptures and related commentaries, personal and family prayer, attendance at public worship services, association with fellow believers, and attempts (however imperfect) to communicate my understanding of these matters to others without in any way seeking to impose my convictions upon them.

For years my main public channel for such communications was my father's religious radio broadcast, and the speaking opportunities which flowed from that. My usual themes were The Meaning of Faith, Faith and Business, Faith and Politics, Faith and Science, and Faith and Conflict Resolution.

It is quite appropriate for people trying to understand where I am coming from to ask, "What does a contemporary evangelical Christian believe?" It is also appropriate to ask how my evangelical faith affects my life in general and my politics in particular. Because the trustworthiness

---

1. People sometimes ask me for a short list of books which have influenced or in some way reflect my own thinking on matters of faith. Besides the Bible itself, I would suggest: *Eerdmans' Handbook to the Bible,* edited by David and Pat Alexander (Grand Rapids, Michigan: William B. Eerdmans Publishing Co., 1973); Jacques Ellul, *The Politics of God and the Politics of Man* (Grand Rapids, Michigan: William B. Eerdmans Publishing Company, 1972); A. B. Bruce, *The Training of the Twelve* (Grand Rapids, Michigan: Kregel Publications, 1971); Fydor Dostoyevsky, *The Brothers Karamozov* (New York: North Point Press, 1990), particularly the "Grand Inquisitor" chapter; C. S. Lewis, *Surprised by Joy: The Shape of My Early Life* (New York: Harcourt, Brace, 1955); Malcolm Muggeridge, *Chronicles of Wasted Time: The Green Stick* (London: Collins, 1972) and *The Third Testament* (Boston: Little, Brown, 1976); and Ronald S. Wallace, *The Message of Daniel: The Lord Is King* (Leicester, England: Inter-Varsity Press, 1979).

of elected people is becoming a major issue in Canada, I believe that voters have every right to inquire of a candidate for public office, "What are your most deeply held values and beliefs, and how might these affect your personal and political behaviour?" Voters asking such questions should not accept many of the superficial and incomplete answers that have been given to such inquiries in the past. It is insufficient, for example, for politicians to respond to such questions by saying, "My most deeply held values and beliefs are a private matter and have no bearing on my political behaviour."

When I am asked for a definition of my most deeply held values (that is, for a statement of faith), I could respond by reciting the Apostles' Creed or the statement of faith of any of the various churches (Baptist, and Christian and Missionary Alliance) that my family and I have attended.

Such a statement would not be very meaningful, however, to Canadians who have abandoned or who have never subscribed to this country's Christian heritage. When asked to define my Christian beliefs, therefore, I try to do so in terms that will be intelligible to non-religious people as well as to those of other faiths.

I start with the proposition that the most important thing in life is relationships—the relationships between God and humankind, parents and children, husbands and wives, employers and employees, and so forth—and that strained and broken relationships are the principal sources of frustration, pain, and despair in our modern world.

Through my political involvements, I attend hundreds of meetings in which people seek political solutions to their concerns about jobs, incomes, taxes, trade, or national unity. But I am acutely conscious that most political programs are only dealing with symptoms. If one could get inside the heads and hearts of Canadians we would find that most have another set of problems and concerns that are deeper and more trouble-some than those dealt with by the politicians—strained relationships, problems of self-esteem, alienation from others.

There are, of course, many different approaches to dealing with such problems—from the teachings of religion and philosophies old and new to the contributions of modern medicine and the social sciences—and I disparage none of these. But the explanation of the causes of broken relationships and the path toward better relationships that has been most meaningful to me is that presented by the Judaeo-Christian scriptures and embodied in Jesus Christ.

When I read those scriptures and the great commentaries about them, and when I talk to people for whom faith in Christ is a living reality, one theme emerges time and time again. That is the theme that human relationships are incomplete without a relationship with God. Or, put another way, at the root of strained and broken relationships between people lies a strained and broken relationship with God. To me, this is the great theme of the opening chapters of the book of Genesis, although it is easy to miss it by getting sidetracked onto arguments about creation versus evolution or whether God is male or female.

This proposition is very hard for intellectuals and opinion leaders with a scientific and materialistic worldview to swallow, although public opinion studies indicate that faith in the existence of God is still a part of the worldview of the common people. For all our modernity, however, we have not done a particularly good job of handling our relationships. And the fact that the Christian explanation and remedy for the human condition has survived for two thousand years and has been embraced by millions of people from a vast array of backgrounds and national cultures, ought to commend this explanation and remedy to our examination.

If we accept the necessity of a relationship with God, or even suspect that such a relationship may be possible and important, the instinctive reaction of most people is to "get religious" in some way. We try to work our way toward God by keeping rules and regulations like the Ten Commandments or the Golden Rule and by participating in various religious exercises such as attending church and taking communion. All major religions propose ways in which people can reach toward God. What is unique about the Judaeo-Christian tradition, and represented by Jesus Christ, is the idea that God himself has taken some initiatives to reach out to us.

To me, this is the central, revolutionary truth embodied in the Christian gospel—that human beings can be restored to a right relationship with God, thereby opening up the way to the renewal of their other relationships, not by their own religious efforts, but by believing and responding to the initiatives that God himself has taken. This is rightly referred to as "the way of faith" because belief, rather than effort, is its starting point.

I liken all this to the discovery that we are lost in the woods. Our first instinct is to try to find our own way out, to take the initiative ourselves. Many of us have already tried that and found ourselves even more lost than before. We have been given a survival manual, however, by our forefathers, although it is rarely consulted by our generation. It says, "If lost spiritually, stay where you are and trust that One who cares, and knows you are lost, will take the initiative to rescue you." Whether we choose to believe that or not is the critical issue.

But what, then, are these great initiatives that Christians believe God has taken to restore human beings to himself? In my attempts to discuss and communicate my faith, I usually focus on two of them: a "legal initiative" and a "mediation initiative."

The Old Testament scriptures contain a detailed account of what might be called God's legal initiative. This is the record of a set of laws that were given to a man named Moses, leader of the ancient Hebrew nation. These laws, if obeyed, promised to restore and preserve the relationship of the people to God and to each other.

I might add that the story of this legal initiative to restore relationships is one of the most instructive that anyone pursuing a career in politics or lawmaking could examine. The law of God, and subsidiary regulations derived from it, sought to govern every aspect of the Hebrews' economic, social, political, and personal life. And this exercise was conducted for hundreds of years, with lasting peace and great prosperity promised to those who would obey the laws, and the most dire penalties meted out to those who failed to keep them.

The most significant thing about this whole socio-religious exercise is that it did not succeed in attaining its objective. The latter-day prophets of this ancient people came to a sobering conclusion: unless laws can be inscribed on the human heart, and not merely written on parchment or tablets of stone, law by itself is insufficient to restore or regulate relationships between people and God or among themselves. In other words, the Hebrews came up against the limits to law, and to the conclusion that something more than rules and regulations is required to heal and restore strained and broken relationships.

The prophets, therefore, began to look forward to another divine initiative, an initiative which Christians believe found its fulfilment in Jesus Christ. This, the "mediation initiative," is the major subject matter of the New Testament scriptures. Here God is portrayed as sending, not another lawgiver, but a unique and divine mediator to restore our relationship to him and to one another. We are told that this mediation is motivated by love, and love is portrayed as action to establish and restore relationships, turning bad relationships into good. This is the very opposite of evil, which might be defined as actions that strain and destroy relationships, turning good relationships into bad.

The New Testament makes clear that this greatest of divine initiatives is noncoercive. People are free to accept or reject it. In fact, if there is one test for distinguishing genuine Christianity from spurious Christianity (and this test should be rigorously applied to Christian people seeking public office), it is that genuine Christianity never seeks to impose itself or its solutions on those who do not choose to receive it.

At the heart of this mediation is Jesus Christ. He is not a judicial mediator, harsh and impersonal, distancing himself from the parties to be reconciled so as to avoid conflict of interest. Instead, he is intimately related to the alienated parties, calling God his father and the people his brothers and sisters. Rather than avoiding the conflict of interests between them, he accepts and resolves it.

Initially, his mediation effort focuses on restoring communication between the alienated parties. The mediator represents the people to God in prayer, and represents God to the people through teaching. The restoration of communication, in this case through a third party, is necessary for the healing and restoration of relationships.

Finally, the climax of the mediation effort is sacrifice. The mediator sacrifices himself in order to restore the relationship between God and the people, and asks the alienated parties to accept his sacrifice as payment of the price of reconciling with each other.

Examples abound to illustrate the principle that sacrifice can restore relationships. A mundane example, but one which is relevant to many of my consulting clients, goes as follows: a group of oil companies, encouraged by high petroleum prices, enter into a joint development project. Oil prices decline and the cash flow of all the participants is restricted. A small cost overrun on the joint project, which under normal conditions would not be a problem, becomes the subject of a bitter dispute concerning who is responsible and who should pay. The dispute threatens to destroy the companies' working relationship. They are on their way to court when a mediator—not an outside arbitrator, but one of the participants—makes the following declaration: "I'll cover the cost overrun. Let's not allow this dispute to destroy our relationship and the project." The mediator's willingness to pay the cost of reconciliation himself opens up a way to reconcile the parties to the dispute. All they need to do is to accept the sacrifice the mediator made on their behalf.

A more current and relevant example is the following. Leaders of a government find themselves mediating between public service unions who want higher pay and more job security, and taxpayers who refuse to pay higher taxes. They must reconcile both to the idea of receiving less (less service for the taxpayers and less money and job security for the unions). The only possible way for those mediating such a dispute to gain a hearing from the disputants is for government leaders to visibly take less themselves (lower pay, fewer benefits). Visible sacrifice by the mediator is essential to credibility and gaining a hearing if one wants others to make sacrifices for the sake of better relations.

Christians believe that the resurrection of Jesus Christ from the dead was the sign that God himself accepted his mediation effort. Whether you or I accept his mediation effort on our behalf—that is, whether we decide to submit our strained, broken, or incomplete relationships with God and one another to mediation by Jesus Christ—is up to us.

I made a decision many years ago to accept mediation of my relationships by Jesus Christ. By this I mean that I began to acknowledge as evil and destructive those things in my own life which damage or destroy relations with God and with others; to seek forgiveness, make restitution, and take corrective action where appropriate; and to trust that the sacrificial mediation of Jesus Christ somehow renders such responses on my part effective in restoring and maintaining peace with God and with others. I believe that my efforts to practise the Christian faith in this way have affected the kind of person I am, my relations with my wife and family, my relationship to God and others, and my own approach to conflict resolution.

In my twenty-five years of married life, and in my twenty years of management consulting, I have studied and observed many different models and approaches to reconciling conflicting interests and restoring broken and strained relationships. Of all the reconciliation approaches I have encountered—and I disparage none of them—none has struck me as being more profound and more directly addressed to the human condition than that taught and lived by Jesus of Nazareth.

American anthropologist Ashley Montagu once wrote: "The only measure of what you believe is what you do. If you want to know what people believe, don't read what they write, don't ask them what they believe, just observe what they do."

A few years ago, in looking back over our consulting files, I noted that almost every project we undertook involved some attempt to reconcile conflicting interests—utility company interests with competing interests, oil company interests with native and community interests, public interests with private interests. I subsequently began to pay more attention to the various mechanisms available in both the public and private sectors—from markets, to courts, to regulation, to negotiation and arbitration—for the harmonization and reconciliation of conflicting interests. This function is at the heart of contemporary politics.

In 1983, I attempted to develop a conflict-resolution model based on the Christian doctrine of reconciliation but expressed in systems language and stripped of any religious terminology. I used this model to some extent in my consulting work. For example, if asked to look for individuals or mechanisms to improve relations between the owners and managers of energy projects and the communities where such projects were located, I would place little emphasis on legalistic mechanisms and search instead for individuals (executives, community leaders) who identified with both sides of the issue. I also made several presentations of this model to seminars on "Christians in the Market Place" sponsored by Regent College in Vancouver.[2]

I called my conflict-resolution model "The Model of Last Resort" and sent draft copies to a number of eminent practitioners of the art of conflict resolution.[3] One of these experts was Charles Malik, Lebanese statesman and former president of the United Nations General Assembly. Mr. Malik offered the following comments, which I have since taken to heart:

> Nothing replaces actual, responsible, political involvement. Only in and through concrete political participation can any reconciliation or peace between parties in conflict be achieved. . . . Even your ideas you owe not to some a priori theoretical thinking about models, methods, and processes, but to some experience you have had, or to your knowledge of the experience that others may have had, in concrete political responsibility and decision making. You should plunge therefore into the concrete arena of politics by running for office or seeking some important political appointment, to be able really to contribute to the "Reconciliation of Parties in Conflict."

This overview reveals my most deeply held values and religious convictions but leads to the following questions: What role, if any, does my personal faith play in my decision making on public issues and my attitudes to public policy questions? Is the Reform Party of Canada a religious party because it happens to have a leader with religious convictions? Does the Reform Party have a hidden religious agenda?

The answer to the second and third questions is No. The Reform Party of Canada is not a religious party, nor does it have a hidden religious

---

2. Regent College is a transdenominational postgraduate theological school located on the campus of the University of British Columbia. It specializes in helping Christians relate their faith to contemporary life and work. For several years I sat on its Board of Governors.

3. An abbreviated version of "The Model of Last Resort" was printed in a Regent publication entitled *With Heart, Mind and Strength*, Vol. 1, (Langley, B.C.: Credo Publishing Corp., 1990), p. 237.

agenda. As a populist and democratic party, the Reform Party of Canada draws its agenda from consultations with Canadians, and although it has chosen me, a practising Christian, as its first leader, no doubt the party will one day be led by someone with different convictions.

There *is* a relationship between private and public morality, between what one believes and how one responds to public policy issues, between personal spiritual resources (or the lack of them) and how one copes with political stress. And these relationships should be openly explored.

In many parts of the world, people with deeply held values that have been ignored or rejected by pragmatic and supposedly "value-free" politicians have organized themselves into political movements or interest groups to bring their values more effectively to bear on public policy making through concerted political action. The rise of Islamic fundamentalism in the Middle East and the Moral Majority movement in the United States are prominent examples of this phenomenon.

The distinguishing feature of "fundamentalism" is its unwillingness to compromise on matters of moral principle. In Canada, it is secular fundamentalism rather than religious fundamentalism that is on the rise and that is demanding recognition and accommodation from the political system. Secular fundamentalists (and I do not use this term in a derogatory sense) include people who hold uncompromising convictions on everything from the role of women in society to environmental conservation, and they are demanding recognition by the political system.

The challenge that fundamentalism—whether secular or religious—presents to a representative democracy is one of providing value-driven people a place to stand in the political system and an opportunity to contribute to public policy, while at the same time preventing value-driven minorities, or even majorities, from imposing their convictions on all of society.

My own experiences, and those of other western Canadians who have been involved in efforts to deal responsibly with the intersection of faith and politics, may shed some light on various approaches to dealing with this issue.

When I have been asked to address audiences of professing Christian people on Christian involvement in politics, I usually suggest that there are two approaches. One is to develop an explicitly Christian political agenda and to implement it through direct political action. This is the approach that was taken by the so-called "Christian left" in North America in the early part of this century, when liberal Christians in the United States developed a political agenda, rooted mainly in a social interpretation of the Christian faith, which placed a heavy emphasis on civil rights and social justice. They pursued that agenda by employing all the available instruments of modern politics, from demonstrations, to voter registrations, to political action groups, to attempts to influence and even take over the Democratic Party.

Similarly in Canada, many Christian people, motivated by their commitment to the social gospel, developed an agenda with a heavy emphasis on social justice for the old, the sick, and the poor, and pursued it through direct political action and the advocacy of social legislation.

Then, in the 1970s, the so-called "Christian right" began to do exactly the same thing. Informed by a different perspective on the Christian faith, these Christians drew up another explicit political agenda emphasizing the protection of the unborn, reduction of the influence of secular humanism in education, and opposition to government intervention in family life. In the United States, this agenda was pursued by pro-life and pro-family political action groups, the best known of which was the Moral Majority movement. In Canada, a similar agenda is being pursued by similar political action groups and by a new political party, the Christian Heritage Party.

Although I do not deny Christians of the right or the left the right to develop such agendas and to pursue them through political action, including the formation of political parties dedicated to such agendas, this is *not* the approach that I have taken to politics, nor is the Reform Party of Canada a product of such an approach.

A different approach to Christian involvement in politics, and the one that I personally favour, might be described as "working Christianly with the urgent or existing public agenda." This involves accepting the present political agenda as a legitimate starting point for one's involvement in politics—whether presented as the ideological agenda of a party like the NDP, or as the pragmatic agenda of a party like the Liberals or the Conservatives, or as the populist agenda of something like the Reform movement—and trying to influence it from within by the application of one's most deeply held values.

As a populist political party, the Reform Party accepts a political agenda that comes from its consultations with Canadians. Since most Canadians do not have a strong or explicit Christian commitment, that agenda will not be a specifically Christian agenda. Instead, it will be rooted in a complex mixture of personal, regional, and national interests. However, as a practising Christian, I chose to participate in the formation of the Reform Party and to contribute to the development of its policies and positions.

Of course my perspective and contributions will reflect Christian convictions such as the following: that human beings are of infinite value, that all human beings are of equal value in the sight of God and entitled to equal treatment under law, that relationships are the most important thing in life, that truth and right and wrong are not matters of personal or public opinion, that evil is a reality to be constrained and justice (right relations) an end to be pursued, that man is called to be a steward and not an exploiter of the environment, that there are limits to what can be achieved by law, that communication and sacrifice are essential to reconciling conflicting interests, that service to others is a worthy pursuit, and that human beings will be held accountable to God for their actions.

But in so doing, even though I am the party leader, I am seeking to influence from a minority position. The final positions of the party on major issues of public policy will be decided by a majority vote in democratically constituted assemblies in which those sharing my evangelical Christian views will be a minority. Of course, all sectors of the party have the right to express their views.

The concept of working constructively with the agenda of a majority, from the perspective and position of a minority, may be illustrated by some famous examples from history.

The early Christians, for example, did not found a political party, even though most of the first disciples of Jesus hoped that he would prove to be a political Messiah. The idea that this little band of men from the obscure province of Galilee could somehow "storm Jerusalem" or "storm Rome," seize the levers of power, and impose their agenda on an unreceptive majority would be preposterous and is nowhere advocated in the New Testament, least of all by the founder of their faith. Instead he told them to function as salt seasoning a greater whole, as leaven leavening a larger loaf, as lights penetrating a greater gloom.

My favourite example of this concept, however, is a famous one from the history of the Jewish people. When the ancient kingdom of Judah was at its pinnacle in the days of King David and King Solomon, the Jewish people were of course a majority in their own land with their own king, their own temple, their own way of worship, and their own laws.

But when Judah and Jerusalem fell to the Babylonians in 587 B.C., and many of the Jewish people were carried off into exile in Babylon, their political, cultural, and spiritual positions dramatically changed. They were now a tiny minority living in the midst of a hostile majority, and the question presented itself, as it presents itself to all minorities living against their will in the midst of majorities, how can we preserve our political, cultural, and religious distinctiveness in these circumstances?

Nothing could have been more preposterous than to suggest that the Jewish exiles should somehow "storm Babylon," seize power, and impose their views and values on a hostile majority. Certainly this metaphor ("storming Babylon") does *not* describe my own views on how religious minorities should relate to secular or other majorities.

The Jewish exiles, in fact, were plunged at first into hopeless gloom. No doubt many of them felt there was no way that they could now preserve their values, language, and worship, and they raised the sad lament recorded in the Book of Psalms, "How shall we sing the Lord's song in a strange land?"

Into their gloom, however, came a shaft of light, a strange letter from the prophet Jeremiah. It called upon them to "Build houses and live in them; plant gardens and eat their produce. Marry wives and beget sons and daughters; take wives for your sons and give your daughters to husbands, so that they may bear sons and daughters and you may increase there and not dwindle away. Seek the welfare of the city to which [God] has carried you off, and pray to the Lord for it; on its welfare your welfare will depend."

On a deeper level, Jeremiah called upon the Jewish exiles in Babylon to radically alter and vastly expand their conception of sovereignty, in particular their view of national sovereignty and the sovereignty of God. This prophet, and other leaders after him, called upon the Jewish exiles to believe that they were in the hand of their God whether they were in their own land or in Babylon. God, the source of their national identity and being, could not only guide the hand and inspire the visions of a David or a Solomon, but of a Nebuchadnezzar as well. Moreover, he could be worshipped not only in a great temple near the banks of the Jordan, but also in humble homes near the banks of the Euphrates.

And based on that faith and expanded conception of sovereignty, they were able to develop and implement strategies, illustrated in the exploits of Daniel and Esther, for bringing a minority view to bear on a pagan and hostile majority. This faith and these strategies would enable them to survive as a distinct and influential people, even in the absence of territory and political institutions upon which the experience of sovereignty is usually thought to depend.

The focus therefore is not on "storming Babylon" and seeking to achieve or maintain national sovereignty by imposing acceptance of a minority view on a majority. The focus rather is on defining and achieving a sovereignty of the spirit, not confined to territory or political institutions, and in the strength of that sovereignty to exert a significant influence on the majority culture.

It is a position which Jesus Christ was centuries later to describe as "being in the world [or a culture], but not of it." It is a position which I seek to occupy as a member of an invisible minority (a practising Christian) living and working politically in a majority culture that is essentially secular and humanist. It is a legitimate position for the Québécois to occupy as members of a French-speaking minority living and working in a North American culture that is predominantly English-speaking.

In my travels across Canada, I find a genuine longing among many Canadians to get more people with a strong sense of values or ethics into politics. This is a reaction against pragmatic politicians who seem to have no values at all other than a single-minded dedication to their own re-election.

At the same time, those who long for a higher standard of values in politics express a legitimate and understandable fear. What if the values espoused by the politicians are different from my values? Is there not a danger that such politicians will use the power and processes of politics and government to impose their values on me? How can we get more people into politics who will hold fast to their values (whether those values pertain to higher ethical standards, or to a deeper commitment to environmental conservation, or to the role of women in society, or to fiscal responsibility) and still protect ourselves against value-driven minorities imposing their ideas on everyone else?

The Reform Party has addressed this issue by endorsing two distinct principles, incorporated into its Constitution (see Appendix I, Statement of Principles).

One of these affirms the right of Canadians and party members "to advocate, without fear of intimidation or suppression, public policies which reflect their most deeply held values." In my case these would include the values of a practising Christian; in your case they might be something else.

But the party also upholds the principle that "public policies in democratic societies should reflect the will of the majority of the citizens as determined by free and fair elections, referendums, and the decisions of legally constituted and representative parliaments and assemblies elected by the people." It is this principle which guarantees that minorities cannot impose their will on the majority. The only way any minority can prevail in determining a Reform Party policy is for it to persuade at least a majority of the members of a properly constituted assembly to endorse its position.

Thus, when the abortion issue was raised during my campaign in Yellowhead, I advised voters that my Christian views on the sanctity of life led me personally to support a pro-life position. Second, I said that were I the MP, I would seek to determine whether a consensus existed on the issue in the riding, using such mechanisms as surveys, a constituent assembly, or a referendum. In any debate in the constituency, I would argue the pro-life case. If a consensus existed in the riding and could be determined, I would vote in accordance with it in the House of Commons; if no consensus existed, I would vote in accordance with my personal view, which I would previously have made known.

Obviously, if my constituents continually forced me to vote against my better judgment, we would soon come to a parting of the ways. On the other hand, my willingness to represent their view in the House, even when it differed from my own, would give me an opportunity to present my position and to gain a hearing I would not have received had I indicated I would vote my own view regardless of what constituents wanted.

To the charge (from the Christian Heritage candidate in Yellowhead) that the Reform Party believed matters of right and wrong (moral issues) could be determined by referendum, I answered that this was not the case. Obviously majorities can be and have been wrong. All a referendum tells you is what position a majority (rightly or wrongly) is prepared to support, so that you can tell what course of action has sufficient public support to be implemented. And if a majority makes a wrong decision through a referendum, then at least it can be held morally accountable. On the other hand, if some "principled" minority is always permitted to make moral judgments on behalf of majorities, the majority cannot be held accountable for the course pursued.

This, then, is the Reform Party's response to the twofold demand for more principled approaches to politics and for protection from the imposition of minority positions on majorities. I also believe it is a more thoughtful and workable approach than that offered by the traditional parties, and one more attuned to the demands of the twenty-first century. Its dominant characteristic is principled flexibility.

As a practising Christian, it gives me a place to stand in the political process from which I can attempt to influence public policy. It likewise gives you a place to stand, though your values may differ from mine. But it also gives those who do not share my values or yours, and who subscribe to other values, protection against our values being imposed upon them. If to these positions we add the checks and limitations of a constitution and bill of rights which protect minorities from majorities, the picture is complete.

In reforming our practice of democracy in Canada to meet the demands of the twenty-first century, would we be wiser to encourage greater participation by value-oriented politicians, including those with strong moral convictions, or should we continue to allow politics to be dominated by supposedly "value-free" pragmatic politicians?

My own inclination would be to support the conclusion of British historian D.C. Somervell on this issue—a conclusion drawn from his study of two great nineteenth-century British statesmen, William Gladstone (the moralist) and Benjamin Disraeli (the pragmatist):

> For Gladstone, every important political issue was a contest between good and evil; and if he could not discover good on the one side and evil on the other, he failed to discover importance and was not interested. Sometimes his hearers could not fail to find it thrillingly appropriate. At other times the note seemed forced, and the speaker pharisaical; he might even seem insincere.... To Disraeli on the other hand, even when he was most convinced of the importance of the task he was undertaking, his opponents appeared as no more than perverse and wrong headed. Political questions were to him, as he often said, matters of opinion and not of right and wrong.... Disraeli was inclined to err on the Machiavellian side, Gladstone on the other; for it is an error to discover moral issues where none are in fact at stake, though a lesser error than to be blind to them when moral issues really arise.[4]

---

4. D.C. Somervell, *Gladstone and Disraeli* (Garden City: Garden City Publishing Co., 1928), pp. 65-66.

CHAPTER FIVE

The Importance of Home

Besides my religious commitment, the greatest single factor that has enabled me to pursue my business and political objectives has been the security and freedom of my home.

For the first twenty years of my life, this combination of security and freedom was provided in the home established by my parents for themselves, my brother Keith, and me. For the past twenty-five years, my wife Sandra and I have tried to provide that same environment for ourselves and our five children in our home.

If there is some place, no matter how modest, where you feel truly at home—accepted, secure in relationships, and free to be yourself—then you have a base from which to tackle and withstand all the challenges and vicissitudes of life. If there is no place where you feel at home—or if the security and freedom of home is shattered by violence or financial crises or broken relationships—then meeting the challenges of life is infinitely more difficult.

For me, trying to understand another person's experience and conception of home is not only a key to better understanding the individual, but it also contributes to my vision of the type of society we should be striving to create in Canada politically as we approach the twenty-first century.

The word "home" is the fourth word of the English version of our national anthem and the first metaphor used in that anthem to describe our country. "O Canada, our home . . . ." (In the French version, Canada is described as "the land of our ancestors," and in the chorus the "value" of Canada is invoked to protect "our homes and our rights.") However we define Canada—economically, culturally, constitutionally, politically—it must in the final analysis be a place where our people feel "at home."

The Reform Party of Canada was created to provide a new political home for people who no longer feel at home in Old Canada's traditional political parties or in the divided and dissension-plagued house that Canada has become. Our vision of a New Canada is a country where a greater number of Canadians will feel truly at home. It is appropriate therefore to conclude this first section on my own roots and beginnings with a brief description of my own home life and a few reflections on the meaning and importance of home.

I don't know whether this was a general characteristic of young couples in the late 1960s, or just us, but when we got married, Sandra and I really thought we could do just about anything and everything, and without a lot of planning. We thought we could feed, care for, and educate a large family without any problem at all. Sandra would continue with her music (she was both a singer and a pianist). We would be active in the church (we led a youth group of forty teenagers at one point). We would start an after-school child-care program in the community because one was needed. I would master the systems management business and pioneer its introduction in Alberta. We would start a consulting firm and make a million dollars sooner or later. Of course we would travel. And to top it off, we would participate in political revolutions—perhaps a provincial one to revitalize the Socreds or initiate the Social Conservative movement, and another on the federal level.

We have done a number of these things (except make the million dollars), but of course it has taken a lot more effort and time than we originally anticipated.

Our first daughter, Andrea, was born in 1968, and is now a pre-law student at the University of Calgary. Our second daughter, Avryll, was born in 1971, and is now pursuing nursing at Mount Royal College in Calgary. Our third daughter, Mary Joy, was born in 1974, and is currently in grade twelve at Bishop Carroll High School (a flex-time high school for artists and athletes) in Calgary. Our older son, Nathan, was born in 1977, and our younger son, David, in 1980. Both boys attended French immersion schools when we lived in St. Albert north of Edmonton. They now go to Glenmore Christian Academy in Calgary.

In 1977, we moved to St. Albert, a bedroom community north of Edmonton with a strong francophone heritage and population. Eight years after that we moved to an acreage east of St. Albert. In 1989 we moved to Calgary to be closer to the head offices of the Reform Party.

Sandra's sisters married one by one, and at one time were scattered across the country. By the time we moved to St. Albert, however, all the Beavis girls and their husbands and families, as well as Sandra's parents, ended up living within about six blocks of each other. For a number of years, the entire clan would gather at least once a week for a meal at the Beavis residence—four couples with sixteen children altogether.

Sandra has made the care of the children and our home her full-time profession, although she has worked out of the home from time to time when extra money has been required to support the children's many activities.

When I began my long association with Slave Lake Developments Ltd., Sandra found and purchased a lake lot twenty miles along the north shore of Lesser Slave Lake from the town of Slave Lake, at a place called Marten River. We set up a mobile home there, and named the place Nor'Westerlea (after our farm, which had been called Westerlea). It became our family retreat, especially loved by the children. We formed a small community association to bring in electric power and provide a mechanism for dealing with the growth and development of the community. In those days, if asked by media folk whether I had any political ambitions, my reply was that I had my eye on being deputy mayor of Marten River.

When the girls were young, we enrolled the two oldest in a seemingly innocuous program at the YWCA in Edmonton—synchronized swimming for one hour a week. But the girls got hooked on the sport. All three swam with the Edmonton Auroras synchronized swim club under coach Leslie Sproule, reaching the provincial, national, and international competitive levels, which require up to thirty-five hours of training per week.

For more than ten years now, someone at our house has been getting up at 5:30 in the morning to go swimming, often swimming twice a day. The girls have travelled all over Canada, the United States, and Europe to represent Alberta and Canada at synchronized swimming meets, and have learned discipline, poise, and teamwork in the process. Although the two oldest girls are now "retired," the youngest, Mary Joy, is still competing, swimming now with the Calgary Aquabelles.

Sandra has participated in the activities of the Canadian Amateur Synchronized Swimming Association, and claims that federal politics is a Sunday School picnic compared to the politics of amateur sport. For a brief period, I was president of the Edmonton synchro club, and had a treasurer who was so efficient and budget-conscious that other members of the executive were actually afraid to spend club money. Her name was Nadia Poulowsky, and she would make a good role model for some future finance minister of Canada.

My move from being a private consultant to the more public position of the leader of a new federal political party has not particularly affected my three older children. It is the boys who have made the greatest sacrifice to accommodate my change of work and location.

At an age when I left the city for the wide open spaces of the farm, our boys have moved from an acreage with a large house, a ravine, a dog, room to shoot air rifles and bows and arrows, and friends with a "quad" (a four-wheel-drive, all-terrain vehicle) and a snowmobile, to a smaller home with no yard and no dog, in Calgary. There are compensations—new friends, and being closer to the mountains, with more opportunities to fish, trail ride, and ski—but they still miss the acreage and cheer for the Edmonton Oilers and Eskimos.

One of the most vexing adjustments for Sandra has been having to cope with the assumption of uninformed media people and even well-meaning friends that our family is independently wealthy and thus unacquainted with the struggles of others to make ends meet. While my parents were able to increase their net worth considerably once they were out of public life, our own family has been primarily dependent upon my income as a management consultant (and now as an unelected politician) to sustain ourselves. Sandra has had to practise many economies (downsizing our home, transportation, and clothing budgets) to cope with the closing of my consulting practice, and the older children are all working to pay for their higher education. My shift from private to public life has had a more significant effect on their standard of living than on mine.

I do want to acknowledge publicly the adjustments to politics the family has been willing to make thus far, and pray that any further adjustments that may be demanded will not prove too onerous. I also want to thank the many Reformers who have gone out of their way to recognize the needs and contributions of Sandra and my children.

Our family unit would be classified by my social science friends as a traditional family, whereas the Reform Party must take into account many other definitions of family unit in its approach to social policy. It would be a mistake, however, to consider the traditional family as linked only to the past. Through our children and their friends, my wife and I feel we have a direct and constant link with the future and the generation that will inhabit it.

Over the past four years I have spent many hours on the road, attending hundreds of public meetings and media events in scores of communities across Canada, communicating the concerns and proposals for change that are at the heart of the Reform Party program. On average, I am away four or five days at a time, then I return to Calgary and head office for follow-up and other activities there.

Each time I start out, there is the exhilaration of meeting new people and responding to a genuine grassroots interest in fundamental political change. I know what it is like for politics to be "barren and lifeless" and I know what it is like for politics to be "alive." And to be actively engaged in political activity at a time when there is raw political energy welling up from the electorate is a rare privilege.

But by mid-tour, no matter how well things are going—and sooner if they are not going well—my attitude changes. I find myself counting the days and the hours until I will be at home again with Sandra and the children. There is no substitute for the freedom and security of home, if one wants to challenge and change the world.

Erik Nielsen, the former Conservative MP from the Yukon, has done a great public service by the recent publication of his memoirs, particularly the chapter where he openly and courageously shares the negative impact that his public duties had on his family life. This section of Nielsen's book and related material should be required reading for any potential candidate for the House of Commons, in particular his concluding comment, under the heading, "Keep your family with you":

> My own case leads, again, to this final bit of painfully learned wisdom. The married politician may well feel that he or she cannot afford to move his or her family to Ottawa, but I discovered that you cannot afford not to. Do not become a commuting politician; do not tolerate separation from your family. If you do, you will lose them and learn, too late, that the House is not a home.[1]

At the conclusion of this personal memoir, I want to stress that whatever New Canada is, it must be home to the twenty-six million or more people who choose to live on the northern half of the North American continent. All of us can contribute to the definition of New Canada as home. What must happen for you and your family to feel more at home in this country? What must remain the same, what must be changed? What are you prepared to do to make others as well as yourself feel more at home in New Canada?

I realize, of course, that for many Canadians, their experience of home at a personal and family level has been anything but positive. Shattered

---

1. Erik Nielsen, *The House Is Not a Home* (Toronto: Macmillan, 1989), p. 278.

and dysfunctional homes abound and there are thousands of homeless people on the streets of our larger cities and towns. Your contribution to redefining Canada may well be to make clear what a home must *not* be.

In my case, I attach substance and meaning to the concept of Canada as home by reminding myself that it must be a home for all the people and interests I have met thus far on my personal journey towards New Canada, and the thousands more that I and my fellow Reformers have yet to meet as the Reform Party expands from sea to sea to sea.

This means that New Canada must be a home for all the schoolchildren attending the equivalents of Garneau and Horse Hill High across the country. It must be a home for the successors of those sons and daughters of farmers who met on the Horse Hill playground. It must be a homeland for all the August Osises and their families, the immigrants who give character and strength to countless communities across the country.

New Canada must be a home for the soft hearts/soft heads, and hard heads/hard hearts who populate the political parties. It must be a home for those who want to preserve the best features of Old Canada and those who want fundamental change. It must be a home for both the dreamers and the pragmatists.

New Canada must be a home for those native businessmen and oilmen who met in convention to find a way to work together. It must be a home for all those Indian and Métis people I met in the course of my consulting work. It must be a home for all the Ernestines and their children.

New Canada must be a home for all the men and women who populate thousands of resource service towns like Slave Lake and operate all the resource and manufacturing industries, without whom this country would grind to a halt.

New Canada must be a home for all those workers and managers in the utility companies who keep the lights on and the furnaces burning. It must be a home for all the workers and managers in the service industries everywhere, which have become our chief providers of employment.

New Canada must be a home for all the regulators, arbitrators, and conflict resolvers without whom we would sink in a sea of conflict. It must be a home for those who live by religious faith as well as for those who draw their inspiration and reason for living from other sources.

New Canada must be made a home for all those who feel "left out" or "driven out." Above all, New Canada must be a home for the young—for all the contemporaries of Andrea, Avryll, Mary Joy, Nathan, and David—the Canadians who will live most of their lives in the twenty-first century on the foundations and within the frameworks that we have bequeathed to them.

Part Two

The Reform Party of Canada

CHAPTER SIX

Regional Alienation

Whenever populism has become a force to be reckoned with in western Canadian politics, it has been energized by "western alienation"—a conviction shared by generations of western Canadians that their region and interests have not achieved equality with the constitutional and economic interests of Quebec and Ontario, and that systemic change is necessary to achieve such equality.

In the case of Riel in 1870, the constitutional future of the West in general and the Red River colony in particular was being decided by a distant federal government with no regard for the wishes or rights of the people who inhabited that region. Riel organized his Métis people with some support from other settlers, and the resulting rebellion sufficiently challenged the position of the federal government to change the constitutional status of Manitoba. This was the first of what was to be a continuous series of confrontations between the federal government and western Canadians—not over religion, language, or education (although those confrontations would occur too)—but over resources. The right to ownership and control of land (resources) was a central feature of Riel's list of rights, and has been a basic concern of all the western populist movements ever since.

Western alienation was also at the root of the Autonomy Movement led by Haultain and others who demanded provincial status for the old North West Territories, not on terms that would leave those provinces inferior to the older provinces of Canada as the federal government proposed, but on terms that would make them equal. In this case, "equality" meant granting the western provinces ownership of the public lands and natural resources within their boundaries and allowing them to settle educational issues (including minority educational rights) in accordance with the wishes of their own people, rather than in accordance with some formula prescribed by the federal government.

During the 1920s, when the Progressive movement was in full bloom, the rallying cry was again "economic equality." Every Progressive candidate and farmers' advocate raised two basic questions: (1) Why should the western Canadian farmer pay 20 percent more for everything he buys?—a reference to the cost to western farmers of the tariff imposed by the federal government to protect and encourage central Canadian industry at the expense of Canadian consumers; and (2) Why should the western Canadian farmer receive 20 percent less for everything he sells?—a reference to the cost to western farmers of discriminatory and exorbitant freight rates charged by the railway monopolies on grain shipped to seaboard. The platform of the Progressives consisted primarily of reforms intended to redress these grievances, and their appeal to the electors was that they addressed these roots of western alienation more directly and more faithfully than did either of the traditional federal parties.

As the western provinces became more prosperous, western alienation abated, but with the great Depression it returned with a vengeance. The social and economic injustices of that era led people to examine the defects of an economic and political system that permitted poverty in the midst of potential plenty.

The leaders of the Canadian Commonwealth Federation (CCF) blamed the capitalist system itself, a system based in central Canada and supported by the policies of the federal government. They called for the abolition of this system, public ownership of the means of production, centralized economic planning by governments, and a vast expansion of government-operated social services.

The leaders of the Social Credit Movement also blamed the Depression on defects in the capitalist system, in particular the financial system. Once again, the object of their wrath was based outside the West and supported by the policies of the federal government. Unlike the CCF leaders, the Social Credit leadership called for the reform of the capitalist financial system, rather than its abolition. They argued that if credit could be nationalized, or "socialized," it would be unnecessary to socialize anything else.

During the war years and the postwar boom, western alienation went into the background again, only to resurface periodically in the 1960s, 1970s, and 1980s, mainly as a reaction to federal constitutional and economic policies. In an insightful editorial in the March 30, 1991, edition of the *Globe and Mail*, William Thorsell reluctantly expressed the view that Canada may have made a fundamental error in the mid-1960s when its elites so wholeheartedly embraced the concept of Canada as an equal partnership of two founding races, cultures, and languages: the English and the French. I distinctly recall sitting in the office of the premier of Alberta twenty-five years ago and hearing him express exactly the same opinion, just half an hour after receiving a telegram from Prime Minister Pearson outlining the proposed terms of reference of the Royal Commission on Bilingualism and Biculturalism. The working definition of Canada which the federal government intended to use to guide future constitutional development was the old Upper Canada/Lower Canada definition that had proved so harmful to Canadian unity in the colonial Parliament from 1840 to 1866. The B and B definition of Canada did not even acknowledge, let alone embrace, the real political aspirations of most western Canadian communities. In fact, since the mid-1960s, virtually every constitutional initiative taken by the federal government to make Quebec feel more at home in confederation has increased western alienation and made an ever-increasing number of other Canadians feel less at home in confederation.

At the same time, the Trudeau administration added fuel to the smouldering fires of western alienation through its economic policies, especially the National Energy Program and related taxation policies. In the late 1970s, the policies of the OPEC cartel and the Iranian revolution made international oil prices soar. The petroleum companies and the western producing provinces had hoped to benefit from this transformation of what had been a buyer's market into a seller's market. But the federal and provincial governments would not allow the industry to keep the lion's share of the increased revenues. Joe Clark's short-lived administration could not negotiate a satisfactory pricing and revenue-sharing arrangement with the Lougheed government, and was defeated in the 1980 federal election (in which its controversial proposal to impose an eighteen-cent excise tax on gasoline was a key issue). On October 28, 1980, the Trudeau government introduced the National Energy Program (NEP) as part of its first budget after the 1980 general election. The immediate effect of this policy was to force western producers to sell oil and gas to Canadian consumers at substantially less than the world price. The NEP also imposed new taxes such as the Petroleum Gas Revenue Tax (a tax, not on the net incomes of petroleum producers, but on gross revenues), and attempted to increase Canadian ownership of the petroleum sector by establishing rules and incentives that favoured Canadian-owned companies over foreign-owned firms.

Many western Canadians saw the National Energy Program as a massive raid by a spendthrift federal government (the Trudeau government's accumulated deficit at that point was $72 billion) on the resource wealth of western Canada, as well as a massive federal intrusion (through the use of federal taxing, pricing, and regulatory powers) into provincial jurisdiction over natural resources.

By 1985, figures compiled by economist Robert Mansell at the University of Calgary showed that the National Energy Program and related tax policies had resulted in a net transfer of wealth from the producing provinces to the federal treasury and the energy consumers of central and eastern Canada of approximately *$100 billion*. About 60 percent of this figure represented wealth transferred through the sale of oil and gas at prices below the world price as a result of federal regulation and pricing policies. The other 40 percent, or $40 billion, represented transfers from federal taxes on western energy resources and producers.

The inability of many western Canadian energy producers and service companies to withstand the drop in oil prices and the collapse of the boom in 1981—a collapse which led to the bankruptcies of hundreds of companies and the loss of over fifty thousand jobs—was also blamed in large measure on the NEP and related policies.

The effect of the National Energy Program on so many western Canadians led some to question the equity of the whole federal system and the benefits of confederation itself. What type of a system, they asked, would permit a hundred-billion-dollar raid on the resource wealth of one region by the federal government in the name of the national interest? Where is the equity, particularly for the private investor, in a federal economic regime that lets market forces allocate resources *when market prices are low,* but insists on government intervention in the market place when prices are high? Why is it acceptable national policy to impose a special revenue tax on companies engaged in developing the petroleum resources of western Canada while exempting the largest energy companies in the country, Ontario Hydro and Hydro-Québec, from taxation? Why is the accumulation of capital in Alberta's Heritage Trust Fund a menace to confederation, while the accumulation of similar amounts of capital in the accounts of Ontario Hydro and Hydro-Québec is supposed to be in the national interest? How do people who are always talking about the need for justice and equity in federal-provincial relations explain the fiscal inequities in the regional distribution of federal fiscal balances in Canada?

(These fiscal inequities show up clearly in a series of tables prepared by economists at the University of Calgary.[1] These tables show the differences, in 1990 dollars, between all federal revenues collected in each province, and what the federal government spent in each province. Over the period 1961 to 1988, largely as a result of federal energy and related taxation policies, the difference between what the federal government collected from Alberta and what the federal government spent in that province was more than *$145 billion,* or $2,519 per capita. Over the same period, the difference between what the federal government collected and what the federal government spent in British Columbia was over $9 billion, or $205 per capita. For all other provinces, including the central Canadian provinces of Quebec and Ontario, federal expenditures and transfers received exceeded the contributions of those provinces to federal revenues. Net federal *contributions to* the people of these provinces from the federal government ranged from $69 per capita for Ontario, to $757 for Quebec, to $3,451 for Prince Edward Island.)

The inability of representatives of the federal Liberal Party to answer these questions in the 1970s and 1980s, combined with the bias of Liberal constitutional policies, virtually destroyed the federal Liberals in western Canada. By 1984, there were only two Liberal members of Parliament west of the Lakehead—Lloyd Axworthy in Winnipeg-South Centre (and his political life was only sustained by massive infusions of patronage money under the guise of regional development funding), and John Turner in Vancouver Quadra.

One further dimension of western alienation, most pronounced in Alberta, must be noted. Albertans are very competitive, and to a large extent are competing against themselves. They do not simply compare their economic and political standing with that of the other provinces, but they compare the Alberta that "is" with the Alberta that "could have been" or "could still be." In other words, part of western alienation stems from frustrated ambitions, unfulfilled expectations, and the tragedy of unrealized potentials—the crop that might have been if the hail had not come, the fortune that might have been made if the well had been drilled three miles farther north. Such sentiments deeply affect how many westerners think about themselves and the country as a whole.

The problem of western alienation and the demands for equality it engenders poses a larger and more fundamental question, which is of

1. Robert L. Mansell and Ronald C. Schlenker, *An Analysis of the Regional Distribution of Federal Fiscal Balances: Updated Data,* Department of Economics, University of Calgary, 1990.

significance to all Canadians, no matter where they live. Several years ago, when the Reform Party of Canada was in its infancy, I addressed a public meeting at Fort St. John in the Peace River country of British Columbia on the need for more fairness and balance in national decision making. (This is a particularly relevant subject in the Peace River Country, because the people there often feel doubly alienated. They identify with western alienation from central Canada, but they suffer from north-south alienation as well.) At the conclusion of my address, a woman stood up to ask a question. I found out later that her name was Mrs. Woolley. (No audio or video record of the meeting was kept, so I am quoting and paraphrasing Mrs. Woolley from memory.)

> You have been talking about the need for more "fairness" for the West and the North. I agree that we need fairer treatment from the federal government. But a number of years ago another gentleman named Mr. Trudeau came through here and he also talked about fairness—a Just Society he called it. We thought that when he talked about "justice" he meant justice for everyone, and perhaps in a sense he did. But later on it appeared that what he was especially concerned about was "justice for Quebec"—the province where he was born and raised.
>
> Now my question for you is this: When you talk about "more fairness in national decision making," are you talking about fairness, period—more fairness for everyone? Or are you just talking about "more fairness for the West," the way Mr. Trudeau was really talking about "more justice for Quebec"?

I answered that if western Canadians want to avoid dividing the nation in the name of justice as the Trudeau Liberals did, then we (and the Reform Party) must address the need for "fairness, period"—more fairness for everyone in confederation, not just more fairness for the West. (Please note that I like to use the word "fairness" rather than "justice." Ernestine would call "justice" a "high word," easily used by professors and constitutional lawyers and interest-group spokespersons addressing the media. But the street word is "fair" and it is on the street that the concept of "fairness for all Canadians" must be sold and implemented.)

Western Canadians, given their experience with regional inequities and national politics, are aware of something that other Canadians are beginning to realize as well, and which may enable us to achieve more equitable constitutional arrangements and federal policies for the future. We realize that the concept of justice or "fairness" is not really divisible.

And if you try to divide it—by talking about justice for one region, but not for all; or justice for one ethnic or economic group, but not for all—you end up pursuing special status rather than justice. And in a country as diverse as Canada, where the one thing we may all have in common is a feeling that our group has been hard done by in some way, the pursuit of special status for some, rather than equality and justice for all, is a formula for national disunity and disintegration.

You can't be concerned about regional alienation in western Canada and not be concerned about regional alienation in northern and rural Ontario, northern and rural Quebec, northern Canada, and Atlantic Canada. You can't be concerned about securing constitutional equality for the West or Quebec and not be concerned about securing constitutional equality for all other Canadians, including aboriginal Canadians. You can't be concerned about economic justice or constitutional justice and not be concerned about social justice.

Western alienation is really a particular case of a more general phenomenon of inequities, real and imagined, experienced by other regions and groups in Canadian society. And any populist reform program generated to address this particular case must be broad and deep enough in its concerns and its prescriptions to address the more general phenomenon.

CHAPTER SEVEN

The Vancouver Assembly

All during the 1970s and early 1980s, I had studied and explored proposals for bringing about fundamental political change in the federal arena either by seeking to influence existing parties or by creating a new party. I soon realized, however, that there were two barriers to creating a new political party. The first was the fact that the most natural and logical vehicles for pursuing change in federal politics, especially in the West, were the traditional opposition parties, the Progressive Conservatives and the NDP. The second was that, as far as I could tell, there was no broad public constituency emerging to support the fundamental changes in the federal system that I considered necessary. I often found interest groups, clients, and personal friends with an interest in these matters, but there was as yet no evidence that a genuine populist base was emerging to support a new political alternative.

In 1984, therefore, when the electorate finally decided to put an end to the Liberal era, it did the predictable and expected thing. On September 4, 1984, it gave the Progressive Conservative Party of Canada under the leadership of Brian Mulroney an overwhelming mandate to govern and lead the country in new directions.

By 1986, however, it was becoming clear to me and to others in western Canada that the federal Conservatives, despite the presence in their ranks of some very able people, could not meet the expectations they had actively and deliberately raised in the 1984 campaign. The federal Conservatives, Mulroney in particular, had grossly underestimated the desire for systemic change which lay behind public support of the Conservatives in the 1984 election. So when the Conservatives failed to adopt any new model for constitutional reform, when they held onto the NEP until the drop in world oil prices rendered it financially expendable, when they failed to address the demand for Senate reform, when they merely extended and refined the Liberals' official language policy, and when they failed to come to grips with federal overspending to the extent westerners expected, a political vacuum began to open up, capable of calling into being another populist movement in the western reform tradition.

The federal Conservatives resorted to an extremely weak argument in self-defence. They pointed to the numbers of western ministers at the cabinet table and spoke about the enormous influence that these ministers had on federal policy. Except in the case of Don Mazankowski, however, these arguments cut little ice with western voters. If these western ministers really had influence, why didn't Senate reform move to the top of the government's constitutional agenda? Why wasn't the government rethinking the objectionable aspects of the Liberal approach to language and cultural policy? Why were western MPs from Conservative ridings unable to exert more effective pressure to curtail public spending?

If western ministers had any influence at the cabinet table, how was it being used? An increasing number of westerners came to believe that western ministers used their "influence" primarily to represent unacceptable Ottawa positions to their western constituents, rather than to represent legitimate western concerns and aspirations to Ottawa.

The growing suspicion on the part of many westerners that the Mulroney government had the same old central-Canadian bias as the Trudeau regime when it came to economic development was confirmed for many in October 1986 by the CF-18 affair.

Earlier in the year, the federal government had called for tenders for the maintenance of Canada's fleet of 136 CF-18 fighter aircraft. Bidders anticipated that the contract would be awarded to the company with the lowest tender and the highest technical competence. The principal competition was between Montreal-based Canadair Ltd. and Bristol Aerospace Ltd. of Winnipeg. Bristol Aerospace submitted the lower bid ($100.5 million to Canadair's $104 million), and received a higher rating for technical competence (926 evaluation points out of a possible 1,000, compared to 833 for Canadair) from a team of seventy-five civil servants from three federal departments. However, Quebec cabinet ministers intervened in the tendering process and the government was persuaded to award the contract to Canadair. Treasury Board President Robert de

Cotret announced that this decision was in the "national interest," since Canadair could better use technology transfers resulting from the contract to develop the country's industrial base.

For many westerners, the CF-18 decision had the same odour as the NEP, only this policy was instituted not by the Liberals but by the new Conservative government, which was supposed to be introducing more regional fairness and balance into national decision making. The CF-18 decision also showed westerners exactly how much influence their PC members and cabinet ministers had in the new government when push came to shove. To add insult to injury, instead of sending de Cotret to Winnipeg to deliver the bad news, the government told Jake Epp, the senior cabinet minister from Manitoba, to explain to Manitobans how awarding the contract to Canadair instead of to Bristol was "in the national interest."

Other westerners noticed the contrast between the clout exercised in the power circles of the new government by the fifty-eight PC members from Quebec (most of them rookies) compared to that of the fifty-eight PC members from the West (many of them veterans). And for the supporters of an elected Senate with equal numbers of senators from all provinces, the CF-18 decision provided another clear-cut argument as to why Canada needs a reformed Senate to safeguard and advance regional interests. "How did Seattle, Washington, home of Boeing—many miles farther from Washington than Winnipeg is from Ottawa—ever become the huge and sophisticated aircraft maintenance and development centre that it is?" they asked. Because in the United States Senate, thinly populated Washington has just as many senators as industrialized New York or heavily populated California; the United States Senate thus provides a far stronger mechanism for balancing regional allocations of defence spending than does the Canadian Parliament with its impotent and unaccountable Upper House.

The best commentary on the CF-18 decision, and one that Reformers used most effectively to illustrate the inequities involved, was a column by Les MacPherson of the Saskatoon *Star Phoenix* entitled "Giving cup to Quebec a typically capital idea."

> OTTAWA —The federal government today announced it would award the Stanley Cup to Quebec, even though Alberta's Calgary Flames won the competition.
>
> The cup will go instead to Quebec's Montreal Canadiens, who were defeated by the Flames four games to two in the best-of-seven series.

Prime Minister Brian Mulroney said the hockey series was "only a guideline," and not binding. He conceded that Calgary might have the best hockey team, "but we have to look at what's best for all Canada." "We have to support Canada's hockey industry, which is centred in Montreal," said the prime minister. "Montreal is in the best position to take full advantage of the Stanley Cup."

He said the decision to overrule the playoff results was "difficult and painful" but the national interest had to prevail over petty regional considerations.

Loss of the coveted trophy left most of Alberta seething with rage.

"It's another example of Quebec getting the goodies and the West getting the shaft," said Ted Byfield, editor of the stridently regionalist newsmagazine Western Report.

Western Tory MPs were not so hostile. They shuffled their feet, clenched their buttocks, pursed their lips and said nothing at all. Neither did Alberta Premier Don Getty, who was golfing and unavailable for comment. However, reliable sources indicated he "seemed quite upset" and was "way off his game."

Indignant Quebec MPs who lobbied long and hard for the Stanley Cup vehemently denied that the decision had anything to do with politics.

"It's not as if the West isn't getting its fair share of federal support," sniffed Benoit Bouchard, the Tories' senior Quebec cabinet minister. "We've announced the Lloydminster upgrader eight or nine times. The West received the very lucrative contract for air in the CF-18s' tires. And let's not forget about all that rain for western farmers this spring."

Quebec Industry Minister Pierre Johnson dismissed western complaints as "anti-French hysteria from Alberta dinosaurs."

"Quebec absolutely deserves this," he said. "The Montreal Canadiens have extensive experience as Stanley Cup champions, while the Calgary Flames have none at all. Sure, Calgary won this particular series with a couple of fluke goals and lucky saves, but the Canadiens have proven themselves over the long haul."

"If we're denied the Stanley Cup now, it could only rejuvenate Quebec separatism and threaten the integrity of all Canada."

Saskatchewan Premier Grant Devine said sending the Cup to Quebec "seems fair enough."

"Ottawa has done plenty for the West," he said. "Just look at the Dundurn army base. They could have shut it down, and they didn't. They let Swift Current keep the Memorial Cup. And there's a darn good chance we'll get to keep our Via Rail service too."

David Orchard blamed it all on free trade.

Quebec Premier Robert Bourassa was delighted to see the Cup go to Montreal. He said the trophy will be re-engraved with its new name—"la Coupe Stanley"—to comply with Quebec sign laws.[1]

One of the indications that the time is ripe for a new idea or movement is that different people in quite different circumstances come to roughly the same conclusions at the same time. In 1986, when I started to explore with some of my business and political contacts across the West whether the time was finally ripe for a new federal political option to emerge, several other groups of westerners were coming to similar conclusions.

In Edmonton, Ted Byfield, magazine editor, publisher, and long-time crusader for a Triple-E Senate and other western causes, was calling for a new, moderate, western-based federal political party to demand a fair deal for the hinterland regions of the country. In a column in *Alberta Report,* August 25, 1986, he stated, "The West needs its own party" to push for economic and constitutional reforms. In Calgary, a small group of oilpatch lawyers and executives began in September 1986 to meet regularly to discuss ways and means, including political action, to secure greater constitutional equality for the resource-producing regions through Senate reform and political action. The group included Jules Poscente, chief executive officer of Canada Northwest Energy; Doug Hilland, a lawyer and director of CNWE; and Bob Muir, a lawyer and former general counsel for Dome Petroleum. And on Vancouver Island, retired Edmonton businessman Francis Winspear assembled a small group to discuss the shortcomings of the Conservative administration from a western perspective and to consider alternatives.

Francis Winspear had been a lifelong supporter of the Liberal Party, but had finally broken with the party over the central-Canadian bias and fiscally irresponsible behaviour of the Trudeau administration. In 1984, for the first time in his life, he had backed the federal Conservatives, financially as well as verbally, but by 1986 he was as disillusioned with Mulroney's administration as he had been with Trudeau's. Winspear had been a long-time supporter of the Canada West Foundation and a member of its governing council. Through this association he had met

---

1. Saskatoon *Star Phoenix,* 22 June 1989. Reprinted with permission.

Stan Roberts, the former Liberal leader and MLA from Manitoba who became the first president of Canada West, and left the foundation to become president of the Canadian Chamber of Commerce.

When Winspear and his Vancouver Island colleagues decided to explore new political options in the federal arena, Winspear contacted Roberts (then living in Burnaby) and asked him to investigate the possibilities. Winspear later wrote out a cheque for $50,000 to aid the process. Roberts began to get in touch with many of his old friends and associates from his Canada West days. These included Jo Anne Hillier from Beausejour, Manitoba, who had been a Canada West director; Alan Beachell, a farmer at Rosser, Manitoba, and president of the Union of Manitoba Municipalities; and Wally Nelson of Avonlea, Saskatchewan, one of the founders of the Palliser Grain Growers' Association.

Meanwhile, through my consulting contacts with various political and economic interests across the West, I too had been finding rapid disillusionment with the new Progressive Conservative government. But where was the evidence that this political unrest and willingness to look at new alternatives existed, not just among certain opinion leaders, but among ordinary "grassroots" westerners? Was a populist base emerging on which a political movement might be built?

I did not have a great deal of confidence that these questions could be answered simply by looking at the opinion polls. My awareness that there was "a stirring among the grassroots" came to me through my contacts with municipal politicians in Alberta. (Stan Roberts was getting similar impressions from his contacts with municipal politicians in Manitoba.) Of the three levels of politicians in this country—municipal, provincial, and federal—it is usually the municipal ones, especially in the rural areas, who are closest to ordinary citizens. By attending several conventions and seminars of the Alberta Association of Municipal Districts and Counties, and talking with the various municipal politicians who visited my consulting office, I began to get the message that political unrest and the willingness to search for alternatives were even more pronounced at the grassroots level than they were at the executive and interest-group level.

Cliff Breitkreuz, a municipal councillor from Onoway, in Joe Clark's constituency, was particularly insistent that "the time was ripe" for a populist movement at the federal level and that I, because of my background, should help initiate it. He kept asking me, "When are you going to stop studying and talking about a western-based reform movement, and start doing something about it?"

On September 5, 1986, partly to test the waters and partly to get people like Cliff Breitkreuz off my back, I wrote a memorandum entitled, "A Western Reform Movement: The Responsible Alternative to Western Separatism." After reviewing the evidence of growing disillusionment with the traditional federal parties and the West's propensity for producing new movements in such circumstances, I concluded with the following observations:

> Many of the policies, plans, ideas, and ingredients required to construct the platform of a responsible Western Reform Movement already exist, articulated by respected and thoughtful spokesmen like Jim Gray of the oil patch, David Elton of the Canada West Foundation, Ted Byfield of *Western Report,* and the late Hu Harries.
>
> The ingredients missing to date are: (1) the will to turn ideas, discussions, hopes, and fears into *political actions;* (2) strong and respected leadership; and (3) the funds necessary to do the job.
>
> Perhaps it is time that someone gave a little talk to the potential leaders of the next Western Reform Movement similar to that which Napoleon is reported to have given to a group of France's up and coming generals. He told them that in pursuing the military interests of France they would sometimes be confronted with "real alternatives." In such situations, it was imperative that they carefully consider, discuss, and evaluate the options before proceeding. But on other occasions they would find themselves in situations where there were no real alternatives, or where all the apparent alternatives were unacceptable. In such cases, Napoleon concluded, they must remember that it would be "bold actions, not further calculations, which will carry the day."
>
> The western Canadian who views the federal political scene today sees nothing but unacceptable alternatives. There is therefore no point in further analysis or debate as to whether supporting the federal Conservatives, Liberals, or NDP in the next federal election is the lesser of the three evils. Politically, we are now in one of those situations where it is "bold actions, not further calculations, which will carry the day."

I mailed copies of this memorandum, along with Ted Byfield's editorial calling for a "Western Canadian Party," to Ted himself, Jim Gray, and Dr. David Elton.

At the time, Jim Gray was a member of the Canadian Committee for a Triple-E Senate, vice-president of Canadian Hunter Exploration Ltd., and a strong Conservative. Jim is also a hard-driving innovator with a great concern for advancing the interests of western Canada within confederation and for advancing Canada's interests in the international marketplace. Dr. David Elton, a political scientist at the University of Lethbridge, had succeeded Stan Roberts as president of the Canada West Foundation.

In the covering letter accompanying my memorandum, I proposed a meeting in Calgary to discuss "bold actions." I suggested Calgary was an appropriate meeting place, not just because it had become a symbol of what misguided federal resource policies could do to the West, but also because it was the place where the initial organizational meetings for the last two western reform movements (both the CCF and Social Credit) were held.

Eventually this meeting was held on October 17, 1986, in Jim Gray's boardroom. David Elton was present but Ted Byfield was ill and unable to attend, although he made it clear that he thought the time was ripe to "do something." Jim Gray had also invited Bob Muir and Doug Hilland from the Hilland group to attend.

In the draft agenda for the meeting I had listed four options for discussion: (1) continue to work within the present system of traditional federal parties, provincial governments, and interest groups; (2) ignore, oppose, or encourage the separatists; (3) organize a new western-based federal political party to run Reform candidates in the next federal election (my preference); (4) organize a "Parliament of the West" for the spring or the fall of 1987 to debate the issues and recommend a course of action.

Jim Gray believed that the federal Conservatives had made some grave mistakes, but that it was still too early to conclude that they would not change course and recover. He was not prepared to endorse a course of political action that might simply divide Conservative support in the West and frustrate the pursuit of the free trade initiative, which many oilpatch people considered to be their only real safeguard against another National Energy Program.

I argued that the time was ripe to create a new federal political movement in the West dedicated to systemic changes that would make the West an equal partner in confederation. I especially stressed the fact that I thought there was grassroots support for such a movement.

Although Ted Byfield was not present, he had expressed himself quite clearly through the editorial pages of his magazine, and we assumed that he was in favour of a new political movement. If there was any question about Ted's position, it was whether he favoured a genuinely federalist movement, or one that would rely on the threat of secession as its principal means of getting attention.

David Elton agreed that the policies being pursued by the federal Conservatives were not addressing the concerns of the West, in particular the demands for systemic change. His reading of the polls, however (and David was a pollster himself and had supervised regular polling by Canada West), did not confirm my assertions that the public would support some new initiative. David generally favoured more study rather than precipitate action.

Muir and Hilland did not say much during the meeting, although they remarked that some members of the oilpatch had been badly burned by prematurely backing the separatist Western Canada Concept movement in the late 1970s and early 1980s, and would be much more guarded toward any new movements in the future.

And so once again it appeared that there would be no consensus on what to do, even within so small a group, and a group which was generally agreed that western alienation was deepening and needed to be addressed by political action of some kind.

Not wanting this get-together to be a total loss, we then turned our attention to the fourth option. Surely the one thing we could all agree on was that westerners should have a big meeting somewhere in the near future, to see if we could at least identify the major changes that would be necessary to solve the present discontents and to make the West an equal partner in confederation, and discuss how such a list of reforms might best be promoted in the federal political arena. No one strenuously objected to this proposal, although Gray and Elton had their reservations.

After the meeting, Muir and Hilland advised me that their group consisted of "doers" rather than "talkers," and would probably help "get something going." They invited me to make a presentation to this group, which I did on November 13, 1986. My presentation was entitled "Proposal for the Creation of a Western-Based Political Party to Run Candidates in the 1988 Federal Election."

Shortly afterward, Stan Roberts came to see me at our Edmonton consulting offices and brought me up to date on Francis Winspear's thinking and his own explorations. I told Stan that about the only thing I thought we could get the various Calgary groups to agree to was "a big meeting somewhere to address the issues and alternative courses of action." Stan felt such a meeting would at least be a step in the right direction. He volunteered his organizational assistance and offered to talk further to Winspear about the necessary financial backing.

I also talked to Ted Byfield about the Calgary discussions and the proposal for a big meeting. He agreed to promote the idea through his magazine, and suggested that the big meeting be held in Vancouver rather than Calgary, since Calgary had hosted more than its fair share of "wild and woolly" political gatherings.

Thus, by a very uneven and tortuous process, the idea and the means for organizing the Western Assembly on Canada's Economic and Political Future came together. The assembly was to be held on May 29-31, 1987, at the Hyatt Regency Hotel in Vancouver.

Stan Roberts agreed to supervise the facilities and accommodation arrangements through his Vancouver office, and to help get a cross-section of delegates from across the West to attend.

Francis Winspear agreed to provide the financial backing required to book the hotel and finance the organization of the meeting. (As a prairie populist, I would have preferred that the assembly be held in more humble surroundings, but Winspear wanted it to be done "first class" and in the end the Hyatt in Vancouver proved to be a good choice.) The Reform Association of Canada was created to sponsor the meeting and collected funds to defray expenses.

Ted Byfield agreed to write the main advertisements for the assembly. This included a four-page supplement that ran the first week of April in the *Alberta Report* and *Western Report,* as well as smaller ads for other western publications such as the *Western Producer* and the *Manitoba Cooperator.* The ads asked westerners to address a basic question: "What does the West want, anyway? The time has come to provide an answer. We need economic change. We need constitutional change. We need political change. We need you!" The ads invited readers to nominate delegates to represent their province and federal constituency at the assembly. Nominees were to be "eligible to vote in a federal election, knowledgeable in at least one of the subject areas to be dealt with by the Assembly, committed to seeking fundamental change in Canada, and open minded (not narrowly partisan) with respect to the choice of political vehicles." Readers were also invited to join the Reform Association of Canada for a twenty-five-dollar fee, to make a financial contribution to the assembly, and to attend a public rally at the conclusion of the assembly if they were able to do so.

It was Ted who coined the Reform slogan, "The West Wants In," to make clear that what we were doing was not intended to revive western separatism but to establish more fairness and balance in the Canadian confederation.

Provincial delegate selection committees were set up to choose delegates from among those nominated by the public, and to recruit additional delegates if this was necessary to round out the representation. The registration fee per delegate was $200, and delegates had to pay their travel costs to and from Vancouver.

I agreed to help draft the assembly agenda and to get some credible resource people, drawing on my contacts with Canada West and some of our consulting clients. I also offered our consulting office address and phone number in Edmonton as the main contact point for people who wanted to attend the assembly.

People such as Jo Anne Hillier and Allan Beachell undertook to stimulate interest in the assembly in Manitoba. Wally Nelson and Bill Duke of the Western Canadian Wheat Growers' Association agreed to do the same in Saskatchewan. The Hilland group from Calgary would be responsible for southern Alberta, and I would work on northern Alberta.

Others—Bob Grbavac, a farmer and rancher from Raymond with Liberal connections; Marshall Copithorne, a well-known rancher from Cochrane with Conservative credentials; Ray Speaker, my old friend and the member of the Alberta Legislature for Little Bow; and Howard Thompson, the former Socred and WCC organizer from Innisfail—helped recruit delegates from rural Alberta. David Elton suggested possible resource people to work on papers, particularly on the economic issues. Bert Brown, chairman of the Canadian Committee for a Triple-E Senate and a prominent Conservative, agreed to come and make a presentation on that concept. Stan Roberts and Francis Winspear used their prairie and British Columbia contacts to get representation from their circle, especially on the West Coast.

Eventually, 58 official delegates from British Columbia, 100 from Alberta, and 38 from Saskatchewan and Manitoba, along with 23 observers and resource people, 350 delegates-at-large, and about 100 visitors, attended the Western Assembly in Vancouver. Most of them had been connected at one time or another with one of the three traditional parties. Of the Albertans, most had been Conservatives, while those from Manitoba, Saskatchewan, and British Columbia represented a greater mix, in which disaffected Liberals and Conservatives predominated. Some of the delegates would have described themselves as uninvolved or unaligned, having been disenchanted for some time with all three of the traditional federal parties.

The Vancouver Assembly had two goals. First, we wanted to develop a "Western Agenda for Change" that a majority of western Canadians could support. Second, the assembly was to answer the question, "What would be the best political vehicle to advance the West's agenda for change over the next few years, including the next federal election?"

The Assembly opened on the morning of May 29, 1987, with some words of welcome by Stan Roberts. I explained the agenda, then Ted Byfield gave a rousing address on the need for fundamental change in Canada. The assembly delegates received a number of brief presentations by task forces and special speakers dealing with economic, constitutional, and social reform, each report concluding with some draft resolutions. Delegates then broke into workshops to review and revise the task force recommendations, and, if necessary, suggest alternatives. The recommendations of the task forces and workshop sessions were then reduced to a short list of "proposed reforms" for inclusion on a summary ballot.

Sunday morning, May 30, was devoted to a final discussion of the summary ballot and voting. Delegates were asked to indicate on their ballots whether they agreed in principle, disagreed in principle, or suggested modification, for each proposed reform on the ballot.

As the person responsible for developing the agenda and coordinating the task forces, I had a hand in framing most of the original resolutions. On Saturday night, while delegates and observers assembled for a dinner and an address by Peter Brimelow, author of *The Patriot Game*, the workshop coordinators, our small administrative staff, and I worked long into the night to collate the results and complete the summary ballot.

The entire assembly was open to the media, and there were many observers wandering around—academics, politicians, and curious citizens who wanted to see what was going on but were not certain whether they wanted to be directly identified with the outcome.

During the presentations of the first day, I could not help but observe a disturbing but predictable phenomenon which symbolized one of the major difficulties faced by any constructive reform movement attempting to communicate its message through the mass media.

At the opening session, Ted Byfield led off with an appropriate and hard-hitting presentation on the need for reform. Naturally, given his subject, he presented a stinging critique of the current imbalances within confederation, and their negative effects (especially economic effects) on the West. Then Bob Grbavac presented a paper prepared by the assembly's economic task force, which focused on what the West itself could do to improve its own economic position by removing interprovincial barriers to trade and capturing more of the advantages of freer trade.[2] The paper used an idea originally suggested by Dr. Clay Gilson of the University of Manitoba, that reformers should take the old Treaty of Rome, which established the initial European Common Market in the 1950s, and substitute the names of Manitoba, Saskatchewan, Alberta, and British Columbia for those of the original European signatories. In other words, it used the treaty as an "idea generator" to identify various steps that might be taken to establish an economic common market in western Canada, to expand our own domestic market potential, and to prepare the way for freer trade on a broader scale.

There were about thirty-five media people in the assembly hall at the time (the assembly by this time had become something of a media event). At the conclusion of the session in which these two presentations (one a negative critique, the other a positive solution to the problems raised by the first) were made, thirty-three of the media people clustered around Ted, while only two had follow-up questions for Bob.

The communications challenge faced by reform movements the world over and illustrated by this incident is this: in the modern communications business, particularly in the case of television, negative is more newsworthy than positive; short-term is more newsworthy than long-term; disagreement is more newsworthy than agreement; emotion-laden critiques are more newsworthy than well-reasoned proposals for constructive change; discord, threats to order, and bad government are much more newsworthy than peace, order, and good government.

Thus a reform movement's criticisms of the existing order, particularly if these are expressed in vigorous and emotional language, will be amplified by the mass media, while its constructive proposals for change—the elements that distinguish a genuine reform movement from a mere protest movement—will be dampened and filtered by the same media.

This peculiar bias of modern mass communications systems arises from the markets that drive them and the technology they employ. It has very little to do with the ideological or other biases of particular reporters or

---

2. This paper had been prepared from input provided by Dr. David Elton in his capacity as Professor of Political Science at the University of Lethbridge; Dr. Clay Gilson of the Department of Agriculture and Farm Management at the University of Manitoba; Gordon Engbloom, an energy consultant with whom I had worked in the past and the President of Confer Consulting Ltd.; Dr. Brian Scarfe, Professor and Chairman of the Department of Economics at the University of Alberta; and myself.

news organizations. How to cope with and compensate for this bias of the mass media in the reporting of "reform politics" is one of the major challenges facing any reform initiative aimed at the general public.

In the workshop sessions, however, delegates demonstrated a willingness to move beyond criticism of the status quo to a serious consideration of constructive proposals for change, even though, as is often the case at these types of gatherings, they were often too rushed to allow for serious debate and reflection on the task force reports. They did, however, bring together in a small-group setting people from different political backgrounds and localities to discuss subjects of common interest and to discover whether or not they had any common political purposes.

The interactions between these small groups and the task forces also represented the first organized attempt by the leaders of the Reform Movement to establish the cooperation between "expert opinion" and "grassroots common sense" that I consider essential to the maintenance of an informed and intelligent populist movement.

Far too often in Canadian politics, academics and policy makers with professional expertise are unwilling to submit their ideas, reasoning, and conclusions to thorough and open scrutiny by ordinary Canadians. "Why should I?" asks the expert. "The average citizen isn't interested, or doesn't have the knowledge and training to understand. Or worse yet, the rank and file will corrupt my elegant and thoughtful theses with questions and suggestions rooted in ignorance, or prejudice, or short-term self-interest." This attitude discounts the fact that it is that "average citizen" whose life will be affected by the adoption of that policy and who will probably have to pay for its implementation through his or her taxes. Also, if the public doesn't understand a policy or disagrees with a policy, the chances of implementing it successfully are very low. The Meech Lake Accord was a good example of a proposed public policy approved by almost everybody except the people to whom the constitution belongs.

At the same time, I am equally impatient with citizens who are prejudiced towards professional policy-making expertise. "These so-called experts," they say, "are usually boring and often hard to understand. They raise difficult questions on matters we think are quite straightforward. They challenge our basic assumptions and are not always sympathetic to our partisan interests. Why should we even listen to them, let alone seek out their advice?" My answer in this case is to say that in attempting to frame workable and forward-looking public policy, you and I need all the help we can get. If there is someone in our community or our country, or even someone from abroad, who has devoted his or her life to studying and thinking about a particular policy issue or subject matter, why not at least listen to what that person has to say? We can always reject what we don't agree with or consider impractical or contrary to our conception of the public interest. But to overlook expert opinion when framing public policy is as great an error as to ignore common sense and public opinion.

The papers and workshops that commanded the most active interest from delegates to the Vancouver Assembly were those on Senate reform and proposals for freer trade—both east-west within Canada and north-south with the United States—as a means of dismantling the last vestiges of the old heartland/hinterland economic model that has dominated federal economic policy for more than a century.

A presentation by Stan Roberts on "completing the West's economic agenda" was well received, although delegates were lukewarm to proposals for measures to increase the western population base as a means of securing more clout in confederation. Delegates also responded positively to a presentation by the assembly's constitutional task force on the need for Senate reform to remedy the centralist bias of the current constitution, and the need to include a definition of economic rights in the Charter of Rights and Freedoms.

Dr. John Richards, former professor of business administration at Simon Fraser University who had been an NDP member of the Saskatchewan legislature and later sat as an independent, made a strong presentation to the effect that the status of aboriginal people in the West constituted our most serious unresolved social challenge.

The only subject area considered by the assembly where I felt I had not done a good job in securing the necessary input was the area of social reform. I had looked for resource persons and contributors who combined the "hard head" and "soft heart" necessary to generate constructive alternatives to the welfare-state approach to dealing with the old, the young, the sick, and the poor, but I had not been very successful.

The greatest challenge facing the delegates to the Vancouver Assembly was not in defining a list of reforms required to make the West an equal partner in confederation. An immense amount of work had already been done on this subject over the previous ten years by provincial governments, think tanks, interest groups, academics, and consultants. We simply identified items on which there was general consensus. The real challenge was the political question. If the West could come up with a list of reforms, how could these be promoted in the federal political arena?

In order to ensure that all the options were presented fairly at the Vancouver Assembly, I had written at the very outset to Brian Mulroney, John Turner, and Ed Broadbent, advising them of our intentions to hold the assembly. I invited each of them not simply to send observers, but to send a senior representative to explain why western Canadians should still consider the traditional federal parties as adequate vehicles for expressing and promoting western demands for change in the federal arena.

Both Turner and Broadbent expressed polite interest in the assembly and indicated that they would have observers present, although they declined to send official representatives. Each asked to be kept informed of the assembly's conclusions. NDP member of Parliament Simon de Jong did attend as an observer, and several well-connected Liberals from the Vancouver area also sat in on the proceedings.

Brian Mulroney wrote to say that he welcomed any proposals the assembly might make on western economic diversification, promised that his government would submit "a specific proposal for Senate reform" to the first ministers (a promise the government has taken more than two years to fulfil partially), and alluded again to "the unprecedented positions of power and influence" held by western MPs in Ottawa. The third paragraph of his letter, however, was the most interesting. It said: "The topic for your main dinner on Saturday evening is 'presentation on the concept of a new federal political party,' and it is clear that this is the principal reason you are convening the meeting. It seems to me that another regional party risks fracturing and reducing the influence of western Canadians on national policy. That would be contrary to Canadian interests, and contrary to western Canada's interests, so you will understand that I would not wish to designate representatives to a conference with such a purpose."

Mulroney told western Conservative MPs that he would look with disfavour on any who attended the assembly, and only Dr. Alex Kindy, MP from Calgary Northeast (who marches to the beat of his own drum) attended as an observer.

Thus, by the time the assembly was held, no official representative of the position of "working within the traditional party system" had emerged. A panel discussion involving journalists was held to explore the pros and cons of a new initiative, and the field was then left wide open for me to make a presentation to the assembly arguing in favour of a new party.

My forty-minute presentation, which was delivered on the afternoon of Saturday, May 30, to the full assembly, was entitled, "Choosing a

Political Vehicle to Represent the West." I began by saying that we were *not* talking about creating another splinter party, or single-issue party, or party of the strange and extreme. Rather, we were talking about a new expression of the great reform tradition of Canadian politics. I then summarized the reasons why a new federal party had to be considered. "The West is in deep trouble economically, but no existing party makes our needs its number one priority. The West is in need of new instruments to advance new solutions, but the traditional political instruments at its disposal are flawed and unsympathetic. The present leaders of the federal parties offer no fresh vision for Canada and the West. If a federal election were held today, 50 percent of our people would not vote because they do not like any of the options."

Next I dealt with the objections to a new federal party, in particular: the argument that it was better to "work for reform from within a traditional party" (I mentioned the track record of those who had advocated this position in the past); the argument that a new party would simply split the Conservative vote (I argued that the new party must be positioned so as to draw support from across the political spectrum, using the strength of its positions on constitutional and parliamentary reform); the argument that there was no time to organize a new party before the next election (I said that our task was not to create a new political movement but to provide a channel for the expression of the energies of a new populist movement that already existed); and the argument that there was no charismatic leader among us (I suggested that leadership of this type was not essential, but that leadership dedicated to the service of reform and of the public could be found).

Finally, I recommended that if the assembly endorsed the new party option, it should give some specific "guidelines to the architects" based on lessons to be learned from previous western attempts to create new political movements. In particular, I recommended that the new party have a positive orientation and vision (it must be more than a party of protest). It should establish standards of performance, policy, and ethical behaviour exceeding those of the traditional parties. It should be ideologically balanced, moving beyond the old categories of left and right. It should be truly federalist, committed to preserving and strengthening Canada through reform. And it should aspire to become a truly national party, not simply a regional party, avoiding actions in its early stages of conception and birth that might prevent it from gaining support all across Canada, including Quebec.

Although I have given hundreds of presentations on the subject of reform, I feel that this was one of the four or five most important speeches I have ever been called upon to make. This particular occasion did not call for me to say anything original. It only called for me to express the concerns and aspirations of people who were already thinking seriously along the same lines, and to apply the wisdom and precedents from past political movements that I had studied and admired since childhood.

Immediately after my speech I went back to collating the input from the workshops in order to have the summary ballot available for voting the next day. I understand from others, however, that there was lively discussion at the dinner that evening and far into the night, not so much on whether to create a new party, but on exactly how it was to be done.

There were still a number of delegates who favoured "working for reform from within a traditional party," but by now they were a distinct minority. Perhaps the most damaging arguments against continuing to work for change within the traditional parties were made, not by myself, but by those who had already tried that option. Time and time again during discussions of this issue, delegates would say something to this effect: "I have worked for twenty-five years within the Liberal Party, and if you think you are going to get that party committed to genuine Senate reform along the lines favoured by western Canadians, you're crazy." Or "I have worked for, voted for, and supported the federal Conservatives all my life, but if you think that party under its current leadership is going to adopt a 'reform agenda' coming out of western Canada, you need your head examined."

On Sunday morning, after all the presentations, panels, workshops, luncheons, dinners, and discussions had been completed, it was time to stop talking and start voting. The summary ballot asked the delegates to approve, reject, or suggest modifications to a short list of constitutional, economic, and social reforms. It also asked delegates to express themselves on the all-important political question:

RESOLVED that this Assembly recommend that Western Canadians seek to advance the West's Agenda for Change by (choose one):
    ☐ Working within an existing federal party
    ☐ Creating/supporting a new, broadly-based pressure group
    ☐ Creating/supporting a new, broadly-based federal political
      party
    ☐ Other

Immediately after the voting, while the delegates went to lunch, the ballots were counted and the results summarized. The results were both predictable and encouraging because of their decisiveness. There was strong support for an elected Senate, economic rights protection, a western common market, and question ballots or referendums. And 77 percent voted in favour of creating and supporting a new broadly based federal political party with its roots in the West.

Delegates quickly approved the establishment of a steering committee to plan a founding assembly for the new party in Winnipeg before November 30, 1987. The committee consisted of Jo Anne Hiller, Stan Roberts, Henry Carroll, and me.

As soon as the formal assembly was over, a public meeting was convened in the assembly room for people in the Vancouver area who had not wanted to sit through the entire assembly (and pay the hefty delegate fee), but who wanted to get a synopsis of the proceedings.

The Vancouver media had given the pre-assembly preparations very little publicity. In fact, the Vancouver dailies had not even intended to cover it at all, until they began to notice the national and out-of-province media arriving the day before. By the end of the assembly, however, the local media were giving it substantial coverage, and this perhaps explained the fact that more than six hundred people jammed into the public briefing.

After another rousing introduction by Ted Byfield and a brief synopsis of the proceedings, this larger group of delegates, delegates-at-large, and observers were asked whether the time had come for a new political party at the federal level, or whether westerners should continue to operate within the three traditional parties.

Those attending the public meeting were probably more representative of the "grassroots," at least in the Vancouver area, than the official delegates. They had come of their own volition, whether out of curiosity or conviction, and had not been "pre-programmed" by the assembly presentations. When their ballots were counted later that night, I was pleased to see that they had voted even more strongly (81 percent) in favour of the creation of a new party along the lines discussed by the assembly.

For me, the Vancouver Assembly was the culmination of eight months of political work that had begun with that meeting in Calgary in September 1986. I was very tired, and Sandra had to leave on the Sunday afternoon to take care of things on the home front and bring the children up to date on what had happened, so I was at loose ends. So was Ken Whyte, an editor with *Western Report,* who had to stay over until the next day.

It was Stanley Cup time, and the Edmonton Oilers were playing the final game in the 1987 Stanley Cup series against Philadelphia. Ken and I ended the day, a politically auspicious day for Reformers, in a typically Canadian way—watching hockey on TV. The Oilers, the first World Hockey Association team (a new league formed by people who were denied an opportunity to play the national game within the traditional NHL) won the game 3-2. It was their third Stanley Cup. If you believe in the "hockey model" of Canada, you might say the Oiler victory boded well for our future.

Because the Vancouver Assembly grew out of concerns that had occurred to a number of different groups at roughly the same time, there has developed a friendly rivalry among Reformers as to who really were the first "fathers and mothers" of the Reform movement. While acknowledging the significant early contributions of a number of people, if I had to single out one individual for special recognition, I would probably choose Dr. Francis Winspear—for two reasons. First, Winspear and his Vancouver Island friends certainly held some of the earliest discussions leading to the Vancouver Assembly, and Winspear was the first to offer financial support for the undertaking. Secondly, what was remarkable about Winspear's willingness to participate in such an adventure was the fact that he was eighty-four years old at the time. It is one thing for younger people, at the peak of their powers or burning with unfulfilled idealism or ambition, to launch out on such an uncertain undertaking. It is quite another for a man well into his eighties, who has every right to leave political entrepreneurship to others, to take the lead in such matters. For this I believe that Francis Winspear deserves special recognition.

CHAPTER EIGHT

The Founding Assembly

The Vancouver Assembly generated a lot of publicity in western Canada for the Reform Association of Canada and those associated with it. The membership mailing list increased to more than three thousand names, and requests for information on the association and the results of the Assembly began to pour in. The next milestone was the Founding Assembly for the new party, scheduled for October 30, 31, and November 1, 1987, at the Winnipeg Convention Centre. A small assembly office was established in Winnipeg under the direction of Jo Anne Hillier to help organize it.

The assembly steering committee sent out guidelines for the selection of delegates for the Founding Assembly to everyone on the mailing list and to inquirers. These guidelines called for Reform Association members to choose up to eight delegates per federal riding. At that stage there were no known Reformers in many ridings, especially in Saskatchewan, Manitoba, and northern British Columbia, so this was quite a tall order.

Eventually the process resulted in an official registration for the Founding Assembly of 305 voting delegates: 140 from Alberta, 90 from British Columbia, 65 from Manitoba, and 10 from Saskatchewan. Once again, delegates had to pay a registration fee of two hundred dollars, in addition to travel and accommodation expenses.[1]

The Assembly agenda called for the delegates to decide on a party name, to adopt a constitution and statement of principles, to agree on an initial party policy platform, and to elect a party leader and governing council. This was a handful, particularly for a group of people who didn't

---

1. Not all of those who registered showed up, so the actual number of participating delegates was 262: 129 from Alberta, 76 from British Columbia, 51 from Manitoba, and 6 from Saskatchewan.

know each other, drawn from four different provinces and having different party backgrounds.

While the assembly was being organized, none of the traditional federal parties considered the Reform movement significant (remember, political intelligence is the ability to recognize that which is significant), so most of our organizational work and meetings were ignored rather than criticized.

On the morning of Friday, October 30, at 9:00 a.m., the Founding Assembly that was to produce the Reform Party of Canada got under way, chaired by Winnipeg businesswoman and volunteer activist Joan Tait. I talked about the need for a new federal political party, briefly summarizing the results and conclusions of the Vancouver Assembly. Then Stan Roberts moved, and Francis Winspear seconded, the formal motion to create a new federal political party. The motion was carried unanimously by a show of hands; that was what the delegates had come to Winnipeg from all across the West to do.

The first item of business was to consider suggestions for a party name. This was potentially contentious. The name raised the whole issue of whether we had come together to found a *regional party* to represent the West exclusively, or to found a *national party* with its roots in the West but possessing the potential for and intention of expanding. There had already been a considerable amount of discussion about this issue by the steering committee and among association members, so we had come to Winnipeg with a list of names for the delegates to consider. These included the following:

Acumen Party	Federal Reform Party
All Canada Party	First Canada Party
All Canadian Party	First National Party of Canada
Alliance Party	Forum Party
Canada First Party	New Reform Party
Canada Party	Next Canada Party
Canadian Confederation Party	One Canada Party
Canadian Equality Party	Progressive Confederation Party
Canadian Forum Party	Progressive Reform Party
Canadian National Reform Party	Reform Party of Canada
Canadian Progressive Party	Representative Party
Canadian Reform Party	United Party
Confederation Reform Party	United Progressive Party
Confederation Party of Canada	Western Reform Alliance
Conservative Reform Party	Western Reform Party

It is significant that of these thirty names, twenty incorporated national terminology—Canada, National, Confederation, United—whereas only two (Western Reform Party and Western Reform Alliance) included regional adjectives.

Not everyone was enthusiastic about the word "reform." Some delegates felt it had moral connotations, as in "the Reformation," which would be misunderstood. Someone else remarked that if this name was adopted, our candidate training programs would come to be known as "Reform schools." However, the idea of incorporating the word "reform" in the party name already had a considerable amount of acceptance, in that we had been referring to ourselves as the Reform Association of Canada (and using the whole maple leaf as a symbol) for more than six months.

After a lively discussion of the suggested names, delegates reduced the list to four, from which the name "Reform Party of Canada" was eventually chosen by a wide majority.

The delegates then turned their attention to a clause-by-clause review of a draft party constitution. Bob Muir and his committee had drafted the heart of the constitution and I had drafted the Preamble and the Statement of Principles, using materials I had been collecting for the past twenty years (see Appendix I).

The preamble recapped the reform tradition of Canadian politics, identifying contemporary reformers with the "reform tradition in Canadian politics whereby far-sighted and courageous men and women have sought to correct injustices and inequities and to achieve more responsible and representative government in Canada" and giving examples such as Joseph Howe in Nova Scotia, Louis Lafontaine in Lower Canada, and Robert Baldwin and Egerton Ryerson in Upper Canada; the Fathers of Confederation; western reformers, including Louis Riel and F.W.G. Haultain, and the members of the Progressive Party, the Cooperative Commonwealth Federation (CCF), and the Social Credit Movement; the leaders and supporters of the Quiet Revolution in the province of Quebec; the members of groups such as the Confederation of Regions Party, Canadians for One Canada, Western Canada Concept, the Canada West Foundation, and the Committee for a Triple-E Senate; and the members of political parties and interest groups working for the attainment of provincial status for Yukon and the Northwest Territories.

The constitution presented by Muir was that of a national political party. Recognizing that some delegates would have preferred that the party establish a regional identity before expanding into the more populous regions of Canada, a clause was included to confine party candidates to eighty-nine federal ridings north and west of the Manitoba-Ontario border. This restriction could only be removed by a two-thirds vote of the membership in a special party referendum. But the constitution made it clear that the party was a federal party, not a provincial party, and that it was a federalist party, not a separatist party. Ringing endorsements were given to the slogan that "the West wants in," not out.

The principal changes made by the delegates to Muir's draft involved strengthening the powers of the constituency associations and reducing the powers of the executive council of the party. This was very much in keeping with the populist tone of the meeting and the discussions.

This original party constitution required delegates to constituency nominating meetings to become party members at least forty-five days before the meeting, to prevent the stacking of such meetings by "instant Reformers." It laid a heavy responsibility on constituency associations to recruit and assess candidates, rather than allowing this process to be driven solely by the personal ambitions of potential candidates. It provided for internal party referendums. And it contained a unique sunset clause declaring that the party constitution would be dead in the year 2000 unless two-thirds of delegates at an assembly voted to re-enact it. This latter clause was included because so many of the delegates had belonged to political parties that had outlived their usefulness.

Presentations, panels, and workshops helped complete the draft platform of the newly formed party. Presentations were made on Senate reform and Meech Lake by Bert Brown of the Canadian Committee for a Triple-E Senate and John Lamont, past chairman of the Constitutional Law Section of the Canadian Bar Association; on parliamentary and party system reform by Jo Hillier, Jack Horner, the former Alberta MP, and Ray Speaker, Alberta MLA; on free trade by David Elton of the Canada West Foundation; on economic justice by Stephen Harper, economics lecturer at the University of Calgary; and on the CF-18 affair by Dorothy Dobbie, then president of the Winnipeg Chamber of Commerce.

If anyone in Ottawa had been paying attention, the resolutions passed concerning Meech Lake identified most of the reasons why Meech ultimately failed to get the endorsement of a majority of western Canadians, notwithstanding the support for Meech by three of the western premiers. In particular, delegates sought to make any western support of Quebec's constitutional demands conditional on federal, Ontario, and Quebec support for Senate reform.

Delegates strongly supported resolutions calling for parliamentary and democratic reforms, in particular the provision in Canadian law for referendum and recall mechanisms, and the adoption of a policy stipulating that the defeat of a government measure in the House of Commons should not automatically mean the defeat of the government.

The best speech and most influential presentation at the Founding Assembly of the Reform Party of Canada—and there were numerous strong presentations—was that given by Stephen Harper on the subject of "Achieving Economic Justice."

When the Vancouver Assembly was being organized, I had asked Dr. Bob Mansell, professor of economics at the University of Calgary, to send one of his brightest and best graduate students as an observer. Bob encouraged Stephen Harper to attend.

Stephen was raised and educated in Toronto and completed his undergraduate work at the University of Calgary. During 1985-86, he took leave from his studies to go to Ottawa as an executive assistant to Calgary West MP Jim Hawkes before beginning work on his master's degree in economics at the University of Calgary. Unlike many of the delegates to Vancouver and Winnipeg, Harper had observed the operations of the Conservative government from close up as well as from a distance; but the effect was the same—profound disillusionment.

Harper's address to the Winnipeg Assembly was more germane to western concerns and more detailed in its analysis and its policy prescriptions than any speech by any cabinet minister to a western audience since the Conservatives came to power. At the same time, Harper's delivery was eloquent and understandable to those not well versed in economics, marking him as a potential spokesman, candidate, and member of Parliament. People who have been told that the Reform Party consists of well-meaning simpletons mouthing naive solutions to complex problems should study Harper's speeches on behalf of Reform.

Harper began by introducing the topic of justice and injustice, fairness and unfairness, in the economic treatment of western Canada within confederation. He buttressed his argument that confederation has failed to provide economic and constitutional equality across the country with figures on job creation funds, Supply and Services procurement, CBC programming, civil service employment, federal government offices, federal expenditure/taxation balances and regional allocations of federal development grants, and federal government policy priorities.

He then went on to argue that applying fairness criteria to national decision-making structures and processes required such things as more effective regional representation in national institutions; regional impact assessments of major federal policy initiatives by Treasury Board; the removal of interprovincial as well as international barriers to trade; reform of the welfare state to balance taxpayers' interests with client interests and to focus social spending on those with the greatest needs, not those with the loudest voices; and an end to public subsidization of special-interest lobby groups, including political parties. He ended with a direct and stirring appeal for westerners and Reformers to become "the essential element of a new political majority that will promote fairness for all Canadians."

Harper's address shattered all the stereotypes (reactionary, backward-looking, narrow, simplistic, extreme) that are often applied to a new political party struggling for legitimacy from a western base. It combined youthful enthusiasm and idealism with wisdom, breadth of vision, and practical solutions to real problems. It was greeted with a prolonged standing ovation from all who heard it, and I knew that the party had found a potential policy chief.

Harper's speech was immediately followed by one from Dorothy Dobbie, president of the Winnipeg Chamber of Commerce. She gave a blow-by-blow account of the CF-18 affair as a practical and timely example of the unfairness to which Harper referred and the need for fundamental reform in federal government procurement processes. You can imagine the surprise of Reformers and many others in the Winnipeg business community when, less than one year later, Dobbie agreed to run for the Conservatives in Winnipeg South in the 1988 federal election and was elected by a majority of 715 votes.

Reformers maintain that such behaviour by key spokespersons for western economic interests and by the electorate confirms the view of the big federal parties that although local business, labour, and political leaders will protest discriminatory decisions for a time, they can usually be silenced or co-opted. Simply remind the businesspeople and local politicians that if they protest too much, they may lose more government business in the future. Invite them to a pleasant luncheon with the prime minister or one of those ministers with "unprecedented positions of power and influence in Ottawa," and they can easily be defanged. They will even swallow the old argument that has been used with disastrous effect in the Maritimes that "since you can't beat us, and you have no alternatives, if you know what's good for you, you'll join us and play the game by our rules." Such behaviour also reminds the governing party that electors have extremely short memories.

Dorothy Dobbie's presentation to the Founding Assembly of the Reform Party, combined with her subsequent actions, taught us a valuable lesson. It strengthened our resolve to recruit a new breed of people into public life who cannot be silenced or co-opted so easily by "the system." It underlined the need to change the party system itself so that respected regional spokespersons cannot be turned into Ottawa's representatives to the regions. And it gave us an incentive to raise sky-high the political price of regionally discriminatory decision making by the federal government.

The final task of the delegates to the Winnipeg Assembly was to elect a leader. Although I had made it known right after the Vancouver Assembly that I would be a candidate, I had not spent much time directly on a party leadership campaign. At that stage, when the Reform movement was so frail and its future so uncertain, there was virtually no chance that some high-profile political figure would seek its leadership. This meant that the leader would probably be chosen from among those who had helped bring the Reform movement to its current stage of development.

I had suggested to the assembly steering committee that we ought to put most of our energies into organizing the assembly itself and trust the judgment of the delegates when it came to the leadership question. Jo Hillier, as chairman of the steering committee, felt that a contest for the party leadership would add some excitement to the proceedings and increase media attention. The logical candidates were Stan Roberts, Ted Byfield, and myself.

Ted, however, said that he wanted to preserve his role as an editorialist and journalist, supporting the Reform movement in principle, but retaining his freedom to write on national and regional issues without being tied directly to any particular party.

Hillier repeatedly urged Stan Roberts to declare himself as a candidate if that was his intention, so that the leadership contest could be used to boost delegate interest in the assembly. Stan delayed his announcement, however, until the middle of October, and by then a good number of the delegates, especially from the prairies where I had been most active, had already decided that I was the logical choice.

An informal committee of my supporters got together to promote my candidacy. I advised this committee that I thought we should keep our campaign low-key and straightforward. Many of our delegates were refugees from the traditional federal parties and would be turned off by any campaign that emphasized image over substance or ambition over willingness and ability to serve.

In any event, when we all got to Winnipeg, I had a good network of delegates committed to my campaign and willing to put in a word on my behalf with fellow delegates. But in terms of the normal trappings of a leadership campaign we had virtually nothing, other than some buttons and a printed resume about my background. Bill Kurchak, a communications consultant from Calgary whom I had met in the course of peddling my COMMUNICATE 500 program, brought over his portable desktop publishing equipment, and produced several promotional pieces on my behalf throughout the assembly.

Stan Roberts took a more traditional approach, with posters, embossed scarves, twice-daily news releases, and a hospitality suite. This approach, as I had suspected, was not particularly well received by the delegates, who were leery of anything that reminded them of the traditional parties.

By the Friday evening, Stan sensed that his campaign was not going well, and some unpleasantness developed. He hinted in a speech at the Friday night banquet that about a hundred more of his supporters had not yet registered, whereas the steering committee was under the impression that there were fewer than two dozen official delegates left to register. This aroused the suspicion among my supporters that an effort might be made to pack the assembly prior to the leadership vote. A motion was moved on the assembly floor to cut off official registration at 9:00 a.m. on the Saturday morning, and it was carried by a large majority.

Upset by this, Stan charged that the interim executive had lost control of the assembly and threatened to withdraw. This put Jo Hillier in a very awkward position. She was a long-time friend of Stan's, but had always been cordial to me, and wanted to preserve the impartiality of the steering committee while at the same time avoiding further unpleasantness over the leadership question. She asked Stan and me to meet privately with her on Sunday morning to see if something could be worked out. The meeting was held in a basement room of the Winnipeg Convention Centre. I was accompanied by Bob Muir, and Stan was accompanied by Francis Winspear.

Jo proposed that a separate leadership assembly be held in a year's time, with Stan and me serving as co-leaders in the interim. Stan said that a year was too long, and recommended a mail-in ballot within six months to decide the leadership question. My position was simply to let the assembly itself decide the issue. Most of the delegates had come to Winnipeg expecting to choose a leader. They could postpone the leadership vote if they wanted to, but if they preferred to get on with it, they should be given that opportunity.

Shortly after our meeting, Stan asked the chairman of the Sunday morning session on "Winning the West," Ray Speaker, if he could make a special announcement. Stan then announced his withdrawal from the leadership race, alleging irregularities in the registration of delegates and the handling of funds. Then he left the assembly hall.

Ray Speaker, a veteran politician who attends more weddings, funerals, political breakfasts, lunches, dinners, meetings, and conventions in a year than most people do in a lifetime, was not particularly surprised by these strange proceedings. He simply asked me to come to the podium where, under these rather inauspicious conditions, I was acclaimed leader of the new Reform Party of Canada.

A pessimist would say it was a bad beginning; an optimist would say we had nowhere to go but up. But the delegates seemed pleased with the result. That was all that really mattered.

It would be unfair to leave this description of the selection of the first leader of the Reform Party of Canada without a note on Stan Roberts. I had known Stan for many years. When he was president of the Canada West Foundation, he had supported my development of the Deal Model of Confederation. He was an able and articulate advocate of western and national causes. After leaving the assembly, Stan had very little to do with the Reform Party. He sought the party's nomination in the federal riding of Saanich-Gulf Islands before the federal election in 1988, but was defeated by Dr. Bob Slavik. In August 1990 he was diagnosed as suffering from a brain tumour and he died very suddenly on the 30th of that month.

Those who knew Stan well, including Dr. Winspear, Jo Hillier, and me, felt that Stan's conduct at the Reform Party assembly was out of character. Perhaps the medical condition that ultimately ended his life was already having some effect on him. Those who knew Stan as a strong advocate of measures to strengthen the West as an equal partner in confederation, and thereby to strengthen and preserve confederation itself, will remember him for his long record of public service to both the West and Canada.

The Founding Assembly of the Reform Party of Canada ended on an upbeat note with the election of its first executive council. These were the unsung heroes of our original organizational development, whom the founding members and delegates were prepared to entrust with the daunting task of working with me to build a national federal political party.

The people elected to that first council included: Diane Ablonczy, a former teacher and practising lawyer from Calgary; Alan Beachell, a

Manitoba farmer and municipal politician; Henry Carroll, a Brandon lawyer; Ron Gamble, a Vancouver businessman; Ian McClelland, an Edmonton businessman; Valerie Meredith, a real estate agent from White Rock; Bob Muir; Werner Schmidt; Gordon Shaw, a retired oil company executive; Joan Tait; and Short Tompkins, a retired contractor from northern British Columbia.

While some misinformed commentators on the genesis of the Reform movement immediately asserted that the party council was dominated by people with a political and religious heritage similar to my own, only two (Meredith and Schmidt) had had any connection with Alberta Social Credit, and only two (Ablonczy and Meredith) held religious convictions similar to my own.

Immediately after the Founding Assembly, a short meeting of the new council was held in my hotel room. We were all exhausted and did not know each other well. We did little business, other than to select Diane Ablonczy as our chairman and Gordon Shaw as our vice-chairman, and to appoint some committee chairmen. There was nevertheless a sense that the Reform Party of Canada, no matter how humble its beginnings, was an expression of something much larger than ourselves. The rivulets of Reform had become a stream, and the potential existed for that stream to become a river. We were on our way.

CHAPTER NINE

The 1988 Federal Election

My principal task, and that of the newly elected executive council, was to get the Reform Party into a position to make a credible showing in the next federal general election, which was about one year away. I discontinued my personal consulting work, mothballed Manning Consultants Limited, and on January 1, 1988, began working full time for the party.

The Edmonton offices of my consulting firm were converted into the head office of the party. Jeanie Clemenger, my secretary and researcher, who was as familiar with the background of the Reform movement as I was, agreed to continue to work with me. My consulting associate, David Berger, continued to carry out some of his consulting projects, but found himself spending as much time on Reform Party work. Stephen Harper, who was pursuing his studies at the University of Calgary, agreed to serve on a volunteer basis as our first policy chief.

Immediately after the Founding Assembly, the Reform Association of Canada turned over its assets to the Reform Party of Canada. These included all the research, organizational, and policy files associated with the Vancouver and Winnipeg assemblies, the legal work related to developing the party constitution and registering a new federal party, and a mailing list of five thousand names.

By January 1988, Bob Muir and Murray Smith, a Calgary lawyer and former PC member of Parliament, secured the preliminary registration of the Reform Party of Canada with Elections Canada. Full registration, enabling the party to offer tax-deductible receipts for contributions, could not be achieved until the party had officially nominated candidates in fifty electoral districts at the next federal election.

A not-for-profit company called Reform Fund Canada was incorporated under the Canada Corporations Act to serve as the official agent of the party and to be responsible for the collection and disbursement of funds.

Because the initial staff of the party was so small, and primarily concerned with administrative work (handling memberships and donations), it was the volunteer members of the executive council who not only planned the organizational development of the party, but also were actively engaged in implementing those plans.

Ron Gamble ran a small Vancouver office, and he and Gordon Shaw took on the preliminary organization of most of British Columbia's thirty-two federal ridings. Short Tompkins of Fort St. John began organizing what we referred to as the "Big Eight" ridings. These were the huge northern ridings that required special attention and an airplane to service. In Manitoba, Alan Beachell, Henry Carroll, and Joan Tait assumed responsibility for constituency organization, with Joan, a former president of the provincial Progressive Conservative women's organization in Manitoba, supervising a small office in Winnipeg. In Saskatchewan we were still very weak in terms of membership, and constituency development was deferred until this could be remedied. In Alberta, we had a strong organizational group in Calgary where chairman Diane Ablonczy, Bob Muir, and Stephen Harper lived. Edmonton was in good shape because the head office was located there, and Werner Schmidt and I lived there. We also had access to the services of people like Howard Thompson in central Alberta, and Neil Weir, who had experience in organizing constituencies for other parties.

To help recruit members and develop constituency associations, we designed a small promotional brochure and a seven-point constituency development package to distribute to party members. In April 1988 we started up a party news tabloid called *The Reformer.* The first editor of *The Reformer* was a nineteen-year-old University of Alberta student with an interest in journalism, movies, and theatre, named Jaie Laplante. He not only edited *The Reformer* but also promoted it vigorously with our constituency people, so that it shortly became our most effective communications tool.

Neil Weir, who had a background with the Navy and in small business, became head office administrator and our federal election coordinator. Neil had an approach to personnel recruitment and management that was quite different from mine. His philosophy was that if there was a job to be done, you grabbed the first warm body you could find, and shoved that person into the slot. If things didn't work out, you shuffled the first body somewhere else (you could not and should not "fire" volunteers) and found another one to fill the original slot. You kept doing this until you finally had a complement of competent people capable of working together. By this process we gradually built up an organization composed largely of volunteers, many with very little past political experience, with which to do battle with the traditional federal parties in the 1988 federal election.

From January 1988 to October 1 when the election was called, I focused on three main tasks, leaving most of the constituency development work to council members, the fund raising to Reform Fund Canada, and the administrative work to head office staff. My first task was to explain what the Reform Party was all about to as many western Canadians as possible. This was done mainly through speaking engagements and media interviews. The second was to flesh out our policy platform and to rebut the charge that we were offering simplistic solutions to complex problems. The third was to develop our strategy for the 1988 federal election and to start putting it into practice.

My speaking engagements, and those of other Reform Party spokespersons, took us all over the West. In many communities it would take us three meetings before we could get an audience of more than one hundred people. Often the first meeting would be held in a restaurant or in someone's home. We would explain to half a dozen people what we were trying to do and ask for their help. The next meeting would be a public one, often with thirty or forty people in a hall much too large for that number. Finally, by the third meeting, the numbers would be more respectable, there would be some media coverage, and our local organizers would be gaining more confidence in their ability to organize public political gatherings.

The themes of my public addresses during the first part of 1988 were the core of the Reform platform: the need for more effective regional representation in national decision making through Senate reform; the need for greater fairness toward the resource-producing regions through the performance of regional fairness tests on major federal policies; and the need for parliamentary reform to make MPs more accountable to the people who elected them.

These themes were often adapted to the special interests of different audiences. For example, in Manitoba the need for more effective regional representation and greater regional fairness was illustrated in terms of the CF-18 decision. Our Manitoba Reformers distributed a pamphlet at the Bristol Aerospace plant in Winnipeg entitled, "Don't Get Mad, Get Even." Senate reform was presented, not as an academic subject of interest only to constitutional lawyers, but as a practical measure leading to more jobs, better incomes, and economic diversification.

In Alberta, Reformers were already well into the free trade debate, arguing that "free and fair trade, east-west as well as north-south," together with genuine Senate reform, were necessary to safeguard against the imposition of another National Energy Program as soon as petroleum prices began to recover.

In British Columbia we tackled the problem of illegal immigration and the insensitivity of federal immigration policy to public opinion and the overheated state of the lower mainland economy. Such issues, on which western MPs from all parties had failed (with a few notable exceptions) to represent the views of constituents faithfully when these differed from the party line, were effectively used by Reformers to illustrate the need for parliamentary and political reform.

In the past, when the West produced new political movements, they were invariably labelled extreme, eccentric, and potentially separatist by editorialists and political critics. Riel and the Métis were said to be both fanatical and traitorous. Haultain and the Autonomy Movement were accused of frustrating the grand design of the Fathers of Confederation. The Progressives were labelled as dangerous radicals bent on destroying the established order of society. The founders of the CCF were called communists. And Social Credit was frequently portrayed as a dangerous mixture of monetary unorthodoxy, religious fundamentalism, and grassroots fascism. It therefore came as no surprise that the Reform Party was labelled, particularly in the early stages, as "fringe," "extremely right wing," potentially racist, and separatist.

Rather than simply denying that we were separatists, we continued to express our federalist positions strongly. Our official position was that the West wanted into Confederation as an equal partner, and that the West would support a strong federal government *if that government could be made regionally sensitive and accountable* through Senate reform and other measures. As we learned to communicate this federalist position more widely and effectively, our critics were simply unable to make the spurious separatist label stick.

In spring 1988, we launched a major constitutional initiative that gave us ample opportunity to stress our federalist position, to get a good reading on public opposition to the Meech Lake Accord across the West, and to establish ourselves as the leading political advocates of Senate reform in the federal arena.

For almost ten years, western think-tanks, interest groups, provincial governments, some western Conservatives, and some western Liberals had been talking about the merits of a Triple-E Senate or variations thereof—reforming the upper chamber of the Canadian parliament to make it *E*lected, with powers to make it *E*ffective in safeguarding regional interests, and with *E*qual representation from each province. Yet no one, least of all the western Conservative ministers and MPs "occupying unprecedented positions of power and influence in Ottawa" had translated this desire for Senate reform into a draft constitutional amendment.

Westerners had begun to ask at public meetings: "How come it took the Mulroney government less than six months to translate Robert Bourassa's five constitutional demands into a draft constitutional amendment, while it has done absolutely nothing to respond to our demands for a Senate reform amendment, demands which the Conservatives have known about for almost ten years?"

In response to these concerns, the Reform Party's constitutional committee, under the chairmanship of Calgary lawyer Vic Burstall, undertook to draft a full-blown Senate reform amendment embodying the Triple-E Senate concept. The committee also planned to submit this amendment to a series of public workshops across the West, and to the Western Premiers' Conference in Parksville, British Columbia, on May 18-21, 1988.

I was on Burstall's committee, along with Bert Brown, chairman of the Canadian Committee for a Triple-E Senate and a prominent Conservative; Dr. Peter McCormick of the political science department at the University of Lethbridge and co-author of a Canada West Foundation study on regional representation; John Lamont, a Winnipeg lawyer with strong Liberal connections and former chairman of the Constitutional Law Section of the Canadian Bar Association; Stephen Harper, our policy chief; and Sian Stephenson, another Calgary lawyer who was doing an increasing amount of legal work for the party. The actual drafting of the amendment was done by Mel Smith, former deputy minister of constitutional affairs for the government of British Columbia.

Once the committee finished its draft, the document was submitted to a series of advertised public workshops in Winnipeg, Saskatoon, Edmonton, Calgary, Vancouver, and Victoria, which generated some useful suggestions. I was particularly impressed by the call for "downsizing" all federal institutions, and the strong desire on the prairies for ensuring that the territories be given a fair shake in any future constitutional development.

Our draft amendment provided for equal representation of each province by ten elected senators, as well as four each for Yukon and the

Northwest Territories. The accompanying notes acknowledged that many people at the workshops preferred a smaller Senate of six to eight senators per province and two per territory. Procedures for Senate elections would be established by provincial law and senators would be elected for a six-year term. Senate elections would be held throughout Canada on a fixed date every three years, with half the senators being elected each time, using a single transferable ballot. To ensure its independence from the House of Commons and the office of the prime minister, members of the reformed Senate would be barred from accepting appointments to the cabinet.

The powers of the reformed Senate would safeguard and enhance provincial and regional interests, but the reformed Senate would not have the power to defeat the government. It would ratify treaties, appointments to the Supreme Court of Canada, and appointments to major federal boards and commissions. It would retain its existing fiscal powers, including the right to veto the budget or budgetary items, but it would not have the right to veto bills providing for the ordinary annual essential services of the government. (In other words, the reformed Senate could not bring down the government by withholding supply, as was done by the Australian Senate in 1975.)

Our meetings on Senate reform also gave us a chance to address the question, "Why not abolish the Senate altogether?" Abolition rather than reform has been the official position of the NDP. We pointed out that if the Senate were abolished, the Canadian Parliament would consist of a single house, in which southern Quebec and southern Ontario, by virtue of their populations, would have an absolute majority of seats. Without a Senate, it would be impossible to safeguard the interests of the thinly populated areas of the rest of the country.

At the conclusion of several of our Triple-E workshop sessions, I asked what should be done with the current senators once the Senate had been reformed. The kindest suggestion was: "Grant them immunity from future prosecution, if they go peacefully."

Before our Triple-E workshop tour I had had a leather briefcase emblazoned with the words "Western Constitutional Amendment." At each workshop, we circulated a petition calling for Parliament and the legislatures to formally begin passage of the Triple-E Senate amendment. As we moved across the West, my briefcase slowly filled with signed petition sheets. In Victoria, late on the night of May 17, after the last workshop, we put the finishing touches on the draft amendment in Richie Martin's law office. Our British Columbia Reformers chartered a train, calling it the Constitutional Express, to take a crowd of Reformers, together with our committee, up-Island to Parksville to present our amendment and petitions to the Western Premiers' Conference. In Parksville, we had a short rally and lunch attended by several hundred enthusiastic Reformers. (Half the Reform Party's British Columbia membership at that time was on Vancouver Island. I suppose that the farther away from Ottawa you lived, the more likely you were to be alienated— and Vancouver Island was about as far away as you could get.)

The premiers—Bill Vander Zalm of British Columbia, Don Getty of Alberta, Grant Devine of Saskatchewan, and Gary Filmon of Manitoba— were still extremely dubious about the Reformers (we had yet to register in the public opinion polls), but an official at the Premiers' Conference agreed to accept my briefcase, which contained a memo to each of the premiers, the draft Triple-E amendment, and the petitions. He assured us that the briefcase and its contents would reach the premiers. (I also told him that the Reform Party had to watch its nickels and dimes and that we would like the briefcase back. A few days later, the briefcase was returned to me, empty.)

Only Vander Zalm acknowledged receiving its contents. No provincial minister or MLA or federal MP to whom copies of this draft amendment were distributed took any action whatsoever to advance it in caucus or in a provincial legislature. The Reform Party, however, gained considerably from the exercise. If we could develop positions on other major issues with the same level of expertise, openness, and thoroughness, we could give a good account of ourselves in an election.

Our strategy for the 1988 federal election was based on a realistic assessment of our limitations as well as our potential. By the summer of 1988, our membership was up to about twelve thousand, with some thirty constituency associations ready to participate in an election campaign. Although some of our people had been involved in elections with other parties, many had not and were learning on the job. I had once read in an old military manual something to the effect of "Never attempt to execute complex strategies with raw troops." Our basic strategy therefore had to be simple.

We anticipated fielding from sixty to seventy-five candidates. Each one would run a "guerilla" campaign under the control of a local constituency association and campaign team. These campaigns would be linked together by some common literature and advertising, a common platform, access to the services of our head office in Edmonton, and public appearances by myself as leader. Otherwise, every constituency was virtually on its own.

But we needed something to draw national media attention to our existence and our efforts, and it was the electors of the federal riding of Yellowhead who gave us that opportunity. Stretching from just west of Edmonton to the British Columbia border, Yellowhead was a big hinterland riding, in which the Reform emphasis on more fairness for the resource-producing regions found a receptive audience. Yellowhead was also a riding, in which the voting record of the sitting member, External Affairs Minister Joe Clark, was at considerable variance with the views of his constituents. Early in the year, five of Clark's constituency executives had resigned and joined the Reform Party. They told the local media that Clark had lost touch with the riding and was better suited to represent central Canadian bureaucrats in Ottawa than he was to represent the farmers, oil patch people, forestry workers, miners, and small business-people of Yellowhead.

On March 26, a Reform Party constituency association was formed in Yellowhead, and the new executive asked me to be their candidate. The executive included Marg Johnson, an Edson businesswoman, as president; Cliff Breitkreuz, the farmer and municipal councillor from Onoway who had urged me to "do something" in 1986; and Duane Aide, an Edson accountant. On May 27, after meeting with the executive in Edson, I announced that I would seek the Reform nomination in Yellowhead. In a short speech to local Reformers I suggested that the principal issue in a contest between Clark and me would be whether western Canadians would be better served in the next parliament by politicians representing traditional political parties, or by western Reformers dedicated to changing the system.

The executive had scheduled nominating meetings for June 21 and 22 at five different communities throughout the riding. Nominations closed on June 15 and, there being no nominations besides my own, I was declared to be the Reform Party's candidate by acclamation. On June 21 and 22 I toured the riding, giving short speeches in Drayton Valley, Whitecourt, Barrhead, Jasper, and Edson. What the media were to call the Battle of Yellowhead had begun.

We didn't worry about the prospect of ultimately losing the Battle of Yellowhead. We were underdogs anyway, and the likelihood of Reformers winning seats the first time out was low. Better to lose to a high-profile candidate like Clark whom no one expected us to beat, than to a lesser light like Walter Van De Walle in St. Albert (where I had also been invited to run). In any case, if I could not go to Ottawa with a fairly strong contingent of members, I'd be better off to stay out of the House and give my full attention to building and promoting the party in the field.

I should make clear that, having known him since university days, I had no personal animosity toward Joe Clark, nor do I today. Joe is an able and intelligent individual who has made significant contributions to Canada, and who has persevered politically with dignity in the face of great obstacles. My main quarrel with Joe would be that he did not faithfully and vigorously represent the views of his constituents or the West, particularly when those views conflicted with the conventional wisdom embraced by the traditional parties on issues like the constitution and how to relate to Quebec.

When Joe was active in university and provincial politics in the 1960s, he developed a reputation for being interested and able when it came to political organization and tactics, but not very strong when it came to ideology or policy. In fact, it was said, unkindly, that "Joe's strongest conviction is that a politician should not have strong convictions." I believe, however, that there is another reason for Joe's failure to represent the interests of the people of his home region and bringing a western perspective to bear on national issues.

When Joe finally broke into federal politics in the early 1970s, western Conservatives were in disfavour within the federal Conservative party. The western PCs had dominated the party during the Diefenbaker era, and they were held partially responsible for the party's fall from power. The new hierarchy, those close to Robert Stanfield and Dalton Camp, did not want to hear anything more about western alienation or western perspectives. Young and ambitious MPs from the West were told, directly and indirectly, to "scrape the manure off their boots" if they expected to get anywhere in national politics.

Of course, the wheel of federal politics has come full circle, and today it is possible to function successfully in federal politics without shedding one's regional identity. But it is extremely difficult for politicians like Clark, having severed their regional roots, to reestablish them again with any credibility.

Some will argue that a federal politician without deep commitments to ideology, policy, or region is the ideal person to broker a new constitutional arrangement for Canada. I do not share that view. A politician whose vision of Canada is one that attempts to accommodate everyone may in the end fail to accommodate anyone.

There is a reason why Joe Clark was unable to get an energy agreement with Alberta, whereas Pierre Trudeau succeeded. It is the same reason why Lester Pearson was unable to get agreement on a constitutional amending formula, whereas Pierre Trudeau succeeded there, too.

Pearson was seen by officials of my father's government (and if by them, then also by officials and politicians of other governments) as essentially a "diplomat." And in their view the essence of diplomacy was a willingness to accommodate. Thus they never took any position articulated by Pearson as "the last word" or "the bottom line." There was always the feeling that if you held out long enough, or hit him hard enough, he could be moved off his original position ten or fifteen degrees. Thus his very willingness to accommodate became an obstacle to closing a constitutional deal.

This is also why Clark failed in 1979 when he attempted to negotiate an energy agreement with the government of Peter Lougheed. To Lougheed, Joe Clark was the young fellow who organized his meetings for him at the University of Alberta in the late 1960s and ran errands for him as an executive assistant. Everyone in Lougheed's Alberta delegation who knew anything about Joe knew that he had never "gone to the wall" on anything, let alone on a matter of policy. There was an unspoken assumption that no offer he made was really a final offer, and in the final analysis this made agreement more difficult rather than easier to reach.

With someone like Trudeau, on the other hand, whether you agreed with him or not (and I disagreed with his government's positions on both the constitution and energy), you sensed that there was a point beyond which he could not be pushed, particularly if you were trying to modify his constitutional vision. In the end, Trudeau's apparent intransigence proved more conducive to securing agreement on fundamental constitutional and economic issues than did the pliability of Pearson or Clark.

In fall 1988, Reformers in federal ridings all over the West were preparing for the election. Meetings to gather members, establish constituency associations, raise funds, or recruit candidates were held with the knowledge that we had no time to lose.

Our vice-chairman, Gordon Shaw, had vowed that British Columbia, with its thirty-two federal ridings, would nominate more candidates than Alberta, with its twenty-six. Shaw, with his friendly and enthusiastic manner, assisted by his equally talented wife Mary-Jane, had rapidly become one of our most effective organizers and was in increasing demand as a speaker at organizational and public meetings. The first official Reform Party nomination meeting in the West was held not in Alberta, but in the federal riding of Saanich-Gulf Islands in British Columbia on June 19, 1988.

Dr. Bob Slavik, a fifty-three-year-old retired military doctor with a good sense of humour and a deep commitment to grassroots political organization, became the first officially nominated Reform candidate for the 1988 federal election. Bob had lived in all ten provinces of Canada and both territories, as well as in Europe and Egypt, before retiring to Vancouver Island. His broad perspective on Canada served him well as a candidate, as a member of the party's executive council after the election, and as organizer of the first Reform meetings in Atlantic Canada.

Elsewhere in British Columbia, a number of ridings came up with strong candidates who had credible campaigning capabilities. These included Surrey-White Rock, where Val Meredith was the candidate; Okanagan Centre, where Werner Schmidt (who had moved to British Columbia) was nominated; and Prince George-Peace River, where Short Tompkins had recruited a young farmer named Jay Hill to carry the Reform banner.

Strong candidates and campaign organizations also emerged in central Alberta and the Calgary area. In Wetaskiwin we were represented by Jim Henderson, a former provincial minister of health; in Wild Rose by Dal Brown; in Crowfoot by Jack Ramsay, the former WCC leader-turned-Reformer; in Calgary West by Stephen Harper; in Calgary North by Murray Smith, a former Progressive Conservative MP; and in MacLeod by Ken Copithorne of the Copithorne ranching family.

In Edmonton-Strathcona our profile was raised considerably when Doug Main, a well-known TV anchor man for ITV, was nominated. In the huge Athabasca riding, Betty Lebsack, whom I knew as the wife of the manager of Slave Lake Developments (my old consulting client), carried our banner. In Beaver River, a schoolteacher named Deborah Grey agreed to represent Reform, even though our membership in that constituency was less than two hundred.

In Manitoba, our strongest association was in the Portage-Interlake riding, where Alan Beachell was nominated. In Saskatchewan, our best prospect for progress was in Kindersley-Lloydminster, where our candidate was a young farmer from Beechy (near Lake Diefenbaker) named Elwin Hermanson. He was later to be of enormous help in organizing for Reform throughout Saskatchewan.

Behind each individual who represented the Reform Party in the 1988 federal election (see Appendix II) there is a personal story, a constituency organizational story, and a campaign story to which I cannot do justice here. Suffice it to say that, although the Reform Party will have more and larger candidate slates in the future, there will be only one slate of "first candidates to run under the Reform banner," and these individuals deserve special recognition.

When the 1988 federal general election was announced on October 1, the Reform Party of Canada had twenty-eight candidates officially nominated, and on October 24, when nominations closed, the number had increased to seventy-two. Because we had nominated more than fifty candidates, contributors to Reform Fund Canada became eligible for the federal income tax credit for political contributions. And, yes, in the end, British Columbia nominated thirty candidates to Alberta's twenty-six.

There were only three ridings in which we had serious problems with nominations, and these had to do with the predictable issues of expediency and extremism—two issues that often bedevil a new party.

The executive council was initially concerned that traditional party people (particularly Conservatives in Alberta) who lost their own party's nomination might seek Reform nominations, making us look like a refuge for other parties' rejects. In the federal constituency of Red Deer, Dan Lawrence, who had finished second to Doug Fee for the Conservative nomination, had a large organization ready to back his bid for the Reform nomination. When I expressed my concern about how this might appear, he graciously withdrew. The Reform Party nominating meeting, however, selected as their candidate Michael Roth, the man who had finished fourth in the Conservative nomination race.

Some members wanted the executive council of the party to intervene and set the nomination aside. In the end, since there were no irregularities in the nominating meeting itself, we decided not to interfere, nevertheless recognizing that Lawrence had been unfairly treated. Roth ran a respectable campaign, finishing second to Doug Fee.

In the Alberta riding of Crowfoot we had a different problem. There, one of the leading contenders for our nomination was Jack Ramsay, the former leader of the separatist Western Canada Concept party in Alberta. Some people felt that Jack was too much of an extremist and that I should not sign his nomination papers even if he was successful at the nominating meeting. Others, including some of the local media, asked how we could distance ourselves from separatism if we nominated a former separatist as our candidate.

Fortunately, in Crowfoot we had a broadly based constituency association with a lot of political experience and common sense. Many of them had known Ramsay for some time. They felt he was a man who held his convictions very strongly and only changed them with great reluctance. But if he did change them, and openly acknowledged that he had, then he could be trusted. They were convinced that Ramsay's public declarations favouring reform of the federal system rather than separation from it were genuine.

Ramsay was nominated, and since then he has become one of the hardest workers for Reform in central Alberta. Since one of my initial motivations for promoting the Reform Party was to provide an effective and constructive alternative for westerners who were leaning toward the separatist option out of frustration, I was pleased with the way the Crowfoot situation worked out. At the same time, I was saddened that we lost the support of some good people and strong federalists over this incident.

The most serious problem we faced over nominations was in the Capilano-Howe Sound riding in West Vancouver. In that constituency, a number of our members and the executive had been initially enthusiastic about the prospective candidacy of Doug Collins, a well-known author and columnist with the *North Shore News*. Collins was a colourful personality, with strong views on everything, including official language policy and immigration. When the news got out that he would probably seek our nomination, we began to get calls from some Reformers expressing alarm that some of Collins's statements might be viewed as racist and that they would leave the party if he became one of its spokespersons.

Gordon Shaw, our vice-chairman, arranged for me to meet Collins before the Capilano-Howe Sound nominating meeting. I told Collins frankly about my concern. Without passing judgment on his statements and positions, with which I was not familiar, I told him that I would ask the constituency association to pass a resolution that neither they nor their candidate supported any public policy that discriminated against people on the basis of race. If Collins was prepared to sign such a resolution, I would not oppose his pursuit of our nomination and we would use the resolution to try to combat unfair charges against him and us. On the other hand, if the constituency association or he were not prepared to distance themselves publicly from the racist accusations in this way, then I would not sign his nomination papers.

Collins did not take this well. He said the issue was not racism, but his own integrity. He was not going to be singled out for special treatment and embarrassed by this type of demand and he refused to support such a resolution. I replied that I could not then sign his nomination papers.

When the Capilano-Howe Sound nomination meeting was held on October 18, 1988, there was a large crowd in attendance. According to the constituency executive, there were 178 members of the Capilano-Howe Sound constituency registered to vote out of a total membership of approximately 500, and of the others present, more than 600 were simply Doug Collins supporters. When the constituency executive attempted to read out my letter requesting the resolution on racism and Collins' assent to it, they were hooted and voted down by these non-members. Collins made a speech that was wildly applauded by his supporters, who proceeded to "nominate" him anyway. The whole meeting got out of hand. Five days later, at another nominating meeting attended only by Reform Party members, Neil Thompson, a West Vancouver businessman, was unanimously nominated to carry the Reform banner in Capilano-Howe Sound.

The Reform Party of Canada was then and is today prepared to go to extraordinary lengths to distance itself from people whose involvement lays us open to the charge that we tolerate policies that discriminate against people on the basis of race. We oppose the traditional parties' model of confederation (the definition of Canada as a partnership of two founding races, languages, and cultures) because it uses race to define the relationship between the citizen and the state. We oppose any use of immigration policy, no matter how well intended, to preserve a French-English balance—or any other ethnic balance—on the same grounds. We oppose any approach to multiculturalism that directs federal government support to particular groups on the basis of race or ethnicity.

The Collins affair generated a great deal of publicity for us on the west coast, some bad and some good. I am convinced that the long-term result was positive. By clearly taking steps, no matter how crude, to distance ourselves from racism—real or alleged—we lost the support of some who thought the rights of the "grassroots" to nominate whomever they pleased, Reformer or not, were violated. But we gained the support of many others who had been wondering whether Reformers could distinguish between the grassroots and the weeds. We also gained ground with thoughtful people who noticed the double standard that some of our critics use when it comes to extremism and racism. If Collins had become our candidate, we would have been severely criticized by at least half the commentators and special interest groups on the lower mainland for tolerating a spokesperson whom they regarded (rightly or wrongly) as racist. But when we did take decisive action, we got no support from those who are so keen at detecting prejudices in others.

The Reform Party's election campaign began with the adoption of an official party platform at a special policy assembly held in Calgary on August 12-14. The draft platform, drawn up for the most part by Stephen Harper, was discussed, modified, and approved by some 250 delegates from across the West. The completed thirty-six-page election platform of the Reform Party of Canada, entitled "The West Wants In," was divided into four sections.

The constitutional section included establishment of a Triple-E Senate, rejection of the Meech Lake Accord, entrenchment of property rights, public referendums on constitutional change, and the right of the territories to provincial status. The economic section included market-driven economic policies, regional fairness tests on all federal economic decisions, free trade within Canada as well as without, privatization of Petro-Canada and reforms to the postal service, more competitive and regionalized banking, reforms to federal spending and MPs' pensions, cooperative labour-management relations, and a balanced budget. The social section included free and recorded votes in the House of Commons and in a Reform Party caucus, plebiscites on moral and social issues, lessening of party discipline and pressure-group power, targeting of critical social spending to those who need the help, mobilization of private sources of social responsibility, a strong system of criminal justice, and new approaches to official languages and immigration. The environment section included commitment to sustainable economic development, and opposition to economic development undertaken without regard to long-term environmental costs and implications and to environmental regulations made without regard to economic costs and social implications.

A highlight of the Calgary policy assembly was a report from Short Tompkins, our executive council member from Fort St. John, and Bob Van Wegen, a Calgary university student, on their twenty-six-day journey in Short's Cessna 185 to spread the Reform message through the "Big Eight" northern ridings. Their trip had covered more than six thousand miles and more than thirty stops, from the Peace River country of British Columbia and Alberta, to Prince Rupert on the west coast, to Whitehorse in the Yukon, Inuvik on the Mackenzie Delta, to Yellowknife, then through Uranium City in northern Saskatchewan over to Churchill, Manitoba, and back to Calgary.

The plane was initially loaded down with ninety thousand copies of a special northern edition of *The Reformer* news tabloid. When Short and Bob landed in Mackenzie, they blew their tail wheel tire and had to call a local Reform contact, whom they had never met, for help. Syd Johnston, the proprietor of the local hotel, came to the airport, picked them up, bought them lunch, introduced them to the local newspaper editor, arranged for the distribution of *The Reformer* in Mackenzie, and gave them a donation that kept them in aviation fuel for some time. They reported many similar instances of help and support from northern communities, completing their Big Eight report with the message that "the North wants in."

I, too, did a lot of travelling that fall, thanks to the services of the "Reform Air Force"—an assortment of small planes, from crop sprayers to two-engine executive aircraft, piloted by businesspeople, lawyers, and flying farmers sympathetic to the cause. Apart from these forays to rally the troops and raise our profile, most of my time was spent on the Battle of Yellowhead. It was there that I worked out answers to questions and responses to issues in greater detail, for distribution by memo and fax to other ridings where similar questions and issues were being encountered.

The two main pillars of our campaign were to be personal contacts with as many constituents as possible through door-knocking and meetings, and the media attention to be gained through six all-candidate forums, at which we would contrast the Reform approach to key issues with that of Joe Clark and the Conservatives.

In July I had contacted Ginny and Dale Assmus in Edson to see if Ginny would be my campaign manager. Dale is an accountant and Ginny is a homemaker and businesswoman. They had had previous political experience in provincial election campaigns and with Joe Clark's organization in Yellowhead. No one in Yellowhead worked harder or longer on my behalf over the next four months than Ginny and Dale.

I was also assisted by a corps of dedicated volunteers—people whose interest, advice, and friendship made the whole campaign worthwhile, regardless of the outcome. All of them deserve to be acknowledged, but to avoid a long list of names, I can mention only a few.

In Edson, where our main campaign office was located, Randy and Donna Murray made their motorhome available for our constituency tours, and knocked on as many doors as I did. Randy had been a druggist in Edson for many years, was outspoken in his opinions, and worked very hard. He and Donna were one of the first couples in Edson to express a serious interest in Reform.

Ray Gideon, also in Edson, was in charge of signs, and was our most prolific membership salesman. Ray had been in the contracting business for thirty years, and still retained a trap-line territory along the Athabasca River that has been in the family since 1921. He knew the woods and the back roads of Yellowhead like the back of his hand, and was as close to the grassroots in the west and north end of that riding as anyone could possibly be.

Ray was blunt and would no doubt be labelled a redneck by those who enjoy attaching labels to others. He was a vociferous critic of Joe Clark and most politicians, although years ago, if Joe had ever asked him, he probably would have agreed to show Joe a side of Yellowhead that simply cannot be seen from podiums or through the reports of executive assistants in three-piece suits. Ray probably hired and worked with more Métis and Indian people than any businessperson I know, and it was largely due to his efforts that the Reform Party did so well in the predominantly Métis community of Marlborough.

Another character who enlivened our Edson operations was Slim Martin. Slim was over seventy and used to be a rodeo rider and clown, as well as the town constable in Barrhead and Edson. He earned the respect of the people of those communities by tempering toughness and fairness with a good sense of humour. Like Ray Gideon, Slim was blunt and outspoken, a fountain of knowledge concerning the people and the politics of the West, and a great repository of plain common sense.

People from other constituencies also came to help. Virgil Anderson set aside his Calgary law practice for three months, rented a basement suite in Edson, and worked night and day along with his wife Lea on my behalf. Ken and Margaret Suitor, from Edmonton, who owned and operated a hotel at Fort Assiniboine in Yellowhead, assisted us there, and Ken also volunteered to run as a "spear carrier" candidate for the Reform Party in the huge northern-Saskatchewan riding of Prince Albert-Churchill River, where he also had business and personal contacts. And Keith Cummings, a Calgary communications consultant, came on staff for the campaign period to help us with our media relations, advertising, and tour coordination.

I encouraged our Reform candidates to keep what I called "The Diary of a Door-knocker"—a record of the interesting experiences that invariably occur when one goes door to door during an election campaign. I often used extracts from such diaries to entertain crowds at public meetings.

On one of our first calls early in the campaign, Randy Murray and I knocked on a door and introduced ourselves to the lady who opened it. Before we could say anything more, she asked, "What is your position on the ozone layer?" As I contemplated a scientifically correct answer, Randy declared, "We're in favour of it, at least the western portion." We probably lost our first vote then and there.

On another occasion, Randy was heading for the next house while I finished my conversation with the occupant of the last one. In the yard of the next house, however, was an extremely large lady, heavily tattooed, trimming a tree with a chainsaw. Randy ambled by, took a hard look, turned, and walked back towards me. As we met, he whispered, "Compared to some of the slogans tattooed on that lady, 'The West Wants In' looks pretty tame."

In Edson one morning we started up the walkway to a house when someone yelled out, "If it's religion or politics, I don't want it." To which Randy replied, "Actually, we're from Lotto Canada, but if you don't want to be disturbed, we'll leave."

Trailer courts, of which there are many in resource service towns, presented quite a challenge to our door-knocking efforts. There seemed to be about as many dogs as people, and given my love of dogs, I often got sidetracked. I had to be reminded that since the federal government had not yet extended the franchise to canines, perhaps we had better focus more on the voters and less on the dogs.

Later in the campaign we heard a tale of perhaps the most confused voter in Yellowhead. Two stories carried by the Edmonton media had apparently caught this man's attention. One dealt with the possible northward movement of killer bees from Brazil, the other with the possible movement of PCB-contaminated oil from Quebec to Alberta for incineration at the Swan Hills waste-disposal facility. Somehow he had got the two mixed up, and when a Reformer knocked on his door, the first thing he wanted to know was, "Why are the PCs bringing in all these bees? And from Quebec yet?"

My most traumatic door-knocking experience occurred in the town of Swan Hills. It was getting late, the sky was threatening rain, and we were tired. As I leaped up the porch steps to greet a man at his door, his puppy ran across the step, and I stepped on its paw. The poor thing started to howl. The owner, glowering at me, swept up the dog and disappeared into the house, to be replaced after a few seconds by his bewildered wife. Here is the great test of a political door-knocker. What do you say in such a situation, in a town where dogs are more highly valued than politicians? Of course, there is only one thing you can say: "Good evening, my name is Joe Clark and I'm running for Parliament."

The real benefit of door-knocking, however, is not the entertainment value, but exposure to the real questions and concerns of real people, not on the politicians' terms and turf, but on theirs. We had questions on everything from abortion to Meech Lake, from language policy to free trade. Underlying many of these questions, however, partly because our own inquiries encouraged it, was the representation issue: "What difference does it make what we think or who we vote for? Politicians just go ahead and do what they want to do anyway."

At the outset of the campaign I had challenged Joe to a one-on-one debate on the question, "Who is best able to represent the real interests of this constituency and the West in the next Parliament?" Several media outlets, including *Alberta Report,* had expressed interest in sponsoring and promoting such a debate, but Joe was not enthusiastic about the proposal. His people favoured the all-candidate forum approach, and in due course these were arranged in Whitecourt, Hinton, Drayton Valley, Barrhead, Edson, and Jasper.

There were seven candidates running in Yellowhead: Joe Clark for the Progressive Conservatives; myself for the Reform Party; John Higgerty, a Crown prosecutor from Hinton, for the Liberals; Muriel Stanley-Venne for the New Democratic Party; John Torringa for the Christian Heritage Party; Pat O'Hara, an auctioneer, for the Western Canada Concept; and Peter Hope for the Confederation of Regions Party.

The large number of candidates meant that debate at the all-candidate forums was diffused. They also gave Clark the opportunity to lump me and the Reform Party into the "fringe" category with the CHP, WCC, and COR. Our challenge was to turn the forums into sharply focused debates between myself and Clark and to get the crowds involved in that debate.

As it turned out, the first forum in Whitecourt went our way. It was sponsored by the Chamber of Commerce, and because it had been hyped as "the first round in the Battle of Yellowhead," both the national and the local media were present. I was casually dressed in a leather jacket, slacks, and boots; Joe was dressed as if he was attending the opening of the United Nations. (This was a small thing, but I knew it was on some people's minds because a fellow in Drayton Valley had asked me, "Are you going to dress like him, or are you going to dress like us?")

We drew numbers to determine the order of speaking. We were allowed six minutes each, with another two minutes each for rebuttal. I spoke right after Joe, which was good, because it allowed me to compare and contrast my positions with his. After briefly introducing myself and the Reform Party, I listed the distinctions between Clark's position and the Reform position on such subjects as federal spending, Meech Lake, language legislation, Senate reform, party discipline, and patronage. I ended by asserting that the key issue facing Yellowhead electors was "real representation" of their interests and positions in Parliament. Replacing Joe Clark with a Reformer would send an unmistakable message to every traditional politician in the country, namely, "We don't care who you are or what positions you've held. We don't care how long you've been in Parliament. We don't even care if you're a former prime minister. If you will not faithfully and accurately represent the views of the people who elected you, you'll be replaced by someone who will!''

There were about 250 people packed into a fairly small room. At least twenty to thirty of these were dedicated Reformers who had come to cheer me and boo Joe at every opportunity. The Whitecourt Reformers were there in force; but so were others from out of town, including the Gideons, the Assmuses, the Murrays, the Suitors, and the Stuffcos.

During the question period, a man from Fox Creek zeroed in on the one question that Joe could not readily answer: "Mr. Clark, could you tell us why we should vote for you when you won't vote for us?" And before Joe could stop him, he started down the list: Meech Lake, Senate reform, the CF-18 contract, language legislation, federal spending, capital punishment—all the items on which Joe's positions were miles away from those of a majority of the people in that room. As he ploughed through the list, the crowd started to cheer each item. Gideon was bouncing up and down like a wolverine on a chain. Assmus and Stuffco were whooping like cowboys and Indians (which is quite accurate, because Dale Assmus is part cowboy and Phil Stuffco is part Indian).

When Joe tried to respond to the specifics—saying, for example, that Meech Lake would bring Senate reform—they laughed. When Joe tried to generalize, saying he owed them "his judgment" rather than his vote, they started to boo. When Joe got flustered, they booed even louder. The journalists in the front row were scribbling furiously.

The headlines ("Clark in trouble in Yellowhead") and the national TV coverage gave the Reform campaign across the West a much-needed boost at precisely the right time. I told myself we should enjoy it while we could; knowing Joe Clark, it was unlikely that he would let anything like that happen a second time.

The Whitecourt forum gave us a theme and a slogan that we would use again and again across the West and throughout the campaign. The theme was real representation and the slogan was "Why should we vote for you, when you won't vote for us?" These were more effective than anything an advertising professional could have thought up.

The next all-candidate forum was scheduled for Hinton two weeks later. The media were there in force, hoping for some more fireworks, but they were to be disappointed. This time Joe's people were better prepared and much more in control. The crowd was larger, about 350, with my supporters filling the front seats on one side of the hall, and Joe's filling the front seats on the other side. The boos and the cheers, for both Clark and myself, were about even this time.

After talking about my background and the positive aspects of the Reform option, I raised the representation issue again, this time in terms of Joe's failure to represent Hinton's interests in a freight rate increase that had threatened the expansion of the Champion Forest Products mill. In 1986, just as Champion Forest Products was planning a major expansion and modernization of its Hinton mill, CN and CP announced an 8 percent freight rate increase (in two stages) on all wood pulp from origins in western Canada to destinations in the United States.

Repeated attempts by the Hinton Survival Committee to secure Joe's interest in representing their concerns had been unsuccessful. It was actually the Liberal transport critic André Ouellet who finally raised the matter in the House, but when the matter was eventually resolved to Hinton's satisfaction, Joe was on hand to take the credit. Many of the local business and union people in Hinton were quite familiar with the facts of the case, although the outside media were not. My point was simply that "Hinton and other mine and mill communities in Yellowhead cannot afford an MP who is uninterested, unwilling, or unable to tackle freight-rate issues affecting the jobs, wages, businesses, and livelihoods of the people of this riding."

Joe knew that I would be raising the freight-rate business, and was ready with a comeback. He read out a letter from the Hinton Survival Committee thanking him for his efforts, a nominal thank-you note that had been sent to anyone and everyone on their mailing list once the issue had been resolved. The local people who knew the whole story were not impressed, but most of this was lost on the outside media, who didn't really know what either of us was talking about.

My greater concern with the Hinton forum was with the weak performance of the Liberal and NDP candidates. If we couldn't win in Hinton ourselves, it was very important that the NDP and Liberals do well there and take votes away from Clark. The Liberal candidate, John Higgerty, talked almost exclusively against the free trade deal. He made no effort, however, to relate the issue to Yellowhead, where many of the export-oriented forestry and oil patch people rightly regarded free trade as protecting their access to the export market and safeguarding them from another national energy program. John's one good line, which reinforced the representation issue, was that Yellowhead residents were as likely to see Elvis Presley in their riding as they were to see Joe Clark.

Joe had to be pleased with the Hinton forum. The question period was tightly controlled, with written questions screened by a panel; the crowd didn't really get involved; and the media had nothing exciting to report. For the incumbent, a draw is always as good as a win.

One amusing thing happened at Hinton, which my wife and Ginny Assmus, with an eye for issues of style, noticed. Joe's handlers were starting to think about "dressing him down." But on this occasion he arrived with a rather large and conspicuous corsage pinned to his lapel. One of Joe's aides sidled up to him just before the meeting and must have said something to the effect that "in Hinton, Joe, the boys do not usually go around with a lot of foliage pinned to their chests." He then disappeared into the men's washroom. There was a loud flush, and he emerged minus the flower arrangement.

The next forum was in the oilfield service town of Drayton Valley and was attended by more than 650 people. Joe led off by reminding the good people of Drayton Valley that it was the Conservative government of Brian Mulroney that had done away with the iniquitous National Energy Program. He recounted how he and the Conservatives had fought the NEP tooth and nail while in opposition, and had removed it completely when they formed the government.

I countered with a handout and some figures which suggested that this was misrepresentation. The truth of the matter was that when the Conservatives were elected, they did *not* immediately do away with the NEP or the hated Petroleum Gas Revenue Tax (PGRT), despite intense pressure from energy companies and the Alberta government. In fact, in 1985 they collected more than $2 billion from 114 producing companies (many of which were active in the Drayton Valley area), almost as much as the Liberals had collected the year before. Only when the fall in world oil prices reduced revenues from the PGRT to less than $400 million a year did the federal Conservatives finally consent to the removal of the tax.

Clark, of course, countered with righteous indignation, demanding to know what I had been doing while he was valiantly fighting the NEP tooth and nail from the opposition benches. I replied that I had been trying to make a living, the same thing that everybody else in this room and in the energy business had been attempting to do during that period.

By now the all-candidate forums were becoming predictable and the media were losing interest. There was a large crowd at Barrhead, relatively friendly to me, but no fireworks.

The Edson forum was also well attended, and could probably be described as a draw. The highlight of the evening came when the NDP candidate, having castigated the energy industry for supporting free trade, asked rhetorically, "How many of you are senior executives of multinational oil companies, the only ones who will benefit from this deal?" A roar of laughter went through the hall as Slim Martin, the ex-constable and rodeo clown, slowly rocked to his feet and, removing his hat, bowed low to the crowd.

The last all-candidate forum was held in the town of Jasper. Surrounded by mountains, it is one of the most beautifully situated communities in all of Canada. For me, there is no better way to escape the tensions of business or politics than to round up some saddle horses and fishing rods and spend some time with the family trail riding in the foothills or the Rocky Mountains. If I had been successful in winning the Yellowhead election, Sandra and I would have seriously considered moving to Jasper.

The forum in Jasper was not well attended and Clark himself was absent on other business. Nevertheless, two incidents gave our campaign team some pleasant memories of electioneering in that community.

Randy Murray had a loudspeaker attached to the top of the recreational vehicle that was the mobile headquarters of our door-knocking campaign. When we first got to a town, we usually drove slowly up and down the streets, Reform banners and "Elect Manning" signs in plain view, advertising our public meetings or forums, or loudly inquiring whether Joe Clark had been seen in those parts since the last election.

When we got to Jasper, our door-knocking crew began to make bets on how long it would take the authorities to shut down our loudspeaker (Jasper was the only community in Yellowhead where this was expected to occur). Someone said fifteen minutes, someone else said thirty minutes, and so on. But two minutes after we had driven slowly down the main street advertising our meeting, a parks official in a government vehicle pulled us over and, after citing the appropriate regulation, ordered us to cease and desist. The Charter of Rights and Freedoms notwithstanding, it would be unseemly to disturb the tourists or the wildlife with the propaganda of democracy.

The other incident that enlivened our Jasper campaigning involved the first public appearance of the "Reform Posse." The steam train *Royal Hudson* was scheduled to arrive in Jasper from British Columbia as part of a tourism promotion. One of our Jasper contacts heard that Joe Clark was going to get on the train on the British Columbia side and ride to the Jasper station, where the media would be waiting to cover his arrival.

As a counterattack, our people wanted to put together a mounted Reform Posse to meet the train when it pulled into Jasper station. The posse, led by myself, would have banners and saddle blankets emblazoned with Reform logos, and would distribute "Wanted" posters indicating that the posse and Sheriff Manning were in pursuit of the notorious Joe Clark, who was wanted for failure to represent Yellowhead properly in the federal Parliament. I could tell by the enthusiasm with which this scheme was presented that it would provide some welcome relief for many of our key workers from the routine campaign activities of meetings, forums, and the endless door-knocking.

I also couldn't help being reminded of stories I had heard long ago of the "political horse races" that were a feature of some of the early campaigns conducted by the Social Credit and CCF movements in an era when political campaigns were much more entertaining than they are today. These horse races had usually been held at political picnics or country fairs. Three or four horses and riders would be dressed up in colours and other paraphernalia to represent the various political parties contesting a provincial election. If it was a Social Credit picnic or rally, the UFA horse representing the government party would be a broken-down old nag. The Liberals might be represented by a mule, and the Conservative jockey might be sitting backwards on a ponderous work horse pulling a "Bennett buggy."

If William Aberhart was the guest speaker, he would be invited to introduce each horse and jockey with some appropriate comments, and then the race would begin. As the animals rounded the track, whoever was calling the race would make further remarks about their progress and relative fitness for finishing the race. Then, just as they were rounding the last turn, a beautiful dark horse (the Social Credit horse in Alberta, the CCF horse in Saskatchewan) would gallop onto the track, leaving the rest in its dust and crossing the finishing line first, to the cheers of the partisan crowd.

What stuck in my mind about these events was that when you talked to the old-timers who had participated in those early campaigns, it was those crazy horse races—not the formal meetings, speeches, or debates— that they remembered most fondly. So when the Yellowhead campaign crew came up with the idea of the Reform Posse, what could I say but "Let's do it"?

The horses were obtained from the Jasper Park Lodge, and there was no shortage of volunteers for the posse itself. Even Slim Martin, who was pretty stiff with rheumatism, volunteered to ride—an impressive sight because of his size and the huge buffalo coat that was part of his outfit.

Then, on the day of the event, we got the news. The steam train had lost a wheel in British Columbia, and would be delayed more than twenty-four hours. Because of the delay, Joe Clark would not be on board.

We went ahead with the Reform Posse ride anyway. The horses were assembled in a parking lot not far from the Jasper station. The banners and signs were all in place, and we had our posters. Our fifteen-horse Reform Posse then rode through the streets of Jasper inquiring after the presence of the notorious Joe Clark, handing out our posters, and posing for pictures with tourists, some of whom were sure they were participating in a quaint local custom.

We got our picture taken by the local paper, and then headed for the Jasper train station. It was almost vacant except for a CBC cameraman and reporter who had not yet heard that the arrival of the train had been delayed. They had been sent to film the train and Clark, not the Reform Posse, and no amount of persuasion could get those representatives of the people's network to turn on their camera to record our posse for posterity.

After it was all over, we took a leisurely ride along the Athabasca River back to the Jasper Park stables and all had dinner together at the Overlander Lodge. Twenty-five years from now, when all the forums and speeches of the Battle of Yellowhead have long been forgotten, those who participated in the ride of the Reform Posse will still tell their grandchildren about the time they almost captured Joe Clark.

I have dwelt on the grassroots aspects of my personal campaign in Yellowhead because it was important to me. This campaign was amazingly successful (it shifted almost 30 percent of the popular vote away from Joe Clark and the Conservatives toward myself and Reform). It did not, however, really address the more basic interests that tie certain voters to an incumbent representing a governing party. In Yellowhead, as in every federal constituency, there are scores of interest groups, associations, and communities that receive funds or specific attention from the federal government and that are susceptible to the suggestion that, if they want that financial support or attention to continue, they had better support the government candidate. As a veteran politician of the old school, Joe Clark keeps meticulous records of every voter and interest group whose vote can be influenced in this way and he uses it to full advantage at election time.

Of greater concern to the Reform Party campaign in Yellowhead, and indeed throughout the West, was the domination of the latter stages of the 1988 federal general election by the free trade issue. As a party, we supported free trade in principle and argued that Canada's best course of action in the light of the worldwide movement toward freer markets and trade liberalization was to enter into a North American free trade arrangement and make it work. We pointed out that the whole world was dividing into huge trading blocs—the European Community, the Asia-Pacific Community, and the Americas community; that future trade laws would increasingly be negotiated between these communities rather than between individual nation-states; that Canada had to belong to one of these; and that the most natural one to belong to was the one that included the United States and eventually other countries in Central and South America.

To distinguish ourselves from the Progressive Conservatives on this issue, we argued that it was not sufficient simply to negotiate a framework agreement to make free trade work for Canada. There was an equally urgent necessity for complementary actions on other policy fronts. These should include reducing the cost of government as reflected in high deficits and high taxes; lowering interest rates so that monetary policy reinforced rather than contradicted the free trade initiative; removing interprovincial barriers to trade; and improving labour-force transition programs (retraining, relocation allowances, income support) to help workers switch from less productive sectors of the economy to more competitive ones.

In Alberta, we tended to brush aside the NDP complaint that freer trade was going to destroy the social safety networks by insisting that a strong, internationally competitive economy was itself the best social safety network you could have. In other western provinces, where the opposition to free trade was stronger, our candidates had a harder time defending our position.

Although our free trade position was clearly distinguishable from that of the Conservatives on paper, it got lost in the shuffle as the election polarized between the Conservatives and the Liberals over this issue. It also became almost impossible in the latter stages of the campaign to direct the voters' attention to any other concern. Statements on Meech Lake, Senate reform, the deficit, the impending GST, and parliamentary reform were drowned out by the noise of the free trade debate.

Finally, mercifully, the 1988 federal election campaign ground to a halt, and election day, November 21, was upon us. The day was spent on "getting-out-the-vote" activities, and as the polls closed Sandra and I went to our motel in Edson with our boys to wait for the results.

In Yellowhead, the vote totals, compared with those of the 1984 election, were:

PARTY	1984	1988
Conservative	37,462	17,847
NDP	6,906	6,174
Liberal	4,097	3,997
Reform	—	11,136
Other	2,156	880

A year-old party, running against a senior minister and former prime minister, had picked up 29 percent of the vote and reduced the incumbent's percentage of the total vote from 74 percent to 45 percent.

My campaign manager Ginny Assmus, who had done a superb job in pulling together an organization from scratch across the huge Yellowhead constituency, couldn't resist pointing out to me one significant item among the poll-by-poll results. In Neerlandia, where I had not spoken during the campaign, but Sandra had, the results were 197 votes for me and 23 for Joe.

In total, 275,000 western Canadians voted for the Reform Party of Canada, although no Reform candidates were elected. This was about twelve votes for every name on our membership lists. In Alberta, Reform Party candidates received more than 178,000 votes, or 15.4 percent of the popular vote in the province, compared to 17.4 percent for the NDP and only 13.7 percent for the Liberals. Nine finished second in their ridings. Doug Main in Edmonton-Strathcona came closer to winning his riding than any other Reformer—within 6,063 votes. Dal Brown in Wild Rose polled the largest number of votes (13,865) of any Reform Party candidate, and also received the largest percentage of the popular vote (33 percent).

In British Columbia, Reform Party candidates received almost 75,000 votes, or 5 percent of the popular vote. In three ridings, commentators attributed the defeat of Conservative candidates to their loss of votes to the Reform Party, although Reformers, particularly on the Island, were encouraged by their ability to draw votes away from both the Conservatives and the NDP.

Approximately 22,000 votes were received by the Reform Party in Manitoba and Saskatchewan, where our constituency associations were still very much in the formative stages.

Generally speaking, there was a significant protest vote against the Mulroney government across the West. But in typically western fashion, the protest vote had been split among three parties. In Manitoba, many voters turned against the federal PCs and free trade, but voted for the

Liberals to show their displeasure. In Saskatchewan and British Columbia, the protest vote went strongly to the NDP, whereas in Alberta (which was pro-free-trade) it came to the Reform Party. There were comments that old Progressives were turning over in their graves at the idea that western Canadians would vote against trade liberalization, but of course they had never met Brian Mulroney.

As the results of the election became clearer, Sandra, Nathan, David, and I went down to the Glenwood Hall in Edson, where our workers and campaign team had gathered to watch the results. We were joined there by the rest of our family and other friends and supporters. I gave a brief speech congratulating Joe, thanking our workers, and expressing my general satisfaction with the results. I concluded by saying, "The Reform Party is here to stay. We are building for the future, and tonight we have made a significant step forward."

The mood of our workers and supporters was quite upbeat, and reporters who were scurrying between our hall and Joe's said it was hard to tell who had won, on the basis of the post-election celebrations. Joe's party shut down quite early, whereas our people carried on until the wee hours. When I got Joe on the phone to congratulate him, I felt he was pleased about his own showing and that of the government, but disappointed that his wife Maureen McTeer had not been successful in the Ottawa riding of Carleton-Gloucester.

In election contests, candidates with families often have a concern as to how family members, especially younger children, may react to losing a contest on which so much time and energy has been expended. Sandra and I were fortunate, however, in not having much to worry about along these lines. All our children are competitive athletes. We have driven home from swim meets and hockey games where the girls have won gold medals and the boys have scored winning goals; but we have come away from many more where exactly the same amount of effort and desire had only produced silver, bronze, or nothing at all, or where it was "the other guys" who scored the winning goal.

When I arrived at the party head office in Edmonton the next day, the mood there was optimistic as well. Neil Weir and his crew, whom I had hardly seen for weeks on end, were exhausted but encouraged. Phone calls and letters of congratulation had been pouring in, as well as many calls from people apologizing that at the last minute they had decided to vote Conservative instead of Reform out of fear that the Liberals might be rallying.

Media commentary, at least in western Canada, on the performance of the Reform Party in the federal election made it clear that it was

Myself, aged three and a half

The farmhand, aged thirteen

"Touchdown," my calf, 4H Northern Alberta champion

My father, me, my mother, and my brother Keith in 1950

With my parents in 1966

University graduation photo

Wedding day, March 23, 1967

In Hong Kong, 1968

Brand-new father:
with Andrea,
1968

The family in 1983. Front: Mary Joy, Nathan, and David. Back: me, Sandra, Andrea, and Avryll

The acreage overlooking Sturgeon River Valley

With Dave Berger and
a friend of Ernestine
Gibot's at Fort Chip

With my father-in-law,
Gordon Beavis, at
Nor'Westerlea

Campaign photo from the 1988 federal election

With my family in 1988. Front: David, Sandra, me, and Avryll. Back: Nathan, Mary Joy, and Andrea

The famous Reform Posse, with Virgil Anderson on the far left, and Dale Assmus on the far right

"Sheriff" Manning

Doorknocking with Donna Murray during the 1988 campaign

Congratulating newly elected Reform MP Deborah Grey after her swearing-in at the House of Commons in July 1990

Members of the Reform Party's Executive Council, 1989–91: Front row: Wayne Smith, Diane Ablonczy, me, Jeanie Clemenger (secretary to council), Neil Weir, Short Tompkins. Back row: Elwin Hermanson, Lee Morrison, Cliff Fryers, Lloyd Kirkham, Gordon Shaw, Gordon Duncan, John Cummins.

Stan Waters, Deborah Grey, and me at the press conference in Ottawa at which Stan and Deborah announced that they were taking a 10 percent pay cut in support of their demands for reductions in federal spending

Stan Waters speaking at the 1991 Assembly

Voting at the 1991 Assembly

A little impromptu mainstreeting in Smiths Falls, Ontario

Together with Sandra, 1990

becoming inappropriate to keep describing Reformers as a "fringe party." The Reform Party had obtained more votes in that federal election than any other non-traditional party, and more votes in western Canada than all other non-traditional parties combined. In Alberta, the party took more votes than the federal Liberal party.

At the end of the year, when we closed our books on 1988 and the election campaign, the financial results were also encouraging. Reform Fund Canada had received $799,000, almost all of it from membership sales and contributions from members. Total expenditures, including those to support the head office and its role in the election campaign, amounted to $713,000, leaving a surplus of about $86,000 for the year.

At the constituency level, we had collected $848,000 and spent $923,000 on the campaign. In eleven Alberta ridings, however, Reform candidates received more than 15 percent of the popular vote, thereby qualifying for the recovery of 50 percent of approved expenses, or approximately $173,000. At the constituency level, therefore, we ended up with an overall positive balance of $98,000, although some candidates and constituency associations had to dig deep again to make up for cost overruns in their ridings.

Perhaps the most encouraging thing was that in the six weeks after the federal general election—an election in which we had fought the good fight, but had not won a single seat—we took in almost three thousand new memberships, many of them unsolicited. I found I was repeating, to myself and to others, the same words with which I had cheered the Yellowhead gang: "We are here to stay."

CHAPTER TEN

By-Election in Beaver River

Five days after the November 21, 1988, federal general election, John Dahmer, the Progressive Conservative MP-elect for the Alberta federal riding of Beaver River, died of cancer. Since federal law required that a by-election be held within six months to fill the seat, the Reform Party's Beaver River constituency association scheduled a nominating meeting for January 9, 1989.

That night, two hundred people gathered in the Ukrainian National Hall in Smoky Lake to hear nomination speeches by Deborah Grey and Cold Lake medical doctor Richard Johnson. Deborah was well known to the Beaver River Reformers, having represented the party in the federal general election two months before. She had finished fourth after the Liberal candidate and the NDP candidate. At the nomination meeting, she was declared the winner by a large majority.

On January 21, 1989, only two months after the general election, the Prime Minister announced that the Beaver River by-election would be held on March 13, and once again Reformers were on the campaign trail.

Deborah Grey was born on July 1, 1952, in Vancouver, and received all her early and high school education in the Vancouver area. She attended the Burrard Inlet Bible Institute at Port Moody and Trinity Western College at Langley, B.C. In April 1978 she graduated from the University of Alberta with a double B.A. degree in Sociology and English, and in 1979 she obtained her Bachelor of Education degree, also from the University of Alberta.

In 1977 she took a summer job with Alberta Transportation, working as a government checker on a runway paving project at the airport in Fort Chipewyan in northern Alberta. It was there that she fell in love with Alberta's northern bush country, and in 1979 she accepted a teaching position at the Frog Lake Indian Reserve in northeastern Alberta.

In 1980 she began teaching junior and senior high school classes at the nearby Dewberry School, where she was employed at the time of the 1988 general election and the 1989 by-election.

Deborah had a general interest in Canadian politics, and had studied and taught Canadian politics as part of the social studies curriculum. In September 1988, she was talking to Liz White, a local nurse, and the discussion turned to the upcoming federal election. Deb asked Liz if she knew anything about the Reform Party and who their candidate might be in the new federal riding of Beaver River. Liz told Deb that she herself had joined the party and that as yet no candidate had emerged. Suddenly she said, "Why don't you run, Deb?"

Liz got on the phone to Pat Chern, director of nursing at the Smoky Lake hospital, and soon to be president of the Reform Party's Beaver River constituency association. Pat (whom I had once spoken to about considering a candidacy herself) encouraged Deb to check out the party and sent her the party platform.

The next week, Deb had to travel through Edmonton to catch a plane to attend her brother's wedding in Vancouver. In the airport waiting area she pulled out a copy of the party platform and started leafing through it. Gordon Shaw, the vice-chairman of the party, who was returning to Vancouver from an executive council meeting in Edmonton, happened to be sitting nearby. When he saw Deborah reading Reform Party material, he introduced himself to her and they arranged to sit together on the flight to Vancouver. After talking to Deborah for a while, he strongly encouraged her to seek the party's nomination in Beaver River for the federal general election.

Shortly before the deadline for close of nominations, Deborah agreed to carry the Reform Party banner in Beaver River, and the fledgling constituency association acclaimed her as their candidate on October 12, 1988.

Although she finished fourth in that campaign, she had gained a lot of exposure by participating in a number of all-candidate forums and information meetings. The local media and various people throughout the riding began to notice and comment on the fact that she was an excellent communicator—a better communicator, in fact, than many local politicians with much more public experience.

The campaign team assembled to fight the by-election included some old and some new faces. Neil Weir agreed to serve as campaign manager, and a campaign office was established in St. Paul, the second-oldest francophone community in Alberta. Tom Holliday of Elk Point became Deborah's official agent. Erna Holliday, Tom's wife and a registered nurse, managed the St. Paul office and became our most efficient mobilizer of volunteers.

The federal constituency of Beaver River is another of those large hinterland ridings that present a physical challenge to campaign orga- nizers and the people elected to represent such constituencies. The riding covers twenty-eight thousand square kilometres, stretching from just east of Edmonton all the way to the Saskatchewan border, and from the North Saskatchewan River in the south to well beyond Lac la Biche in the north. Like Yellowhead, Beaver River is not dominated by one large community, but includes a number of smaller towns (none larger than 5,200 people), which service the agricultural, forestry, and petroleum activity that is at the heart of the local and regional economy. The riding also includes a number of Métis communities and seven Indian reserves, and almost one-third of the residents of the riding have some native ancestry. The seven Indian bands were the very same bands that were the subject of my socio-economic impact assessment work for Esso years before.

Some political professionals and the media suggested that if I was serious about advancing the Reform cause, I should run in Beaver River myself. There was also speculation that several of the other parties might choose to run high-profile parachute candidates there. Ray Hnatyshyn, who had lost his Saskatoon seat in the general election, was mentioned as a possible Conservative candidate. Even Jean Chrétien, who claimed to have relatives in St. Paul and was contemplating his re-entry into federal politics, was mentioned as a potential Liberal candidate.

After receiving all this advice from numerous people "in the know," I asked my contacts in Beaver River, in particular our Reform group there, what they thought should be done. They replied that if, for strategic reasons, the party felt the leader should run in the by-election, they would be happy to comply and to help me as much as possible. But I could also sense that they felt they had gone out and found a very credible candidate from their own community, that she had done exceptionally well in the federal general election with very limited resources, and that they honestly believed they could win with Deborah if they could get the resources required to run a proper campaign.

Once Deborah was nominated, no time was lost in hitting the cam- paign trail, and our first target was the Progressive Conservative nominat- ing meeting itself. It was held in the town of Glendon in the eastern part of the riding on the night of January 28, and was attended by more than four thousand people. We knew that there would be a large number of unhappy Conservative members after the PC nominating meeting, because of regional rivalry for the nomination. Deborah, who is not bashful, therefore showed up at the meeting, shaking hands in between ballots and receiving a considerable amount of media attention. While she worked the floor, members of her campaign team placed letters under the wipers of the hundreds of cars outside, saying, "If your candidate didn't win the PC nomination and you are unhappy, perhaps you would consider supporting Deborah Grey." The PCs finally nominated real estate agent Dave Broda from Redwater, at the west end of the riding.

The Liberal nominating meeting was held in Smoky Lake, and was conducted with the usual Liberal attentiveness to both official languages, notwithstanding the fact that Smoky Lake is one of Alberta's oldest Ukrainian communities. Ernie Brousseau, a baker from Smoky Lake, was nominated to carry the Liberal banner. Ernie is well respected locally, but he was put at a great disadvantage by his own party's insensitivity to the demographics of the constituency. In Beaver River, next to the English-speaking majority, the largest minority language groups are Cree first, Ukrainian second, and French third. Nevertheless, the local Liberal candidate is expected to stand up in his own home town or on the border between the Cree and Chipewyan reserves and faithfully affirm language and constitutional positions that flow from the proposition that "Canada is an equal partnership between two founding races, languages, and cultures, the English and the French."

The NDP, who had finished third in the federal general election, nominated Barb Bonneau from Newbrook, also in the westerly part of the riding. The NDP MP from Edmonton, Ross Harvey, declared that the NDP was prepared to lead a crusade, starting with the Beaver River by-election, against the Conservatives' proposed Goods and Services Tax (GST). Our response was that "sending a New Democrat to fight a tax increase was like sending an arsonist to fight a fire. For thirty years NDP members of Parliament have consistently advocated increased public spending, which leads to increased taxes, as the universal solution to virtually every issue faced by the federal government. They are part of the fiscal and taxation problem, not part of the solution."

By the time all the nominations for the Beaver River by-election were complete, Deborah Grey was as well positioned as we could possibly have hoped for. The PC, Liberal, and NDP candidates were all from the westerly end of the riding, where we had a good base, and Deborah was the only candidate from the easterly portion. Also, Deborah was the only candidate who had run in the federal general election just two months before. She was beginning to be referred to affectionately as "the Iron Snowbird," a Beaver River combination of Anne Murray and Margaret Thatcher.

Deborah's platform and speeches, and my speeches on her behalf, focused heavily on the representation issue and the fact that the Beaver River by-election was an opportunity to "send the government a message it won't forget, in the only language it understands, and that language is neither French nor English, but the number of votes its candidate receives or fails to receive on election day." We then emphasized that by electing a Reformer on election day instead of a traditional party candidate, Beaver River would be saying "Yes to Senate Reform and No to Meech Lake, Yes to reduced federal spending and taxation and No to the Conservatives' GST and high-interest-rate policy, Yes to a fair language policy and No to inappropriate language policies such as those contained in the Conservatives' Bill C-72, Yes to a candidate who would represent Beaver River in Ottawa and No to candidates whose fate under traditional party discipline would be to represent Ottawa to Beaver River."

In the middle of the Beaver River by-election campaign, Mr. Mulroney, with typical sensitivity to the West's interest in Senate reform, announced that he would not abide by the results of any proposed election in Alberta to fill the province's vacant Senate seat. This weakened Dave Broda's pronouncements on the PCs' commitment to Senate reform, while allowing Deborah to ask the people of Beaver River to teach the prime minister a needed lesson on the meaning of democracy by voting Reform in the by-election.

As for the proposed GST, we accepted the argument that Canada had to do away with the old federal manufacturers' sales tax to make us more competitive under the new free trade agreement. But our position was that the revenue shortfall should be compensated for through spending cuts, rather than a new tax. Our basic position was that "the federal government should not be given any additional tax revenues or levers unless and until it controls its own spending."

The local concern over high interest rates gave us one of our few opportunities to get some coverage for Deborah from the urban media, which until then had virtually ignored the by-election campaign in Beaver River. At the time the Bank of Canada was defending its high-interest-rate policy by insisting it was necessary to control inflation, particularly the inflation associated with the overheating of the economy of southern Ontario and southern Quebec. At the same time, the economy of most of the rest of Canada, including that of Beaver River, was experiencing a recession that was aggravated by high interest rates.

Western Reformers were not advocating simplistic or unworkable solutions to this problem, such as regionally differentiated interest rates. We did, however, feel that the Bank of Canada should consider a more regionally sensitive mix of fiscal and monetary policy than the one it and the finance department were pursuing. More specifically, we believed that at least part of the overheating problem in southern Ontario was caused by overspending by the federal and Ontario governments themselves in that region. For example, in 1987-88, regional development spending by the federal government in Quebec and Ontario was up to 71 percent of total federal spending on regional development, and per capita federal procurement in Ontario and Quebec was three to four times the level in Alberta.

In other words, while the Bank of Canada was trying to pour water on the inflationary fire in southern Ontario and Quebec through high interest rates, other federal departments and the Ontario government were pouring gasoline on the same fire. Our argument was that if government overspending in southern Ontario and southern Quebec could be reduced, or even redistributed, this would ease inflationary pressures to some degree and perhaps permit some lowering of interest rates.

These views were incorporated into a four-page letter to Bank of Canada Governor John Crow and a covering news release. Deborah then flew down to Calgary, courtesy of the Reform Air Force, and we held a press conference explaining our concerns outside the Bank of Canada offices in Calgary. After the news conference, Deborah and I walked into the Bank of Canada building, followed by a phalanx of reporters and TV cameras, to present our letter to someone who would deliver it to Governor Crow.

Of all the institutions of the government of Canada, perhaps the least well equipped to deal with requests for information and explanations from ordinary people, or to handle face-to-face encounters with citizens affected by its policies, is the Bank of Canada. Once inside the building, we were confronted with two wickets, behind which two Bank of Canada employees eyed us suspiciously while summoning the security guards. We explained that all we wanted to do was "deposit" a letter for the governor of the Bank of Canada on behalf of voters in Beaver River and other parts of western Canada who were suffering adversity from the bank's high-interest-rate policy.

While one of the tellers gingerly accepted the letter, the tension was broken by two of the security guards who recognized Deborah and me and rushed up to assure us that they themselves were card-carrying

Reformers. While the cameras rolled and the scribes scribbled, they wished us success on whatever mission had brought us to the central bank.

The resulting media coverage of our visit to the Bank of Canada helped some of us to become less intimidated by institutions that appear on the surface to be hostile to populist political initiatives. Time and time again we have visited editorial boards of large newspapers, or the producers of public affairs television programs, or the offices of interest groups or other organizations that are cool to the Reform Party and its positions. But in these places we invariably find technicians, secretaries, make-up people, chauffeurs, maintenance workers, or security guards who wholeheartedly support what we are doing, despite continuous exposure to criticism of our activities and positions. The common people are all-pervasive, and a political party that can win their hearts has friends and eyes and ears in the most unlikely places.

Because language was also an issue in the Beaver River by-election, we had our "fair language policy" printed up in four languages—English, Cree, Ukrainian, and French—and distributed throughout the riding. Our pamphlets criticized the government's official languages policy for being inappropriate for a riding like Beaver River and potentially discrim-inatory against unilingual Canadians and Canadians whose mother tongue or second language was neither English nor French. In its place we called for a fair language policy that recognized French in Quebec and English elsewhere as the predominant language of work and society, with bilingual services at the national (Parliament, Supreme Court) and local levels where market demand and common sense dictated. Our policy also called for recognition of freedom of speech as the basis of any language policy and an end to "forced language legislation" (such as Quebec's Bill 101, and the rule adopted by the Alberta legislature requiring a member to get permission from the Speaker before speaking in a language other than English). We also called for generous public and private support for second-language education on a voluntary basis.

Our fair language policy was in an embryonic state at the time of the Beaver River by-election. However, no fair-minded person who took the time to find out what our position was could characterize it as anti-French or anti-Quebec. We emphasized that our language policy could be taken to any community or home in Beaver River—English-speaking, Ukrainian-speaking, Cree- or Chipewyan-speaking, or French-speaking— and presented and defended as fair, whereas the official languages policy of the three traditional parties could not.

The policy positions of the Reform Party, and efforts to communicate these through the distribution of literature and extensive door-knocking (despite the minus-twenty-to-thirty-degree temperatures), played a significant role in the Beaver River by-election campaign. Our strongest asset, however, was Deborah herself. As in the general election campaign, the all-candidate forums provided good community exposure for Deborah's quick wit, common sense, and superior communication skills. Deborah made frequent reference to the fact that Beaver River and the West would not be well served by simply sending more "PCBs"—Progressive Conservative Backbenchers—to Ottawa. She concluded many of her talks with a reference to Shakespeare's *Julius Caesar,* warning Mulroney to "Beware the Ides of March, because Beaver River has a surprise for you."

I did not attend the all-candidate forums, as we did not want to give the impression that Deborah needed to have her hand held by the party leader, nor did we want to divert media attention from Deborah as the chief spokesperson for the Reform Party in Beaver River. Deborah and I did, however, address a number of public meetings together, and we door-knocked throughout the riding.

I usually heard about the results of the all-candidate forums the morning after, from our own workers or from voters who had attended. For example, we were canvassing the town of Waskatenau shortly after the Redwater forum. It was a bitterly cold morning and the only signs of life on the main street were two pick-ups, motors idling, parked outside the local hotel beer parlour. I stepped inside, introduced myself to two grizzled Ukrainian farmers, and asked them what they thought of our candidate Deborah Grey. One expressed some scepticism about the effectiveness of a woman candidate, but the other said he had heard and seen Deborah at the Redwater forum and had changed his mind. "She talks common sense," he said, "and she speaks better than all the rest."

While Deborah gained support through all the forums, it was Redwater that gave us a unique opportunity to deal head-on with the charge of racism that the Liberals (naturally) tried to introduce into the campaign. Ernie Brousseau was unfortunately saddled with some advisers from the city, who had recommended that he attack the Reformers. They had written an article for Ernie's campaign paper charging the Reform Party with racism and placing us "to the right of the Nazis." The piece relied for its evidence on extensive quotations from Doug Collins, the West Coast columnist whose nomination I had refused to endorse over this very issue.

At the Redwater forum, during the question period, Colleen Everitt, a member of Deborah's campaign team and a West Coast Indian, got up and asked Ernie about this article. "If the Reform Party was racist," she asked, "how is it that people like myself are not only members of the party, but hold key positions on the local party executive and campaign team? Do you yourself actually believe that Reformers are racists, or is this something that a few smart-aleck lawyers in Edmonton put into your campaign literature?"

To the amusement of the crowd, by the time Colleen was through with Ernie, he had not only dissociated himself from the article in his campaign literature, but also apologized to anyone whom it might have offended and offered to print retractions in several of the local papers. Colleen's actions at Redwater and her involvement in the campaign were far more effective in squelching accusations of racism than any formal statements or denials by Deborah or myself would have been.

Deborah's campaign was further aided by four effective television commercials produced by Randy Lennon Management Inc. of Edmonton. I had met Randy years before when he was just out of high school and had become the innovative editor of a widely read community newspaper. He had since become a telethon host, promoter, and television executive producer. With the help of his technical producer, John Berry, he provided us with high-quality, low-budget television commercials which were especially helpful in establishing the legitimacy of the Reform option with those people for whom nothing is "for real" unless they see it on television.

During the last weekend of the campaign, Reformers from all over the riding and from all over Alberta converged on key targets in Beaver River with posters, placards, and banners on their vehicles. They drove, honking and waving, up and down the streets of a dozen key communities, ultimately converging on St. Paul. Their purpose was to remind the electors of Beaver River to vote on March 13, and, by voting Reform, "to send Ottawa a message it won't forget, in the only language it understands."

On the evening of March 13, we all gathered in the Reform Party's St. Paul campaign office. The media, regional as well as local, were sensing an upset. They had decided to focus their coverage on St. Paul where our headquarters were located, rather than Radway, where the PCs had gathered to await the election results.

As the poll-by-poll results came in, Jack Ramsay from Crowfoot, who had campaigned extensively for Deborah during the by-election, stood on a chair reading them out. In my hand, I had the poll-by-poll results from the recent general election in order to make comparisons. Right from the beginning it was evident that Deborah was on her way to Ottawa. Whoops and cheers from the assembled workers and well-wishers greeted each announcement. When the final results were in, the totals were Deborah Grey, Reform Party, 11,154 votes; David Broda, Progressive Conservative, 6,912 votes; Ernie Brousseau, Liberal, 2,756 votes; and Barb Bonneau, NDP, 2,081 votes.

In St. Paul itself, the second-oldest francophone community in Alberta, the party and the candidate that had been consistently mislabelled by its opponents as anti-French and anti-Quebec finished first in ten of the twelve polls.

Less than sixteen months after the birth of the Reform Party of Canada in Winnipeg, the electors of Beaver River had given us our first elected representative in the Parliament of Canada. On March 14, instead of reporting to Dewberry School for teaching duties, Deborah Grey would be packing her bags for Ottawa, and starting a whole new chapter in her personal and political life.

Late that night, as Sandra and I drove back to Edmonton from St. Paul, we couldn't help but marvel at the Reform Party's good fortune. Of all the potential candidates who could have been the first Reformer to get to Ottawa, we could not have hand-picked a better initial representative than Deborah Grey. Not only was she young and female and from a riding not given to radical political action, she was also stable, an excellent communicator, and a genuine populist.

Five days later, a special send-off dinner was held in Deborah's honour in Calgary. It was organized by the Calgary Reformers and chaired by Stan Waters, former commander of the Canadian Armed Forces and a prominent Calgary businessman.

Two of the special guests at that dinner, who represented the previous populist movements of the West and came to "pass the torch" to a new generation of Reformers, were my father, Ernest C. Manning, and Douglas Campbell, one of the original Progressives and a former Liberal premier of Manitoba. My father was eighty-one and represented the populist uprising in the West during the Great Depression, an uprising that sent seventeen Social Credit and seven CCF members to Parliament in the 1935 federal election. Doug Campbell was almost ninety-three and sharp as a tack. He was introduced as representing the great Progressive tradition of Canadian politics. Elected to the Manitoba legislature in 1922 as a Farmers' candidate, he became minister of agriculture in the Liberal Progressive government of John Bracken in 1936 and went on to become premier of Manitoba in 1948. He continued in office until 1958.

Doug Campbell and my father had a number of things in common, besides being card-carrying members of the Reform Party. When they were premiers of their respective provinces, they rode the trains together to attend the postwar federal-provincial conferences in Ottawa. Both claim that the West had its act together better in those days because the western premiers had to spend several days together in close quarters before and after the conferences.

When Doug Campbell got up to speak, he recalled the 1921 by-election in Medicine Hat, in which the first Progressive candidate was elected to Parliament, and the following general election, which sent sixty-five Progressives to the federal Parliament. He also recalled the fact that the first woman member of Parliament (Agnes Campbell Macphail, a Progressive) did not get to Ottawa by representing the traditional parties, and remarked that he thought it significant that the first Reformer in Parliament would be a woman. He paid personal tribute to Deborah, and wished her every success on behalf of all Reformers past and present.

He concluded by reciting by heart a short poem. It linked the present Reform Party with past populist movements, describing both as "builders of bridges" between the past and the future. It also answered most eloquently the unspoken question "What are senior citizens like Campbell, my father, Francis Winspear, and countless others doing in a new political party dedicated to sending people like Deborah Grey (thirty-six years old at the time) to Ottawa to reform the system?"

The Bridge Builder
(Miss) Will Allen Dromgoole

An old man, going a lone highway,
Came at the evening, cold and gray,
To a chasm, vast and deep and wide,
Through which was flowing a sullen tide.
The old man crossed in the twilight dim—
That sullen stream had no fears for him;
But he turned, when he reached the other side,
And built a bridge to span the tide.

"Old man," said a fellow pilgrim near,
"You are wasting strength in building here.
Your journey will end with the ending day;
You never again must pass this way.
You have crossed the chasm, deep and wide,
Why build you the bridge at the eventide?"

The builder lifted his old gray head.
"Good friend, in the path I have come," he said,
"There followeth after me today
A youth whose feet must pass this way.
This chasm that has been naught to me
To that fair-haired youth may a pitfall be.
He, too, must cross in the twilight dim;
Good friend, I am building the bridge for *him*."

CHAPTER ELEVEN

The Alberta Senate Election

Every large nation with an uneven population distribution must answer the following question if its national government is to be effective: how can the interests of both the thinly populated and the heavily populated regions of the country be effectively represented and balanced in national decision making?

The classic federalist response to this question has been to establish two levels of government, one national and the other local or provincial, with a balanced and functional division of powers between the two. A democratic bicameral national parliament is also established, in which the composition of the lower house is based on representation by population, the composition of the upper house is based on representation by region, and legislative proposals do not become law until they are approved by both houses.

In Canada, balancing the interests of the thinly populated resource-producing regions such as the West, the North, Atlantic Canada, and rural and northern Ontario and Quebec with those of the heavily populated regions of southern Ontario and southern Quebec has been frustrated by the fact that the Senate is undemocratic (its members are appointed by the prime minister rather than being elected by the people), regionally unbalanced (more than 50 percent of the senators come from the more heavily populated areas of the country), and unable to safeguard or advance regional interests as effectively as the upper chambers of other large federations such as the United States or Australia.

The fact that successive federal administrations in Canada have been able to secure parliamentary approval to pursue numerous national policies and decisions (such as the National Energy Program, official languages legislation, the CF-18 decision, the high interest rate policy, and the Meech Lake constitutional proposals) that have ignored or grossly offended the interests of significant numbers of Canadians living in the thinly populated regions of the country, is ample proof that the Canadian Senate is not doing its job and needs to be reformed.

In the mid-1970s, Premier Lougheed of Alberta appointed a Citizens' Advisory Committee on the Constitution to make recommendations on Alberta's position in future constitutional talks. The committee was chaired by Dr. Peter Meekison, then deputy minister of intergovernmental affairs, and included Professor Gene Dais, a professor of constitutional law at the University of Calgary. It was Professor Dais who convinced the committee (which included Ted Byfield and several others) that an elected Senate with equal numbers of senators from each province was needed to improve representation of regional interests in the Canadian Parliament. The committee recommended a higher priority for this type of Senate reform to the caucus and the cabinet, and "Senate reform" became an item on the province's constitutional negotiating list.

In 1981, Dr. Peter McCormick of the University of Lethbridge; Gordon Gibson, a Vancouver businessman and columnist and former executive assistant to Prime Minister Trudeau; and my father (then a senator) produced a study for the Canada West Foundation entitled *Regional Representation: The Canadian Partnership*. It argued that reforming the Senate of Canada to make it Elected, with Equal representation from each province, and Effective powers to advance and protect regional interests would go a long way toward addressing the need for regional fairness and balance in national decision making.

An Alberta Committee for an Elected Senate was created to popularize the concept in August 1983. Bert Brown, a farmer and political activist from the town of Kathryn, was elected as chairman. Ted Byfield coined the shorthand phrase "Triple-E" to summarize the committee's Senate reform proposals. When interest in the committee's work spread to Saskatchewan and British Columbia, its name was changed to the Canadian Committee for a Triple-E Senate.

In 1984, the spring convention of the Alberta Progressive Conservative Party strongly supported a resolution calling for the Alberta government to support the Triple-E Senate proposal. In March 1985, the Alberta government's Special Select Committee on Senate Reform recommended that the Alberta Government commit itself to the Triple-E Senate concept. That same year, the Canadian Committee for a Triple-E Senate began to promote the concept to all provincial political parties across Canada, with increasing success.

I provide this background on all the effort that went into the development and promotion of the Triple-E Senate concept from 1975 to 1986 to make the point that Senate reform had a strong claim on the interest and attention of many western Canadians long before the unveiling of the Meech Lake constitutional proposals in 1987. Neither the federal Conservatives nor anyone else made a fraction of the effort to explain or promote the contents of the Meech Lake Accord to westerners. This in part explains why so many westerners found Meech Lake's token references to Senate reform so inadequate and why they resented the off-hand dismissal by the federal government and central Canadian commentators of attempts by Premiers Filmon and Wells to make their support of Meech conditional on a stronger commitment to Senate reform.

In the early 1980s the Triple-E Senate proposal had no real champion among the provincial premiers, although several had expressed guarded interest in the concept. This was to change, however, when Donald Ross Getty succeeded Peter Lougheed as premier of Alberta on November 1, 1985.

At the first convention of the Alberta Progressive Conservative Party after Getty replaced Lougheed, the new premier was under a lot of pressure to assert his own leadership and put his own mark on the party. He tried to do this by strongly committing the party to Senate reform, in particular the promotion of a Triple-E Senate. Many Albertans still cannot understand why Getty did not make Senate reform a condition of his signing the Meech Lake Accord. Meech Lake did, however, contain one small concession to the Senate reform movement: the federal government agreed to appoint senators from lists provided by the provinces. This was later to prove critical to securing the appointment of Canada's first democratically selected senator.

In August 1988 Getty called for a first ministers' conference on Senate reform. The federal government and the governments of Ontario and Quebec would not agree to such a conference, however, until all provinces had ratified the Meech Lake Accord. Getty then appointed a Senate Reform Task Force to travel to all the other provinces and to meet with their premiers and intergovernmental affairs ministers to promote the Triple-E Senate concept. The task force was to be chaired by the deputy premier and intergovernmental affairs minister for Alberta, Jim Horsman, and included Bert Brown.

The idea of an Alberta Senate election, to fill an Alberta vacancy in the upper house and to force the issue of Senate reform, was first suggested (to my knowledge) by Nick Taylor, the former Alberta Liberal leader and

MLA for Westlock-Sturgeon. Nick made this suggestion in 1987 shortly after the signing of the Meech Lake Accord. The Alberta government rejected Taylor's suggestion, but the idea lingered as a possible option to be pursued.

In fall 1988, with a provincial election looming, and the provincial Conservatives worried about losing the initiative on Senate reform to the Reform Party, David Elton and Bert Brown strongly lobbied the Alberta cabinet on the issue of attempting to fill an Alberta Senate vacancy by direct election. (The seat had been left vacant by the death of Senator Donald Cameron of Calgary.)

In February 1989, while we were fighting the Beaver River by-election, the Alberta government's speech from the throne promised an Alberta Senatorial Selection Act, a draft of which was tabled in the house. Brown had wanted the Senate election to be held concurrently with the provincial election. Getty, however, called the provincial election for March 20, 1989, the legislature was prorogued, and the Senatorial Selection Act died without being debated.

The Reform Party's reaction to all of this was frustration. We believed that the Senate of Canada had to be completely reformed from top to bottom and that this could be done only by the passage of a comprehensive constitutional amendment. We also believed that this could be done if the western provincial governments took the position that Meech Lake would not pass unless it was modified to include clauses establishing a Triple-E Senate. We had also objected to the draft Alberta Senatorial Selection Act, in particular the provisions that required the Reform Party of Canada to form a provincial political party if we wanted to participate in an Alberta Senate election. The way the bill was worded, we could not offer the Alberta political tax credit to financial contributors to a Senate election campaign, nor could the word "Reform" appear under our candidate's name on the ballot, unless we were registered as a provincial party under the provisions of the Alberta Elections Act.

The Alberta Conservatives were re-elected with a reduced majority in the March 1989 provincial election. Don Getty was defeated in his Edmonton-Whitemud constituency, and had to seek re-election in a by-election in the Stettler riding. All this took time, and it appeared that the government's enthusiasm for a special election to fill the Alberta Senate vacancy was waning. The next opportunity would be to combine the Senate election with province-wide municipal elections scheduled for October 16, but this meant that the Alberta Senatorial Selection Act would have to be reintroduced and passed forthwith.

Bert Brown, David Elton, and Peter McCormick sent a strongly worded letter to all the Alberta MLAs urging action on the Alberta Senatorial Selection Act. Brown went to see Horsman and Getty, armed with a list of seven reasons (later expanded to eleven) for immediate action. He was indirectly aided by the fact that the Reform Party, after its Beaver River by-election victory, was growing by leaps and bounds in Alberta, and was in a position to seize the initiative as the leading advocate of Senate reform in the province.

One of the more persuasive arguments for proceeding with the strategy of a single Senate election to force the issue of Senate reform onto the national stage was an appeal to the Oregon precedent. Originally the United States Senate was not directly elected; senators were appointed by the state legislatures. This led to considerable abuse along party lines. Then the State of Oregon took the unprecedented step of directly electing a senator in 1904. This move was universally opposed by the political establishment of the day, including Congress and the President. Oregon's enabling legislation was challenged in the courts, and the first directly elected senator never did get to Washington. But the American people liked the idea of directly electing their senators, and they began to express their dislike for the appointed senators. Within six years, more than half the United States senators appointed in 1909 had been elected by the states they represented. And in 1913 the American Congress ratified the seventeenth amendment to the constitution, giving the United States a Triple-E Senate.

To Don Getty's credit, he rejected the counsel of those who told him to forget about the Alberta Senatorial Selection Act, and reintroduced it in the legislature. He did so knowing that it would be unlikely that a Conservative would be elected to fill Alberta's Senate vacancy. The Alberta Senatorial Selection Act received third reading, and was proclaimed on August 18, 1989. Canada's first democratic election to fill a seat in the Senate of Canada was scheduled for October 16.

After the Beaver River by-election, our executive council under the chairmanship of Diane Ablonczy had authorized a number of changes in the party's administrative machinery to cope with the expanding workload. Wes McLeod, who had been the Reform candidate in Edmonton Southeast in the federal general election, became the chief administrative officer of the party, managing the head office in Edmonton. Tony Kryzanowski, a weekly newspaper editor whom I had met during the Yellowhead campaign, had also joined us as media coordinator and editor of *The Reformer*. Stephen Harper went to Ottawa as Deborah Grey's legislative assistant while continuing to serve as the party's chief policy officer. Cliff Fryers, a Calgary tax lawyer who had become increasingly involved with the party, was appointed chief executive officer of Reform Fund Canada. Donna Larson, who had joined the party as a volunteer working on Wes McLeod's campaign in Edmonton, became our full-time fundraiser.

In anticipation of the Alberta Senate election, the executive council also approved the establishment of a Senate Election Committee for Alberta under the chairmanship of Virgil Anderson of Calgary. The initial task of the committee was to canvass the twenty-six federal Reform constituency associations across Alberta on three important questions. First, should the Reform Party run an official candidate in the Alberta Senate election? Second, if so, how should our candidate be selected? Third, whom should we approach as potential candidates? All but two of our constituency associations felt that we should run a Reform candidate for senator (one felt we should run an Independent backed by the Reform Party; the other thought we should not participate because there was no guarantee from the federal government that the winner would actually be appointed to the Senate).

At the same time, party legal counsel Bob Muir was supervising arrangements to register the Reform Party under Alberta's electoral laws so that we could take part in the Senate election. This involved securing more than 4,650 signatures from eligible voters on a petition for submission to the province's chief electoral officer.

The Reform Party's Senate Nomination Meeting was scheduled for Monday, August 28, 1989, at the Red Deer Lodge in central Alberta. Each of the party's twenty-six federal constituency associations in Alberta was eligible to send ten voting delegates and as many observers as would like to attend.

About a dozen names of potential candidates were suggested by our members and constituency associations. I contacted all of them to determine their interest and eligibility. When nominations closed on August 21, four well-known Reformers had filed nomination papers with our Senate Election Committee. These included Vic Burstall, Calgary lawyer and chairman of the Reform Party's Constitutional Task Force; Bob Matheson, former Edmonton alderman and long-time western rights advocate who had been active in organizing the Reform Party in Edmonton and had chaired our first party task force on expansion; Murray Smith, Calgary lawyer, former PC member of Parliament and Reform Party candidate in Calgary North in the 1988 federal general election;

and Stan Waters, former commander of the Canadian Armed Forces, and a Calgary businessman.

On August 28, some 850 Reformers, including 210 voting delegates chosen by the Reform constituency associations, packed into the main ballroom of the Red Deer Lodge for the nominating meeting.

Each candidate made a brief speech reflecting his area of expertise and interest. Vic Burstall stressed the importance of using the Alberta Senate election to advance the overall concept of Senate reform. Bob Matheson reflected on his long involvement with previous attempts to secure more fairness and balance in confederation, and the importance of Senate reform as a means to that end. Murray Smith viewed the Senate election as a vehicle to send messages to Ottawa that our MPs and provincial government seemed unable or unwilling to communicate. And Stan Waters gave equal emphasis to the themes of Senate reform and fiscal responsibility, pausing to state with strong emphasis and great effect: "If I could carve two words into the heart of every federal politician, those two words would be, 'Cut Spending.'"

On the night of the Senate nomination meeting, Reform Party of Canada membership in Alberta stood at about fifteen thousand, and we had already secured the signatures of some seven thousand voters on our petition for provincial registration. By the time the petition was actually filed, we had about fourteen thousand signatures.

When all the ballots had been counted, Stan Waters had received 74 percent of the votes cast on the first ballot and was officially declared the Reform Party's candidate in the Alberta Senate election.

Stanley C. Waters was born in Winnipeg on June 14, 1920, of English immigrant parents. He was educated in prairie schools, including Garneau Elementary and Strathcona High School in Edmonton, but spent one year, 1933, at school in England. In 1938, he entered the University of Alberta, but as with many young men of that period, his education was interrupted by World War II. In 1941 he joined B Squadron of the King's Own Calgary Regiment as a private, and later that year went overseas as a corporal with his regiment. On being commissioned in 1942, he volunteered for the newly formed Canadian Parachute Corps and was assigned to the United States-Canadian First Special Services Force which specialized in commando and parachute operations behind enemy lines. Stan fought in southern Italy and took part in the assault landing at Anzio. His unit was the first to enter Rome on June 4, 1944.

Stan had attained the rank of major when his unit was disbanded. He then joined the 1st Canadian Parachute Battalion and fought in northwest Europe in 1945. After the war, Stan served in a wide range of command and staff appointments, including command of the Princess Patricia Canadian Light Infantry and the 1st Canadian Infantry Brigade in Calgary. He also served Canada on United Nations Peacekeeping assignments and on NATO duties in Europe. In 1971 he was promoted to Lieutenant General. From 1973 to 1975 Stan Waters commanded the Canadian Army.

Stan's thirty-four years of service to Canada as a member and leader of the Canadian Armed Forces took him to every part and province of the country, and to many nations around the world. His years in Ottawa (which he affectionately referred to as Fort Fumble on the Rideau), also gave him a unique insight into the operations of the government of Canada from the inside out and at the highest levels. No other candidate in the Alberta Senate election had his breadth or depth of national and international experience.

Upon Stan's retirement from the military, he joined the Mannix organization in Calgary. Within six months he had been appointed president of part of that organization, the Loram Group, which engaged in national and international activities in heavy construction, oil and gas, coal, engineering, and manufacturing. Later he helped create the Bowfort Group of companies, which were engaged in farming, real estate, venture capital, and investment operations. He retired from the Mannix organization in 1989.

Like many of our Calgary members, Stan had vigorously supported the Progressive Conservatives in 1984 (particularly in fund raising), but had become profoundly disillusioned with their performance in office. Besides sharing the view that systemic changes like Senate reform were needed for more fairness and balance in national decisions and policies affecting the resource-producing regions, Stan had been particularly disillusioned by the Conservatives' inability to bring federal spending under control. When Stan talked about "cutting federal spending" he was not talking about generalities, but had some very specific expenditures in mind based on his own experiences and observations as a senior civil servant and personal and corporate taxpayer.

Stan also had a long record of community involvement, especially in Calgary, which stood him in good stead once he decided to get into politics. He had been deputy chairman of the Calgary United Way Campaign, president of the Calgary Chamber of Commerce, a director of the Canadian Chamber of Commerce, president of the Sir Winston Churchill Society, a member of the YMCA board of governors, a member of the University of Calgary Chancellor's Club, a member of the National Citizens' Coalition, a member of the Fraser Institute, a member of the Centre for Conflict Studies and the Canadian Institute of Strategic Studies, a director of the Calgary Military Museums Society, and founder of the Calgary Native Opportunities Committee.

The fact that Stan was sixty-nine years old at the time of the Alberta Senate election was also important. Many of our members had expressed reservations about nominating an ambitious younger candidate because, until the Senate was reformed along the lines which we advocated, under the current appointment system this could mean handing someone a lifetime meal ticket and benefit package to which many of our people were opposed in principle. Our Senate reform amendment called for senators to be elected for six-year terms. Since Stan was sixty-nine, and the mandatory retirement age for senators was seventy-five, he would in effect, if elected and appointed, have one six-year term, and this would be acceptable to voters who opposed longer-term appointments.

By the close of nominations for the Alberta Senate election, six candidates had filed nomination papers. Besides Stan Waters of the Reform Party, these included William Code for the Liberals, Bert Brown for the Conservatives, and three Independents—Gladys Taylor, Dr. Ken Paproski, and Tom Sindlinger. The provincial NDP toyed with the idea of fielding a candidate, but then declined to do so, acceding to the position of the federal NDP that the Senate should be abolished altogether. The Alberta NDP leadership did not attempt to explain to its own members or the Alberta electorate how the regional interests of the West would be better represented in a one-house Parliament where a majority of the members come from southern Ontario and Quebec.

In the case of the provincial Liberals, William Code, a prominent Calgary lawyer, was simply appointed as the Senate election candidate by provincial Liberal leader Laurence Decore, an inauspicious beginning to a campaign that would focus on the need to replace appointed senators with elected ones. Code's nomination, however, was to be expected. As someone had remarked earlier, the likely Liberal approach to candidate selection would be to have a news-monitoring service compile a list of Albertans whose names appeared most frequently in the newspapers and on television. They had only to go down the list until they found a Liberal, or someone willing to become one, and that would be their most likely choice for a candidate. For two years, Bill Code had been conducting the highly publicized inquiry into the failure of the Principal Group of investment companies. By spring 1989, his was a household name in Alberta, and the Liberals hoped to capitalize on that fact.

The nomination for the provincial Conservatives did not take place until September 16. There were only two potential candidates: Bert Brown and Brian Heidecker, a cattleman from Coronation and a Mulroney appointee to the board of the Bank of Canada. Given his track record in promoting the Triple-E Senate concept and the Alberta Senate election itself, Brown was the logical choice, and he was duly nominated.

Some Albertans wondered why Brown didn't seek the Reform Party nomination rather than the Conservative nomination, but his party affiliation had been with the Conservatives for some time. Having helped persuade Getty to pass the Senatorial Selection Act, he could hardly have turned around and run for us without appearing to be stabbing Getty in the back.

Although Bert was well known as the primary promoter of the Triple-E Senate concept, by standing for the Conservatives, he had three heavy millstones around his neck. Those were the Meech Lake Accord, which the provincial government continued to support, the growing unpopularity of the Getty government itself (which had just raised the salaries of MLAs and cabinet ministers following the provincial election), and the growing unpopularity of the Mulroney Conservatives, who were in the process of introducing the GST.

In addition, neither the federal nor the provincial Conservatives had a good track record with respect to "reforming" anything. Our line would continue to be, "If you want to *reform* something—a policy like deficit financing or an institution like the Senate—send a *Reformer* to do the job!"

The three Independent candidates were all interesting people, each of whom argued that Senate elections should be conducted on a nonpartisan basis so that excessive party discipline would not eventually corrupt the upper chamber the way it had the House of Commons. Tom Sindlinger, an engineer and former Progressive Conservative MLA from Calgary, had broken with Lougheed in the early 1980s over party discipline, sat as an Independent, and tried to start his own provincial party called the Alberta Reform Movement. Tom had recently written a book on Senate reform, and he still had a network of contacts across the province. Gladys Taylor, a feisty weekly newspaper publisher from Irricana, had been supportive of the Reform Party in the beginning. At one point we thought Gladys might seek the Reform nomination, but she preferred the independent route. Dr. Ken Paproski, a former

Progressive Conservative MLA from Edmonton and brother of Progressive Conservative MP Steve Paproski, was the only one who was not from southern Alberta.

The Reform Party had wrestled with the issue of whether candidates for election to a reformed Senate should be Independents, free from party discipline, rather than candidates aligned with the federal political parties. In 1988, our workshops to develop the Triple-E Senate amendment had addressed the question of whether or not there was some way of keeping the federal parties out of Senate elections so the elected senators would be freer to vote in accordance with the interests of their constituents. Our legal advisers' answer was that reforms could be implemented to *reduce* the partisan influence on a reformed Senate. These included making elected senators ineligible for appointment to the cabinet or federal boards and tribunals, and thus less susceptible to the patronage-granting powers of the prime minister or party in power. Provisions could also be included in the constitutional amendment to ensure that the Senate did not function as a "confidence chamber," that is, to ensure that the defeat of a government motion in the reformed Senate would not bring about the defeat of the government.

But to attempt to eliminate partisan influence on the reformed Senate altogether or to expressly prohibit organized political parties from running candidates in Senate elections would be impractical and unwise. In order to raise funds and organize workers for Senate elections, candidates would need some form of organization, which in time would take on most of the characteristics of a political party. More importantly, any measures to keep the federal political parties out of Senate elections would infringe on the right of Canadians to freedom of association for political purposes; in other words, the proposed cure for excessive partisanship would prove to be worse than the disease.

Stan Waters's Senate election campaign team was headed up by Muntz Jensen of Calgary, who served as campaign chairman and managed the Calgary Senate campaign office. Jan Jessop, who had run as the Reform candidate in Calgary Southwest in the 1988 general election, became volunteer coordinator, and David Salmon, a lawyer from Calgary North, acted as Stan's official agent. Mark Waters and Ron McCallum organized the fundraising and accounting activities. They soon realized that financing a province-wide senatorial election campaign was like financing a mini-provincial election campaign. To send one piece of campaign literature to every household in Alberta could cost about $75,000. The original campaign budget was eventually increased to $250,000, a total which included almost $90,000 for television advertising.

A strategic planning group, including Diane Ablonczy, Jim Denis, former president of the Association of Professional Engineers, Geologists, and Geophysicists of Alberta, and me, met regularly to monitor progress and adjust strategy.

Stan also took a major role in fundraising, something he had once done very successfully for the Progressive Conservatives. A number of prominent Calgarians, who had declined to contribute to our election financing in 1988, were now more than willing to contribute to Stan's campaign and to be publicly identified as supporting Reform.

A Senate election pamphlet, inviting voters to "Elect a Reformer to the Canadian Senate on October 16," was produced, along with a special Senate campaign edition of *The Reformer.* Two hundred and fifty thousand of these pieces were printed and distributed by our members and federal constituency associations across the province. *The Reformer* invited voters to send four messages to Ottawa by electing Stan Waters. Those messages were: YES to Senate Reform, NO to the Meech Lake Constitutional Accord, YES to reduced federal spending, NO to the proposed Goods and Services Tax. It concluded by stating, "If Albertans want the Senate reformed, they should send a Reformer to get the ball rolling. The Conservatives and the Liberals have had 122 years to begin reforming the Senate, and have not done so."

Randy Lennon produced four up-beat ads showing Stan in conversation with Albertans of all ages and descriptions on such themes as effective representation, regional representation, federal overspending, and federal taxation. These were aired repeatedly all over the province, especially during the last ten days of the campaign.

Stan put in dozens of personal speaking appearances and participated in all-candidate forums all over the province. While the forums did not draw large crowds, they did get some media attention and made clear that the issue in the election was not so much Senate reform itself (all the candidates were agreed on the need to establish a Triple-E Senate), but which candidate would be the most effective representative on federal issues of immediate concern to voters.

During the Senate campaign I did extensive speaking on Stan's behalf and made telephone calls and wrote letters to key contacts who could help us deliver the vote. Sometimes Stan and I appeared together, but for the most part we split up in order to contact more people. Our joint appearances gave us an opportunity to compare notes and discuss strategy. On one occasion we were travelling back to Calgary late at night when Stan told me that if I had been a soldier, I probably would have got myself shot on my very first night patrol. He had observed that whenever I am approached by a potentially hostile voter, I would carefully question that voter and make sure he or she was really an enemy before engaging in combat. Stan, on the other hand, if approached by a potential political enemy, was inclined to shoot first and ask questions later. I responded by observing that in political combat it is more difficult to tell a potential friend from an enemy. We agreed that perhaps between the two of us, me questioning first and shooting second, and Stan shooting first and questioning second, we might make a good team.

On another occasion, I was introducing Stan, as I frequently did, at a large party barbecue in Calgary. In giving his background, I made the mistake of saying that Stan had left the University of Alberta to join the Canadian military during the *First* World War, rather than the *Second* World War. Before I could recover and correct myself, someone at a table of Stan's friends near the front of the room called out, "No, it wasn't the First World War, it was the Boer War." "No," called out another of Stan's pals, "it was the Crimean War." By the time order had been restored they had Stan leaving university to participate in the Battle of Hastings in 1066.

Stan also gave me the idea of including in many of my own talks, and in this account of the development of the Reform Party of Canada, a tribute to "the unknown volunteer." In this book, I have been able to mention by name only a small number of the hundreds of people who made the emergence of the Reform Party possible, and of those, I have only been able to devote a few words to describing their involvements—words which do not begin to describe their motivations, abilities, and contributions.

Contemporary politics in Canada, especially grassroots democratic politics, would grind to a halt if it were not for those unsung and unheralded volunteers, who do what they do without credit or tangible reward to advance some cause or candidacy in which they believe. These are the unknown volunteers to whom every democracy should pay tribute, just as most armies pay tribute to the "unknown soldier" whose efforts and sacrifices are the essence of all military achievements. If you have done something for the cause of political reform in Canada over the past five years, and I have failed to note your name or your contribution, please regard this tribute as especially yours.

As the summer of 1989 drew to a close, I was not only heavily involved in the preparations for the Alberta Senate election, but Sandra and I had also decided that we should move to Calgary. As much as we loved our acreage just east of St. Albert, it was becoming impossible for me to maintain it properly. In addition, the executive council had decided to move the head office of the party from Edmonton to Calgary in the new year, mainly because our largest reservoir of volunteers, including volunteers with professional skills (accountants, computer programmers, and lawyers), was located there.

For Sandra, the move to Calgary meant giving up a house that she had completely remodelled and a large yard full of trees, which she had thought would make a lovely setting for wedding receptions some day. The move also meant finding a new place in Calgary and sorting out all the logistics of meeting the educational and other needs of our five active children. For our girls, the move was potentially exciting. The two older girls were interested in attending the University of Calgary, and our youngest girl, Mary Joy, would be able to carry on her synchronized swimming activities with the highly competitive Calgary Aquabelles. For the boys, however, the move from country to city was a real sacrifice. The acreage was the home in which they had grown up. As we drove out the driveway for the last time, a drive that looked out on a grainfield with two rocking-horse oil pumps silhouetted against the sky, I was conscious again that "the unknown volunteers" in this political crusade also included spouses, teenagers, and small boys whose sacrifices were every bit as great as those who received the plaudits at Reform Party rallies.

If there was one federal issue that helped fuel the interest in the Alberta Senate election, particularly in Stan Waters' candidacy, it was the federal government's introduction of the Goods and Services Tax and the fact that Alberta's Conservative MPs (with two exceptions, David Kilgour and Alex Kindy) were prepared to vote for it when 85 percent of their constituents wanted them to do otherwise.

Our position (no additional tax revenues or levers until government spending was controlled) had been pressed by Deborah Grey during the House of Commons budget debate in May. She observed that the federal government would spend $10 billion more in 1989-90 than it had in 1988-89, and that the federal deficit would increase by another $1.5 billion. "I may be a political novice," she concluded, "but I am not politically stupid. We cannot ask people to support a deficit-reduction program that does not reduce the deficit."

As the federal government went ahead with the implementation of the GST, the makings of a grassroots tax revolt began to appear, especially in Alberta (the one province that had no provincial sales tax). *Alberta Report* sponsored what it called the "Resolution One" campaign. This Canadian version of California's famous Proposition Thirteen called on the federal government to "forthwith enact a law under which all future increases in total revenue must be exceeded by reductions in overall expenditure until the budget is balanced." Axe the Tax rallies were held in a number of cities across the West, with Reformers actively involved in their promotion.

Many out-of-province politicians and spokespersons fail to appreciate Albertans' deep-seated hatred of commodity taxes, and retail sales taxes in particular. My father and others with a historical perspective on this matter say that this sentiment has its roots in the Depression years, when the only taxes that governments were able to collect were commodity taxes such as the fuel tax. People could avoid income tax because they had no taxable incomes, and they could default on property taxes, but they couldn't escape commodity taxes on essentials as long as they had any income to spend at all. This aversion to sales taxes has become ingrained in the Alberta political psyche. Of course Albertans are well aware that they have been paying federal sales taxes for years, but the idea of an explicit commodity tax still evokes a swift and bitter negative reaction.

On October 10, less than a week before the Senate election, more than two thousand people attended an anti-GST rally in Red Deer, organized by a group calling itself Canadians AGAST (Against Goods And Services Tax). Deborah Grey represented the Reform Party and was heartily cheered when she was introduced as a crusader for reduced federal spending and taxation. Jack Shields, one of the two Conservative MPs who dared to show up (Red Deer MP Doug Fee was also there), almost needed a police escort to enter and leave the building, and Bert Brown received a chilly reception as well.

To those who criticized us for making the Alberta Senate election a referendum on Meech Lake and the GST as well as on Senate reform, we explained that the elected people who were supposed to be representing Albertans' views on these issues were not doing so. Alberta MPs were prepared to vote for the GST even though a majority of their constituents wanted the government to solve its financial problems through lower spending; and both the provincial government and the federal Conservative MPs insisted on supporting the Meech Lake Accord, despite the fact that it enjoyed the unqualified support of less than 10 percent of the Alberta electorate.

We also argued that as Canada moved toward democratizing the upper house, it would become increasingly important to know where prospective senators stood on all the major issues of the day. Future senators would ultimately be accountable for their legislative actions to the people who elected them, and Alberta voters therefore had a right to ask the Senate candidates where they stood on any federal issue before casting their ballots on October 16.

In the end, the greatest opposition faced by the Reform Party in the Alberta Senate election was mounted not by the other candidates, but by what might be called "the wet blanket syndrome." The Triple-E Senate concept is, by Canadian standards, an innovative constitutional idea, and holding an election to fill a vacant Senate seat was an innovative act. But the initial reaction of many of our opinion leaders to any innovative proposal—technological, economic, social, or political—is to pour cold water on it or smother it under a wet blanket. Later on, of course, after much discussion and sober second thought, our opinion leaders may grudgingly "warm" to the innovation and concede that it deserves a second look. But by then, the innovator has usually been driven to despair or to the United States.

The electronic media in the larger centres virtually ignored the Senate election campaign until the last week, when it became apparent to even the most obtuse that the public was taking it seriously. The large city dailies and most of their editorialists declared over and over again that the Alberta Senate election was "a non-event" or "a yawner," the results of which would be completely ignored by the powers that be and which therefore ought to be ignored by the people as well.

Worse yet were the negative reactions to the Alberta Senate election from some members of Alberta's political elite, including many Alberta Conservative MPs. Harvie Andre, Calgary Centre MP and then minister of regional industrial expansion, declared that Alberta's Senatorial Selection Act was unconstitutional, implying that Albertans who participated in the election were doing something illegal. Other prominent Conservatives, true democrats all, went out of their way to emphasize that the prime minister was under no obligation whatsoever to appoint the winner of the Alberta Senate election to the upper chamber.

Tory Whip Jim Hawkes, representing the Calgary West constituency (which contained the University of Calgary, where students had demonstrated in support of the democracy movement in China), went the furthest of all. He was quoted as describing the Alberta Senate election as a meaningless plebiscite that would induce more yawns than interest, predicting that those Albertans who did go to the polls would either spoil or reject their Senate ballots.

How can the "wet blanket syndrome" be prevented from smothering other innovative constitutional reform proposals in the future? First, we must recognize that the syndrome is a feature of our national psyche and discount the stream of negative commentary that initially greets any populist proposals for constitutional reform. Second, we should take heart from the evidence that on many of the public policy initiatives required to get Canada's constitutional, economic, and parliamentary houses in order in the 1990s, the people are not as instinctively negative as are their would-be leaders.

On October 16, 1989, despite minimal publicity, more than 620,000 Albertans voted in Canada's first Senate election. The turnout, 40 percent of the eligible voters, was slightly higher than the average turnout for Alberta municipal elections. Those who discount the significance of these figures have never attempted to get 600,000 people to do something new politically.

When the ballots were counted, Reformer Stan Waters had received 257,523 of those votes, or about 42 percent of the total. Because of the size of his constituency—the entire province of Alberta—Waters personally received more votes in support of his bid to go to Ottawa than any other candidate for federal office has ever received in any Canadian election.

Stan finished almost 120,000 votes ahead of his higher-profile competitor, Bill Code, and more than 130,000 votes ahead of Bert Brown. For the second time, the Reform Party had won an election with a candidate who was not well known to the general public before the election, which explains in part why our search for candidates for the next federal election is not focused heavily on recruiting recycled politicians or opinion leaders.

Once again, Stan Waters's Senate election victory, like Deborah Grey's by-election victory in Beaver River, helped destroy another set of stereotypes concerning the Reform Party. Stan had finished with more than 50 percent of the vote in all rural polls. But he had finished with more than 47 percent of the vote in Calgary (Code was next with 20 percent), 31 percent of the vote in Edmonton (to Code's 34 percent), and came first in virtually every other urban centre in the province. To finish as well as he did in Edmonton, where the NDP candidate for mayor, Jan Reimer, had topped the municipal polls, a significant number of NDP people must have voted Reform, despite their party's official boycotting of the Senate election and commitment to Senate abolition rather than reform.

On the evening of October 16, I noted from the election returns that Stan was doing very well in Calgary, which was not unexpected. I wanted to be assured, however, that we were at least holding our own against

Code in Edmonton and against Brown in the country, before starting to celebrate. While I was still looking suspiciously for snipers in the trees, however, Stan and his people had already run up the victory flag. By the time Sandra and I got to the election night headquarters at the Glenmore Inn in Calgary, the media had already declared Stan elected and he was busy giving interviews.

That evening, Jim Denis and I presented Stan to the assembled crowd of workers and well-wishers as Canada's first democratically elected Senate nominee (one had to be careful to get the correct description). Stan then gave a brief thank-you speech, which was interrupted frequently by whoops and yells from the Calgary Reformers.

Premier Getty called to congratulate Stan and we made an appointment to confer with him the next day on how best to present the results of the Senate election to the prime minister. Stan also received best wishes from the other senatorial candidates, several of whom came down to Stan's hotel to congratulate him in person. All the candidates had helped to generate public interest and support for the concept of Senate reform and had a sense that they had participated in a historic event. In fact, a national poll released by Telepoll Research Inc. of Montreal several weeks later reported that 48 percent of all Canadians (63 percent on the prairies) "strongly agreed" that the members of the Senate of Canada should be elected.

The next day Stan and I flew to Edmonton to meet with and thank our northern Alberta workers. We then went over to the legislature building, where I found myself sitting about thirty feet away from where the little side room used to be when my father had occupied that same office many years before. If that room had still existed, and if a small boy had been inside listening to the goings-on in the premier's office through the crack in the door, he probably would have heard a sound like the grinding of an axe.

Stan and I thanked Getty sincerely for proceeding with the Alberta Senate election. The task now was to get a reluctant prime minister to respect the results and appoint Waters to the Senate immediately. We knew that we could not count on much help from the Alberta Conservative MPs in pressing our case. We did, however, express the strong hope that the Alberta government would use all of its influence, including threatening to withdraw its support of the Meech Lake Accord, to secure Waters's appointment and recognition of the legitimacy of Alberta's demand for a democratically elected Senate.

Don Getty was very gracious, though unwavering in his support of the Meech Lake Accord, and he and Stan established a good relationship.

Getty said that he was drafting a letter to the prime minister communicating the results of the Alberta Senate election, and urging him to appoint Waters to the Canadian Senate. We told Getty that we intended to go to Ottawa ourselves to put our brand on that Senate seat while our iron was still hot.

On Friday, October 20, 1989, Stan, Deborah Grey, and I held a news conference in Ottawa to introduce the Reform Party's "senator elect," or "senator-in-waiting" as Stan called himself, to the national media. After the news conference we took a stroll down the main hall of the Centre Block of the Parliament Buildings (Parliament was not in session) toward the Senate. Stan paused at the threshold of the Red Chamber to express, on behalf of the 620,000 Albertans who had participated in the Senate election, his commitment to the proposition that "the Senate of Canada must be reformed." On our way out, one of the security guards with whom Deborah was on good terms winked and whispered, "You should have grabbed the seat and run."

Earlier that day, Premier Getty's letter to the prime minister had arrived in Ottawa. It formally advised the prime minister that "the people of Alberta have selected Mr. Stanley Charles Waters as the person to represent them in the Canadian Senate," listing the names of all the Senate election candidates and their vote totals. "I am forwarding the choice of the people of Alberta for your immediate attention," the Premier concluded, "and I urge you to appoint Mr. Waters without delay." Little did anyone realize how long the "delay" would be.

CHAPTER TWELVE

Expanding the Base

All during the Beaver River by-election and Senate election campaigns, another dedicated band of Reformers in Edmonton, headed by insurance and financial consultant Wayne Smith, had been organizing the third assembly of the Reform Party of Canada—our first since the federal general election of 1988.

Reformers all across the West, and especially in Alberta, were on a "high." Our membership had increased to more than 26,000 across the West. Reform Fund Canada would collect more than $1.1 million in revenue by the end of the year, spending about $900,000 and achieving a net operating surplus of more than $200,000. And in the short period of one year, the Reform Party had received more than 540,000 votes from western Canadians and elected two representatives to the Canadian Parliament. Last-minute registrations poured in for the 1989 Edmonton Assembly until they had to be cut off for lack of space.

On the morning of October 27, when the assembly opened, more than one thousand voting delegates, delegates at large, and observers had jammed into the convention facilities of the Edmonton Inn. The assembly opened on a rousing note, as delegates unanimously passed a resolution calling for Prime Minister Mulroney to appoint Senator-elect Stan Waters to the Senate without delay.

The primary purpose of this assembly was to consolidate our hold on the political ground that we had come to occupy as a result of our participation in the federal general election, the by-election, and the Senate election. We were rapidly becoming the leading federal exponents in western Canada of fiscal (spending) reform, constitutional reform (alternatives to Meech Lake), and parliamentary (particularly Senate) reform. We also wanted to expand our policy base, particularly on environmental issues, and lay the foundations for dealing with issues of organizational growth, such as provincial involvement, executive-grassroots relations, and party expansion outside the West.

Both Deborah and Stan were greeted with cheers and standing ovations every time they spoke. In Deborah's luncheon address she reported on the highlights of her first six months as the lone Reformer in Parliament. These included her official swearing-in on April 3, 1989, and her maiden speech to the House of Commons on April 12. In that speech she had made it clear that Reformers represented a fundamentally different perspective on constitutional matters from that represented by the traditional parties. She had concluded her speech with the affirmation that "The Beaver River . . . is not a tributary of Meech Lake. Its waters come from different sources and flow in a different direction."

Deborah also reported on her response to Michael Wilson's budget speech, her participation in attempts to halt the imposition of the GST, and her comprehensive efforts, including the distribution of a question-naire to every household in her riding, to consult her constituents before voting against the government's abortion bill.

The next day the delegates formally endorsed the approach taken in Beaver River to directing the vote of a member of Parliament on issues like abortion, namely, "that the MP state clearly and publicly his or her personal views and moral beliefs on the issue; that the MP ask all constituents to develop, express, and debate their views on the matter; that the MP seek the consensus of the constituency that emerges from this process, utilizing such mechanisms as constituency referendums; that if such a consensus exists and can be determined, the MP faithfully vote this consensus in the appropriate divisions in the House of Com-mons; that should such a consensus not exist or be unclear, the MP vote in accordance with his or her own publicly recorded statements on the issue; and that the MP urge other honourable members to conduct themselves in a similar manner."

Deborah proved again at the Edmonton Assembly that understanding and representing the people who elected her is her first political priority. At the very outset, Deborah and I had decided that since Beaver River and not Ottawa was her home base, she should spend 30 to 40 percent of her time in the riding, even if this meant missing time in the House. I had also cautioned our party executive about the danger of trying to make Deborah our spokesperson on any and every issue of importance to the Reform Party. Her priorities were to represent Beaver River first, and the Reform Party second.

My reason for this approach went back to a sad experience that I had witnessed in 1966 when the NDP elected its first and (at that time) only member to the Alberta Legislature in a by-election in Pincher Creek-Crowsnest. Neil Reimer was the unelected leader of the Alberta NDP at the time, Grant Notley was the secretary and chief organizer, and Garth Turcott was the new MLA. Unfortunately, Reimer and Notley tried to make Turcott the spokesperson for the NDP on every issue. Many of these issues were of little or no interest to Turcott's constituents and he was not equipped to deal with each one competently. Not only was Turcott given an impossible burden to carry by his own party (he once collapsed in the House from nervous and physical exhaustion), but he became increasingly unrecognizable to his own constituents. After working his heart out, he was defeated at the next general provincial election.

The afternoon session of the assembly was spent in plenary and workshop sessions designed to flesh out the party's positions on environmental issues. Although some positive work was done on developing the Reform Party's commitment to sustainable development, this is a policy area where I feel fresh approaches are required. Unless contemporary political parties have something new and worthwhile to contribute to the environmental conservation issue, they would be better advised to work on it rather than to scramble on the green band wagon. By "fresh approaches" I mean approaches that do not rely exclusively on government regulation to protect the environment, but effectively harness consumer purchasing power ("green buying") and marketplace mechanisms and technologies ("green businesses" and "green processes") to the goal of sustainable development. At the same time, governments should focus on getting their own regulatory role sorted out, by integrating their environmental regulatory powers rather than further dividing them among competing jurisdictions and agencies.

The last day and a half of the Edmonton Assembly was devoted to issues related to our own organizational growth, including the relationship of the executive to the grassroots constituency, and demands for expansion into provincial politics and outside the West.

As the party had grown, some of our original members had become uneasy about the executive and administrative structures required to serve these greater numbers. People who wanted to be in on all the decisions of the party now had to learn to delegate. People who wanted to be big fishes in a small pond felt their own relative importance and influence diminished. Changes were required in our own party constitution, including clarification of the roles of the leader, executive council, and constituency associations. But because of conflict between those who feared expansion and change, and those who welcomed it, competing proposals for revising the party constitution had to be referred to a task force on the party constitution chaired by Vic Burstall.

I felt concerned enough about these internal strains to say something to our delegates on the subject of "the government of ourselves." The English poet John Milton described a statesman (Oliver Cromwell) as one who had "first acquired the government of himself, and over himself acquired the most signal victories, so that on the first day he took the field against the external enemy, he was a veteran in arms, consummately practised in the toils and exigencies of war."[1] If we can't govern ourselves effectively as a party, I asked our delegates, how can we pretend to be fit to govern others? If we can't reconcile conflicting interests among Reformers over nominations or changes to our party constitution, how can we pretend to be fit to reconcile conflicting interests among Canadians to reform the Canadian constitution?

Wise, democratic decision making in the tradition of western populism requires four basic ingredients to work well. These are: a good cross-section of people (numbers), adequate information and advice, enough time to digest the information and advice, and—most importantly—a willingness on the part of the participants to accept the decision of the majority. But if even one of these ingredients is missing, the grassroots democratic decision-making process doesn't work, and ends up discrediting itself through dissension or bad decisions.

On a more positive note, delegates were able to deal constructively and expeditiously with questions about expanding the Reform Party into provincial politics and beyond the West. I had provided a memorandum to the delegates discussing the pros and cons of provincial involvement. It acknowledged a growing political vacuum at the provincial level, particularly in Alberta and British Columbia, which could very well call forth a new party. It also noted that many people had urged the Reform Party to expand into provincial politics because the opportunity existed, because it would give Reformers an organizational focus between federal elections, and because some of our key constitutional reforms required provincial as well as parliamentary support. On the other hand, I pointed out that our original focus and mandate was to reform the federal system by political action at the federal level. We had a long way to go to achieve

---

1. John Milton, "The Second Defense of the People of England," in Merritt Y. Hughes, ed., *John Milton: Complete Poems and Major Prose* (New York: The Odyssey Press, 1957), p. 832.

this objective and only limited resources to apply to the task. I noted that many of our members already belonged to one of four different provincial parties, and that historically Canadians have preferred to have different parties rather than the same party running their provincial and federal governments.

After debate, delegates voted down a resolution calling for the Reform Party of Canada to form provincial parties and constituency associations, but also voted down a resolution that would have slammed the door on provincial involvement. They then voted in favour of establishing a task force to evaluate the benefits, costs, and organizational processes that might be involved in the formation of provincial Reform parties, with the task force to report to the membership by May 1990.

As for Reform Party expansion beyond the West, delegates listened to a report from a task force chaired by Bob Matheson, a memorandum I had written listing the pros and cons, and a letter from Stephen Harper, who had been assessing the Ontario situation from his base in Ottawa.

This issue prompted lively discussion. Those opposed to expansion were not so much opposed in principle, as concerned about timing and the need to protect the party's ability to represent western regional interests. They cautioned against the dangers of spreading ourselves too thin, recommended building up the western base first, and suggested revisiting the question after the next federal election. They also expressed the legitimate fear that we could end up repeating the mistakes of the CCF, a western protest party that had expanded into central Canada (changing its name to the NDP) and was now led by a former York University professor and dominated by the influence of the central Canadian unions.

Those in favour of expansion pointed out that the original aim of the Reform Party was to be a national party, and that key elements of our platform (fiscal responsibility, rejection of Meech Lake, and provisions for more fairness and balance in national decision making) had obvious appeal beyond the West.

Stephen Harper, commenting on our slogan that "the West wants in," made the telling point that "the West will never get in by keeping others out." He also argued that the principal consequence of not expanding was that the Reform Party would then never be anything more than a protest party. The electorate could never be expected to consider it as a potential governing party. This latter point concerned me as well. I agree with Lord Acton's famous aphorism, "Power corrupts, and absolute power corrupts absolutely," but I also believe that "powerlessness corrupts"—that the complete absence of power or governing responsibility can lead to complete irresponsibility. If a political party is never in a position to act on its proposals, it may adopt irresponsible positions (promising to spend more money, for example, when there is no more money) because it knows it will never be called upon to deliver. This is in part the explanation behind some of the more irresponsible aspects of the platform of the federal NDP (its ignoring of Canada's defence requirements, for example, and its tendency to take wealth creation for granted while fixating on wealth redistribution).

On the question of timing, however, Harper also advised caution. He too wanted to see safeguards in place, to ensure effective regional representation in the party's decision-making structures and to protect embryonic constituency associations from being hijacked by extremist elements in the early stages of any expansion.

The last word in this debate went to Jim Purdie, a delegate from Calgary who had spent a lot of time in northern Ontario. "They've heard about Reform in northern Ontario," he said. "It's like a big truck heading down the Trans-Canada highway. And they're asking me to tell you, 'Don't stop that truck at the Manitoba-Ontario border!' " When the debating and voting was finished, delegates to the Edmonton Assembly had voted in favour of a motion reaffirming the commitment of Reformers to create a national party, and defeated a resolution calling for the party to remain western only.

A new executive council was elected to govern the party until the next assembly and to carry out the policy and strategic directions that had been established. Seven new councillors were elected: Lloyd Kirkham, a supervisor with the City of Winnipeg; Gordon Duncan, a professional engineer and developer from La Salle, Manitoba; Wayne Smith, the chairman of the Edmonton Assembly Committee; Neil Weir, our veteran organizer from Sherwood Park; John Cummins, a teacher and fisherman from Delta, British Columbia; Lee Morrison, a rancher and mining engineer from Robsart, Saskatchewan; and Ted Krause, a retired businessman from Grande Prairie, Alberta. (Ted resigned for personal reasons shortly after his election, and was replaced by Marguerite Stack of Kelowna.) Diane Ablonczy, Gordon Shaw, Short Tompkins, and Elwin Hermanson won election for second terms.

Few people besides myself and a number of key staff had any idea how much our first executive council members had contributed to advancing the Reform movement in its early stages. While there will be many more executive councils and councillors for the Reform Party of Canada, there was only one "first council," and it had done its job amazingly well.

The original Reform Party constitution called for delegates to the first Assembly after a federal general election to vote on the question "Do you want a leadership Assembly to be called?" This question was voted on by secret ballot and answered in the negative, thus affirming me as leader of the party.

The overall theme of the Edmonton Assembly was "Leadership for Changing Times." Because the Reform Party was doing so well in Alberta, many of the local media commentators assumed our main thrust would now be to push into provincial politics and that this would be the subject of my main address to the assembly on the night of October 28. But when my turn came, I focused on the issue of leadership for a nation "divided against itself," and what a new party based in the West might contribute to the provision of such leadership.

I readily acknowledge that in the back of my mind when I prepared this address was Abraham Lincoln's famous "house divided" speech. This was the speech he had given to members of the newly created, regionally based Republican Party in 1858, a party born out of the political turmoil preceding the American Civil War. The American secession crisis is the one great historical example of a full-blown secession attempt by one part of a federation in the North American context, and I had studied it ever since the threat of a Quebec separation became a political reality in the 1960s. Although the economic and moral *causes* that lay behind the secession of the southern states were very different from those that lie behind the possible secession of Quebec from the Canadian confederation, there are lessons to be learned from the attempts that were made to prevent the secession of the southern states through judicial, constitutional, and political compromises in the twenty-five-year period preceding the American Civil War. And there are lessons to be learned from the American experience concerning the impact that a full-blown secession crisis can have on national political party structures.[2]

Before 1850, the two main federal political parties in the United States were the Democrats and the Whigs. But the forces that divided the country divided the national political parties as well. In 1860 the Democratic Party split into a northern and a southern section, each of which ran a candidate for president. It was the resulting split in the

2. Two references I have found particularly instructive on this subject are Carl Sandburg's multi-volume biography of Lincoln, in particular, *Abraham Lincoln: The Prairie Years* (New York: Dell Publishing Co. Inc., 1959) and Abraham Lincoln's *Speeches and Writings*, especially Volume One, 1832-1858 (New York: Literary Classics of the United States, Inc., 1989).

Democratic vote that made possible Lincoln's election as the first Republican president with less than 40 percent of the popular vote. The Whig Party, on the other hand, disintegrated. A number of smaller parties such as the Free Soil Party and the Nativist, or "Know Nothing," party, appeared on the scene in the 1850s.

Out of all this division and political confusion emerged a new party with the potential to displace the Whigs. Its name was the Republican Party, and it started as a "sectional party." In the beginning it had little or no support in the older parts of the country—the south and New England. But it found acceptance, and its first successful candidate for president, in the newer part of the country, namely the West (what would now be called the American Midwest).

It does not require too vivid an imagination to speculate that if Canada went through a full-blown secession crisis, we too could experience a division and disintegration of some of our national political party structures. For example, one could see the federal Liberal Party dividing in two, with the Quebec federal Liberals (those sympathizing with the aspirations of Quebec secessionists) going one way, and those outside Quebec going another under the leadership of someone like Clyde Wells. One could also see that the federal Progressive Conservative Party might disintegrate, its western base eroded by the Reform Party, its Quebec base eroded by the Bloc Québécois, and Ontario and Atlantic Canada abandoning the sinking ship.

If something like this were to happen, what newer party would most likely displace the most grievously injured of the two traditional parties? The two most likely candidates would be the federal New Democratic Party and (if we could develop fast enough into a serious contender) the Reform Party of Canada. And where do these two parties have their origins and roots? Not in Upper and Lower Canada, the older parts of Canada whose ancient antagonisms over French-English relations would be at the root of any secession crisis, but in the "newer" parts of the country, the West and the North.

This is not to say that the Reform Party aspires to be the Canadian equivalent of the Republican Party or that I am trying to pass myself off as a modern-day Lincoln. The only reason I had no qualms about borrowing the theme of Lincoln's "house divided" speech is that Lincoln himself had borrowed the phrase from another great Reformer, Jesus Christ, whose influence on my own life I have already acknowledged.

Under the heading of "Leadership for a House Divided," I therefore addressed the following words to the Edmonton Assembly:

Of all the troublesome issues which will face Canada in the next decade, I can think of none which are more in need of a blast of fresh air from the West than the issue of relations between Quebec and the rest of Canada.

It is now more than a quarter of a century since the Pearson administration committed Canada to governing itself as an equal partnership between the English and the French. It is now more than twenty years since the Trudeau administration declared the federal government rather than the Quebec government to be the primary guardian and promoter of the French fact in Canada. ...

Has this approach produced a more united, less divided, Canada? No, it has not. Has this approach produced a more contented Quebec? No, it has not! Has this approach reduced the use of Quebec separatism as a threat to wring more concessions out of the rest of Canada? No, it has not! Has this approach engendered in Quebec politicians an emotional as well as an economic commitment to Canada? No, it has not! Has this approach produced in Canadians a new sense of national identity, pride, and purpose sufficient to guide us into the 21st century? No, it has not!

Instead, what the Pearson-Trudeau-Mulroney approach to constitutional development has produced is a house divided against itself. And as a great reformer once said long ago, "a house divided against itself cannot stand."

Now if this is the unvarnished truth as we see it, then leadership demands that we rise to our feet in the federal political arena, and say at least three things on behalf of Western Canadians:

First, we do not want to live, nor do we want our children to live, in a house divided against itself, particularly one divided along racial and linguistic lines.

Second, we do not want nor do we intend to leave this house ourselves (even though we have spent most of our constitutional lives on the back porch). We will, however, insist that it cease to be divided.

Third, either all Canadians, including the people of Quebec, make a clear commitment to Canada as one nation, or Quebec and the rest of Canada should explore whether there exists a better but more separate relationship between the two. . . .

In making these statements, we must brace ourselves against the flood of misinterpretations which will be placed upon them.

It will be said, for example, that Reformers want to break up the country and that our constitutional position is motivated by ill-will towards Quebec. Let the record show that this is not the case.

Our preference is for a united Canada in which Quebec is prosperous and culturally secure. The loss of Quebec will diminish Canada. If, however, we continue to make unacceptable constitutional, economic, and linguistic concessions to Quebec at the expense of the rest of Canada, it is those concessions themselves which will tear the country apart and poison French-English relations beyond remedy.

If Canada is to be maintained as one undivided house, the government of Canada must ask the people of Quebec to commit to three foundational principles of confederation:

- That the demands and aspirations of all regions of the country are entitled to equal status in constitutional and political negotiations.
- That freedom of expression is fully accepted as the basis of any language policy.
- That every citizen is entitled to equality of treatment by governments, without regard to race, language, or culture.

If these principles are accepted, our goal of one united Canada is achievable. But if these principles of confederation are rejected by Quebec, if the house cannot be united on such a basis, then Quebec and the rest of Canada should openly examine the feasibility of establishing a better but more separate relationship between them, on equitable and mutually acceptable terms.

The next day the delegates strongly endorsed a resolution embodying these views. It was labelled the "Quebec Resolution" and had been prepared by Stephen Harper, Tam Deachman (a British Columbia Reformer), and me. Tam is a retired advertising man who has worked for several international agencies in Montreal, New York, and Vancouver. Tam was particularly helpful in establishing the "tone" of the Quebec Resolution, not too harsh on the one hand, but not too soft on the other.

The Quebec Resolution officially started the Reform Party down the road to representing the quest for a New Canada to replace the Old Canada, which had become a "house divided." It anticipated the collapse of the Meech Lake constitutional discussions, and thus gave us a seven-month jump on the traditional federal parties in developing constitutional alternatives.

In November and December I received numerous invitations from across the West to speak on the federal spending and taxation issue, and addressed Axe the Tax rallies in Alberta, British Columbia, and Saskatchewan. In March of the following year, our Manitoba Reformers organized their own anti-GST rally, which drew over a thousand people in Winnipeg to hear Deborah, Stan, and myself, and helped raise our profile in Manitoba.

By spring 1990 we also began to see growing signs of interest in the Reform option in Saskatchewan, where before we had received a fairly cool reception. At the outset, we had attracted very few people who were interested in protest for its own sake or who were motivated by single-issue concerns such as language or immigration. But through the efforts of people like Elwin Hermanson, we managed slowly to secure the support of a few key individuals here and there across the province until a fairly solid nucleus had been established. By the time our public profile began to rise, largely as a result of events and media attention outside the province, people in Saskatchewan began to take an interest and were impressed with the quality and balance of our local representatives.

In some other parts of the West, we had grown quickly by attracting many disaffected and single-issue people early on. But beyond a certain point, solid growth and expansion by attracting people from the political mainstream was not possible until after a considerable amount of "weeding out" had been done at the local level. This process involved considerable dissension in areas like the Lower Mainland in British Columbia, the city of Winnipeg, and some Alberta constituencies.

The varying types of response to the Reform Party across the West illustrate a cardinal principle governing political organization in western Canada (indeed all of Canada)—namely, the importance of recognizing distinctive regional reactions to proposals for political change and harnessing them to work for you rather than against you. For example, south-central Alberta is likely to be the first off the mark in energetically supporting a political protest or political innovation. Saskatchewan (and to some extent northern Alberta) is more likely to play the role of "the chamber of second thought," carefully evaluating proposals for change. Manitoba is literally the "keystone province." More than any other western province, Manitoba, especially Winnipeg, looks both ways (east and west) before crossing the political street.

Thus, predictably, it has been from Winnipeg that the Reform Party has received the message, "If you are just a regional rump party, based in Alberta and British Columbia, we are probably not interested. (Calgary and Vancouver are not that much closer to us than Toronto and Montreal.) If, however, you aspire to be a truly national party, based in the West but willing to cross the Canadian Shield, our reaction may be quite different."

And then there are "the six provinces of British Columbia." There are many political similarities between the prairies and the British Columbia interior (the Okanagan and the Caribou), the Peace River country, and parts of the Fraser Valley. But much of the Lower Mainland, Vancouver Island, and northwestern British Columbia are very different politically. British Columbia is the home of the "West Pole" (as distinct from the North Pole and the South Pole) and "polarization" is the distinguishing characteristic of its politics. British Columbia will either be indifferent to a political innovation ("Let's ignore it and go to the beach") or embrace it with a vengeance. I thus tend to think of British Columbia as the "make-or-break" province for Reform in the West. With its thirty-two federal seats (more than one-third of the federal seats west of the Manitoba-Ontario border), British Columbia can tip the political balance either in favour of fundamental change or in favour of maintaining the status quo. Thus, the main challenge to the Reform Party was to use the strengths of each region.

In the first half of 1990, the organizational efforts of the Reform Party of Canada received a substantial boost from an unexpected source. The party had considered launching a contest to identify the "Reformer of the Year"—the individual who did the most to increase membership sales and financial contributions during 1990. Upon consulting our constituency people, however, we found that the winner would be one Brian Mulroney of Ottawa.

Instead of respecting the will of Alberta voters and the request of the Alberta government that Stan Waters be appointed to the Senate immediately, the prime minister dragged his feet. And not one of those Alberta ministers or MPs "occupying unprecedented positions of power and influence in Ottawa," seemed able to convince him to act.

During January and February 1990, Stan and I toured Alberta to increase public support for his appointment to the Canadian Senate. Our theme was "democracy delayed is democracy denied." We carried petitions to the prime minister calling for Waters's immediate appointment, petitions to the Alberta Legislature calling for the rescinding of its resolution supporting Meech Lake, and a petition asking Parliament to withhold its support for the government's Goods and Services Tax and redirect the efforts of the government into effective control of federal spending.

Our "appoint Waters now" campaign drew even more people than the Senate election campaign meetings, despite the fact that it was conducted in the dead of winter. More than seven thousand people attended public meetings in thirty Alberta communities, from Fort McMurray in the north to Lethbridge and Pincher Creek in the south, and from Jasper in the west to Lloydminster in the east. They came to meet their new "senator in waiting" and to hear him talk about what the West meant by substantive Senate reform as compared with the pale and paltry version of Senate reform apparently envisioned by the Meech Lake gang. They also came to vent their frustration over the unwillingness of their MPs to register their constituents' opposition to the GST in the federal Parliament, and to listen to Stan talk about ways and means of reducing federal spending.

We read quotes from western Conservative MPs patting themselves on the back for having the "courage" to impose an unpopular tax. But we asked why this same courage could not have been demonstrated by making unpopular spending cuts instead. We quoted the finance minister as saying that "there was no more fat left to cut," and then Stan would read off lists of federal government expenditures that most taxpayers consider imprudent or unnecessary. This reading usually culminated in a quotation from Erik Nielsen's book on the federal government's efforts to finance a piano manufacturing plant in the Yukon Community of Cracker Creek.

At a breakfast meeting in St. Albert, my lawyer brother-in-law Phil Stuffco got up and said, "I want to fire my member of Parliament (Walter Van De Walle) for failing to represent me in the House of Commons. I want to send him a pink slip. Do you people have a pink slip for firing MPs?" This idea brought a roar of approval from the crowd. So the Reform Party produced a formal "Notice of Termination of Employment for Cause" which could be mailed postage-free to your MP. It included a number of boxes that you could check off to indicate the reasons for dismissal—support of Meech Lake, support of GST, failure to respect the Alberta Senate Election results, and "Other." There was also a tear-off coupon that you could mail to the Reform Party, advising us that you had just sent a pink slip to your MP and wanted to add your name to our mailing list because you would be looking for a replacement at the next election. More than sixty thousand of those pink slips were eventually distributed, thousands at the Calgary Stampede and local rodeos all over Alberta, and many of the tear-off coupons were returned to us.

By May 1990, the head office move was completed. Brenda Nelson, who had a background in administration and finance in the oil industry and with the Alberta Special Waste Management Corporation, became our new chief administrator. Ron Wood, a Calgary radio man who was born in Ontario, educated in Calgary, and worked for many years in media relations and public relations in Ottawa, joined us as our communications director. Ken Warenko, who had managed policy chief Stephen Harper's 1988 campaign in Calgary West as well as organizing city-wide meetings and publicity, assumed responsibility for coordinating party policy development.

Lloyd Mackey, a journalist, publisher, and president of DoMac Publications Ltd. based in Vancouver, was appointed the new editor of *The Reformer,* which by now had become a major undertaking, with press runs of several hundred thousand copies for some editions, and a network of supplier and staff connections across the west. Editing and copy production was now coordinated out of Vancouver, the paper was printed in St. Albert, labelling and primary distribution was handled from Edmonton, and constituency associations were becoming increasingly involved in secondary distribution.

Once every eight weeks, Donna Larson and I, with help from Diane Ablonczy and Cliff Fryers, produced a long, newsy fundraising and information letter for distribution to our entire membership. These letters were vitally important to keep our members informed as the party expanded, and as a means of soliciting feedback. Almost 80 percent of our revenue was also generated by these letters.

Throughout 1990, the members of our executive council dedicated themselves to constituency development and ensuring that the Reform Party had properly functioning constituency associations at the grassroots level to conduct membership and fundraising drives, and to service our own membership once people became committed to the party. This included writing a constituency development manual and organizing a workshop program, and with the help of local coordinators, putting on constituency development seminars across the west. Reform Clubs were organized at the University of Calgary and the University of Alberta in Edmonton. Soon there was similar activity on other campuses across the West.

At the community and constituency level, many of our members were developing innovative means of creating and sustaining interest and support for the party. In Calgary, a small group led by Jack Mackenzie and Daphne Pirie began to organize what they called "lunches for the curious." The organizers all had a background in the oil business, and they applied the same drive and enthusiasm to organizing support for Reform that they had used in building their respective companies from scratch.

The lunches were usually held at the Palliser Hotel or Glencoe Club in Calgary. They were especially designed to encourage uncommitted people—professionals, businesspeople, youth, members of special-interest groups—to find out what the Reform Party was all about. Tables of eight were sponsored or pre-sold. The lunches began at noon, key party people were introduced, I said a few words, there was time for questions, literature was distributed, and it would all be over by 1:30. Some of these luncheons were attended by more than three hundred people, and one held during the Liberal leadership convention in Calgary in June attracted more curious Liberals than some of the leadership events.

In Vancouver, Reformers in the federal constituency of Quadra (John Turner's riding, where we were hoping for a by-election) put on a fundraising dinner that drew people from across the city and raised $30,000. Stan and Deborah gave inspirational accounts of their electoral successes, and I spoke on the theme that "something old is dying in Canada, and something new is being born." But the highlight was an auction which contributed considerably to the election war chest in Quadra. This was a few weeks after it had been announced that the federal government had paid $1.1 million for a painting consisting of three broad stripes on a piece of canvas and named "Voice of Fire." Not to be outdone, the Quadra Reformers produced a facsimile of this painting called "Voice of Waters," signed by none other than our Senator-elect.

The auctioneer, Fred Cavanagh, a Vancouver businessman who had been with us from the very beginning, soberly explained how the artist whose name appeared on this magnificent painting had begun his artistic career as a humble soldier painting camouflage designs on tanks. Gradually he had perfected his technique and raised his sights until he had produced this masterpiece. Fred also explained that while the federal government had determined that paintings of this type were worth more than a million dollars, he was prepared to allow the bidding to begin at a mere $200,000.

Buoyed by his success at auctioning off "Voice of Waters" (it sold to a generous supporter for $500), Fred went on to auction a donated gourmet dinner for two aboard a luxury cabin cruiser. This had been arranged by the hard-working president of our Capilano-Howe Sound Association, Darrell Frith, and his wife Kris. The TV lights were shining in Fred's eyes so he couldn't see very well who was actually doing the bidding. This didn't bother him, however, as he had spotters circulating in the crowd to identify the bidders, and his smile grew broader and broader as someone kept raising the bid until it was over $1,000.

I heard someone at the head table whisper, "Isn't that your wife, Fred, that's raising the ante?" but Fred was flying too high to hear. He came back to earth in a hurry, however, when a spotter ushered Sylvia Cavanagh to the front to claim her gourmet dinner for two.

Any technique to raise membership, money, and support that worked was written up in *The Reformer* or disseminated via the constituency development workshops or the party grapevine. Well-intended efforts to raise membership, money, and support that didn't work were also passed along, so that others could avoid making the same mistakes. In this way, well-endowed ridings helped others that were struggling.

The Edmonton Assembly had given the new executive council a clear mandate to explore all aspects of the eastern expansion issue through the establishment of a permanent committee. The committee's initial membership consisted of party vice-chairman Gordon Shaw, George Carter of Halifax, policy chief Stephen Harper, Bob Matheson of Edmonton, Jim Purdie of Calgary, and me.

Our job was to look for opportunities and assess the dangers of expansion east of the Manitoba-Ontario border, and investigate the possibility of expansion of the party's interests into those regions, with a minimum investment of human and financial resources from the western base. We developed informational materials, analyzed the most promising regions, identified likely individuals to assist in local organizational efforts, and organized an exploratory tour for me to Ontario and Atlantic Canada in March 1990. On this initial trip I visited Thunder Bay, Sudbury, Kleinburg, Richmond Hill, Toronto, London, Cambridge, Kitchener, Belleville, and Ottawa. Then I went on to Halifax and Fredericton to meet some people who had shown some initial interest in the relevance of the Reform option to Atlantic Canada.

Because the Reform Party was not yet organized in Ontario, most of my meetings there followed invitations from service clubs or university classes that had expressed curiosity concerning this new political phenomenon from the West. It was not surprising that many of the service club invitations came from northern and western Ontario, where regional alienation was as strong as in the West. What was somewhat surprising was that about one-third of the invitations came from universities (usually journalism, political science, or law classes). In the West, inquiries and invitations to speak had been slow in coming from these sources.

At Thunder Bay, Ron Wood and I were joined by Stephen Harper. We were also met by a small group of media people, including a reporter from the *Toronto Star.* They were there because my trip to Ontario coincided with the controversy aroused when several northern and western Ontario municipalities passed "English-only" resolutions. It was assumed, particularly by the Toronto media, that I was going to exploit anti-French sentiment, and there was some obvious disappointment when this did not prove to be part of my talk at all.

In Thunder Bay I addressed the Rotary Club and received a warm reception. When I made some introductory remark about "being glad to be in central Canada," a man sitting at one of the front tables interrupted to say, "You aren't in central Canada, boy, you're in western Ontario." Regionalism was obviously alive and well in Thunder Bay!

While the northern Ontario media (local papers, radio stations, and TV stations) had a number of questions about the language issue, their questions covered a wide range of topics, from the economy to the constitution. Later, in Toronto, at a meeting with some editorial people at the *Toronto Star,* almost all the questions were about linguistic and cultural policy, based on the clear suspicion that these were the main focus of the Reform program and that our views were tinged by racism.

From Thunder Bay we went to Sudbury and a meeting at Laurentian University, then on to small meetings at Kleinburg and Richmond Hill. The next day I addressed Peter Desbarats's journalism class at the University of Western Ontario. From London we went to Cambridge for another service club speech, and then to Wilfrid Laurier University at Waterloo, where I addressed Professor John Redekop's political science class. John is a respected political scientist and a committed Christian of Mennonite background, whose views on how to handle the interface between faith and politics are very similar to my own. From Waterloo we returned to Toronto, where all our contacts, on this trip, were with media people.

After a meeting in Belleville, we moved on to Ottawa to attend a news conference with Deborah Grey, more media interviews, and a reception at a room in the West Block.

As a result of our meetings in Ontario, we became convinced that there was obvious political discontent, and that the concerns respecting the economy, federal spending, the constitutional drift, and the performance of Parliament, were very similar to those in the West. While there was significant interest in Reform, there were many misconceptions that would require hard work to correct.

We had assumed that the organizational pace and pattern in Ontario might be the same as in the West, and that we would need three meetings in a community before we could get more than one hundred people to a public gathering. This assumption was soon proved wrong, as the higher level of media coverage received by Reform in Ontario and the fact that many of the people we were attracting had previous political experience with the traditional parties greatly accelerated our organizational progress.

From Ottawa, Ron Wood and I travelled to Nova Scotia, where I addressed a Rotary meeting in Halifax, a public meeting in Truro, and a class of law students at Dalhousie University. Then it was on to Fredericton, New Brunswick, for media interviews and an address at the University of New Brunswick. One of my main objectives here was to make clear that the Reform Party of Canada was not connected to, and was quite different from, the Confederation of Regions (COR) Party, which at that time was attracting considerable attention at the provincial level in New Brunswick. I pointed out that the Reform Party was exclusively a federal party, whereas COR in New Brunswick was a provincial party. I also described our fair language policy, stressing the differences between our policy and COR's more strident call for English-only language legislation.[3]

At the University of New Brunswick I met Eric Kipping, a former cabinet minister in the Hatfield government, who one year later would make the long journey to the Reform Party assembly in Saskatoon as part of a delegation to present the view that the Reform Party should expand into Atlantic Canada.

Because both western Canada and Atlantic Canada are thinly populated resource-producing regions, many of the main planks of the Reform platform pertaining to regional fairness resonated well with our eastern audiences. The difficulty we encountered was a sense of political

---

3. In September 1991, the provincial COR party won eight seats in the New Brunswick provincial election, and finished second in eighteen others. As the official opposition in New Brunswick, this will provide COR with an opportunity to broaden itself beyond the language issue if it is so inclined. From the standpoint of the federal Reform Party of Canada, the fact that New Brunswick voters were willing to break old voting patterns and vote for something new augurs well for the future.

depression, related in part to the depressing economic circumstances of Atlantic Canada. People would say to us: "Of course there is regional imbalance. Atlantic Canada has suffered from it far longer than the West. And of course 'the system' should be changed. But what can we do about it? We have limited resources and only thirty-two seats in the Parliament. Even if we gave them all to you, it wouldn't be enough to make any real difference. The big provinces and the big parties make the rules of the political game. Aren't we better to play along, and get what we can, rather than to buck the system?"

I stressed that the recipients of large federal-provincial transfer payments also had a vested interest in bringing federal spending under control, because the ability of the federal government to make such transfers would be impaired if the debt and its interest payments continued to rise at the current rate. I also maintained that the regional development programs of the twenty-first century would be based more and more on exploiting the regional benefits of greater north-south trade, and less and less on east-west transfer payments originating from Ottawa.

The only significant change that I made in my "appeal for Reform" when addressing Atlantic Canada audiences, was in my concluding remarks. I would usually end by saying that all over the world—China, eastern Europe, even the Soviet Union—people in far more depressing circumstances than exist anywhere in Canada are demanding systemic change. And where people want to change the system, they are turning in significant numbers, not to traditional parties (which are part of the system they want to change) but to so-called "reform movements." Here in Canada, if we examine our own history and are prepared to learn from it, we too have a reform tradition upon which we can draw. "In your part of the country (and here is where I would tailor my pitch to the people of the region I was addressing) there once were 'Reform Parties'—the Reform Party of Nova Scotia, for example. These were the parties that brought about the change from authoritarian, top-down, colonial government to more representative and responsible government in most of the old colonies. So when I ask you, 'Should we revive the reform tradition and harness it to the task of getting Canada's constitutional, fiscal, and parliamentary houses in order?' I am not asking you to support some transient political novelty from the West. I am asking you to revive and harness to the task of systemic change one of the oldest and best of your own political traditions." As Ron Wood and I got on our plane for the long flight to Calgary, I couldn't help wondering what Joseph Howe would have thought about the Reform Party of Canada.

CHAPTER THIRTEEN

The Eventful Summer of 1990

As the federal government continued to ignore the results of the Alberta Senate election, despite pleas for action from the Alberta government, and as Albertans became more uneasy about Premier Getty's continued support of the Meech Lake Accord, the pressure increased for the Reform Party to get involved in Alberta provincial politics. This pressure came not so much from party members as from angry citizens and commentators outside the party. It was clear, however, that we had to respond to it, and the Edmonton Assembly had proposed a mechanism for doing so.

An Angus Reid poll commissioned by the *Calgary Herald* in March 1990 reported that if the federal Reform Party entered provincial politics in Alberta, it could count on support from 43 percent of decided voters, as compared with 20 percent for the provincial Liberals, 19 percent for the New Democrats (the official opposition), and 18 percent for the ruling Progressive Conservatives.

The apparent willingness of Albertans to replace the governing provincial party (which had been in power nineteen years) with a completely new party, which had never contested a provincial election, might strike some observers as unusual. But for anyone familiar with the historic pattern of Alberta provincial politics, such a development was quite believable. Ever since it became a province in 1905, Alberta's provincial politics have exhibited a distinctive pattern of long periods of one-party government with the periodic replacement of the governing party, not by its traditional opposition, but by a new party. Also, unlike the case in provinces with a stable two-party system, no governing party in Alberta has ever regained office once it has been defeated.

Professor Maurice Pinard of McGill University has studied the phenomenon of Alberta provincial politics extensively and suggests an explanation for this pattern.[1] During long periods of one-party government, the traditional opposition parties gradually come to be seen as "losers," rather than as constructive alternatives to the government. Thus when the voters eventually tire of the governing party, they tend to pass over the traditional opposition in favour of a new party offering what appears to be a fresher and more vigorous alternative.

By 1990, the Progressive Conservatives had governed Alberta for almost twenty years. Many signs apart from the public opinion polls indicated that Albertans might be getting ready to do their periodic house cleaning at the Legislature. Despite all the dissatisfaction with the governing party, the more traditional opposition parties (the Liberals and NDP) were scarcely any more popular. If the historic pattern held, there was a strong probability that the provincial Conservatives would be replaced by a new group.

In 1990, Alberta was the only western province in which opinion polls indicated substantial public interest in a provincial Reform option. The executive council of the federal party therefore established a task force to examine provincial involvement in Alberta. It promised to make the results available to all Reform members and constituency associations across the West, and, based on their reactions, to decide whether similar task forces should be set up for the other western provinces.

The Alberta Task Force on the Reform of Provincial Politics was chaired by Marshall Copithorne, the Cochrane rancher. Marshall was close enough to the voting public to know that there really was a demand for some kind of reform at the provincial level in Alberta. He also had a long association with both the federal and the provincial Conservatives. If his task force concluded that the provincial Conservatives were finished, and the options were either to replace them with a new party or to turn the province over to the Liberals or NDP, this would carry considerable weight with many Conservatives as well as Reformers.

The Task Force was to find answers to three questions and to consult as many Albertans as possible (not just Reformers) in arriving at its conclusions.

The first question was: "What are the prospects that the Alberta Progressive Conservative Party will be able to make the changes necessary to enable it to gain the confidence of Alberta voters before the next

---

1. Maurice Pinard, *The Rise of a Third Party: A Study in Crisis Politics* (Montreal: McGill-Queen's University Press, 1975).

provincial election?" In particular, how likely was it to withdraw its support of the Meech Lake Accord, balance the provincial budget, balance its economic diversification efforts with more sensitivity toward the environment, provide more value per dollar spent on health, education, and social services, and become more sensitive to the wishes of Alberta voters?

The second was: "What are the prospects for the emergence of a new provincial party to provide the changes desired by Albertans?" In particular, could a new party assemble the workers, volunteers, campaign managers, candidates, and finances necessary to fight a provincial election, win the support of Alberta voters, and find someone capable of leading a new provincial party and government? (With respect to the leadership question, I had made it clear that it was my intention to run as a candidate for the Reform Party of Canada in the next federal election, which would likely precede the next Alberta provincial election, and therefore should not be considered a potential candidate for the leadership of any provincial party.)

The third question was: "Should the Reform Party of Canada (a) encourage and support efforts to renew from within any one of the present provincial parties in Alberta? and, if yes, which party? (b) continue to focus on organizing for the next federal election and defer any decision to enter provincial politics until a later date? (c) enter provincial politics now?"

The task force held eleven town hall meetings across the province to discuss these questions with interested Albertans. Letters were also written to all the provincial Progressive Conservative constituency associations soliciting input (only a few responded). The work of the task force was reported in the media and over two hundred written submissions were received from various individuals and groups.

The work of the Alberta Task Force on the Reform of Provincial Politics was carried out during the months of March, April, and May 1990 while the Alberta government was preparing for its participation in the final round of negotiations on the Meech Lake Accord. We had hoped that Progressive Conservative members of the legislature might persuade the government to rethink its position on Meech Lake in light of the fact that Reformers who opposed Meech were the preferred choice of 43 percent of the committed voters to run the provincial government.

At the end of May the task force submitted its report, along with statistics on responses to the three key questions raised at the meetings. It concluded that "Albertans have lost confidence in the ruling Progressive Conservative party, and do not feel that that party is capable of regaining their confidence." It went on to say, "There is a political void in the province of Alberta at the present time into which a reasonably responsive new provincial party could step and receive considerable support. There is a good chance of securing a good leader for such a party, and there is a fair chance of it obtaining necessary financing and personnel."

The key recommendations of the task force's report were "that the Reform Party of Canada should not enter provincial politics at this time; that it should continue to pursue its federal aims and objectives, focus on organizing for the next federal election, and defer any decision to enter provincial politics until a later date; and that any decision to enter provincial politics in Alberta or any other province should be made by delegates to a General Assembly of the Reform Party of Canada."

In a nutshell, therefore, the recommended position on provincial involvement in Alberta was "defer the decision but keep the door open." The party's executive council made the task force report public in early June so as to keep pressure on the provincial Conservatives to change their position on Meech.

From 1989 on I had made it a practice to advise the respective offices of the western premiers when the Reform Party was conducting extensive meetings or campaigns in their jurisdictions, and to offer to share any observations or conclusions that might be of interest, particularly when we were talking with voters on constitutional themes. The Reform Party wanted to be in the position of being able to work with any provincial government, regardless of party, to advance constitutional positions that we shared.

I thus had several useful encounters with Clayton Manness, Manitoba's finance minister, and other Manitoba cabinet ministers (the premier himself being unavailable), one discussion with Grant Devine, and several meetings with Bill Vander Zalm. Of all the western premiers, Vander Zalm appeared to be the most genuinely interested in what we were attempting to do. Unlike the others, his provincial party was not directly linked to any federal political party and he could thus afford to associate more openly with Reform positions.

My relations with Don Getty were on a somewhat different footing. The Reform Party had so many members who were Conservatives provincially and Reformers federally that each party usually had a fairly good idea of what the other was doing at any given time. I had also known

Don Getty longer than the other premiers and had a better grasp of many of the provincial issues with which he was wrestling, although our meeting at the conclusion of the Alberta Senate election was the first time I had met him since becoming leader of the Reform Party.

In June 1990 the Meech Lake Accord collapsed. An understanding of why public support for Meech Lake steadily declined in western Canada is essential to understanding that collapse and the lessons to be learned from it. If the same mistakes made over Meech Lake are made in the next round of constitutional negotiations, it will suffer the same fate, with even more serious consequences for the future of Canada.

During the period from April 30, 1987, when Canada's prime minister and ten premiers first unveiled the draft accord, to June 23, 1990, when it collapsed because of the unwillingness of the Manitoba legislature to pass a resolution approving it, no organized political group conducted more discussions with voters in western Canada on the subject of the Canadian constitution than the Reform Party of Canada.

Our founding assemblies in Vancouver and Winnipeg, as well as our 1988 policy assembly in Calgary and the 1989 Edmonton assembly, all occurred within the Meech Lake time frame, and constitutional reform was high on the agendas of those meetings. We were also active participants in hundreds of meetings and discussions from 1987 to 1990 to discuss the type of constitutional reform preferred by western Canadians, namely Triple-E Senate reform. Constitutional discussions with voters were an integral part of our federal election campaign in 1988, our Beaver River by-election campaign in 1989, our Alberta Senate election campaign in 1989, and our Appoint Waters Now campaign in 1990. We distributed more than eighty thousand copies of the text of the Meech Lake accord to interested Canadians, mainly Reformers, in 1989 alone.

Based on our contacts with western Canadians, we found that opinion leaders at the grassroots level in western Canada were both willing and able to understand the accord, despite constant assertions by commentators that unwillingness or inability to understand was at the root of western Canadian opposition to the accord. They understood that in 1981, the government of Quebec under Premier René Lévesque refused to participate in any further federal-provincial conferences on the constitution unless Quebec was given special rights and assurances. They understood that in 1986 Premier Robert Bourassa announced that Quebec would resume a full role in the constitutional councils of Canada if five Quebec demands were met—namely, recognition as a distinct society, the right to opt out of national programs and to be compensated for them, a greater role in immigration regulation, a role in Supreme Court appointments, and a veto on future constitutional amendments. They understood that on April 30, 1987, the prime minister and the ten premiers met in private at Meech Lake, and, without consulting their legislatures or electors, drafted an agreement to meet Quebec's five demands and provide for a second round of discussions on further constitutional changes, including Senate reform. They understood that in order to get other premiers to accede to Quebec's demands, the prime minister had to grant similar rights to the other provinces, including the right to veto future constitutional amendments. They further understood that the accord was then translated into a constitutional amendment and unanimously approved by the first ministers on June 2-3, 1987, in Ottawa, and that the premiers all agreed to return home and push a Meech Lake resolution through their legislatures without amendment as quickly as possible.

Based on this understanding, we found that the majority of western Canadians opposed the accord, and the more they found out about it, the less they liked it. What bothered them more than anything else was the top-down, closed-door approach to constitution making that Meech Lake represented. The process discredited those who participated in it, as well as the content of the accord.

Second, westerners objected to the rigid amending formula. If every province was given the right to veto substantive amendments, the chances of securing a constitutional amendment to reform the Senate, for example, would be drastically reduced.

Third, westerners objected to Meech's token references to Senate reform and the lack of substantive assurances that real progress would be made in this area in any second round of constitutional negotiations. It had taken the federal Conservative government a very short time to translate Quebec's five constitutional demands into a full-blown constitutional amendment. And yet, despite the presence in cabinet and caucus of western MPs whose constituents had been demanding a Triple-E Senate since 1984, the federal government had no Triple-E amendment in preparation, and was even dragging its feet on appointing one directly elected senator.

Note that none of these three objections to the Meech Lake Accord raised by public audiences across western Canada from 1987 to 1990 refers to the province of Quebec. Those who characterize the rejection of Meech by western Canadians as a rejection of the province or the people of Quebec deceive themselves on this point, or deliberately engage in deceiving others. It is, however, true that the reaction of most western Canadian audiences I addressed to recognition of Quebec as a "distinct society" was this: "If by 'recognizing Quebec as a distinct society' you mean that the rest of Canada should acknowledge and take into account in public policy the historical and sociological distinctiveness of Quebec, we agree. But if by 'recognizing Quebec as a distinct society' you mean to confer upon Quebec constitutional rights and powers not enjoyed by other Canadians and provinces, we do not agree."

Behind these reactions to the distinct society clause was a fundamental question, not fully explored during the Meech Lake debate, which will be at the heart of any future attempt to rewrite the Canadian constitution: will we achieve constitutional unity by insisting upon the *equality* of all Canadians and provinces in the constitution and in federal law, or by guaranteeing *special status* to racial, linguistic, cultural, or other groups?

The chances of the distinct society clause being accepted in western Canada were further reduced by the justifiable unwillingness of the public to trust the utterances of the federal Conservatives or the Bourassa government on this subject. The public had the impression that a Conservative MP in Alberta would describe the distinct society clause as a recognition only of the sociological and historical reality of Quebec, while a Conservative MP in Quebec would define it as a virtual guarantee of all the powers and privileges Quebeckers felt were necessary to preserve their linguistic and cultural distinctiveness.

At the root of the rejection of Meech Lake in the West was *mistrust*—of the process, of the politicians involved, and of the words and phrases cobbled together by that process and those politicians.

At the same time, if you were a resident of Quebec and the only way you could judge the position of the people of British Columbia, Alberta, or Saskatchewan on the Meech Lake Accord was to read the official statements of the provincial premiers or Conservative MPs, you would have concluded that 90 percent of westerners agreed with its terms and conditions. And you would have been completely misled, unless you saw specific polls on the subject or went out as the Reform Party did and directly consulted thousands of westerners at the grassroots level.

The Meech Lake fiasco will not go down as a totally negative experience if Canadians learn some lessons from it, and apply these lessons to the future reform of the Canadian constitution. The first lesson, for all Canadians, is that closed-door, top-down approaches to constitution making do not provide the public input or debate necessary to achieve a constitutional consensus that will be supported by the people.

Politicians (including the prime minister) and commentators who blame the failure of Meech Lake on Clyde Wells, or Gary Filmon, or Elijah Harper, are missing the point. Premier Wells was able to take the position he did in opposition to Meech Lake and sustain it in the face of intense pressure, because what he was saying was supported by a huge constituency of Canadians from sea to sea. Meech Lake died on the floor of the Manitoba Legislature, not simply because one lone native MLA, Elijah Harper, exploited a technicality in the rules of that legislature, but because when Harper said "No," he was expressing the view of a majority of his own people (including natives in Quebec) and a majority of Manitobans who would have voted out of office any political leader who tried to force Meech through the legislature contrary to the wishes of that majority.

Even if the Meech Lake Accord had been approved exactly as Prime Minister Mulroney wished, I believe it would have come unravelled within two years, and that most of the provincial governments that approved Meech would have been replaced by governments prepared to repudiate it. As soon as Bourassa used his veto to kill a Triple-E Senate amendment or began to use the distinct society clause to claim additional constitutional powers (as is done in the Allaire Report) or as soon as any other premier used his veto to make any "second round" of constitutional negotiations meaningless, the whole deal would have come undone.

On May 28, I summarized these thoughts in a memorandum to Premiers Filmon, Wells, and McKenna (who were still resisting Meech), with copies to Vander Zalm, Getty, and Devine (who had already capitulated), and Carstairs and Doer (the Liberal and NDP leaders in Manitoba whose views could still influence the decision of the Manitoba Legislature). My concluding paragraph was: "Federal and provincial politicians who support Meech Lake will go down in history as the discredited defenders of a dying constitutional order. Federal and provincial politicians who reject Meech, and seize the positive possibilities beyond it, will go down in history as the fathers of the new Confederation. Please stand firm in your resolve to be numbered among the latter rather than the former. The people of Canada are behind you."

The second lesson to be learned from the collapse of the Meech Lake Accord is that the results of constitutional negotiations are only as trustworthy as the people who negotiate them. Brian Mulroney implied to the people of Quebec that having the signatures of ten premiers on the draft Meech Lake Accord meant there was genuine and widespread public support for the terms and conditions of the accord outside Quebec. This was untrue, certainly with respect to western Canada.

How does a prime minister get provincial governments to support constitutional proposals repugnant to their own electors? The dark side of the Deal Model suggests all kinds of possibilities. Win over a Vander Zalm by telling him that he can use the Meech Lake veto to shoot down any constitutional amendment that might strengthen native land claims in British Columbia. Woo an Alberta premier by hollow promises of Senate reform and by offering federal aid for energy megaprojects. Saskatchewan? A piece of cake. Just make clear to Devine that his signature is expected in return for a generous and timely support payment for Saskatchewan farmers. How about Manitoba, a have-not province? Just draw a not-so-subtle connection between Meech Lake and transfer payments. Got a new premier in New Brunswick who needs to be brought on side? Send Senator Murray to ask him whether he wants fish plants or frigate contracts. And if dollars and cents bribery and blackmail don't work, there's always emotional blackmail—"Pass Meech or you'll drive Quebec out." "Support Meech or you'll be personally responsible for breaking up Canada." Then go back to the people of Quebec and tell them that by hard work and statesmanlike persuasion you have won the principled support of people in the rest of Canada for Quebec's constitutional demands.

After Meech collapsed, did the Mulroney and Bourassa governments accept the lion's share of the responsibility for its collapse? Of course not. Instead they put the blame on anyone and everyone else (Wells, Filmon, Harper). In particular, they told everyone who would listen that the rejection of the Meech Lake Accord, especially by western Canadians, was a rejection of the people and province of Quebec.

The Reform Party of Canada, on behalf of western Canadians at least, wants to communicate this message to the people of Quebec: "Those politicians and commentators who told you that Meech Lake and Bourassa's five demands had been successfully presented and sold to the rest of Canada lied to you, in some cases deliberately, in other cases because they had managed to deceive themselves. And anyone who tells you that the rejection of Meech is a rejection of the people and province of Quebec is lying to you as well."

Surely, then, when these same politicians come back to us with another constitutional package—Son of Meech, Mega Meech, Joe Clark's "save Canada" package—we will all remember to ask whether this new package represents the real constitutional interests and positions of Canadians in all parts of the country, assembled and refined through a democratic, bottom-up constitution-making process. Or has it, too, been cobbled together by arm-twisting and backroom deals with special interests whose support for special status and powers for Quebec does not reflect public support for that concept, but has been secured by promises of special status and powers for themselves?

This time if Mulroney, Clark, Bourassa, and others claim to speak for Quebec, or federalism, or the people of Canada, surely we will make independent inquiries to see if this is indeed the case, and insist that our media eyes and ears do likewise. New constitutional relations among the people of Canada must be founded upon legitimate interests truly represented; they cannot be founded upon lies and misconceptions, least of all the ones that claimed that the rejection of Mulroney and Bourassa's Meech Lake Accord was a rejection of Quebec.

Although the Reform Party of Canada was the only federal political party represented in the House of Commons that opposed the Meech Lake Accord, ironically we were to benefit in a peculiar way from one of its minor provisions. On June 11, 1990, 238 days after the Alberta Senate election and twelve days before the accord collapsed, the prime minister's office called the Waters home in Calgary looking for Stan.

Barbara Waters told them that Stan was in the hands of the Reform Air Force (namely, Short Tompkins and his Cessna 185) flying around northern Canada promoting Senate reform and that his exact whereabouts were uncertain. The PMO persisted, however, and Stan was finally tracked down at the home of Tom Mickey in Whitehorse (Tom now represents Yukon on the Reform Party's executive council). There Stan received the news that his appointment to the Senate had just been recommended to the Governor General.

Waters's appointment was made, not as a concession to Reform or the electors of Alberta, but as a concession to Premier Getty during the intense constitutional discussions held in Ottawa during the first week of June. It was essential that the Alberta government's support for the Meech Lake Accord be maintained, as the federal government made a last-ditch effort to secure unanimous provincial approval of its constitutional package.

When Stan and I finally connected by phone to discuss the good news, we agreed that he had better get to Ottawa and be sworn in as soon as possible, before Meech collapsed and the federal government's enthusiasm for even token Senate reform evaporated.

So it was that on June 19, 1990, Stan and members of his family, along with Deborah Grey, Stephen Harper, myself, and members of the media, assembled in the office of the Clerk of the Senate in Ottawa to witness the swearing in of Canada's first democratically elected Senator, and a doubling of the size of the Reform Party's parliamentary caucus.

As Stan's family, Deborah, and I watched from the gallery, Stan was duly escorted into the Senate Chamber. He was given a seat about as far away from the Speaker as it was possible to be and still be in the room. No matter, at least Stan was there and would soon be seen and heard. As I watched Stan enter, with Alberta's Senator Joyce Fairbairn on one side and Newfoundland's Senator William Doody on the other, someone near me murmured, "All very dignified, but it looks more to me like the chickens escorting the fox into the hen house."

Before leaving Ottawa for the West, I gave Stan a copy of an extract from Will Durant's *Story of Civilization* on the "signature statement" that Cato the Elder, the great Roman soldier and senator, had always used to close his speeches. In those days, the great enemy of the Roman Republic was Carthage. So Cato, no matter what subject he happened to be discussing, would always pause at the end of his remarks and say, "Ceterum censeo delendam esse Carthaginem" ("Besides, I think that Carthage must be destroyed").

When Stan got his first opportunity to speak in the Canadian Senate on October 4 (the Senate had adjourned for the summer shortly after Stan's appointment), it was during the great row over efforts by the Liberal senators to defeat the GST legislation. Stan chastised the Senate over its disgraceful and unparliamentary performance. Then he used what was to become his own personal "signature statement." He told the story of Cato and added, "I will end all my speeches with this statement: 'The Senate must be reformed!'"

When the Meech Lake Accord finally collapsed, a lot of post-Meech hysteria was exhibited, not only by the politicians, but also by many members of the national media who were in Calgary to cover the Liberal leadership convention that brought in Jean Chrétien. It was in response to the hysteria that I composed one final memorandum to the western premiers on the subject of Meech Lake. It contained the Reform Party's assessment of the reasons why Meech failed, in particular our views on the unacceptability of the process, and proposed that the premiers commit themselves to holding regional constitutional conventions as the first step in any future round of constitution making.

I attached for their consideration a 1981 Canada West Foundation publication entitled *Citizens and Constitutions*. Besides its excellent description of the constitutional convention approach, it contained a quotation from Joe Clark strongly endorsing this approach: "... the differences among governments are legitimate, and sometimes, deep. The challenge now is to find a forum where reasonable Canadians will be free to express those differences, understand them, and then resolve them. Conferences of First Ministers are unlikely to resolve the more important differences because, by definition, those conferences are meetings of heads of government who all have vested interests to protect. They bargain at the margins, rather than reaching to the root of reform." Joe had made this statement in 1980 when he was in opposition and busy condemning the Liberals for their high-handed, top-down approach to constitutional change.

I concluded this memorandum to the premiers by paraphrasing some observations made by the American poet and historian Carl Sandburg about the three types of people who emerged on the United States national stage in the decade preceding their nineteenth-century constitutional crisis. First of all, there were the "hysterical" people—would-be leaders who prophesied that the end of the nation was coming and who predicted the most dire consequences if their particular constitutional proposals were not adopted. Then there were those who advocated "grand schemes" for solving the constitutional crisis. Unfortunately, the political confusion and uncertainty of the times made it impossible to get any public consensus for "grand schemes." And then there were those "who sought to link the tangled past to the uncertain future by proposing only that which was workable in the immediate future."

I closed by saying that the proposals outlined in my memorandum, including the proposal for regional constitutional conventions, were not a hysterical reaction to an impending constitutional crisis, nor did they purport to be a "grand scheme" to solve all of Canada's constitutional problems. "They are simply common sense proposals to do 'that which is workable in the immediate present,' and as such I hope that they will commend themselves to you."

By the summer of 1990, membership in the Reform Party of Canada had increased to almost 44,000: 24,000 in Alberta, 14,000 in British Columbia, 5,000 in Saskatchewan/Manitoba, and 1,000 in other parts of Canada. The size of the Alberta membership was a bit misleading. The Beaver River by-election and the Alberta Senate election had kept Reform in the public eye, stimulating interest and membership sales. If we had had two election campaigns in British Columbia or Saskatchewan/Manitoba during the same period, our membership would have been better balanced across the West.

At one point it looked as if we might have precisely that opportunity in British Columbia. A federal by-election was expected in Vancouver Quadra if and when John Turner resigned, and Premier Vander Zalm had introduced a Senate election bill to his legislature. With these possibilities in mind, Sandra and I rented a house in south Vancouver for July and August with our two boys (the two oldest girls had gone to New Zealand and Australia, and the youngest was in Europe). I wanted to visit as many of the British Columbia ridings as possible and to confer with our members and constituency associations on several important issues (provincial involvement, a British Columbia Senate election, expansion). There is no more beautiful place in Canada to spend a summer than British Columbia, and I also hoped to have some holiday time with my family.

It was a highly productive summer. I managed to visit thirty of British Columbia's thirty-two federal ridings, and our British Columbia Reformers organized more than forty-five public meetings, town hall sessions, "lunches for the curious," and informal barbecues, attended by more than eight thousand people. In addition, they arranged thirty sessions with constituency executives and key individuals, and more than a hundred media interviews. The Todd family, who had generously supported the Reform movement in Vancouver since its inception, provided office support for our British Columbia activities. (Ian Todd later became our full-time organizer in British Columbia.)

At the meetings in British Columbia, I encountered an increasing number of questions on foreign policy and aboriginal policy. These were prompted by current interest in the attempts of the Baltic States to secede from the USSR, the decision of the federal cabinet to send Canadian forces to the Persian Gulf on August 10, and the July-to-September confrontation between the Mohawks and the Quebec provincial police (and later, the Canadian military) at Oka in Quebec.

An invitation to speak to the foreign consular corps in Vancouver in May had provided an opportunity to express the Reform view that Canadian foreign policy should be based on the principles of representativeness, modesty, consistency, and flexibility. Since the Reform Party of Canada is a populist, democratic political movement dedicated to the peaceful advocacy of fundamental reforms to Canada's system of government, it is highly appropriate that we support democratic reform movements and reform-minded political leadership in other parts of the world such as China, South Africa, Eastern Europe, and the Soviet Union.

I outlined four practical ways in which Canada could express its support of democratic reform movements abroad: (1) support the pro-democracy movement in China by making continued expansion of Canada's economic relations with that country conditional upon an end to government persecution of the pro-democracy movement; (2) recognize the declarations of independence by the Baltic States, subject to declarations by such states of their willingness to negotiate mutually advantageous terms and conditions of separation with the Soviet Union; (3) encourage the Canadian volunteer and business sectors to respond more positively to requests from the Baltic States and other eastern European countries for humanitarian aid and new trade and economic relations; (4) define and communicate to South African black leaders and the South African government a step-by-step plan for lifting Canadian economic sanctions against South Africa as progress was made toward implementing democratic reforms and eliminating apartheid.

Recognizing that in eastern Europe (as in the Baltic States) national democratic reform movements were in tension with the reform-minded government of Mikhail Gorbachev, and that in South Africa the black reform movement was in tension with the reform-minded government of Frederik de Klerk, I suggested that Canadian foreign policy should focus on "identifying with both sides" rather than "choosing sides." The time for choosing sides would come if those reform-minded governments were replaced with reactionary governments determined to suppress the democratic reform movements.

Later in the summer, after Iraq's August 1 invasion of Kuwait, the federal cabinet, with Parliament recessed, decided to send Canadian forces to the Persian Gulf. They were to be part of the multinational military presence being organized to enforce the United Nations resolution calling for Iraq's withdrawal. Stan, Deborah, and I felt this decision should be supported, even though greater efforts could and should have been made to explain the circumstances and the reasons to the Canadian public. In our view the real choice in the Persian Gulf was not between war and peace, but between limited action now to deal with Iraqi aggression against Kuwait and full-scale action later to deal with an all-out Middle East war that might involve nuclear weapons.

The federal government's reaction to the international crisis in the Gulf underscored the need for Canada to get its constitutional, fiscal, and parliamentary houses in order. If a country is internally divided, if its finances are in such bad shape that the decision to send a few thousand personnel and two ships to the Persian Gulf strains its resources, and if its

Parliament cannot rise above partisan division and bickering even in the face of a Middle East war, obviously its national government is going to be less than effective in dealing with any major crisis or challenge, international or domestic.

Another issue that was constantly in the news as I was touring British Columbia was the confrontation between the Mohawks and the Canadian Armed Forces at Oka, Quebec. Numerous Indian bands in British Columbia had set up roadblocks, real or symbolic, in support of the Mohawks. We encountered several of these on our travels, and I was frequently questioned on the issue of aboriginal policy and native land claims at our public meetings.

My response to the Oka crisis and to the land claims issue in British Columbia (where no formal treaty framework exists and very few outstanding native land claims have been settled) was to categorize both as symptoms of a deeper problem, namely the unsatisfactory and deteriorating relationship between aboriginal peoples and the government of Canada. Until that relationship is fundamentally changed for the better, in our judgment there will be little progress in either resolving the land claims issue or improving the socio-economic status of aboriginal peoples. I suggested that if the constitutional aspirations of Quebec had the effect of "cracking the Canadian constitution wide open," this could very well force a complete rewriting of the constitution and, in the process, open up the door for redefining the relationship between aboriginals and the Canadian government.

I had already written to several of the leaders of the Assembly of First Nations advocating a constitutional convention of aboriginal peoples to define that new relationship from their perspective. I hoped it would result in an expression of willingness on the part of aboriginal people to accept responsibility for their own welfare and development, coupled with a call to do away with the Department of Indian Affairs and transfer its responsibilities to democratic and accountable aboriginal governments and agencies. Establishing a new and less dependent relationship between aboriginals and the federal government should lead to a more expeditious settlement of outstanding land claims and a more rapid improvement in the socio-economic status of aboriginal peoples, two objectives which the Reform Party wholeheartedly supports.

Towards the end of the summer of 1990, rumours of a new constitutional initiative by the federal government made it imperative that the Reform Party stake out its own constitutional ground more explicitly so that our positions could not readily be co-opted or misrepresented by the federal Conservatives. Diane Ablonczy and the executive council of the party had agreed that the central theme of our next party assembly, scheduled for Saskatoon in April 1991, should be "Building the New Canada." And on August 24, at a lunch for the curious held at Vancouver's Bayshore Hotel, I gave the first of what would be many addresses, seeking to more clearly identify the characteristics of a New Canada that Canadians might support.

Over that six-month period I asked my audiences to think long and hard about "two Canadas"—an Old Canada that was dying, and a New Canada that was being born. I had thought long and hard myself on what phrase to use to describe the Reform Party's emerging vision of the future, and had finally settled on "New Canada" after consulting with Tam Deachman in Vancouver.

For a while I had used the phrase "Next Canada," but never felt completely comfortable with it. It seemed too shallow and trendy. I have a personal aversion to political slogans that are just that—empty slogans with no real meaning or substance behind them. In the 1960s, John Diefenbaker's "Vision of the North," suggested to him by an advertising man, was a great slogan. But the Conservative government's inability to give it real substance (other than through the Roads to Resources program and the Pine Point Railway) rendered it ineffective as a lasting source of inspiration or guidance to that generation of Canadians.

Deachman convinced me that "New Canada" was the right phrase to use, if in fact the Reform Party could give it meaning and substance drawn from the aspirations of Canadians themselves. This we were determined to do before our April assembly in Saskatoon.

In my speech at the Bayshore in Vancouver, I characterized Old Canada as a "nation divided against itself," whose federal government was almost $400 billion dollars in debt, and whose federal parliament failed to effectively represent the interests of the people who elected it. This Old Canada was dying, and there were two distinct ways that Canadians could react to its demise. On the one hand, we could become gloomily pessimistic, a state of mind for which many Canadians have a psychological propensity. We could dwell on Quebec's threatened departure, English-speaking Canada's lack of identity, the disintegration of confederation into provincial fragments, the eventual attraction of those fragments into the American orbit, and our complete inability to escape such a fate. On the other hand, we could view our circumstances with a cautious optimism conducive to action. Old Canada may be dying, but something new is being born. A "New Canada" is emerging and it is the task of forward-looking citizens and political leadership in the 1990s to give it shape and substance. This is the perspective of the Reform Party of Canada.

The key question to be answered by Canadians in the 1990s is therefore, "What should be the distinguishing characteristics of New Canada?" The Reform Party had been listening as best it could over the past three years—to the common sense of the common people and to expert advice—and what we thought we heard was something like this.

The New Canada should be a place where governments live within their means; where real jobs and real investment opportunities are provided by financially viable, environmentally sustainable, and internationally competitive businesses and industries; where social services are available for all who truly need them; where Parliament represents and responds to the wishes of those who elect it; and where the national government is dedicated to the proposition that all Canadians should be treated equally.

Translated into everyday language, this means that the New Canada should be a place where taxes and prices are lower not higher; where people have good jobs that provide enough income to support themselves and their families; where people can breathe clean air and drink clean water; where the special needs of the young, the old, the sick, and the poor are met by people who care; where every vote counts; where individuals are treated with respect regardless of race, language, or culture.

At the end of the summer of 1990, I was convinced that Reformers had more of substance to say on the goals toward which future constitutional changes should move the country, than spokespersons for the traditional parties. Our problem, however, would be how to get a large enough public hearing. Of the forty-five public Reform meetings held in British Columbia in the summer of 1990, which attracted a total of eight thousand people, only two were reported in the Vancouver dailies. Television coverage was also extremely spotty, and event oriented rather than substance oriented. While we continued to get extensive coverage from local media in smaller communities and specialized media in the larger centres, it would take a lifetime of community meetings, interest group contacts, and literature campaigns to communicate our emerging vision of a New Canada on a large enough scale to significantly influence the national scene. Obviously we were going to need some higher-profile events, like large rallies and our April Assembly, with extensive television coverage, to make the Reform vision of a New Canada a contender to win the minds and hearts of Canadians.

Unfortunately for our media profile, interest in a British Columbia Senate election was nipped in the bud on August 30, when Prime Minister Mulroney appointed Pat Carney to fill the British Columbia Senate vacancy. The British Columbia Senate election act was so worded that it became operational only if a Senate vacancy existed, so it could not be used to conduct a Senate election once the seat was filled.

A week later, I was in Toronto, at the invitation of publisher and businessman Conrad Black, who asked me to explain what the Reform Party was all about to a group of some fifty friends and associates whom he and financier Hal Jackman had invited to an informal dinner.

I knew something about Conrad Black, although I had not met him. I knew he was an outspoken supporter of free enterprise and free trade, and had read his article on the need for radical constitutional change in the September 1990 *Saturday Night* magazine. I had also read his extensive biography of Quebec Premier Maurice Duplessis, and knew that he had a depth of interest in history and political philosophy that was somewhat unusual in a businessman.

Before the dinner at the Toronto Club on September 5, I had a good chat with Black about his constitutional views. He hoped that Canada would remain united under new constitutional arrangements, which he had specified in his *Saturday Night* article. But if it did not, he also felt that there could be worse fates than for English-speaking Canada to end up in the American orbit.

I said that Reformers wanted a New Canada with a reformed constitution within which Quebec was a culturally secure and economically prosperous province. If Quebec chose to secede, on terms and conditions acceptable to Canada as well as Quebec, our view was that New Canada must be a viable national entity in its own right, and that this was possible if the political will to survive and prosper existed.

By then it was time for dinner, so we went and joined Hal Jackman and the others. I was seated at a table with Black, Jackman, Bill Thorsell (editor of the *Globe and Mail* whom I knew from his Edmonton days), George Eaton, G. Emmett Cardinal Carter, and three senior bank executives.

When the time came for me to be introduced, Black was straightforward. He said the polls indicated that the Reform Party was going to be a player with some influence (how much, no one knew) in the next federal Parliament. That Parliament would be making some crucial decisions affecting Canada's future. It was therefore important that his and Hal's dinner guests, as business and opinion leaders in Canada, be aware of what the Reform Party is and what it stands for, regardless of their personal political persuasions.

I then gave my basic talk, without much modification for this particular audience, on the Reform approach to getting Canada's fiscal and constitutional houses in order. I included the Reform position that Senate reform was essential to dealing with regional alienation, and that control of federal government spending meant drastic reductions in federal grants, hand-outs, and tax concessions to large corporations.

I asked exactly the same questions that I had asked scores of audiences in western Canada in much humbler surroundings. Who in the federal political arena would you trust to put consistent downward pressure on federal spending? Who in the current federal Parliament would you trust to ensure that the economic and constitutional interests of the rest of Canada are protected in any future constitutional negotiations with Quebec? And I received much the same response to these questions that I had received elsewhere—a shaking of heads.

A question period followed, and the concerns raised were very similar to those discussed at similar dinner meetings in the West. After the meal, I had the chance to talk to many of the guests, a few of whom I knew personally and many more who had served on corporate boards with my father.

I was pleased to see Stan Milner, president of Chieftain International Inc., from Edmonton, present. Stan was familiar with what the Reform Party was attempting to do in the West, and if any of our key supporters there were wondering whether I was saying the same things or something different in Toronto, I could suggest they call Stan and find out. I also talked with Anna Porter, whose insistence that I should write a book telling the Reform story more thoroughly eventually led to the writing of this book.

Upon my return to Calgary, I wrote thank-you notes to those who had attended the Toronto dinner, asking each one to comment on our vision of a New Canada, the prospects of selling the Triple-E Senate concept in Ontario, and the likelihood of the Reform Party receiving support in Ontario. This letter generated some useful feedback, advice, and even a few financial contributions. Based on my past associations with big business through my consulting practice, however, I was under no illusion whatsoever that the demand and initiative for any real expansion of the Reform Party of Canada into Ontario would come from the likes of Conrad Black, Hal Jackman, or their dinner guests. Senior business executives, with a few rare exceptions, are not in a position to identify openly at the outset with a populist, bottom-up political movement dedicated to "changing the system." Most are accountable to shareholders from a variety of political persuasions who would frown on such activity until the new movement has proven itself competent and successful.

More importantly, all large companies today are forced, whether they like it or not, into an increasingly intimate relationship with government—government the policy maker, government the customer, government the regulator, government the giver of grants and tax concessions, government the tax collector. Senior executives simply cannot afford, regardless of their personal political inclinations, to "get on the wrong side of the governing party" for long, nor can they risk identification with political innovations that may turn out badly. If a breakthrough were to occur in Ontario, it would occur, as it did in the West, through the efforts and support of ordinary Canadians and organizers who rarely dine at the Toronto Club.

CHAPTER FOURTEEN

Conflict and Consolidation

As I travelled across the country communicating the Reform Party's positions to Canadians, Deborah Grey and Stan Waters were raising our profile in Ottawa. Almost every month the Mulroney administration would do something to provide yet another illustration of the need for fundamental reform, and Deb and Stan were quick to seize on these opportunities. For example, when Brian Mulroney appointed eight new senators to help ram the GST through the upper house and the Senate degenerated into partisan chaos over the issue, the media pumped images of this soap opera into every living room in the country. "It's like a continuous commercial for Senate reform," Stan remarked. In his speeches and media interviews, he directed people to look hard at this spectacle and draw their own conclusions. He warned fans of all the NHL hockey teams (Stan was a great supporter of the Calgary Flames) that the new Ottawa Senators team should be investigated because of a rumoured clause in their NHL charter that would permit their executive to appoint eight new players if the team got into difficulty in the playoffs.

In early September, I again went to Ottawa for a news conference at which Deborah and Stan announced that they were taking a voluntary 10 percent cut in their salaries as of October 1. They called for other MPs to do likewise, as a symbolic demonstration of the principle "that the exercise of fiscal restraint by the federal government must begin at the top," and they strongly criticized the new $6,000 tax-free housing allowance that the House of Commons board of internal economy was recommending for all MPs. Deb and Stan also proposed the establishment of an independent commission to set the compensation and benefit packages for MPs and senators, with a recommendation that the pension provisions in particular should be brought more into line with those of other Canadians.

Predictably, when Stan and Deborah told the appropriate officials in the House of Commons and Senate that they wanted to take a pay cut, they were advised that there was no accounting mechanism to ensure that the savings would be retained by the government. All that could be done was to have the amount of the pay cut deduction sent to a charity designated by Stan and Deb.

This prompted Deb and Stan to call for the establishment of a special account, which they labelled the "National Debt and Deficit Retirement Fund" into which such payments could be made, along with proceeds from the sale of Crown assets and taxes designated for deficit and debt reduction. Eventually the government itself announced the establishment of such a fund in its 1991 budget.

For Deborah especially, who was younger and less financially secure than Stan, the voluntary pay cut was a significant sacrifice, but I admired both of them for making it. The trouble with "sacrifices as symbolic acts" is that the immediate impact on those for whom the sacrifice is made quickly fades, while the impact on those who actually make the sacrifice can go on and on. As leader of the Reform Party, it is my responsibility to make sure that sacrifices made by particular members to demonstrate a commitment to a Reform principle do not unduly penalize those members in the long run.

In fall 1990 I toured Manitoba, Alberta, and Saskatchewan to talk to western Canadians about Old Canada-New Canada and to get feedback on the question, "What should be the distinguishing characteristics of the New Canada?" I had various meetings in rural Manitoba at the beginning of October and several in Winnipeg at the end of the month, and addressed the always politically alive convention of the Union of Manitoba Municipalities. Speaking to a convention of genuine grassroots politicians in a way that resonates with their own thoughts and convictions is like speaking into an amplifier. What is said to them in convention, if it carries their judgment and is expressed in plain language, will be repeated loudly and clearly in scores of other communities and circumstances.

In central Alberta I visited Drumheller, Red Deer, Ponoka, Wetaskiwin (where constituents were attempting to get a ruling from the courts on the legal obligation of their MP to accurately represent their views in Parliament), Camrose, and Lloydminster. I was accompanied on part of this trip by my ten-year-old son David. One afternoon in Ponoka we sneaked away for a meal at McDonald's, but some of the other patrons recognized me and a long political discussion ensued from which David could not escape. That evening when the choice was to come to my public meeting or watch the Edmonton Oilers on TV, David voted for the Oilers.

Our meetings on this tour also included several visits to high schools—a part of the community to which I was giving an increasingly high priority. When I asked the question "What should twenty-first-century Canada, the Canada in which you will live most of your lives, be like?" many of the initial responses focused on the environment—a Canada where you could drink the water and breathe the air, a Canada with forests, a Canada in which the soil was still fertile. This interest in the environment was pragmatic, however, not simply idealistic. When one of our local organizers (no doubt reflecting back on his own youthful idealism in the 1960s) asked a class, "Would you be willing to join a Canadian Service Brigade (like the United States Peace Corps) to work on national projects like environmental conservation?" the class first wanted to know what the pay would be.

The central Alberta tour was followed by visits to the huge Peace River and Athabasca constituencies in the north and a well-attended rally in Lethbridge. Two large rallies in Calgary and Edmonton, the first in October and the second in November, drew more than four thousand people between them. These were crowds of unusual size for an off election year, and were a tribute to the work of our urban organizers and the willingness of people to participate in the Reform Party's efforts to give shape and substance to the phrase "New Canada."

I would begin these larger rallies with a brief recitation of some of the strange political events that had occurred in Canada over the preceding three months, which would be funny if they weren't true.

At the end of June we had the Meech Lake spectacle, with the prime minister and Barbara Frum proclaiming that, if the accord was not signed, Canada would pass away at 12:00 p.m. on June 23, 12:30 in Newfoundland.

Then the Mohawks in Quebec challenged the authority of the Quebec provincial police at Oka, to which the premier of Quebec responded by saying you can't have different laws for people of different races and cultures just because they claim to be distinct, and called in the Canadian army to help solve the problem.

Meanwhile, the democratically elected and supposedly politically accountable House of Commons passed legislation to institute a tax opposed by 85 percent of the Canadian people,

while the undemocratic and unaccountable Senate chose to
oppose the tax in accordance with the will of the people.

The prime minister, who has opposed every major attempt to
make the Senate democratic and accountable over the past six
years, accused the Senate of acting undemocratically, and then
petitioned the Queen for the right to make eight more
undemocratic appointments to the Upper Chamber.

No wonder people and commentators within and without
Canada are saying, "the politicians must be crazy," and asking
the question, "What's happening to Canada?"

I also made several more trips to Saskatchewan. My twelve-year-old son
Nathan came along on one of these. He enjoyed his exposure to my work,
but when we returned to Calgary he told Sandra that I kept repeating the
same jokes over and over again and he was afraid I might be embarrassing
myself. Sandra explained that while the jokes were the same, the audiences were usually different, and my image was somewhat restored.

Towards the end of November 1990, I took a more extensive tour of
Saskatchewan. Besides the local exposure for Reform and elements of
our New Canada concept, a CBC *Journal* crew had arranged to accompany us, and it was hoped that their mini-documentary might give us
broader exposure.

At a University of Saskatchewan Law School meeting, where I was to
outline the Reform Party's position on constitutional reform, I was
introduced by Allan Blakeney, the former premier of Saskatchewan and
an active participant in the federal-provincial negotiations that led to the
1982 constitution. The audience also included several constitutional law
professors and consultants with considerable experience in this field, so I
prefaced my remarks with a story I usually use when I spot people in an
audience who are more knowledgeable than I am on the subject under
discussion. This is the story of the Texan who survived the famous
Johnstown flood. Ever after, when he was asked to say a few words at a
public gathering, he would always ask if he could tell the story of how he
survived the Johnstown flood. Eventually this Texan died and went to
heaven, where he was met by St. Peter. Peter explained that it was a
heavenly custom to welcome newcomers with a reception, at which they
were asked to say a few words about their lives back on earth. The Texan
was delighted, but asked Peter whether it would be all right to say a few
words about the Johnstown flood. To which Peter replied, "Certainly, but
I must remind you that Noah will be in your audience." I intended to

speak on the constitution, but there were several Noahs (such as Allan Blakeney and Professor Doug Schmeiser) in the audience.

The only expectation of our Saskatchewan tour which was not met was our hope for broader coverage from the *Journal*. Unfortunately, the documentary, despite the professionalism and experience of the people preparing it, started off with the preconception that the party was an eccentric collection of potentially dangerous right-wing extremists. The reality, which did not fit the producers' preconceptions, that up to 40 percent of the people attending our Saskatchewan meetings came from a CCF-NDP background and that our positions on constitutional and parliamentary reform cut across the political spectrum, was either ignored or simply misunderstood. Moreover, the *Journal* documentary appeared to take at face value the views of a professor at the University of Regina who saw fascist conspirators behind every Reform position.

During the latter half of 1990, the Reform Party of Canada was paid the compliment of being the subject of significant and specific criticism by Brian Mulroney, Joe Clark, Bill McKnight, Don Mazankowski, Kim Campbell, Jean Chrétien, Sheila Copps, and Audrey McLaughlin. The attacks by leading members of the Mulroney government, who could no longer refer to us as a fringe party, since they were dangerously near the "fringe threshold" themselves in the opinion polls, were predictable, but the attacks from Chrétien and McLaughlin were a new development and a welcome sign.

As long as the federal Liberals and the federal NDP believed that the Reform Party was simply draining off disgruntled Conservatives from the federal PCs, they were quite content to leave us alone, even to silently applaud the supposed splitting of the Conservative vote. But by the second half of 1990, the pollsters for the Liberals and NDP were telling their leadership what we had been maintaining for the last year, that the Reform option was now attracting significant numbers of people who had formerly voted Liberal and NDP. Once this was confirmed, Liberal and NDP spokespersons lost no time in denouncing Reform as the repository of all political evils. We would, according to them, kill medicare, bankrupt farmers, impose strange values on others, attack widows, orphans, mothers, pensioners, immigrants, Quebeckers, aboriginals, and all sacred trusts.

Our best defence was a good offence, so we continued to hammer away on the main points of our platform which had proven so attractive to disenchanted voters, including members of other parties, in the first place. We also printed rebuttals to the main charges of our opponents in

The Reformer, and distributed the newsletter widely to our own members and in constituencies where electors had been favoured by special letters from their MPs (at taxpayers' expense) on the subject of the Reform Party.

At my public meetings, I would sometimes deal with these opposition attacks by explaining that we were a populist party that respected the common sense of the common people and that we were not stupid. Then I would ask the crowd such questions as: How many of you want to kill medicare? No hands would go up. How many of you are in favour of destroying confederation? No hands would go up. How many of you favour federal policies that would discriminate against people on the basis of race? No hands would go up. How many of you, if you were called upon to restrain federal spending, would focus on programs that serve the most vulnerable members of Canadian society—the young, the old, the sick, the poor, the disabled? Again, no hands would go up.

"Obviously then," I would conclude, "there is no constituency for these extreme positions, and no political party in its right mind and no candidate seeking election to the House of Commons would therefore espouse such positions. Certainly I do not, and the Reform Party does not. If our critics are mistaken or misguided on such simple and obvious points as these, on what other matters of political significance are they also mistaken and misguided?"

As far as our own members were concerned, I pointed out that, based on the practical experience of all five previous populist movements in the West, such parties usually go through four distinct phases in relation to the traditional parties. First, the new group is ignored, dismissed as irrelevant ("fringe" is a favourite term). Second, it is ridiculed and disparaged (Riel was called a crazy half-breed traitor; Haultain a "would-be prairie dictator"; the Progressives were "radical farmers and union rabble-rousers"; the CCF were "communists"; and Social Crediters were "fascists, Bible thumpers, and funny-money people"). Third, as the new movement continues to gain support, its basic positions, ideology, and leadership are subjected to systematic attacks, substantive criticism, and deliberate misrepresentation. And fourth, if the new party survives and continues to grow by increasing its "market share" at the expense of others, the traditional parties begin to steal significant portions of the new group's ideas, platform, and language.

In fall 1990, the Reform Party in western Canada was just entering phase three, in central Canada we were still in phase two, and in Quebec and Atlantic Canada we were in phase one. A year later, Don Newman, commenting at the PC national policy convention in Toronto for the CBC news, observed that significant parts of the throne speech, budget speech, and now the PC Policy Resolutions Manual for the convention, looked as if they had been copied from the Reformers' policy blue book. We were getting close to phase four, at least in certain parts of the country.

Of far greater concern to me than any attacks on the Reform Party of Canada by its political competitors from without is the vulnerability of a populist party, because of its openness and bottom-up decision-making processes, to divisions and attacks from within. The perversion of populism, as in the case of Peronism in Argentina, or the disintegration of a populist party, as in the case of the Progressives in Canada, occurs from within rather than from without. Once again, to be forewarned is to be forearmed. I therefore have no hesitation in presenting a few examples of internal strains with which the Reform Party was forced to cope as it grew and expanded.

Three cases came to light in 1990. Chronic dissent by a small group in Manitoba centred in Winnipeg resulted in constant friction with head office, executive council, and other party members, and a demand for a larger number of delegates to the April assembly than Manitoba's membership figures or the party constitution allowed. An unwillingness on the part of a small group within the Wild Rose constituency in Alberta, one of our largest and strongest constituency associations, to participate positively in the party's constitution-amending process resulted in the submission and distribution, at considerable expense to the party, of eighty-five alternative constitutional resolutions for the April assembly. And there were efforts by a small group in British Columbia to promote a provincial Reform Party of British Columbia that would capitalize on the popularity of the federal Reform Party of Canada in British Columbia by passing itself off as the provincial equivalent.

Without getting into the wearisome details of these disputes, I should explain why they are so potentially debilitating for a populist party. In each case, a small group of individuals claimed that their position on the issue in dispute was more legitimately representative of majority opinion within the party than the position of the executive council and leadership, which the membership itself had chosen through a party assembly. Decision making and planning, where such factions were involved, took hours and days instead of minutes, led to strained personal relations between individuals, and diverted precious resources away from the main priorities of the party—namely, membership recruitment, fund raising, and building support for getting Canada's constitutional, fiscal, and parliamentary houses in order.

The decisions of the April assembly in Saskatoon showed how little support there actually was among the party membership for the positions of these small factions. But in the meantime, our overworked executive council was forced to devote large amounts of time and energy to dealing with their claims, and no one knows how many potential supporters of the Reform Party were turned off because their initial exposure to the party unfortunately happened to involve contact with such factions.

All this time, however, party members and executives were learning some lessons that would be invaluable in guiding the future growth and expansion of a populist party.

First, in electing leadership at the constituency level, as well as at other levels, it is vitally important to choose people who will abide by the majority decision of a democratically constituted assembly or decision-making process, even if it conflicts with their personal agenda. The real test of a populist is not how many times or how loudly he or she invokes the name of "the grassroots" in pushing his or her own agenda, but in whether or not he or she is prepared to abide by the majority decision of a democratically constituted assembly or decision-making process, when that decision conflicts with his or her personal preference.

Second, in assigning responsibilities at the constituency and executive council levels of a populist party, it is extremely unwise to select people who suffer from low self-esteem and feelings of personal inadequacy and need to compensate for these feelings by seeking positions in a political organization and engaging in arbitrary exercises of their new-found authority. These are the people who are always concerned about titles, credits, and their position on the organizational chart. If they are not selected for the position they want, they are personally aggrieved and will bear a grudge towards the person who was called upon to fill the position. If their advice is not taken, or some contribution they have made goes unrecognized, they are personally insulted. They feel threatened by growth and an influx of new people, especially if some of those new people have greater talents or experience or knowledge than themselves.

Third, it is an enormous mistake for people of ability and sound judgment to sit back at the local constituency level and let people of lesser abilities and poorer judgment assume positions of responsibility, simply because they are willing or insistent or "need the job to feel wanted." In the long run, the costs of this approach in terms of problems caused, internal wrangling, time delays, bad decisions, and potential support lost, will far outweigh any imagined short-run benefits.

Finally, if a populist political party rejects arbitrary top-down decision making by elites in favour of a system in which those affected by the decision are adequately consulted and represented, it must give a great deal of attention to the construction and operation of its own decision-making structures (assemblies, councils, caucuses) and processes (referendums, voting by representatives in assemblies, councils, caucuses, minority parliaments, and majority parliaments). The failure of the Progressives to adequately address and agree on critical aspects of populist decision making before they were voted into Parliament in large numbers was probably the single most important factor contributing to their ultimate demise. As the Reform Party moved toward its April assembly, senior members of the party devoted increasing attention to this issue.

As 1990 came to a close, it was becoming clear that by the spring of 1991—our party assembly was scheduled for April 1991 in Saskatoon—we would be in a good position to make the policy, strategic, and organizational decisions necessary to facilitate the transition of the Reform Party from a regional party to a national party, if that was what the majority of our membership wanted to do.

It was decided that the first day of the Saskatoon Assembly would be devoted to party organizational matters and practical workshops; the second day would be devoted to policy; and the third day would be devoted to strategic issues and directions—provincial involvement, eastern expansion, revisions to our party constitution, and my own presentation on "Building the New Canada." On the final day of the assembly, we would address the need for resources, financial and human, including a presentation of the Reform Fund Canada report and the election of a new executive council. In addition, Stan Waters would speak on Senate reform, Deborah Grey would speak on the need for more Reformers in Parliament, author Bill Gairdner would be invited to speak on "The Trouble with Canada"; futurist Ruben Nelson would be asked to speak on future trends in social policy; and Sir Roger Douglas, the former finance minister of New Zealand, would be invited to make a presentation on "The Politics of Structural Reform."

In preparation for the April assembly, an assembly committee under the chairmanship of Mike Friese, a life insurance underwriter in Saskatoon, had been recruited to organize what would be one of the largest political events in that city in recent memory. We hoped to use the preparations to build a strong organizational team in Saskatoon, which could transfer its abilities and experience into constituency organization and development once the assembly was over.

In preparation for the April assembly, the expansion committee under the chairmanship of Gordon Shaw tackled the question "How should the Reform Party respond to the interest in the party being shown in Ontario and Atlantic Canada so as to encourage genuine support, while safeguarding our western base and preventing our resources from being spread too thin?" It proposed that interested people in Ontario and Atlantic Canada be advised that expansion of the Reform Party beyond its present base in western Canada depended on four conditions. These conditions were: (1) getting the assembly delegates' approval of constitutional amendments to safeguard the founding principles of the party and permit candidates to run under the Reform Party banner outside western Canada; (2) securing assurances from potential Reformers in Ontario and Atlantic Canada that they appreciate the regional alienation that has fuelled the growth of the Reform Party in the West and are prepared wholeheartedly to support constitutional changes, such as the Triple-E Senate, designed to produce more fairness and balance in national decision making; (3) obtaining sufficient funds in Ontario and Atlantic Canada to make any promotional or organizing activity there "self-financing," so as to not draw away human or financial resources from our organizing activity in the West; and (4) identifying mainstream, responsible people in key communities and ridings from outside the West who could provide the nucleus of constituency organizations and prevent the party from falling into the hands of extreme individuals and interest groups (particularly in the early stages of expansion when we would be most vulnerable).

The party's constitutional review committee, under the chairmanship of Vic Burstall, was asked not only to prepare amendments for updating the entire party constitution, but also to prepare amendments that would permit expansion, if that was what the membership wanted, and safeguard the ability of the party to strongly represent regional interests, including those of the less populated regions.

This latter requirement led Vic's committee to propose entrenching the party's policy commitment to the Triple-E Senate in the party constitution, so that it could not be abandoned or altered by a simple policy resolution at a party assembly. It also led to innovative constitutional proposals, designed to balance the interests of the heavily populated regions of the country like Ontario with those of the thinly populated regions like the West and Atlantic Canada, through changes in the structure and the decision-making processes of the party itself.

It was proposed that party assemblies, like the House of Commons, would be based on delegate representation per riding, which in effect would mean representation by population. The party's executive council, on the other hand, like the Triple-E Senate, would be based on equal representation by province (three or four councillors per province regardless of population). Party decisions and policies would need to carry the judgment of both bodies to be effectively implemented, and each would act as a check and a balance on the other with respect to issues of regional fairness.

An additional safeguard proposal was that resolutions presented to a party assembly dealing with changes to party policy or the constitution would require a "double majority" vote. That is, in order to pass, such resolutions would need to receive a majority vote from the assembly as a whole, as well as a majority vote from delegates from a majority of the provinces.

In addition to these conditions and proposals, the executive council, the expansion committee, the constitution committee, and I had all come to the conclusion that expansion was a strategic question of such intense interest to our membership, that after every effort had been made to present all the arguments for and against and to communicate the judgment of the leadership, it was our rank-and-file members who should have the final say, through a referendum among members west of the Ontario-Manitoba border. We explained this conclusion to the Reformers outside the West, who accepted it with some misgivings, and the constitution and expansion committees were charged with looking after the legalities and the mechanics.

All these conditions and proposals for dealing with expansion were then presented to Reform Party members and constituency associations through *The Reformer* and my pre-Assembly meetings with various constituency association executives.

While preparations for the assembly were under way, I made three commitments. The first was a scheduled trip to Australia to spend some time with our two oldest daughters, who were working in Sydney, and to meet some Australian senators in Canberra to discuss the strengths and weaknesses of their Triple-E Senate. The second was another trip to central Canada, this time to Quebec as well as Toronto. And the third was some time away with Sandra to work on my speeches for the assembly, including the keynote address, "Building the New Canada."

I gained two principal impressions from actually visiting the Australian Senate and talking to some of its members. First, it was obvious that although the Australian Senate was not an ideal model for Canadian Senate reformers, it was certainly more effective as a legislative body and as a safeguard for regional interests than our Senate. Second, the Australian Senate is a party house first and a states-rights house second, and this blunts its effectiveness as a chamber of regional representation. Senate reform is thus best considered in the broader context of parliamentary reform, which includes reducing the powers of the parties and the prime minister's office to force members (whether in the Senate or the House of Commons) to vote contrary to their constituents' wishes.

As one Australian senator explained, however, while the Australian Senate does not lend itself especially well to the promotion of regional interests, its very existence and power discourages national governments from pursuing national policies that would strongly offend all or any of the states. An independent senator from Tasmania, Australia's smallest state, with 450,000 people, also emphasized that his state would not receive the consideration in national decision making that it does if it were not for its standing in the Senate, where it has the same number of seats (twelve) as the State of New South Wales, which has a population of six million.

Upon my return to Canada, after time with my family over Christmas, I prepared for my next trip to central Canada. This included a meeting with Reg Gosse and a number of the key Reformers in Ontario to get a report on interest there and their plans to send a delegation to the April assembly.

Reg Gosse, a certified management accountant, who had become our chief volunteer organizer in Ontario, was born in Newfoundland. He grew up and attended school in Scarborough, then studied at the Universities of Calgary and Western Ontario. In 1986 he and his wife Marnie opened their own printing and publishing business in Kitchener.

When he first heard of the Reform Party, on a CBC *Newsworld* report in March 1990, he called the head office and talked to Ron Wood, who referred him to Diane Ablonczy and Gordon Shaw, head of our expansion committee. At that time, our membership list in Ontario was very small. Reg had asked for the names of some other members, met with Gordon Shaw and eleven other Ontario Reformers in June 1990, and, together with Harry Robertson, Michael Dean, and Bill Gearing, formed an ad hoc Ontario expansion committee in July 1990. He and I first met at a Reform meeting in the Holiday Inn at Brampton in September 1990.

Reg estimated that seventy-five to eighty Reformers from Ontario would make the journey to Saskatoon, at their own expense, to talk about Ontario's interest in Reform and to make a pitch for expansion from an Ontario and national perspective. The Ontario delegation had decided that they didn't want to appear pushy—no bands or Madison Avenue campaign, just common-sense people, with some solid facts and arguments, and buttons saying, "The East Wants In."

Reg and his associates were sincerely motivated to explore the Reform option by many of the same concerns and aspirations as our western Reformers. Even when it came to Senate reform, which some westerners felt would automatically be opposed in Ontario, they could speak from experience about regional alienation in northern, eastern, and western Ontario, and make the argument that no part of Canada has a monopoly on feeling "left out."

Before I could go away to work on my keynote speech on the building of New Canada, I needed one more piece of information, and that was an accurate reading on what was going on in Quebec. This was the one province outside the West where our expansion committee was not active, and for a very good reason. We were exploring expansion in Ontario and Atlantic Canada, not because someone in Calgary had made a strategic decision to do so, but because we had received an increasing number of inquiries and requests for information from concerned people in those areas. We had received very few inquiries or requests from Quebec, and those that we had received were not from the Québécois.

There was of course an explanation for this. Discontent with the operations of the federal system was manifesting itself politically in growing support for the Parti Québécois provincially, and the new Bloc Québécois, led by Lucien Bouchard, federally. In addition, there was the language barrier (I am not bilingual, although some of our key Reformers are). What was more disturbing, most of the early reports concerning the Reform Party in the French-language press had painted us as either western separatists (the western equivalent of the BQ) or anti-French, anti-Quebec extremists who wanted Quebec out of confederation. With the exception of journalist and parliamentary correspondent Michel Vastel, few francophone members of the parliamentary press gallery ever came West to attend our public meetings or to conduct in-depth interviews to find out what we were about.

Therefore, when I received two invitations to come to Quebec to discuss Reform in late fall 1990, I readily accepted. One was from the producers of the television series *The Editors*, which appeared on CBC

Newsworld and on the PBS network in the United States. The other was from Pierre Desmarais of Uni Media, whom I had met at David Sadler's invitation in Vancouver, who suggested that I should visit Quebec and at least give the print media a chance to get the Reform story first hand.

Once it had been confirmed that I was going to Quebec, I wrote to the Bélanger-Campeau Commission, the Commission on the Political and Constitutional Future of Quebec, which had been set up by the Quebec government after the collapse of Meech Lake. Although I knew the commission would be concluding its hearings at the end of January and had been reluctant to listen to any witnesses from outside Quebec, I requested a formal or informal opportunity to do two things. The first was to contribute what I could toward clarifying misconceptions, especially those concerning the attitudes of western Canadians towards Meech Lake, federal language legislation, the people of Quebec, and Quebec's aspirations for a new constitutional deal. The second was to discuss with the commission or its staff a short list of questions that many Canadians outside Quebec were already asking with respect to Quebec's future constitutional aspirations.

I attached to my letter a sample list of questions. As to reasons why the commission should give me a hearing, I could claim no special title or expertise other than that I had probably had more discussions on constitutional matters (including Meech Lake) with rank-and-file westerners over the past three years than anyone who had yet appeared before the commission. Also, if the polls were correct, I could end up in Parliament at the head of a significant contingent of Reformers who would have more than a passing interest in any new constitutional arrangements between Quebec and Canada.

Ron Wood and I arrived in Montreal just a few days after the Allaire Report was released on behalf of the Quebec Liberal Party. The report asserted that the maintenance and preservation of Quebec as a distinct society would require a massive transfer of powers from the federal government to the Quebec government, and suggested that this extreme decentralization ought to be attractive to the other provinces. We had arrived at a propitious time to discuss constitutional matters and the politics of confederation.

My media meetings included sessions with CBC *Midday*, *La Presse*, the Montreal *Gazette* editorial board, CFCF-TV, the editors and writers of *Le Devoir*, the publisher and reporters of *Le Soleil*, CTV's *Sunday Edition*, and the producers of *Le Point* (who had sent a crew out west to gather some footage on the Reform Party there). At most of these sessions I would answer basic questions concerning the Reform Party and its policy positions, particularly on language and the constitution, and ask a few questions myself about how the party was perceived by the Quebec elites and by the public (if it was perceived at all). I tried to make clear that just because the Reform Party rejected as inadequate the two founding nations concept as a constitutional cornerstone, that did not mean we were hostile to Quebec's economic, cultural, or constitutional aspirations.

I said that Quebec and the rest of Canada were headed toward a big constitutional negotiation of profound importance in the 1990s; that we might play a modest role in the federal Parliament in representing at least the views of western Canadians on the aims and conduct of that negotiation; that neither western Canadians nor I had given up on the prospect of a united Canada under new constitutional arrangements; that given what was at stake, it was extremely important that Quebec and the rest of Canada understand exactly what each was after; and since I was not currently soliciting votes in Quebec, perhaps I could be more frank than other federal politicians concerning exactly what Quebec might expect to encounter at that bargaining table from those representing the economic and constitutional interests of Canadians outside Quebec.

On the evening of February 1, Ron Wood and I met for an informal chat with Jean Lapierre, party whip of the Bloc Québécois, who was to appear on the same edition of *The Editors* as myself. The theme of the session was to be the significance of regional parties, with Jean Lapierre representing the BQ, and me representing the Reform Party. I had not met Lapierre before, although Deborah Grey knew most of the BQ members. We felt it was important to meet before the *Editors* taping sessions to discuss our positions. The Reform Party did not want to be portrayed as some western equivalent of the Bloc Québécois; we were federalists.

The moderator of *The Editors* was very accommodating and gave us each a good chance to say our piece. I explained that the people of western Canada and the people of Quebec shared a profound dissatisfaction with the current federal system and a deep longing for fundamental change. The Reform Party and the BQ are products of those dissatisfactions and aspirations. However, the immediate constitutional goal of the Reformers of western Canada was summarized in the slogan "The West Wants In," whereas if I understood the basic constitutional goal of the

BQ, it could be summarized in the slogan "Quebec Wants Out." And it would be harder to find two constitutional positions farther apart than that.

I left Quebec with mixed feelings. I had answered many questions that had been put to me, but had received very few answers to my own questions. In listening to the journalists and editors talk about the post-Meech debate, the Bélanger-Campeau hearings, and the deliberations of the Allaire committee, I got the impression that in the aftermath of Meech Quebec was suffering from many misconceptions as to what the rest of Canada wanted or would agree to in terms of future constitutional arrangements.

Proposals for a New Quebec (whether it was the PQ version, the BQ version, or the Quebec Liberals' version) were being developed in a complete absence of interest or knowledge as to how other Canadians might react, just as proposals for a New Canada could very easily be developed in western Canada in a complete absence of interest or knowledge as to how other Canadians might react.

Obviously the Road to New Canada, hopefully a New Canada incorporating a New Quebec, must wind through every part of Old Canada, with signposts so high and clear that no political dust storm generated by politicians can obscure the directions, and so that all Canadians can judge for themselves whether they want to travel that road or not.

CHAPTER FIFTEEN

A New National Party

The April 1991 assembly of the Reform Party of Canada in Saskatoon was the largest and most important assembly held by the party since its inception. The 1,400 registrants included 823 voting delegates chosen through meetings organized by the constituency associations to represent the membership, which by this time had increased to 62,000 members. In addition, 450 delegates at large had registered, as well as 128 media people and observers. (Unlike the traditional federal parties, whose constitutions allow their executives to "weight" conventions in favour of the party line by giving delegate status to large numbers of party officials and appointed people, the Reform Party's constitution tends to weight its conventions in favour of the rank-and-file membership by allowing any party member in good standing who is willing to pay the registration fee to register as a "delegate at large." While delegates at large are non-voting, they can participate in every other aspect of the assemblies, including debates on resolutions.) This number also included the delegations from Ontario and Atlantic Canada (75 and 3 delegates, respectively).

The observers included people who had paid the registration fee in order to check out the Reform Party before making any deeper commitment, and, for the first time, official representatives of the three traditional parties.

The opening day of the assembly, April 4, had been dedicated to organizational development and election readiness. The morning was set aside for a meeting between the executive council and the constituency association presidents, and the afternoon was dedicated to seminars dealing with fundraising and management, team building and conflict resolution, candidate recruitment and development, and campaign management. It had been expected that these sessions would only be of interest to constituency executives, organizers, and workers. When six hundred delegates showed up for the seminars, the organizational committee had to scramble to accommodate the larger numbers.

In my opening remarks to the presidents and the seminar sessions, I briefly recounted the expectations of those who had attended the first Reform assemblies. I then focused on the challenge at hand, which I framed in the form of a series of questions:

> Can the Reform Party become a major player in federal politics in the 1990s? Can our vision of a New Canada compete with the worn and tattered visions of the traditional parties? Can we keep our focus on essentials? Can we get our own constitutional house in order? Can we resolve internal conflicts and disagreements maturely and discreetly? Can our executives faithfully represent personal and constituent convictions while still becoming team players and leaders? In other words, can a grassroots, bottom-up party maintain the unity and self-discipline necessary to fight a successful election campaign and to act as a cohesive force in a divided Parliament?
>
> The answers to these questions still hang in the balance. Their resolution rests more in the hands of our members, constituency associations, and delegates to this assembly, than it does in the hands of the leader or executive council.

The first day of the April assembly concluded with hospitality and social activities designed to give Reformers from across the West and beyond a chance to meet each other. In a rapidly growing new party, very few of the key people, particularly at the constituency level, know their counterparts in other constituencies and other provinces. Informal activities and social gatherings that bring these people together and develop mutual trust are essential. At these informal sessions, and in the hospitality rooms hosted by delegates from each of the provinces, the Ontario and Atlantic Canada delegates began to introduce themselves, and their reasons for being in Saskatoon, to the delegates from across western Canada.

The second day of the April assembly, April 5, began in earnest with another excellent presentation by Stephen Harper entitled "The Reform Vision of Canada." Stephen reported and reflected on the feedback that the Reform Party had received on constitutional issues from its own members as well as other sources. In his judgment, a majority of

Canadians in large parts of the country "do not want the constitutional status quo. ... [They] do not want special status for Quebec or a special deal for Quebec. ... [They] do not want to establish a highly decentralized confederation [as proposed in the Quebec Liberals' Allaire Report]. ... Canadians do not want to build a country around linguistic and cultural 'facts' defined by the federal government. ... [They] do not want a constitution built around the ideology of the Left or the Right. ... [And they] do not want top-down executive federalism."

What do Canadians want in terms of a new constitutional order? "Reformers," said Stephen, "want a strong country built by those who want in, not by those who want out." At this point he was interrupted by such strong applause that it took several minutes to restore order.

Continuing on the affirmative side (what Reformers want, rather than what Reformers oppose), he declared that: "Reformers want a genuinely federal system, including a strong national government with strong regional representation, and strong provinces to protect cultural identity and regional character. ... Reformers want a constitutional division of powers designed to fulfil the needs that Canadians share, including the need for a competitive economy, a responsible community, a sustainable environment. [And] Reformers want a country that respects the democratic values that Canadians share. ... ."

Stephen then concluded by asking the delegates to answer, by their votes on policy and strategic resolutions over the next three days, three tough questions that the media and the public would insist we answer before the next federal election: "First, we will be asked whether the Reform Party is committed to its vision of Canada. Second, we will be asked whether the Reform Party's agenda is free from extremism, especially on issues like language and immigration. Third, we will be asked whether the Reform Party is a positive and united political movement."

Following Stephen's address, the delegates engaged in more than six hours of policy debate. The results of this debate and the decisions flowing from it are summarized in the Reform Party's "blue book" of principles and policies. The most significant thing about the April assembly's policy decisions was that they strengthened or added important elements to the Reform Party's concept of New Canada, and reflected a conscious effort to move away from positions that could be interpreted as extreme or parochial.

For example, the desire that the Reform Party's language policy "be balanced and positive" was reflected in an amendment rejecting "enforced unilingualism" (French-only laws in Quebec and English-only laws elsewhere), as well as comprehensively legislated official bilingualism. Official bilingualism was supported for key federal institutions (Parliament and the Supreme Court) and "critical federal services where need is sufficient to warrant provision of minority services on a cost-effective basis."

The assembly delegates came down firmly in favour of constitutional conventions as a first step in any future round of constitutional negotiations, and in favour of popular ratification of constitutional changes by referendums as a final step.

The party had already committed itself to a "balanced and positive immigration policy," which rejected the use of racial criteria designed to maintain a French-English ethnic balance in Canada. At Saskatoon, delegates made clear their disapproval of any appeal to race or creed in setting immigration policy. They also declared their support of a policy "accepting the settlement of genuine refugees who find their way to Canada." (A "genuine refugee" was defined as "one who has a well-founded fear of persecution and qualifies under the requirements of the United Nations Convention.")

For the first time a Reform assembly specifically addressed the issues of child abuse and family violence, calling for "the enactment, communication, and enforcement of laws designed to protect family members against such acts and to provide a program of assistance to both victims and abusers through therapy."

Resolutions opposing tax concessions to private corporations, tying change in the GST rate to a referendum requirement, and calling for the establishment of a National Debt Retirement Fund were approved.

Delegates wrestled with clarifying and making more precise the party's position on representation and moving towards freer votes in the House of Commons. The objective was to free MPs from excessive party discipline so that they could more faithfully and accurately represent their constituents' interests, not so that they could simply "do as they please." This, in turn, required a process for determining constituent positions and sanctioning any departure from the party platform on which the MP was elected. After much debate, the following resolution was passed:

> RESOLVED that, having had a full opportunity to express their views and vote freely in caucus, with such caucus vote always made public, Reform MPs shall vote with the Reform Party majority in the House, unless a Member is instructed to abstain or vote otherwise by his/her constituents. The Reform Party of

Canada shall provide criteria for proper processes to elicit the will
of the constituency and such processes shall be initiated by
constituents or by the Member.

Delegates agreed that the Reform Party should support defence policies
based on greater reliance on reserves, adaptable and general-purpose
equipment, reduced overheads, careful and specified commitments to
alliances (including United Nations peacekeeping efforts), and lower costs.

The assembly ratified the general approach to redefining relations
between aboriginals and the government of Canada which I had been
advocating, starting with an aboriginal constitutional convention, and
moving toward greater acceptance of responsibility by aboriginals for
their own well-being, and abolition of the Department of Indian Affairs.

The assembly adopted a clear and unequivocal resolution affirming its
commitment to ensuring that adequate health care insurance and services are available to every Canadian. This statement of the obvious was
made necessary by consistent accusations from many of our opponents,
especially the NDP, that Reformers were out to "kill medicare."

The delegates reaffirmed their opposition to government subsidization
of business and their commitment to increased competition, and called
for the realignment of Canada's domestic economic policies (for example, industrial development policies, science and research policies, regulatory policies, taxation policies, transportation policies, education
policies, fiscal and monetary policies) to be more consistent with Canada's international trade requirements. They also endorsed general resolutions supporting public-private sector partnerships for environmental
conservation, and a greater harmonization and integration of federal and
provincial regulatory powers in relation to environmental protection.
Once again, while the principles were sound, more work was obviously
required on the details.

Delegates made clear that they felt that energy policy should be driven
first and foremost by "the demands of consumers for safe, secure
supplies of energy at competitive prices," as distinct from producer
interests, government interests, or other special interests. The party went
on record as opposing both government subsidization of energy megaprojects and the imposition of discriminatory taxes and ownership
regulations on the energy sector.

Resolutions on gun control were tabled. (In voting on the government's
gun control legislation in the House of Commons, Reform MP Deborah
Grey took the position that the Reform Party's priorities, pending further

guidance from the members, were public safety first, freedom to own firearms for hunting and collection purposes second, and reform of firearms regulation in the direction of stricter enforcement of existing regulations and a greater emphasis on licensing the user.)

The only serious hitch in the policy-making sessions at the Saskatoon assembly was an initial lack of consensus concerning what to do about agricultural policy. This was an extremely important subject to many of our members, and it was essential that a western-based federal party have something distinctive to say on the serious problems facing farmers. The problem was how to get from a highly subsidized agricultural sector operating in an international market in which our competitors could afford higher subsidy levels than Canada, to a more competitive and market-driven agricultural sector, without bankrupting one-third of our farmers in the transition process.

To address this and related agricultural issues, the party had established an agricultural policy task force under the chairmanship of Perry Kirkham, a farmer from Saltcoats, Saskatchewan. Their report and policy recommendations to the assembly were more comprehensive and complex than those submitted by any other task force. Assembly delegates, particularly those from urban areas, did not feel they had the expertise or time to do justice to those recommendations during the policy sessions on April 5. But to simply table them for future discussion would have been a great blow to our agricultural Reformers and would have left the party with a huge hole in its policy manual. I therefore proposed, and the assembly agreed, that we schedule a special policy session at 5:30 on Sunday morning (it was the only time available, and I knew that most farmers get up early anyway) to consider a draft policy statement on agriculture.

Sunday morning, bright and early, more than 150 delegates met in special session for two hours to hammer out an agricultural policy statement acceptable to both our urban and our rural delegates and later ratified by the assembly. Unfortunately, the media were given the impression that this session was closed to them, and so it received no coverage. In many respects it was one of the most interesting sessions of the assembly, combining all the aspirations and tensions of conflicting and cooperating interests, thrown together in the policy-making environment of a Reform assembly.

The policy statement that it produced represents the foundation of the Reform Party's approach to agricultural policy, and is included in Appendix III.

The policy deliberations of the delegates to the Saskatoon assembly were further stimulated by the reflections of Ruben Nelson, a futurist with twenty years of consulting experience in Ottawa, and a concluding address by Sir Roger Douglas, the former finance minister of New Zealand, on the Politics of Structural Reform.

Ruben Nelson described the transition from Old Canada to New Canada as the shift from an industrial to a post-industrial society, and challenged the delegates to consider themselves involved in building Canada's first post-industrial political party. He suggested that in industrial age societies, economics is dominant and social policy is residual, and that social policy involves categorized, institution-based programs delivered by professionals, which are administrative nightmares. He speculated that the shift from Old Canada to a post-industrial New Canada would involve a shift in emphasis from doctors and health-care systems to healthy lives, from schools and educational systems to societal learning, from human rights to responsible relations, from day care and homemakers to community creators, from bilingualism and multi-culturalism to creating a living Canadian culture, from input measures to desired outcomes.

Sir Roger Douglas, who led a major effort by a Labour government to reduce public spending, personifies the fact that changing times and conditions the world over are breaking down the old categories of left and right in politics. His short list of ten guidelines for implementing structural reforms, particularly in the area of financial and economic policy, could help with the transition from Old Canada to New Canada. (1) Quality decisions start with quality people placed in strategic positions. (2) Implement reforms by quantum leaps. Moving step by step lets vested interests mobilize. (3) Speed is essential. It is impossible to move too fast. (4) Once your momentum starts, never let it stop. Set your own goals and deadlines. Within that framework, consult widely in the community to improve detailed implementation. (5) Credibility is crucial. It is hard to win and you can lose it overnight. (6) Make your goals clear. Adjustment is impossible if people don't know where you are going. (7) Stop selling the public short. Voters need and want politicians with a vision and guts to create a better future. (8) Don't blink or wobble. Get the decisions right first time. (9) Opportunity, incentive, and choice mobilize the energy of the people to achieve successful change. (10) When in doubt, ask yourself, "Why am I in politics?"

The morning of April 6, the third day of the assembly, began with an address by Bill Gairdner, author of the best-selling book *The Trouble with*

Canada. Gairdner has a Ph.D. from Stanford University, represented Canada in track and field at the Tokyo Olympics, was president and owner of the Fitness Institute in Toronto, and is a successful businessman and author. From a completely different background and perspective, he had arrived at conclusions on the need for constitutional and fiscal reforms that were very similar to those of the Reform Party. What many Reformers concluded from his remarks was that there was a national constituency for fundamental change in Canada.

The April 6 assembly session on strategic directions proceeded swiftly, the culmination of months of discussion and debate by thousands of Reformers on the issues at hand. Cliff Fryers, our most able chairman when decision making on contentious matters is the task at hand, was in the chair, assisted by Peter Thagard, a Saskatoon lawyer who had agreed to serve as our parliamentarian. First up was Vic Burstall, chairman of our constitutional committee. His job was to lay before the assembly delegates any proposed amendments to the party constitution needed to make decisions on strategic directions, such as a decision to expand eastward. These amendments included the four "safeguard" resolutions—entrenching the commitment to the Triple-E Senate reform in the party constitution, providing for representation by population in the composition of party assemblies and representation by equal numbers of councillors from each province on the executive council, requiring a "double majority" vote at assemblies to carry resolutions designed to change party policy or the party constitution, and providing for a special party referendum on eastward expansion by party members in western Canada. (Many members had said that they would not be prepared to vote on the expansion issue until they had an opportunity first to vote on the safeguard resolutions, and the assembly program had been ordered accordingly.)

Next up was Marshall Copithorne. He briefly reviewed the activities and conclusions of the Alberta task force on provincial involvement and the broader interest in the provincial involvement issue. He then laid before the assembly resolutions incorporating three alternative courses of action. The first option would authorize the council to receive applications for the establishment of provincial and territorial Reform Parties. Acceptance of these applications, however, would be made subject to a number of conditions (which the Assembly could approve, reject, or change). The other two options represented two clear-cut alternatives. One slammed the door on provincial involvement, calling for the Reform Party of Canada not to be involved in provincial politics and to take "all legal means available to protect its name, logos, and trademarks from unauthorized use by other political groups." The other would "leave the door completely alone." It was embodied in a resolution calling for the federal party not to be involved in provincial politics and not to stand in the way of any group attempting to register a provincial Reform Party.

The resolutions concluded with a final one that would enable the Reform Party of Canada to register a provincial Reform Party (as it had done in Alberta) "for the sole purpose of running a Reform candidate in a Senate election."

Last up were Gordon Shaw and Reg Gosse to present the conclusions and recommendations of the expansion committee. For Gordon, this was the last step in a long journey that had started at the Edmonton Assembly in November 1989 and had taken him across Canada. If his committee's recommendations were accepted, not only by the delegates at Saskatoon, but by the membership at large, it would be the first step of an even longer journey that would take the party itself across Canada.

Shaw reported on the growing interest in Reform across the country and the necessity of making a decision on expansion now. A delegation from Atlantic Canada was introduced. Reg Gosse described how the Ontario membership had grown to six thousand with more than fifty interim constituency associations. Reg was accompanied by people like Bill Gearing, Harry Robertson, and Colyne Gibbons from Ontario. Reg and these folks had credibility and they talked common sense. The delegates thought, "They are concerned Canadians, just like us."

Gordon Shaw completed his report by placing before the assembly a resolution seconded by Stephen Harper. It called for an expansion resolution to be submitted to the membership of the party residing west of the Manitoba-Ontario border, through a special party referendum to be held immediately after the Saskatoon assembly, and for the party to adopt that resolution as a course of action, provided it received the affirmative support of a majority of the members casting unspoiled ballots in the special referendum.

The proposed wording of the expansion resolution to be placed on the referendum ballot was: "RESOLVED that the Reform Party of Canada should authorize the establishment of constituency associations and the nomination of Reform candidates in federal electoral districts east of the Manitoba-Ontario border with the regional safeguards as proposed by the expansion and constitutional committees."

The constitutional amendments, including all the safeguard amendments, passed by large majorities. An amendment by the small Wild Rose constituency group that would have restricted the interim representation of Ontario on the Party's executive council was defeated, as was an amendment demanding a two-thirds majority vote for approval of the expansion referendum, instead of the proposed 50 percent majority vote for approval.

Delegates at large, including those from Ontario, participated in the debate on expansion. Eric Kipping from New Brunswick came to the mike to say Atlantic Canada wanted in, and the assembly cheered. There were calls for the question to be put. There had been enough talk. Cliff called for the question and a field of green "Yes" cards waved in the air. This authorized a special party referendum on the question of expansion, the question to be worded in accordance with the resolution passed by the assembly. In debating the resolutions relevant to expansion, however, the delegates had expressed their own views on the issue, and it appeared that a majority were strongly in favour of the party expanding eastward.

The delegates themselves sensed they had done something out of the ordinary, perhaps historic. They stood up and congratulated each other.

Then it started. Someone on the far side of the room started singing "O Canada." It spread across the room until everyone was standing, turning toward the Canadian flag behind Cliff's podium. They sang it, not with that awkward restraint with which the national anthem is so often sung at formal functions in Canada, but as if they meant it. The media were caught by surprise, and so were the assembly officials and those of us at the front. We were witnessing that rarest of events, a spontaneous expression of genuine Canadian patriotism at a federal political meeting.

Cliff Fryers, who had been as moved as anyone by the scene unfolding in front of him, recovered himself and restored peace, order, and good government to the assembly by saying, "You realize, of course, that you are all out of order."

When the laughter had subsided, delegates turned to the last of the strategic issues, provincial involvement. Again the die was already cast; having decided to commit its energies and resources to national expansion, it was highly unlikely that the assembly would authorize simultaneous expansion on the provincial fronts. Voting on the provincial involvement issue was swift and decisive. The compromise resolution, leaving the door open for provincial involvement but stiffening the hinges, was soundly defeated, and the delegates then voted overwhelmingly to "slam the door shut." But before doing so they toughened up the resolution directing the Reform Party of Canada to use all legal means available to protect its name, logos, and trademark from unauthorized use by other political groups. The amended resolution further directed the federal Reform Party to use all legal means available to protect its membership lists from such unauthorized use, and to protect itself from "any group passing itself off as being associated in any way with the Reform Party of Canada."

To allow the delegates to the Saskatoon assembly to express themselves directly on the question of expansion, the expansion committee had proposed that a straw vote be taken at the end of the morning session. The wording on the ballot was the same as the wording approved for the special referendum ballot. The straw vote ballots were to be counted later in the day, with the result being given to me so I could announce it at the beginning of my nationally televised address that evening. The result of the straw vote, the recommendation of the Saskatoon assembly itself on the issue of expansion, was also to be included in the information sent to party members as part of the special party referendum on expansion.

The delegates broke for lunch, where Stan Waters was the keynote speaker. After commending the delegates on their deliberations, Stan outlined some of the steps that he felt would be necessary to put the government of New Canada on a sound financial footing by the year 2000. These measures included actions by the shareholders of Old Canada to put it into "voluntary receivership" by the election of a receiver government at the next federal election, which would oversee a 15 percent downsizing of government operations and other reorganizational measures necessary to make the government of New Canada a viable financial entity. It was a colourful analogy and a powerful address, and in the months ahead we would incorporate important elements of Stan's fiscal recovery plan into the Reform Party's description of the Road to New Canada.

The delegates returned in the afternoon to tackle a long list of further amendments to the party constitution to streamline its operations, balance relations between the grassroots membership and executive levels, and equip the party to conduct its affairs on a national level. Werner Schmidt was chairman. Although the debate of resolutions pertaining to the internal governance of a political party appears dry and boring to most outside observers, I saw many encouraging signs of a growing political maturity in the way this session was conducted. Nit-picking amendments, and amendments prompted by suspicions that the party's greatest enemies were its own elected officials, were impatiently struck down.

I left the constitutional session early, leaving Stephen Harper to speak in my place if necessary, to prepare for my keynote address to the delegates on "The Road to New Canada." In many respects I had been preparing for this address for a long time. But tonight I would have a national audience because the national media were there and CBC *Newsworld* had arranged to carry the speech live across the country.

Before I left the assembly hall, Don Leier, chief scrutineer for the expansion straw vote, handed me the results. The assembly delegates had voted 762, or 96.6 percent, in favour of expansion, and 27, or 3.4 percent, against.

My address on "The Road to New Canada" was a condensation of a seventy-page draft that I had prepared during my time away with Sandra in March. This draft had been circulated for comment to Stephen Harper, Tam Deachman, and my father. It had then been boiled down into a tighter version, with Harper incorporating certain elements into his address and Waters incorporating other elements into his.

This is how I like to prepare for major speeches, time permitting. The actual speech itself should be like the tip of an iceberg, with lots of depth and substance beneath and behind it, even if this is not always evident on the surface. Nothing disturbs me more than superficiality and mere sloganizing on matters of public policy, and the suspicion that what the speaker is saying represents the full extent of his knowledge on the subject.

By the time I arrived backstage at the upper auditorium of the Saskatoon Centennial Auditorium, more than two thousand delegates and others had gathered, although it was difficult to see them behind the bright television lights. Dean Whiteway, a former PC member of Parliament from Manitoba, was master of ceremonies. A brief video prepared by Randy Lennon from clips of our past campaigns and commercials reinforced the fact that Reform was on the move. Then Wayne Smith introduced me, and it was my turn.

I began by releasing to the assembly and the media the results of the straw vote on expansion. Subject to confirmation by our membership through the special party referendum, it was the recommendation of this assembly, by a vote of more than 96 percent in favour, that the Reform Party of Canada expand east of the Manitoba-Ontario border.

Ron Wood and others tell me that I must not be impatient when interrupted by applause at public meetings, so I waited patiently for the cheering to subside. I then launched into the Reform Party's diagnosis of what is killing Old Canada, our vision of the New Canada that is struggling to be born, and our vision of the road to New Canada. I sketched the Reformers' vision of a New Canada in these words:

> First of all, let me say charitably but clearly that I do not look to Quebec or Quebec politicians to define New Canada. New Canada cannot simply be a reaction to Quebec demands and aspirations. New Canada must be open and big enough to include a New Quebec, but it must be more than viable without Quebec.
>
> Once we get New Canada defined, the question of whether New Quebec wishes to be a part of New Canada must be addressed, but that is not our starting point. This is what distinguishes the Reform Party's vision of Canada from those of all three of the traditional federal parties.
>
> If you want a revised definition of Canada and a revised constitution that is essentially a reaction to Quebec's latest demands, then look to the federal PCs, Liberals, or NDP because that is their starting point. That's been their starting point for the last thirty years.
>
> If you want a definition of New Canada and a new constitution that takes as its starting point the needs, aspirations, and common sense of the common people in the other nine provinces and two territories, with an open invitation for input from Quebec federalists, then it is the Reformers' vision of Canada that you should examine.
>
> And when we put our ear to the political ground, and listen hard, which is the one thing a populist party ought to do best, we hear disjointed but meaningful words and phrases—which taken together add up to this forty-two-word definition of New Canada:
>
> "New Canada should be a balanced, democratic federation of provinces, distinguished by the conservation of its magnificent environment, the viability of its economy, the acceptance of its social responsibilities, and recognition of the equality and uniqueness of all its provinces and citizens."
>
> Let me express this definition of New Canada a second way, for those of you who are goal-oriented and respond to "mission statements."
>
> Canada's mission in the twenty-first century will be to create, by

evolution, not revolution, a more balanced society on the
northern half of the North American continent:

- A society where the economy is productive, competitive, and
  prosperous, but in harmony rather than in conflict with the
  environment and social needs of its citizens. (It is this balance, if
  we can achieve it, that will distinguish us from the United
  States.)
- A society where the governmental system is truly federal and
  democratic, recognizing the equality and uniqueness of all the
  provinces and citizens. (This is what will distinguish New
  Canada from Old Canada.)

Let me express this definition of New Canada a third way. Many
Canadians (this is a national trait) are more certain of what they
don't want than of what they do want. This is why negative is
always more newsworthy in Canada than positive. So let me say
what New Canada is not.

New Canada must be a federation of provinces, *not* a federation
of founding races or ethnic groups.

New Canada must be a balanced federation, *not* an unbalanced
federation where one province has special status or a special deal;
not an unbalanced federation where *all* the provinces have special
status and Canada has no status; *not* an unbalanced federation
where one generation centralizes all the power in Ottawa, and the
next generation centralizes it all in the provincial capitals in the
name of decentralization.

New Canada must be a balanced federation where the division
of powers between the federal and provincial governments is fair,
functional, and flexible, *not* a federation where the balance of
powers is simply the product of a tug-of-war between federal and
provincial politicians.

New Canada must be a truly *democratic* federation, *not* a
federation where powerful interest groups on the left or the right
succeed in getting their ideology entrenched in the constitution so
that the public cannot choose a different course even if they want
to.

The proponents of New Canada can safely argue that the
constitution of New Canada should entrench a commitment to
freedom, federalism, and democracy, but any attempt to go much
beyond that—to entrench the concepts of a Swedish-style welfare
state (as Audrey McLaughlin suggests) or an American-style

market economy (as some of us might prefer) cannot, in my judgment, be sold to the Canadian people at this point.

Fourth, let me say that of course further refinements and expansions of this definition of New Canada are required. This is one area where the Reform Party can and must open its arms wide to all Canadians for their contributions, and where you people can help me more than in any other.

If some of you could take this speech—with my conceptual definition of New Canada, imperfect and incomplete as it may be—and broaden it out where it needs broadening, deepen it where it needs deepening, and translate it into the language of the street and the neighbourhood where you live, that could be one of the greatest services that you could render this party and your country in the coming year.

My task, I told our Reformers in Saskatoon, would be not only to share our vision of a New Canada with all Canadians who would listen, but also to provide more specific directions concerning the constitutional, economic, parliamentary, and political roads that could take us there.

In the media scrum afterwards, I was asked how I felt about the day's proceedings. What came to mind was a pride difficult to express; it was a pride in our rank-and-file members and delegates from across the West and beyond, who had acquitted themselves so well that day. These people had been accused by their critics since the very inception of the party of being narrow, negative, reactionary, and parochial. By their words and their decisions that day, however, they had shown themselves to be just the opposite, demonstrating an ability to separate the wheat from the chaff on organizational matters and embracing a vision of Canada that extended far beyond their own personal interests, constituencies, provinces, and regions.

When the Vancouver assembly resolved to create a new federal party, our critics and detractors had said it would never come to pass. When the Winnipeg assembly actually founded the party, they predicted it would falter before the next federal election. When we ran seventy-two candidates in the 1988 federal election, they predicted that no one would vote for them. When we received 275,000 votes, they said we would never elect anyone. When we elected Deborah Grey in the Beaver River by-election, they said she would be the only Reformer to sit in Parliament. When Stan Waters was elected, they said he would never be permitted to take his seat. When we said we were considering expansion, they predicted that our western membership would reject that course and turn to provincial politics instead. Now they would likely predict the failure of our expansion efforts, but we would do everything within our power to ensure that this prediction would prove as untrue as the others.

Sure enough, when I was called away for remote interviews with a CTV panel in Toronto and with Barbara Frum on *The Journal,* there were polite acknowledgments of our expansion decision. But, as experience had led me to expect, these were accompanied by cheerful predictions that no doubt it would all turn out quite badly in the end.

That evening there was a banquet, followed by entertainment featuring Dave Broadfoot, whose monologue on the personal and political idiosyncrasies of Canadians was a welcome relief from the heavy debates of the day. At the banquet we honoured the members of the executive council who would be retiring upon the election of a new council the following day. These included Diane Ablonczy, Lloyd Kirkham, Gordon Shaw, Wayne Smith, Short Tompkins, and Neil Weir. Diane Ablonczy and Gordon Shaw were retiring from council after serving since the founding assembly in 1987 and I gave them a special acknowledgment for their longstanding service to the party and its membership. Nevertheless, I felt each had already received a far more appropriate tribute. For Diane it was the success of our largest assembly ever, and for Gordon it was the overwhelming endorsement of expansion.

The closing day of the assembly featured an address by Deborah Grey on the next great challenge facing our constituency people—that of recruiting a new breed of candidate into public life to represent the Reform option and lead the way to New Canada. Deborah emphasized that a commitment to the reform of Parliament was a prerequisite to attracting new people of vision and competence into federal politics. Such people would be repelled by the current ineffectiveness of a parliament constrained and perverted by executive federalism, the power of the bureaucracy, and party discipline.

I was also scheduled to give a major presentation on candidate recruitment and development, but I shortened this considerably, sensing that our delegates had just about had enough. I concluded this session by asking our constituency executives to stand, and giving them the closest thing they will ever get to a direct order from me, I said: *I charge you this day, in the presence of the delegates to this Assembly, to carry out a candidate recruitment and nomination process which will nominate the very best candidates you can discover to carry the Reform Party banner in the next federal election—candidates who are trustworthy, able, Reform-oriented, and electable.*

Following the financial report from Cliff Fryers on behalf of Reform Fund Canada, the delegates from each province retired to separate rooms to elect their representatives to the new executive council. When the results were finally announced later in the day, the additions to council included new council members Lloyd Davis from Steinbach, Manitoba; Stew Dent from Peace River, Alberta; Mike Friese from Saskatoon; Dick Harris from Prince George, British Columbia; Don Leier from Saskatoon; Myles Novak from Kelowna, British Columbia; Danita Onyebuchi from Winnipeg; Fraser Smith from Vancouver; Monte Solberg from Brooks, Alberta; George Van Den Bosch from Winnipeg; and Gordon Wusyk from Edmonton. They would join continuing councillors John Cummins, Gordon Duncan, Cliff Fryers, Elwin Hermanson, and Lee Morrison.

The Saskatoon assembly formally ended early in the afternoon of April 7. The closing ceremonies included a fast-paced video showing highlights of the assembly, demonstrating again the skills of our electronic media consultants upon whom we will increasingly rely to communicate the Reform vision of a New Canada.

My last official act at the assembly was to present two awards that the party had instituted to recognize outstanding contributions by its own members. The first was our Outstanding Reformer Award for 1991, awarded to Selby and Kathy Thorne of Rimbey, Alberta. Selby, a retired oil company executive, and his wife Kathy had taken on the onerous task of ensuring that all of the Reform Party's constituency associations in the west met the requirements for official registration and recognition prescribed by the party's constitution. At the time of the Saskatoon assembly, eighty-five of the eighty-eight federal ridings north and west of the Manitoba-Ontario border had met these requirements, thanks to Kathy and Selby's efforts and the cooperation of the constituency associations.

The second award was the Bridge-Builder's Award, inaugurated in 1991. I presented it to ninety-six-year-old Douglas Campbell, the former Liberal premier of Manitoba and Progressive MLA, now a dedicated Reformer, who had spoken so eloquently about the importance of "bridge building" at the Calgary reception to honour Deborah Grey two years before. Campbell recalled with humour and vigour the days when the Progressives swept across the West and over the Canadian Shield to elect the second-largest number of members to the Canadian House of Commons in their first fully contested federal election. If the Reform Party could do as well, the road to New Canada could be well under construction by 1992-93.

Saskatoon is divided by the South Saskatchewan River and is known as the City of Bridges, so it is appropriate that the assembly where expansion was approved was held there.

The paradoxical thing about rivers is that they can both unite and divide a country. In the eighteenth and nineteenth centuries, most Canadian cities were built on rivers. But with the passage of time, growth, and changes in our modes of transportation and communications, "the artery that brought our cities into being" became the artery that divides them. To reunite the city, to get from one part of the city to another, Canadians had to build bridges.

Similarly, in the eighteenth and nineteenth centuries, especially during the period from 1840 to 1866, the concept of a partnership between the French and the English brought the colony of Canada into being. But with the passage of time, that concept has become the thing that divides us, and now we must build bridges across it.

The federal Liberals and Conservatives, and more lately the NDP, still following a nineteenth-century map, insist that dredging the old river so that it flows more deeply and swiftly is the way to unite the country. Reformers advocate building new bridges, first between the West, Ontario, and Atlantic Canada, and then across that oldest of national rivers. If the constitutional proposals of the Reform Party appear at first glance to be at complete cross-purposes with those of the traditional parties, it is in the same way that the river dredger and the bridge builder are at cross-purposes with each other.

The Saskatoon assembly was over. It had accomplished everything we could have hoped to accomplish, and the media coverage had raised the profile of the party nationally as well as regionally. None of us knew at the time that it would be the last Reform Assembly for our Senator, Stan Waters. Later that spring, Stan was diagnosed as suffering from cancer, and after a valiant struggle he died on October 25, 1991. He had served his country in war, in peace, in business, through community involvement, and as a pioneer of Senate and fiscal reform. At his funeral in Calgary, where he was buried with full military honours, I was asked to speak about his political career. I closed by saying, "I can think of no more fitting tribute to Stan and his family than for those of us who knew and worked with him to recommit ourselves more firmly to those goals for which he gave the last full measure of devotion." The military chaplain reminded us all that, particularly in times of adversity, it was Stan who would pose the question, "What would the infantry do?" And with his characteristic enthusiasm and willingness to lead, he would answer his own question by saying, "The infantry keeps marching." If Stan had known that his address in Saskatoon in spring 1991 would be his last to a full assembly of the Reform Party of Canada, I am convinced that he would have concluded it with these same words: "Keep marching."

When I was in the consulting business, and we had just concluded a large project involving the expenditure of great amounts of time and energy to meet some deadline, I would sometimes suffer from what Sandra called "the post-project doldrums." In the Reform business, there was literally no time for the doldrums. As soon as one major event was over, there was another to take its place, and as the party grew, there were often three or four major projects going on at once.

Ken Warenko was in charge of implementing the assembly's decision to submit the expansion issue to a special party referendum. The day after the assembly, he drove back to Calgary along with Ron Wood and Stephen Harper, and set the referendum wheels in motion.

An information sheet was printed up, providing our members with the relevant background resolutions on the issue passed by the 1989 and 1991 assemblies, a summary of the pros and cons of expansion, the results of the straw vote on expansion taken at the assembly, and a description of the procedure to be followed in conducting the referendum.

The ballot itself was a tear-off flap on the back of a return envelope on which the referendum resolution was printed. Members were asked to study the resolution, "RESOLVED that the Reform Party of Canada should authorize the establishment of constituency associations and the nomination of Reform candidates in federal electoral districts east of the Manitoba-Ontario border with the regional safeguards as passed by the Saskatoon Assembly," and mark one of two boxes, AGREE or DISAGREE. The membership number of each member was to be shown on the return form so the auditors could verify that each member cast only one official ballot.

Eight days after the assembly, the ballots and information sheets were mailed out to 55,000 paid-up western members and were to be returned to the auditors by May 24. While the expansion referendum was in process, Ron Wood and I travelled to Boston, New York, Toronto, and Yorkton, Saskatchewan.

Earlier in the year I had accepted an invitation to speak at a "Canada Seminar" sponsored by the Centre for International Affairs at Harvard University. This was a monthly seminar attracting a mixed audience of students, faculty, and interested members of the public from the Boston area. From Harvard, we were scheduled to go on to New York for an address to the Americas Society. The society is a nonprofit organization dedicated to Western Hemisphere concerns and, since 1981, had been sponsoring a regular forum for the discussion of Canadian and Canada-United States issues.

We would then return to Toronto for several meetings, including an address to the Scarborough Chamber of Commerce. On our way home, we would stop in Regina and drive to Yorkton for a public meeting there. The Yorkton-Melville constituency was considered one of our "lead ridings" in Saskatchewan, and we wanted to continue to encourage its growth.

At Harvard we stayed at the Faculty Club Residence, toured the campus and some of the bookstores in the morning, had lunch with Dr. John Courtney (a visiting professor of Canadian studies), talked to a CTV crew that had come from Washington to see what we were up to, and then spoke to the "Canada Seminar" in the late afternoon of April 22.

The lecture at Harvard was followed by a wide-ranging question period, which continued with a smaller group over dinner. The most informed questions came from Canadian students studying at Harvard, whose return to Canada depended in part on whether they would be going back to Old Canada or New Canada.

At the Americas Society luncheon in New York, I was introduced by Lansing Lamont, the vice-president and managing director for Canadian affairs, who had had a long association with *Time* magazine. He mentioned that third parties had enjoyed virtually no success in the United States, but perhaps it was different in Canada. I therefore modified my introduction somewhat to remind my audience that the Republican Party, to which the current president of the United States belonged—and some of them as well—had started as a small, sectional party, and had been transformed into a national party by a secession crisis.

The luncheon was covered by both CBC and CTV television. I have never been comfortable with the strategy, used by many Canadian politicians and especially government leaders, of going to the United States to find platforms from which to impress the folks back home. However, coverage of the Reform Party leader speaking to a hundred people in New York seemed to do much more to "legitimize" the Reform Party in the eyes of some of the central Canadian media than coverage of speeches to thousands of western Canadians at our Reform Party meetings there.

After further interviews with American media (the *Wall Street Journal* and the *New York Times*), I had three short but informative sessions with the Czechoslovakian ambassador to the United Nations, the Hungarian ambassador, and the deputy consul at the Polish Embassy. These meetings had been arranged, at our request, by the office of Yves Fortier, Canadian ambassador to the United Nations, so we could get some first-hand information on the progress of the democratic reform movement in eastern Europe.

I listened to these men discuss with enthusiasm the determination of their new governments to change their countries' constitutions, economies, and political systems, all at the same time and in the face of enormous obstacles. Surely the reforms that Canadian Reformers were seeking to achieve, in a country with more than 120 years of peaceful democratic evolution to draw upon, were so modest by comparison that it was almost exaggeration to refer to them as "reforms." And given our freedoms, resources, and opportunities, how could so many of our leading politicians and commentators be so pessimistic about the prospects for systemic change in Canada, forever wringing their hands in public about what an impossible country Canada is to govern?

I had been reading *Disturbing the Peace*, by Vaclav Havel, the Czechoslovakian author and reformer who is now president of his country, and I wondered how our political establishment would react to such a man if he were invited to address the Canadian Parliament on the need for systemic change the world over. Would the title of his book lead to his being dismissed as a dangerous radical in contemporary Canada, where constitutional peace at any price is the watchword of all three traditional parties?

Havel is obviously a man whose resistance to the levelling tyranny of the old order in his own country was rooted in deeply held spiritual (though not explicitly Christian) values. Consider, for example, his response to the question, "How would you describe your present ideas regarding a more meaningful way of organizing the world?" He says: "I think that the reasons for the crisis in which the world now finds itself are lodged in something deeper than a particular way of organizing an economy or a particular political system. The West and the East, though different in so many ways, are going through a single, common crisis. . . . I'm persuaded that this conflict . . . is directly related to the spiritual condition of modern civilization. This condition is characterized by loss: the loss of metaphysical certainties, of an experience of the transcendental, of any super-personal moral authority, and of any kind of higher horizon. It is strange but ultimately quite logical: as soon as man began considering himself the source of the highest meaning in the world and the measure of everything, the world began to lose its human dimension, and man began to lose control of it."[1] If he were to say such things to the Canadian Parliament, however, would Sheila Copps be on her feet, rebuking him for mixing religion and politics, and telling him that in Canada deeply held values are only to be expressed in the personal and private spheres but not in the sphere of public policy?

Ron Wood and I left New York that night for Toronto. As luck or brilliant planning would have it (Ron insists it was the latter), we arrived the night before a national Gallup poll was released showing a dramatic increase in Reform Party support nationally and in Ontario. In Ontario our support among committed voters had increased from 3 percent in March to 15 percent. We were now at 18 percent in British Columbia, 43 percent on the prairies, and 3 percent in Atlantic Canada. Nationally Reform support had more than doubled, from 7 percent in March to 16 percent, while the Progressive Conservatives had dropped to 14 percent. For the first time we were ahead of the governing Conservatives in a national poll.

When it comes to opinion polls, I have told Reformers not to jump up and down too high when the results are favourable, so that we would have less explaining to do when the results are less favourable. Nevertheless it was difficult not to be encouraged by these numbers.

Ticket sales for my address to the Scarborough Chamber of Commerce went up dramatically, and there was a packed house. At this point, I still had to qualify my remarks on the expansion of the Reform Party of Canada into Ontario, explaining that the final decision was now in the hands of our western members voting in the special party referendum. However, the response at the Scarborough meeting to my proposals for getting Canada's constitutional, fiscal, and parliamentary houses in order was as positive and vigorous as that received at any Reform meeting in the West.

On the way home to Calgary, we stopped at Yorkton, Saskatchewan, for a public meeting. Yorkton is represented in the House of Commons by the NDP's Lorne Nystrom. Like Joe Clark, Nystrom had become increasingly distant from the concerns and positions of his constituents on issues like Meech Lake, official languages, and federal spending. At the same time, interest in the Reform Party had grown rapidly

---

1. Vaclav Havel, *Disturbing the Peace: A Conversation with Karel Hvizdala* (New York: Vintage Books, 1990), p.10.

and we had encouraged our constituency association to consider an early nominating meeting.

The Yorkton meeting was attended by more than nine hundred people (our largest Saskatchewan meeting so far), including a good mix of people who supported the NDP or the Conservatives provincially but were checking out Reform federally. Although I had spent the early part of the week speaking to audiences at Harvard and in New York, to end the week in Yorkton was appropriate. These were our people, and, unlike my American audiences, they had the power to elect Reformers to Parliament.

The executive council of the Reform Party, elected at the April assembly, held its first official sessions on the weekend of May 3-4, 1991. After productive team-building and information-sharing sessions to bring new councillors up to speed, the council elected Cliff Fryers as chairman, Don Leier from Saskatoon as vice-chairman, and Mike Friese from Saskatoon as secretary, and appointed four committees and committee chairmen to provide the essential links between the elected officials of the party and its growing full-time administration.

The council also affirmed the reorganization of the party administration into four major departments, each headed by a full-time professional administrator. The departments were Finance and Administration, responsible for Reform Fund Canada, membership services, fundraising, and office administration; Policy, Strategy, and Communications, which worked most closely with me; Constituency Development and Election Readiness, which would be transformed into our National Election Campaign Organization at some time in the future; and Special Projects, whose responsibilities included planning the expansion effort and having our lawyers chase down the various groups who were attempting to capitalize on the Reform Party's popularity by forming provincial parties with similar names.

By the end of the summer, fulltime directors had been recruited to head each of these departments. They included Hal Kupchak, Finance and Administration; Tom Flanagan, Policy, Strategy, and Communications; Virgil Anderson, Constituency Development and Election Readiness; and Gordon Shaw, Special Projects. Although we still had a long way to go in organization, it was no longer possible for our critics to say that we "didn't have the horses" to handle the upsurging interest in Reform or the day-to-day demands on a national political party.

On June 3, Ken Warenko brought into my office a brief note from Norm Knecht of Doane Raymond Pannell, the party's auditors. It contained the results of the special party referendum: 24,042 party members—42.4 percent of those eligible to vote—participated in the mail-ballot referendum on expansion, the highest response ever to any direct-mail appeal undertaken by the party. Of those responding, 92 percent had voted in favour of the resolution to expand eastward.

Two days later, Sandra and I were in Vancouver for the largest Reform Party rally held in the West to date. I announced the results of the expansion referendum that evening and the meeting erupted into thunderous applause. It boded well for the future when these residents and voters of British Columbia, who are so often accused of indifference to the fate of the parts of Canada lying east of the Rockies, so enthusiastically endorsed the eastern expansion of a party conceived at a convention in their city just four years before.

The publicity and media interest generated by the Vancouver rally not only helped raise the party profile in British Columbia but was also a great send-off for our eastern tour the next week. By this time (early June 1991) the membership of the party was over 70,000: 21,000 in British Columbia (an increase of 24 percent since the beginning of the year), 30,000 in Alberta, 10,000 in Saskatchewan/Manitoba, and almost 10,000 in Ontario.

In Thunder Bay, a lunch meeting and a public meeting in the evening were attended by eight hundred people. Membership sales, financial contributions, and media interest were all high. Reform Party expansion into Ontario was off to a good start.

Ron Wood and I then flew to Ottawa and travelled by car to Smiths Falls for a lunch meeting with our new eastern Ontario organizers. Some impromptu mainstreeting and handshaking in Smiths Falls produced a few startled looks, but a generally warm reception, and some colourful media coverage. This Ontario trip was beginning to take on the appearance of an election campaign, rather than the modest introduction of a new party that it was originally intended to be.

That evening, Deborah Grey and I addressed about 2,500 people at the Ottawa Civic Centre at Lansdowne Park. They had paid five dollars each to get in, and people had been turned away. I gave my basic Road to New Canada speech, altering it somewhat to address the accusation by some of our critics that the Reform Party was ignoring or excluding Quebec. I explained that the Reform Party wanted to have a new Quebec as an equal and fully participating province in a New Canada. Membership in the Reform Party is open to Canadian citizens living in Quebec, and we invited Quebec federalists to join us in defining a New Canada. I made clear that it would be our intention to organize and run candidates in Quebec just as soon as we were convinced of the interest and intentions of the Quebec people on participation in a new confederation. I repeated in Ottawa our conviction that the more the *people* of Quebec and the *people* of the rest of Canada are involved in the defining of the New Quebec and the New Canada, the higher the probability that the two visions can be reconciled. This is because people everywhere want more or less the same things for themselves and their children—a safe environment, good jobs with good incomes, high-quality education and health services, respect for their personal values and cultural heritages, and the freedom to live their lives in peace and dignity. On the other hand, the more the defining of either a New Quebec or a New Canada is left to intellectual or political or economic elites, through some top-down process such as that employed at Meech Lake, the lower the probability that the two visions will ever be reconciled.

In closing my remarks on this subject, I directed a short word to my fellow politicians in the traditional parties: "If the only way you can discuss the constitution of Canada is to *react* to the demands of Quebec, are you not in danger of appearing to ignore or exclude the constitutional needs of the rest of the country? And if it is a crime, as some allege, for Reformers to appear to be ignoring for a time (though we deny it) the constitutional demands of one-quarter of the country, what shall we call it when you appear to ignore or exclude the concerns of three-quarters of the country?"

From Ottawa it was back to Toronto for a full day of media interviews, meetings with my publishers, and preparations for a mammoth rally at the Toronto International Centre near the airport. The organizers sold tickets at $5 and had been engaged in a friendly rivalry for weeks with our Vancouver organizers (whose ticket price was $10) as to who could get the largest turn-out.

In Toronto the principal criticism of the Reform Party by those alarmed about our progress was that we were in some way closet racists. One female reporter with a local television station was obsessed with this subject, which made several of the media scrums repetitious and of little value to the other reporters.

That evening, when we arrived at the International Centre, there were about thirty demonstrators outside, organized under the banner of CARP (Coalition Against the Reform Party), who repeated these and similar charges. But there were 6,000 people inside and the mood there, as in Smiths Falls and Ottawa, was more like an election rally.

Reg Gosse, our newly appointed Ontario regional coordinator, was present, looking pleased as punch, as well he should have. Deborah Grey had come over from Ottawa to add her encouragement, and Gordon Shaw was there on his way to some organizational meetings in Atlantic Canada.

I gave my Road to New Canada address, this time adjusting it to reiterate what the Reform Party was *not,* just as I had often had to do in our early days in the West when we were accused of being separatists. This time I stressed that the Reform Party was not a home for people with extreme views; that we reject racism in all its forms; and that we are the only federal party that bases its approach to the constitution, immigration, and culture on *neutral laws and policies not tied to conceptions of race, ethnicity, or ancestry.* In our judgment, this colour-blind approach, abandoning ethnic criteria in defining relations between citizens and the state, is the only formula that will allow different racial groups to live together in peace in a pluralistic society.

I closed this response to the charges of racism with a reference to the literal meaning of prejudice. "The literal meaning of the word prejudice is 'to pre-judge,' to arrive at conclusions concerning the worth of individuals or groups without even knowing who or what they really are. Reformers understand that kind of prejudice because we have been the object of it ourselves. Thus we are more than prepared to unite with others to see that prejudice of every kind is removed from our politics and from this society."

Following the Toronto meeting, which garnered an enormous amount of publicity for the Reform cause in Ontario and across the country, we travelled to London and Peterborough. In London, 1,600 people in total attended a luncheon meeting and a public rally at night, and again the atmosphere was more like an election rally. At our last meeting of the tour, in Peterborough, the crowd and the mood was more like what I had originally expected for our Ontario tour. Most of the people at the Peterborough meeting had come with open minds to find out who these Reformers were and what we were about before making any commitments. They were quiet and attentive, and the question period was long and thorough.

I took the opportunity at this last meeting to sum up the week's results. About 12,000 people had attended five public meetings and two luncheons during the week in Ontario. More than 1,100 memberships had been sold directly at the meetings, representing a 10 percent increase in our membership. Thousands of pieces of literature had been distributed, and we had more than covered our expenses from financial donations received. I had met with representatives of about one-third of the federal constituencies in Ontario, where we now had seventy-seven interim constituency associations and would have eighty-five by the end of June. If our western members had any questions as to how the Reform Party might be received in Ontario, they now had their answer.

Besides repeating the main themes of the Road to New Canada speech, I also took the opportunity to respond to one more general criticism of the Reform Party, with a story Stephen Harper had passed along.

Some commentators had been asking how a new party could possibly hope to convince Canadians that it had all the answers to Canada's problems. I had replied that it was not necessary for us to do that. What Reformers had to do was convince Canadians that we at least had better alternatives to offer than the traditional parties on the main issues of the day. That we could do, and intended to do. We were like the hikers who were going through the woods when they suddenly came upon a grizzly bear in a clearing. The bear grew agitated, rearing on its back legs and sniffing the air. One hiker (the Reformer in the group), threw down his pack sack, took out his running shoes, put them on, and furiously began to lace them up. The other hikers (Liberal, Conservative, and NDP) just stared at him. Then one of them said, "You must be crazy! Don't you know you can't outrun a grizzly bear?" To which the Reformer replied, as he headed down the trail, "I don't have to outrun the grizzly. I just have to outrun you."

Part Three

Roads to New Canada

CHAPTER SIXTEEN

Road Maps, Sign Posts, and Questions

A vision of New Canada as a future destination is not enough. A reliable road map is required to lead us there. Canadians cannot afford to start out for the new world of the twenty-first century like Columbus—without a map. As the story goes, when he started out, he didn't know where he was going; when he got there, he didn't know where he was; when he got back, he didn't know where he had been; and he did it all on borrowed money. This must not be the Canadian experience.

One well-worn road is marked by political signposts that say Party First, Party Patronage, Party Discipline, Executive Federalism, and Traditional Politics. Defenders of the old political order say that this is the surest road to effective government. Reformers disagree, believing that the road to a New Canada with more representative and responsible government is a road marked by signs that say Constituents First, Ability and Integrity, Free Votes, Ask the People, Balanced Federalism, and Reformed Politics.

The traditional road is also marked by constitutional signposts that say Founding Peoples, Official Bilingualism, Government-Supported Multiculturalism, and Special Status. Advocates of these measures claim that this is the road to national identity, national unity, and constitutional peace. Reformers disagree, believing that this road leads in a circle back to Old Canada, a nation divided against itself. The Reformers' road, by contrast, is marked by signs that say Federation of Equal Provinces, Freedom of Speech, Unhyphenated Canadianism, and Equality for all Canadians.

Finally, the old road is marked by economic signposts that say Government Protection, Government Intervention, More Government

Spending, and Higher Taxation. Travellers on this route claim it is the road to economic security for Canadians. But Reformers believe that the road to a New Canada with a viable economy is marked by signs that say Free Trade, Free Markets, Spending Cuts, and Lower Taxes.

At our Vancouver and Toronto rallies, I concluded my outline of the Roads to New Canada with an illustration drawn from my old community development days in the Slave Lake country.

> Along an old back road, there was once a huge timber set in rocks, and a sign affixed to it with heavy bolts. The sign contained one word, "Sawridge," and an arrow pointing west.
>
> That sign did not change or move in over fifty years, no matter how hard the winds blew or how much snow fell. It had always said the same thing and it had always pointed in the same direction. A reliable guide, some might say. And yet, if you followed the directions on that sign, you would never get to the town of Sawridge. Although the message and the direction of that signpost had not changed, everything else around it had changed.
>
> The town of Sawridge changed its name at the beginning of this century. The town itself was relocated—moved to higher ground after a flood in the 1930s. And the roads in that area had been re-routed half a dozen times since the signpost had been planted.
>
> It was the very fact that the signpost had not changed, while everything else around it had, which made it an unreliable guide to anyone travelling that old road.

My appeal to you is simply to ask you to examine the road map to New Canada for yourself and to compare it to those offered by the traditional parties. Make inquiries and ask questions. And if the answers you receive lead you to decide that New Canada is the place where you and your children want to spend the twenty-first century, then I invite you to join with us on that journey into the future.

Many Canadians have questions for me and the Reform Party of Canada concerning our Vision of a New Canada and the roads that will take us there. Perhaps you are among them. In Chapters 17, 18, and 19, I want to answer as many of these as I can.

If you have questions that are not answered here and you would like to be part of our program of consultation and feedback, we invite you to contact us at the address given on page 359.

CHAPTER SEVENTEEN

The Road to Constitutional Peace

If there is a common negative sentiment that divides and demoralizes Canadians, it is the feeling of "being left out," especially of being left out politically, or discriminated against politically within one's own country. And if there is a common aspiration that might unite us, it is that "Canadians want in"—into the life, institutions, and decision making of their country in a new way.

In other words, there is a need for a new and stronger relationship, not only between the West and the rest of Canada, but also between other regions and the rest of Canada, between Quebec and the rest of Canada, between aboriginals and the rest of Canada, between new Canadians and old.

The great debate among Canadians and political parties during the 1990s will be whether this new and stronger relationship is to be found by going down the road of granting "special status" in federal law and the constitution, especially to those groups whose alienation is attributed to racial, linguistic, or cultural factors, or by going down a different road toward a New Canada in which all Canadians will be treated equally in federal law and the constitution regardless of their race, language, and culture.

Question 1: *All three of the traditional parties accept the definition of Canada as an "equal partnership" between founding peoples, and assert that some sort of "special status" for Quebec is essential to constitutional peace. Where do Reformers stand on this issue?*

Reformers disagree with the traditional parties, on the grounds that both historical and more recent attempts to make the French-English partnership and special status for Quebec the cornerstones of Canada's constitutional development have led to a "house divided," rather than to constitutional peace. Even the most cursory review of Canadian constitutional history will bear this out.

Following the battle between the English and the French on the Plains of Abraham, the Royal Proclamation of 1763 created the province of Quebec and tried to integrate its economy and institutions into the British system. This attempt failed, so in 1774 the Quebec Act allowed the Québécois to retain certain distinct institutions (such as the seigneurial land-holding system). When Loyalist migration to Canada created conflict within this system, the British settlers were granted a distinctive province and constitution of their own in the Constitution Act of 1791.

During the first half of the nineteenth century, the failure of the British to encourage the development of representative and responsible government in Upper and Lower Canada produced rebellions and another political crisis, which Lord Durham was sent to resolve.

In his famous report, Lord Durham said he perceived two nations (the English and the French) warring in the bosom of a single state. He wanted to give the English of Upper Canada more representative and responsive political institutions, but was reluctant to do the same for the Québécois of Lower Canada, lest that encourage the development of a separate nation. His proposed solution was to attempt to force the assimilation of the Québécois by the English element by forcing a tighter political integration between Lower Canada (Canada East) and Upper Canada (Canada West).

The Act of Union of 1840 thus integrated Upper and Lower Canada into one colony, the colony of Canada, with one Legislature, in which each region had equal representation, despite the fact that Lower Canada (Quebec) had a much greater population. The Canadian Parliament from 1840 to 1866 thus represented an attempt to accommodate two nations warring within the bosom of a single state by creating an equal partnership between two unequal groups, deliberately designed to favour the minority group. (In this case, and many Canadians need to be reminded of this, it was the English of Upper Canada who were favoured by this arrangement, and the Québécois of Lower Canada who were discriminated against.) The testimony of history is that the arrangement, whatever its intentions, didn't work, for the same reasons that the attempt to govern Canada today as an equal partnership between two unequal groups isn't working.

By the 1860s, these institutions and arrangements were in chaos, and the politicians were desperately seeking a solution. The solution they came up with was the Confederation of 1867.

It is sometimes said that the concept of Canada as an equal partnership between two founding nations is embedded in Confederation and the British North America Act of 1867. The very opposite is true. Confederation came about largely because of the failure of the "two nations" concept.

On the one hand, the BNA Act was an act of union whereby the provinces of Canada, Nova Scotia, and New Brunswick were "federally united into One Dominion under the Crown of the United Kingdom of Great Britain and Ireland." On the other hand, the BNA Act was also an act of separation in that "the Parts of the Province of Canada ... which formerly constituted respectively the Provinces of Upper Canada and Lower Canada shall be deemed to be *severed, and shall form two separate provinces.*"

In other words, the Fathers of Confederation worked to create new constitutional arrangements and structures, which sought to bypass the discredited concept of a partnership between the English and the French, rather than perpetuate it.

A broader constitutional system—a federal system—was devised. Quebec and Ontario were separated, not more tightly integrated. New partners were sought to the east and the west.

The Fathers of Confederation upheld the right of representation by population in the House of Commons, and intended to affirm the right of regional representation in the Senate. Of the 147 sections of the old BNA Act only one (Section 133) dealt directly with the English-French issue.

Macdonald and his associates clearly wanted to end the "two nations" problem, not by the political and constitutional integration of French and English institutions, but by the creation of a new nation from sea to sea which itself would be part of yet a larger entity, the British Empire. The only "special status" granted to Quebec was that of a province free to preserve its language and culture with the provincial powers allotted to it. It was left to the government of Quebec to deal with the "two nations" problem at the provincial level.

If subsequent generations of politicians had left the problem of French-English tension within the provincial confines to which the Fathers of Confederation had relegated it, and expanded and built on the new foundation of Canada as a federation of provinces rather than a federation of founding peoples, Canada might not be in the dilemma it is today. But unfortunately this was not to be.

As each new western province after British Columbia was added—Manitoba, Saskatchewan, and Alberta—there was a controversy as to whether the constitutions of those provinces should provide special status for the French minority in the areas of education and language. These provisions were promoted by federal politicians of the old two-nation school and provincial politicians from Quebec, and generally resisted by western politicians, who fully embraced the new vision of one nation from sea to sea.

Then, nearly a hundred years later, after the disintegration of the British Empire and the emergence of the Quiet Revolution in Quebec, Lester Pearson established the Royal Commission on Bilingualism and Biculturalism and revived the concept of Canada as an equal partnership between two founding races, languages, and cultures—the English and the French. Future historians will no doubt refer to this as "the Great Leap Backward." The federal government, not the government of Quebec, was proclaimed the primary guardian of the French fact in Canada. Pearson "nationalized" the very issue which the Fathers of Confederation had "provincialized" in 1867.

This vision was pursued with vigour by Prime Minister Trudeau, and it continues to shape the thinking of the current prime minister. It was affirmed in the Liberal Official Languages Act of 1969 and the Constitution Act of 1982. It is similarly reflected in the Conservatives' Official Languages Act of 1988 and the terms of the ill-fated Meech Lake Accord.

This revival of the concept of Canada as an equal partnership between founding races was doomed from the start. Even in the 1960s it was profoundly out of step with the times. The Québécois wanted to be "maîtres chez nous" (masters in our own house). Federal politicians responded by trying to bolster a national duality that had been in decline for ninety years. The cultural backgrounds of people in English-speaking Canada were becoming more and more varied. Quebeckers were calling for less bilingualism, not more bilingualism, in their own province and in the other provinces.

Most importantly, Canadians outside Ontario and Quebec were beginning to realize fully the real significance of the "two nations" theory of Canada. A Canada built on a union of the French and the English is a country built on the union of Quebec and Ontario, in which the other provinces are little more than extensions of Ontario. Moreover, arrangements giving special constitutional status to the French and the English as "founding peoples" relegate the twelve million Canadians who are of neither French nor English extraction (including aboriginal peoples) to the status of second-class citizens.

I therefore submit to you as best I can, that when Mulroney, Chrétien, and McLaughlin—when the federal Conservatives, Liberals, and NDP, when Keith Spicer's Dead Poets' Society or any other task force or commission—ask you to affirm the racial, or linguistic, or cultural duality of Canada as a foundation for future constitutional developments or as a solution to our current national unity problem, they are asking you to affirm all the wrong things.

This capsule history describes the constitutional road that federal politicians and their predecessors have travelled for a very long time. It is a road marked by signs in both official languages that say such things as, "equal partnership between French and English," "founding races, languages, and cultures," and "special status based on race." It largely bypasses the constitutional concerns of Atlantic Canada, western Canada, northern Canada, aboriginals, and the twelve million other Canadians who are of neither French nor English extraction.

Once a country starts down this road, granting special status to one or more groups based on race, language, or culture, it comes under increasing pressure to take the same approach to other groups.

In the case of Canada's aboriginal peoples, special status in federal law based on race has been the governing principle since before Confederation. Surely no one would argue that this approach has led to the social, economic, or cultural benefit of aboriginal Canadians. It has been an unmitigated disaster. The approach of Liberal and Conservative governments to multiculturalism has also made race, language, and culture the criteria for determining which groups get how much from the federal government for the preservation of cultural heritages. The concept of multiculturalism as practised by the current government further extends and institutionalizes special status based on race.

Reformers believe that going down the special status road has led to the creation of two full-blown separatist movements in Quebec and to the proposal of the Quebec Liberals to emasculate the federal government as the price of keeping Quebec in a non-confederation. It has led to desires and claims for "nation status" on the part of hundreds of aboriginal groups, claims which, if based on racial, linguistic, and cultural distinctiveness, are just as valid as those of the Québécois, if not more so. It has led to a hyphenated Canadianism that emphasizes our differences and downplays our common ground, by labelling us English-Canadians,

French-Canadians, aboriginal-Canadians, or ethnic-Canadians—but never Canadians, period.

In other words, this road leads to an unbalanced federation of racial and ethnic groups distinguished by constitutional wrangling and dead-lock, regional imbalance, and a fixation with unworkable linguistic and cultural policies to the neglect of weightier matters such as the environ-ment, the economy, and international competitiveness.

Question 2: *If the "equal partnership," "special status" road leads to a constitutional cul-de-sac, how do Reformers propose to get Canada off that road and onto a new one?*

Reformers advocate four essential steps to get out of our present consti-tutional cul-de-sac and onto the road that leads to a New Canada.

Step One: *Let us define new relationships.*
First of all, let those who want new and better relationships between Canadians define their positions in constitutional terms.

Let the people of Quebec define at least three versions of a new Quebec—a new Quebec independent of Canada, a new Quebec with special status within a revamped confederation, and a new Quebec as an equal, unique, and fully participating province in a new Canada. Then let those visions compete for the support of the Quebec people.

Let aboriginal leaders and peoples define a new relationship between themselves and the government of Canada and other Canadians. Re-formers maintain, and will continue to advocate, that an aboriginal constitutional convention would be the best mechanism for doing this.

Let the federal government and the traditional parties, if they so choose, continue to propose constitutional changes based on the old French-English partnership and special-status model.

And finally, let Canadians who want a new constitution for Canada and new relationships among Canadians based on the principle of the equality of all Canadians in federal law and the constitution define and refine that alternative. It is to the development of this alternative, under the banner of New Canada and Reform, that the Reform Party of Canada is dedicated.

Reformers believe that New Canada should be a place where the people themselves take ownership of their own constitution rather than entrusting it to "top-down" constitution makers and dice-rollers such as the Meech Lake gang. We have advocated that this defining of new and better constitutional relations among Canadians should have begun with a series of constitutional conventions into which the Canadian people would have had direct input. The fact that the current government has chosen to start the latest round of constitutional discussions without the benefit of constitutional conventions will make it extremely unlikely that the Canadian people will take ownership of the final product.

Step Two: *Let there be elections.*
Elections, in particular a provincial election in Quebec and a federal general election, will determine whose vision of the future of Canada the people of Canada are prepared to support, and whom they will choose to represent and negotiate on behalf of those visions in the political arena. Reformers believe that, on an issue as significant as the future unity or breakup of the country, referendums alone (such as the one proposed in Quebec) are insufficient to give politicians the necessary mandate to conduct follow-up negotiations.

 The principal issue in the next Quebec provincial election should be, "Who really speaks for the new Quebec and who should be entrusted to negotiate on its behalf with the representatives of New Canada?" The principal issue in the next federal election will be, "Who really speaks for New Canada and who should be entrusted to negotiate on its behalf with the representatives of the new Quebec?" In particular, "Under what circumstances, if any, can we trust a federal political leader whose position in Parliament depends on Quebec seats to represent the constitutional and economic interests of the rest of the country in negotiations with Quebec, if sovereignty-association is on the table?"

Step Three: *Let there be conclusive negotiations.*
Only after elections can the Great Canadian Constitutional Negotiation (the real thing) begin. The object of these negotiations would be to produce a new constitution for Canada—including new relationships between the people of Quebec and Canada, between the centre and the regions, between aboriginal peoples and Canada, and among all other Canadians. If Reformers had anything to do with this negotiation, the principle governing those new relationships would be the equality of all Canadians.

Step Four: *Let the people have the final say.*
Whatever new constitutional negotiations emerge in the mid-1990s from this or a similar process, the final results should be submitted to a national constitutional referendum in a process similar to that provided for in the Australian constitution, where constitutional amendments must receive a majority of votes cast overall, plus a majority in some percentage of the constituent parts of the country.

Question 3: *The timetable for Canada's future constitutional development has already been set by the Quebec and federal governments. What's the point of talking about further definition, elections, comprehensive negotiations, or national referendums when the time is so short?*

There is a tide in the affairs of Canada, and it is not governed by the partisan agendas of Robert Bourassa or Brian Mulroney. If what Quebec is really asking for is some form of sovereignty-association or some new form of special status within confederation, then it needs someone credible to negotiate with.

The timetable for such negotiations must be agreeable to both parties or no such negotiation can take place. In addition, neither the Bourassa administration nor the Mulroney administration has any real mandate to conduct such a negotiation. Real mandates to conduct negotiations of this magnitude require elections. And an agreement negotiated by the federal government or the Quebec government without such a real mandate would be as worthless as the Meech Lake Accord (that is, not worth the paper it is written on). In other words, the great Canadian constitutional development—the real thing, not the charade—cannot proceed in earnest until a Quebec provincial election and a federal general election have been held.

Question 4: *What is the Reform Party's assessment of the federal government's constitutional package entitled "Shaping Canada's Future Together" that was released in September 1991?*

The Reform Party believes that the Mulroney government's constitutional proposals contain elements essential to real constitutional reform. We are not a traditional opposition party that opposes everything the government puts forward for the sake of opposition itself. We believe in identifying and promoting those elements of the government's constitutional package that we believe the Canadian people will support, and in working to clarify and change those which the Canadian public will find ambiguous or unacceptable.

Not surprisingly, the government's constitutional proposals borrow heavily from the Reform Party's platform. Those portions of the government's constitutional package for which we have found significant public support across the country include: the principle of property rights entrenchment, freer votes in the House of Commons, the election of senators and further reform of the Senate, Senate ratification of key federal appointments, removal of interprovincial trade barriers, and the harmonization of fiscal and monetary policies.

The government's proposals also move it away from the principle of constitutional vetoes and a narrow Quebec-only agenda. All of these are positive steps.

Nowhere is the adoption of Reform proposals more obvious than in the area of Senate reform. Less than two years ago, the government strenuously opposed the appointment of even one elected senator, and the prime minister was talking openly about Senate abolition. Now the government is apparently committed to the democratic election of all senators, and has left the door open on the question of equality and effectiveness. While the government's proposals do not provide for equal representation of each province in the Senate, it concedes that the current four-region formula is unfair to outer Canada and that provinces, not regions, are the only basis for representation. The government's proposals also do not go far enough with respect to real effectiveness, but even senior government ministers are now admitting that the potential ability of the Senate to veto major legislation like the National Energy Program will be an important litmus test for the final package.

All of this tells us that Reformers are on the right track, and we will keep pushing for full Senate reform—elected senators, with equal representation from each province, with effective powers to safeguard regional interests.

There are still many ambiguities and deficiencies in the government's constitutional package. There is as yet no overall vision of a new Canada, only a "laundry list" of proposals designed to secure the support of various interests and sections of the country. It will require more than a laundry list to generate public support for the final package.

Many ideas in the government's constitutional package are still vague, especially its proposals for strengthening the Canadian economic union. Most Canadians will also continue to be uneasy about the real purpose and meaning of the "distinct society" clause until it is more clearly defined and limited.

As previously mentioned, the Reform Party conducted hundreds of meetings during the course of the Meech Lake debate, and distributed more than eighty thousand copies of the Meech Lake Accord across the West. While western Canada's principal objections to Meech Lake had to do with the undemocratic process whereby it was developed, its inadequate attention to Senate reform, and its rigid amending formula, doubts were also expressed about the concept that the constitution should be interpreted in light of "Quebec's distinctiveness."

The general feeling in western Canada was that if the distinct society clause simply meant the recognition of the historical, cultural, and political distinctiveness of Quebec, then no one could object. However, if by recognizing Quebec as a distinct society the intention was to confer upon the government of Quebec constitutional powers not conferred on other provinces, then an unlimited distinct society clause was unacceptable.

The other great deficiency in the government's constitutional package is its lack of any provision for direct participation by Canadians in the approval of the final package.

As the government's constitutional proposals are debated and modified, Reformers will continue to push for the equality of the provinces in confederation, for the equality of all citizens before the law regardless of race, language, or culture, and for a decisive voice for Canadians on the constitution through a national constitutional referendum.

At the time of this writing (October 1991) it is far more likely that the government's constitutional package will be rejected out of hand by the politicians of Quebec than by the people of the rest of Canada. The Deal Model of Confederation would suggest that if any "historic compromise" is possible on the basis of the contents of the government's current constitutional package, it would consist of four elements: a limited recognition of Quebec's distinctiveness, a Triple-E Senate, a limited (defined) recognition of the right of aboriginals to self-government, and provision for a national referendum on new constitutional arrangements. On October 1, 1991, I participated in a ninety-minute discussion with Lucien Bouchard, leader of the Bloc Québécois, who, according to public opinion polls, is currently the most trusted politician in Quebec. This discussion was chaired by Peter Gzowski of CBC's *Morningside*. At the end of our debate, Bouchard agreed that the real question for Quebec is not whether Quebec should leave the Old Canada and become independent, but whether Quebec should join the New Canada or become independent. To him, however, the only "New Canada" being offered was that represented by the federal government's current constitutional package, and that, in his judgment, was insufficient to win the hearts and minds of Quebeckers. It remains to be seen whether some "historic compromise" based on the current package, or the Reformers' vision of a New Canada would receive a better reception.

Question 5: *Does your vision of a New Canada include or exclude Quebec?*

One of the principal objectives of the great Canadian constitutional negotiation of the 1990s will be to see if the vision of the new Quebec can be reconciled with the vision of a New Canada within a broader constitutional framework. As Bouchard said, the question for Quebec should not be "Do you want to leave the Old Canada?" but "Do you want to be part of the New Canada?"

The more that the *people* of Quebec and the *people* of the rest of Canada are involved in the defining of the New Quebec and the New Canada, the higher will be the probability that the two visions can be reconciled. If, however, the visions of the New Quebec and the New Canada are the pet projects of intellectual or political elites or self-serving politicians hoping to ride to political power on a wave of Quebec nationalism or Canadian panic, the two visions may never be reconciled.

Reformers welcome the current constitutional ferment in Quebec because it will crack the Canadian constitution wide open and force the rest of Canada to address the task of developing a new one, rather than attempting to patch up the old one. We view as useful the Allaire Report, the deliberations of the Quebec Liberals, the report of the Bélanger-Campeau Commission, and the deliberations of the PQ and BQ on alternative visions of sovereignty-association—not so much for what they attempt to say specifically about the future of Canadian federalism, but for the stimulus they provide to redefining federalism and for what they say about the possible shape of a new Quebec.

At present, Reformers see three different versions of the new Quebec emerging—the BQ version, the PQ version, and the Quebec Liberal version. We wait to see which version, if any, will carry the judgment of the people of Quebec, or whether a constituency for an alternative vision of New Quebec as a strong and equal province in a New Canada will emerge. Our preference is clearly for a New Canada which includes a New Quebec.

Question 6: *How does the western-based Reform Party of Canada, which is currently expanding into Ontario and Atlantic Canada, intend to introduce its vision of a New Canada to the people of Quebec and to prepare for discussions with representatives of the people of that province in future constitutional negotiations?*

First of all, we must listen attentively to all constitutional proposals coming from Quebec; second, we must provide frank and honest feedback on how those proposals are being received in other parts of Canada; and third, we must share our vision of New Canada with those Quebeckers who express interest in it.

Reformers are federalists, not separatists, but we are unhappy federalists, and we believe that this gives us some common ground with those in Quebec who wish to see fundamental constitutional change.

It should be made clear that the purpose of the Reform Party's efforts to communicate with Quebeckers in the immediate future will not be to solicit votes. No decision has been made as yet as to whether the Reform Party should organize politically in Quebec, mainly because we have not received any encouragement to do so from the ordinary people of Quebec.

If representatives of a new Quebec are headed for a major negotiation with members of a Canadian government and Parliament representing fundamentally different views on the nature and future of Canada, I also believe it is imperative that those representatives fully understand what each is seeking, and how the demands of each might be interpreted and received in different parts of the country.

Reformers need to get a much clearer idea of how our vision of a New Canada will be received by the rank and file of people in Quebec as well as by its leadership. The people and leaders of Quebec would also be foolish indeed to proceed much further with their development of alternative visions of a new Quebec without a much more accurate assessment as to how these proposals are being received in other parts of the country. Quebec must also know whether constitutional proposals put to it by the federal government have any real public support behind them.

The following are some of the key questions we would like to explore on our visits to Quebec:

1. How does Quebec propose to deal with regional alienation within the province, that is, the alienation of people in the rural and outlying parts of the province from Montreal and southern Quebec? If changes to the structure or processes of the Quebec Assembly are proposed as solutions, would similar changes in the Parliament of Canada make these parts of Quebec feel more at home in New Canada?

2. What reforms are necessary to make Quebec more democratic and the provincial government more responsive to the wishes of the people? Would similar reforms at the federal level increase the influence of ordinary Quebeckers in Canada and make New Canada more attractive?

3. What importance do Quebeckers, especially young Quebeckers, attach to the conservation of Quebec's environment? Can environmental protection and conservation, especially of ecosystems (for example, the

St. Lawrence River basin) that cross jurisdictional lines, be better achieved by an independent Quebec or within a New Canada with a new commitment to sustainable development?

4. Given the support of the government, businesses, and people of Quebec for measures to make the Canadian economy more competitive, would a more economically competitive Canada (including Quebec), by virtue of its size and diversity, be able to provide greater economic and social security to the people of Quebec than an independent Quebec?

5. How would the people of Quebec make other racial and linguistic minorities feel secure and equal in an independent Quebec in which the majority of the population were Québécois? If a similar approach were incorporated into the constitutional arrangements of New Canada, could the Québécois then be made to feel secure and equal as citizens of New Canada?

6. What powers would the people of an independent Quebec be prepared to give to linguistic and cultural minorities in their midst to enable them to preserve their language and culture? If similar powers were given to a New Quebec within a New Canada, would this be sufficient to guarantee the cultural and linguistic security of the Québécois?

7. In the past, under what political circumstances has Quebec felt most free to be itself within Confederation? For example, has Quebec had more freedom to develop and preserve its distinctiveness under prime ministers like Trudeau and Mulroney (who have strong convictions themselves on what Quebec ought to be) or under prime ministers like Diefenbaker and Pearson who were more inclined to let Quebec "do its own thing"?

8. What should be the distinguishing characteristics of the society in which you and your children would like to live in the twenty-first century? (Reformers discussing this question with Canadians outside Quebec have received such suggestions as: a viable economy with good jobs, good incomes, and good investment opportunities; industries and businesses that are financially viable, internationally competitive, and environmentally sustainable; a balanced, democratic system of government; a genuine commitment to environmental conservation; a reliable and humane system of health, education, pensions, and social services; recognition and protection of personal rights and freedoms; freedom to preserve one's cultural heritage and most deeply held values.

9. Which constitutional arrangements—those of Canada as is, those of an independent Quebec, or those of a New Quebec within a New Canada—offer the greatest opportunities for establishing a society with the characteristics most preferred by the people of Quebec?

Finally, I would like to explore ways to more effectively communicate Quebec's constitutional positions outside Quebec, and to improve understanding in Quebec of the constitutional positions of the rest of Canada by some means other than accepting at face value the representations of federal or provincial politicians who have a vested interest in creating misunderstanding. In particular, I want to find some analogy to discuss the relationship between Quebec and Canada that is more appropriate than the marriage or divorce model.

According to communications experts, analogies are one of the most effective mechanisms for cross-cultural communication *if* the appropriateness of the analogy is accepted by both parties.

In Quebec, where the "equal partnership" model is still accepted, politicians and journalists refer to the relationship between Quebec and the rest of Canada as being comparable to a marriage, and the separation of Quebec from the rest of Canada as being analogous to a divorce, with the suggestion that there is such a thing as an amicable divorce and that is what should be pursued.

In western Canada, there is virtually no acceptance of the concept of Canada as some sort of marriage between the French and the English. If at one time there was such a marriage, both partners (colonial France and colonial England) died a long time ago, leaving the estate under the joint jurisdiction of twelve siblings (ten provinces and two territories) and a paternalistic guardian (the federal government). The current problems are seen more as sibling rivalry than a marriage breakdown. The oldest sister (Quebec) is unhappy living at home and wants to move out. Her primary quarrel is with the other older sibling (Ontario) and the guardian, and she is largely indifferent to the brats of confederation like Alberta and Newfoundland.

Whose analogy best describes the current situation, and if neither, had we not better find appropriate analogies to use?

Even if one accepts the marriage analogy, it breaks down when we come to the question of divorce. The words Lincoln addressed to the seceding South in his first inaugural address are equally applicable to Canada and Quebec.

> Physically speaking, we cannot separate. We cannot remove our respective sections from each other, nor build an impassable wall between them. A husband and wife may be divorced and go out of the presence and beyond the reach of each other, but different parts of the country cannot do this. They cannot but remain face to face;

and intercourse, either amicable or hostile, must continue between them. Is it possible then to make that intercourse more advantageous, or more satisfactory, after separation than before? Can aliens make treaties more easily than friends can make laws? Can treaties be more faithfully enforced between aliens than laws can among friends?

Question 7: *What if the constitutional negotiations proposed by Reformers fail to reconcile divergent visions of New Quebec and New Canada?*

If the vision of a New Quebec within a New Canada cannot be realized, then the great Canadian constitutional negotiation will divide into two sections. One, involving the federal government, nine provinces, two territories, and aboriginal representatives, will focus on the constitution of a New Canada without Quebec. The second would focus on defining mutually advantageous terms and conditions of a more separate relationship between Quebec and New Canada.

I believe that in fairness to the people of Quebec it should be stated that, if the negotiations take this turn, whoever is negotiating on behalf of New Canada is unlikely to be attracted to the concept of sovereignty-association as currently advanced by some Quebec politicians.

The principal object of those negotiating on behalf of New Canada will be to minimize the economic and other costs to New Canada of a Quebec secession, and to enter only into those relationships with an independent Quebec that are clearly in New Canada's interest.

Question 8: *If Reformers say they favour the equality of all Canadians, how do they propose to provide for the treatment of those who are genuinely disadvantaged or discriminated against (the poor or the disabled, for example)? If you simply treat everyone the same, and there is genuine inequality at the outset, the position of the disadvantaged does not improve, and inequities persist.*

Reformers support "equality of opportunity," not "equality of results." We believe that an open, free-market economy, combined with a genuinely democratic political system, offers the best possible chances for individuals to pursue their goals in life. It is true that not everyone starts from the same position, but these inequalities are not necessarily cumulative and inherited. A market economy, open society, and democratic polity are great engines for the destruction of privilege.

I have been particularly impressed by the work of Thomas Sowell,[1] the black American economist who has written so eloquently on ethnic relations around the world. Sowell has shown conclusively, in my view, that disadvantaged minorities can overcome their disadvantages if the system is open; and, conversely, no amount of affirmative action or special status does any good unless the members of that disadvantaged minority are affirming themselves by their own efforts to achieve a better life.

Of course, government plays a key role in all of this. It is to ensure that the economy and society are truly open and competitive, and that the means of self-improvement are available to all. This means a major emphasis on "human resources development": public health, protection of the life and property of citizens, provision of education, job training, and essential infrastructure. It also means avoiding measures that categorize people on the basis of immutable personal characteristics. For example, working women who have children face many obstacles to their careers. Government has a role to play in legislating about such matters as pregnancy and childbirth leave, children's credits in the tax system, and so on. Such legislation would have a direct impact upon more women than men, since only women bear children, and they tend to be more involved in caring for them. But it would not set women in general up as a special class. Some women might never be affected by the legislation, and some men might be.

This exemplifies the Reform vision of how to deal with disadvantage: diagnose the problem and devise specific measures to enable people to take greater control of their own lives. Do not ghettoize society by putting people into legal categories of gender, race, ethnicity, language, or other such characteristics.

Question 9: *How do Reformers propose to establish a new relationship between aboriginals and other Canadians that would be distinguished by greater equality?*

When we ask aboriginal leaders and people to define a new relationship between themselves and the government of Canada, some (for example, the Council of Yukon Indians) say that the basis of that new relationship should be fair and expeditious settlement of land claims, the acceptance by aboriginal people of responsibility for their own welfare and development

---

1. Thomas Sowell, *Preferential Policies: An International Perspective* (New York: William Morrow and Company Inc., 1990).

through aboriginal self-government, and constitutional protection by Canada of agreements on self-government.

When we ask non-aboriginal leaders and people what they think the
new relationship between aboriginals and the government of Canada
should be, many recommend abolishing the Department of Indian
Affairs and transferring its responsibilities to aboriginal agencies and
governments, subject to obtaining satisfactory answers to the following
questions: (1) Would these aboriginal governments and agencies be
democratically accountable to their own people for their actions?
(2) How would these aboriginal governments and agencies relate to other
levels of government and to non-aboriginals? For example, would they take
an independent or cooperative approach to resource management (fish-
eries, forests) and environmental conservation? (3) Who will represent the
interests of non-aboriginals in the settlement of land claims?
(4) How much will all this cost, and who pays? (5) If democratic and
accountable aboriginal governments and agencies are established, and
outstanding land and treaty claims are settled, would we then be closer to
the equality of all Canadians because aboriginals could relate to their local
governments in much the same way as other Canadians relate to their local
governments (receiving services, paying taxes), or would we be further
away than before?

In the months ahead, the Reform Party hopes to get answers to these
questions from aboriginal leaders and to help work toward some practical
and acceptable approach to aboriginal self-government, mainly through
communications with non-aboriginals.

Question 10: *You say that the current constitution and multiculturalism
policy relegates Canadians who are of neither French nor English extraction to
the status of second-class citizens. How do you propose to treat these Canadians
more fairly and still preserve Canada's multicultural heritage?*

The Reform Party's position in this area is based in part on a presentation
made to the party several years ago by Professor Rais Khan, head of the
political science department at the University of Winnipeg. Professor
Khan said:

> People, regardless of their origin, do not emigrate to preserve
> their culture and nurture their ethnic distinctiveness. If they wished
> to do that, they would stay where they were because the
> environment is more conducive to the perpetuation of one's
> culture and ethnicity. Immigrants come here to become Canadians;

to be productive and contributing members of their chosen society. I am one of them. I did not come here to be labelled as an ethnic or a member of the multicultural community, or to be coddled with preferential treatment, nurtured with special grants, and then to sit on the sidelines and watch the world go by. I came here to be a member of the mainstream of the Canadian society. I do not need paternalism; I need opportunity. I do not want affirmative action; I expect fairness. I do not desire special consideration; I wish to be treated equally. . . .Whether or not I preserve my cultural background is my personal choice; whether or not an ethnic group preserves its cultural background is the group's choice. The state has no business in either.

The Reform Party believes that cultural development and preservation ought to be the responsibility of individuals, groups, and, if necessary in certain cases (for example, in the case of Quebec and Canadian aboriginals), of provincial and local governments. The role of the federal government should be neutral toward culture just as it is toward religion.

This does not mean necessarily an abandonment of the mosaic model of Canada, but a different division of labour in order to develop that mosaic. Let individuals, groups, lower levels of governments if necessary, be responsible for cutting and polishing the individual pieces. But let the government of Canada be responsible for the common background on which those pieces are to be stuck, and the glue that holds them together. The elements of that common background and glue may include the rule of law, an open economy, an efficient public administration, guarantees of artistic and other freedoms, and shared symbols such as the national flag and anthem.

Reformers believe that a country solidly built on elements that all Canadians hold in common (interest in a clean environment, a strong economy, a democratic government, a free and caring society) will in the end provide the greatest opportunity for preserving those elements that are unique.

Question 11: *What division of powers do Reformers recommend for the constitution of New Canada? Are Reformers centralizers, decentralizers, or something else?*

The balance of power between the federal and provincial governments should not rest on action and reaction, that is, centralization (as occurred under Trudeau) in the 1970s and reactive decentralization (as proposed by

Mulroney in the Meech Lake Accord) in the 1990s. Reformers want a division of powers designed to fulfil the needs that Canadians share, including the need for a competitive economy, a responsible community, and environmentally sustainable development.

If Canadians believe it is an important national goal to develop a modern, knowledge-based, service-sector economy, then the jurisdiction of the federal government should be strengthened in areas of economic education, such as post-secondary education and manpower training.

If Canadians want to create a common market among the provinces, then we must clarify and expand federal jurisdiction over trade and commerce and include a constitutional provision for a trade settlement mechanism in interprovincial trade.

If Canadians want to maintain a socially responsible community, then the division of powers and responsibilities between the levels of government for social policy must be disentangled. Full authority for income security and income support, including financial access to social services, should be the responsibility of the federal government, while the legislating and administering of social services should rest with the provinces. As well, the federal government should at least retain its existing legislative authority in matters of law and order.

If Canadians want to make sustainable development a national goal, any new constitutional arrangements must allow both levels of government to delegate appropriate powers and create integrated, ecosystem-based agencies, along the lines of the St. Lawrence Seaway Authority, to handle environmental concerns.

If Canadians want to recognize and preserve certain regional distinctions, without sacrificing national unity in the process, then we must strengthen provincial powers over language and culture, and provincial ownership and management of offshore resources.

The most important division of responsibility in the constitution of New Canada will not be the division of responsibility between the federal and provincial governments, but the division of responsibility between the state and its citizens, between the governmental and nongovernmental sectors. Constitutions that permit and encourage governments to command 50 percent or more of the GNP of a nation are a burden, not a boon, to the citizenry. The character of the governments established by the constitution of New Canada should be that of "governments that enable" rather than governments which, because of their size and power, are able to command and dictate.

The constitution of New Canada should create a federal government that does a few things well, rather than a government that attempts everything and succeeds at nothing. That constitution should provide Canadians with all the tools and safeguards, including a Charter of Rights and Responsibilities, necessary to ensure that government of the people, by the people, and for the people is a practical reality.

Question 12: *Your vision of New Canada says nothing about the social or cultural or spiritual aspirations of Canadians, our international role, the role of sciences and the arts, or our northern environment. Do Reformers have plans for addressing these subjects?*

Reformers currently define New Canada as a "balanced, democratic federation of provinces, distinguished by the conservation of its environment, the viability of its economy, the acceptance of its social responsibilities, and the acceptance of the uniqueness and equality of all its citizens and provinces." Our vision of New Canada includes a New Deal for aboriginals, a New Senate to address regional alienation, and a New Quebec.

The fact that our vision statement is still "under construction" at this point is understandable and appropriate. The Reform Party is only four years old and not yet fully organized across the country. It is also our philosophy that politicians, including Reformers, do not have a monopoly on defining the New Canada.

Every Canadian we talk to has comments to make on our vision of New Canada and something to add. It is important for politicians to listen, synthesize, and then sketch a vision of the future to which others can react. It is even more important to provide the institutional foundations and democratic procedures whereby the judgments of millions of other Canadians can be brought to bear on defining the shape of New Canada and the policies that will take us there.

CHAPTER EIGHTEEN

The Road to a
More Democratic Canada

Question 1: *You say that the Canadian Parliament and the decision-making processes of the federal government need to be made more democratic and responsive to the needs of Canadians. What specific reforms do you propose to democratize Canada?*

In the twentieth century, fear of majority rule has become a liberal issue, and constitutional instruments like the Charter of Rights and Freedoms in Canada have been advocated as a way to protect minorities from oppressive majorities. These minorities are usually defined on the basis of race, language, culture, belief, or gender. Political, economic, and cultural minorities have also organized "special interest groups" to represent them and help them participate in the political process.

Although Canadians need constitutional, institutional, and political safeguards against the tyranny of the majority, Reformers believe that safeguards are also needed to protect Canadians against "the tyranny of minorities."

As special interest groups are given more status, privileges, and public funding, they use their bargaining power to exact concessions from governments that are both economically inefficient and politically un-democratic. Business lobby groups, for example, have been able to secure a level of grants, tax concessions, and subsidies for certain sectors which a majority of taxpayers would not support if they were given the opportunity to express their opinion. Linguistic and cultural minorities have been able to secure federal language and cultural policies which, according to opinion polls, do not carry the endorsement of a majority of the people in the country.

The institution in which the tyranny of minorities is most evident is the Parliament of Canada itself. The Senate has become a chamber filled with patronage appointments by the prime minister and party in power. In the House of Commons, the practice of making every vote a partisan confidence vote frequently prevents members from faithfully and accurately representing the wishes of the people who elect them. Its decisions are often completely contrary to majority opinion across the country.

Reformers therefore argue that to get on the road to New Canada we need a fundamental reform of our democratic institutions and processes. In particular, we advocate reforms to the House of Commons and the Senate of Canada, a new theory and practice of "representation" in Parliament, and more direct input by the public into governmental decision making.

In advocating such reforms, Reformers identify themselves with "the reform tradition" in Canadian politics that originally brought this country representative and responsible government. We also identify with the current worldwide movement to democratize undemocratic institutions and processes, and to break the tyranny of modern "Family Compacts" of bureaucrats, politicians, and special interests that exercise the tyranny of a minority over democratic majorities.

Question 2: *Constituents (voters) want their MPs to more faithfully and accurately represent constituents' views in Parliament. Voters also want political parties to keep their platform promises and practise their principles after elections. And voters want MPs to bring their own judgment and experience to bear on public policy decisions. If Reformers are elected to Parliament, how do they propose to reconcile and represent all these conflicting demands?*

Canadians want their members of Parliament to faithfully and accurately represent their views on a major issue when a clear consensus on that issue can be determined in the riding. (This is what political scientists call the "delegate" theory of representation.)

Canadian voters also want their representatives to practise the principles, implement the platforms, and keep the promises on which they were elected to Parliament. In other words, voters not only expect, but will demand, that on many occasions their elected representatives "vote the party line" because that's what they promised to do if elected. (This is what political scientists call the "mandate" theory of representation.)

At the same time, most Canadians are prepared to respect the judgment, conscience, and experience of their individual elected member, particularly if that member shows respect for the judgment, values, and experience of constituents. (This is called the "trustee" theory of representation.)

Effective representation in a modern democracy, therefore, is not a matter of representing "constituent interests only" or "party principles and platform only" or "member's judgment only," but a judicious and practical combination of the three in accordance with well-understood principles and practices.

The Reform Party has drawn on all three models to develop what I, as a former physics student, like to call a "unified field" theory of representation. Our starting point, as a party of principle with a platform to which we are publicly committed, is the mandate model. We will go to the electors committed to a definite set of principles and platform proposals, and those who vote for us will do so because they expect us to try to implement those principles and platform proposals. To do what our electors expect of us, we will have to work together as a caucus.

Our understanding of our mandate, however, differs sharply from that of the traditional parties. First of all, we will have a democratic caucus, in which positions will be adopted by majority decision after open debate, without heavy-handed direction from the party leadership. Moreover, the Reform Party's principles call for us to recognize the duty of members of caucus to represent the will of their constituents in cases where there is a clear consensus within the constituency, and to respect the rights of members to bring their own judgment and values to bear on public policy issues at the constituency and caucus levels. Both the delegate and trustee models will therefore operate within the caucus, subject to certain limits, with party principles and platform providing the general framework for decision making.

A constituency consensus (especially one that called for a Reform MP to depart from the party line) will have to be expressed in some tangible and persuasive way—perhaps by a constituency referendum using electronic technology. The ratification of the Meech Lake Accord and the passage of the GST are two recent cases where invocation of the delegate model of representation could have saved Parliament from implementing decisions that clearly did not conform to the judgment of the public.

Question 3: *You have said a lot about reforming the Senate of Canada. What about reforming the House of Commons?*

The Reform Party advocates that general elections be held every four years at a fixed date, with the possibility of an early election only if the government was defeated in the House on a specific vote of non-confidence. This measure is designed to reduce the influence of the prime minister over the elected representatives of the people.

The simplest, and most important, recommendation of the Reform Party with respect to the House of Commons, however, is a reform of the use of confidence votes. At present, virtually every vote in the Canadian House of Commons is treated as a partisan confidence vote. If a government motion is lost, the government considers itself defeated and may seek a dissolution and an election. This fact is used by the government's whips to force members to vote against their constituents' interests, since defeating a government measure will not just defeat that measure but could also remove the government itself from office.

Under present arrangements, there is less freedom of speech and freedom of political action in the Canadian House of Commons than there is in any other political forum in the country. Defections that embarrass the leaders of the party can lead to expulsions from the caucus, as happened to Alex Kindy and David Kilgour in 1990 after they voted against the GST. Members are censured for representing their constituents' views when those differ from the government or party line, and rewarded for voting against constituents' interests in favour of the party line.

Reformers (and we have no monopoly on this proposal) believe that the defeat of a government measure in the House of Commons should not automatically mean the defeat of the government. Defeat of a government motion should be followed by a formal motion of non-confidence, and only if that formal motion of non-confidence passes would the government be required to resign.

Strictly speaking, no rule change is required to adopt this policy; law, convention, and precedent in other chambers such as the British Parliament already permit what the Reform Party wants to see happen. All that is required is for the government of the day to make a policy statement at the beginning of the session that it will not resign unless a defeat in the house is followed by an explicit vote of non-confidence. This is what Prime Minister Trudeau did during the Liberal minority government in 1972-74. His government was defeated eight times in eighty-one recorded divisions, and he resigned only on the last vote because he was then prepared to go to the polls.

The adoption of this simple change will ensure that a five-party parliament (which may very well exist after the next federal election) can operate efficiently. It will also promote fiscal restraint in government. As Donald Savoie puts it:

> On the face of it, one may well assume that parliament plays a crucial role in the expenditure budget process. Constitutional niceties aside, however, it does not. Parliament does not exercise executive authority and, although spending estimates are tabled annually, parliament seldom even "tampers with them." They are invariably accepted as submitted. Parliament can only introduce motions to reduce the estimates, given the principles that spending must originate with the government. If a spending proposal is rejected, tradition requires that it must be taken as a vote of no confidence in the government and the government must resign—for to challenge the amounts of spending determined by the government would bring into question the confidence of the House of Commons in the cabinet. This is the single most important reason why parliament, particularly with a majority government in place, merely "rubber stamps" the expenditure budget. One Progressive Conservative backbencher recently explained: "If we could change spending plans without bringing down our government, you can safely assume that some departments, agencies, and crown corporations would never get what they receive every year. CBC jumps to mind as an excellent case in point. But believe me there would be others. And I have no doubt whatsoever that I reflect the majority view of the government caucus."[1]

Question 4: *You call for more direct public input into national decision making. What reforms do you propose to bring this about?*

The Reform Party of Canada advocates the passage of a National Referendum and Citizens' Initiative Act (and related constitutional amendments) to provide greater opportunity for more direct input by the people of Canada into major federal government decisions affecting their interests and their future. The act would make it legally and administratively possible for the Parliament of Canada to ask the people of Canada to vote on a matter of public policy or legislation, and enable the people of Canada to demand a public vote on a matter of public policy or legislation if a large number of Canadians wants such a vote to be taken.

---

1. Donald J. Savoie, *The Politics of Public Spending in Canada* (Toronto: University of Toronto Press, 1990), pp. 26-27.

Such legislation should provide for both binding and advisory referendums. To minimize administrative complications and costs, national referendums could be held in conjunction with national elections, with perhaps mid-term referendums on fixed dates. At election time voters would receive two ballots at the poll—one a ballot on which they would mark their choice for member of Parliament, the other a referendum ballot on which they would express their views or directions with respect to certain key federal issues, especially major constitutional issues. Greater use of modern technology (the use of electronic voting versus paper ballots) will also make national referendums in a country like Canada more efficient and less expensive.

The referendum legislation should ensure that the process is fair and confined to dealing with major issues, rather than localized concerns. The enabling legislation should facilitate the conduct of educational campaigns with respect to the pros and cons of the referendum issue, but should not attempt to overregulate these campaigns.

Because Canada is a federal state with an unevenly distributed population, most national referendums should be subject to the "double majority" principle. By this I mean that a referendum ballot should be decided in favour of the position receiving 50 percent plus one of the votes cast overall, and a majority in more than half of the jurisdictions affected.

Because governments may abuse referendum legislation (by conducting referendums only on those issues which enhance the government's position, or manipulating questions so as to get a desired outcome), Reformers support provisions for "citizens' initiatives." This provides the people with an opportunity to place an issue or question on the referendum ballot by filing a petition with a certain number of names with the chief electoral officer.

The number of names required to launch a citizens' initiative should be high enough to prevent frivolous use of the exercise. In the American states, citizens' initiatives require signatures from between 5 and 10 percent of the electorate. Switzerland uses a fixed total of signatures rather than a percentage. We propose a 3 percent minimum for Canada. In 1991, this means approximately 780,000 names.

Reformers also advocate a special initiative generally known as the "recall petition." If a sufficient number of electors in a federal constituency file a recall petition with the chief electoral officer, they can force their elected member to stand down; a by-election would then be held. While I understand and agree with the sentiment that has given rise to the support of recall (that is, the desire for greater accountability of elected officials), Reformers have some more work to do to develop a recall procedure that will not be subject to abuse.

The main value of having a recall provision is its existence as a threat, since its employment is quite cumbersome. Because it is possible for a Canadian MP to get elected in a four-party race with only slightly more than 25 percent of the popular vote, the threshold levels on recall petitions must be quite high, so as not to result in recall being used simply as a partisan device for unseating political opponents. Reformers should also be well aware that if such legislation were ever introduced by a Reform government, its first exercise would be against Reform members of Parliament by their political opponents.

In calling for these simple direct-democracy measures, the Reform Party has made it abundantly clear on numerous occasions that we are not calling for some extreme form of "government by referendum." We do not want to imitate the Swiss system, where citizens vote three times a year on an average of twelve federal issues, in addition to voting in cantonal and municipal referendums as well as elections to office at all three levels of jurisdiction. Not surprisingly, "voter fatigue" is suspected as one of the major reasons for low referendum turnouts in Switzerland.

The Reform Party is talking about Canada—a country that had only one national referendum in the nineteenth century (the prohibition referendum in 1898) and only one national referendum in the twentieth century (the 1942 conscription referendum). We are not saying that a nation that has averaged one national referendum per century should suddenly start to have one every second Tuesday. But we are saying that there must be some reasonable middle ground where, at least from time to time, on important issues, the public can have a direct say in certain key national decisions.

The Reform Party is not calling for direct democracy as an alternative to representative and responsible government as exercised through parliamentary institutions. We advocate these measures as a necessary complement to parliamentary democracy, to make the government more representative and responsible than at present. The aim is to achieve a better balance and to ensure that one set of abuses (the constant ignoring of majority opinion by elected officials and special interests) is not replaced by another set of abuses (the use of referendum votes by majorities to run roughshod over minority rights or special interests).

In order to avoid the problem of majority tyranny, certain safeguards must be built into the referendum process, even though there is little evidence that people acting through referendums are more likely to oppress minorities than are legislatures. The use of double majorities, as in the Australian system, is one mechanism for providing protection of minority interests against majority interests in referendums. For example, if a national referendum in Canada on the National Energy Program had to be carried by majorities in two-thirds of the provinces, consumer interests in the heavily populated or subsidized provinces could not have run roughshod over producer interests in the four western provinces.

The Canadian Charter of Rights and Freedoms already protects minority rights, and direct legislation that went counter to the Charter could be invalidated by the courts. The current wording of the "notwithstanding" clause requires the approval of a legislature to suspend Charter rights. I do not support the idea of allowing portions of the Charter to be suspended by referendums. If people want to change any of the rights entrenched in the Charter, the proper course is to use the initiative to amend the constitution itself, not to suspend its provisions.

As for the criticism that Canadians are not well enough informed to make important decisions by referendum, Reformers agree with that old Democrat, Thomas Jefferson, who said, "I know of no safe depository of the ultimate powers of society but the people themselves, and if we think them not enlightened enough to exercise control with a wholesome discretion, the remedy is not to take it from them, but to inform their discretion."

Question 5: *You talk a lot about "reforming the political system." Isn't it "the people involved in the system" who make the difference?*

The motivation, values, skills, abilities, and dedication of the people we choose to run our democratic institutions of government are just as important as—if not more important than—the rules, procedures, and policies governing those institutions.

The Reform Party of Canada could grow to two hundred thousand members and have $15 million in the bank by the next federal election. It could define a vision of Canada and a road map for getting there that would turn Sir John A. Macdonald green with envy. It could recruit Wayne Gretzky for a leader, and use the best organizational and political technology available in its election campaign. But unless it is able to offer the Canadian people candidates capable of commanding their trust and of translating that vision and platform into reality, all our good intentions and work done to date could go for naught.

One of the great tragedies of our present parliamentary system is that its defects and inefficiencies often drive good people to despair and out of the system. Men and women go to Parliament with high hopes of influencing the future direction of their country for good or advancing some legitimate cause of genuine interest to their constituents. But within a short time they find themselves reduced to the role of glorified clerks, dispensing prepackaged information on government programs and handling complaints, while major decisions on policy and direction are made elsewhere and presented to them for rubber stamping. Party discipline forces them to vote against their constituents' wishes on matters of fundamental importance, straining to the breaking point the friendships, understandings, associations, and trust that made their election to Parliament possible in the first place.

Worst of all, the current pace and seeming futility of much parliamentary activity put severe strains on the MPs' personal and family relations. There are lobbyists in Ottawa whose starting premise is that one out of three MPs has a marital, financial, or drinking problem that makes him or her ineffective or vulnerable to influence and direction by others. I have heard the following lament from spouses of MPs: "It isn't just the long hours and the long absences from home; it isn't just the strain of maintaining two bases, or the constant personal criticism and partisan sniping. In the end, it's the futility of it all, of suspecting that after all the speeches, all the meetings, all the travel, all the phone calls, all the effort and sacrifices, nothing has really been accomplished—that nothing in Canada is fundamentally different, that nothing in the riding is fundamentally different as a result."

There are at least two ways to give greater recognition to the importance of the human factor in the operation of our parliamentary institutions. The first is to get a respected third party whom current members of Parliament and their families might be prepared to trust to conduct a private forum and inquiry on behalf of the members of the House of Commons itself, and propose ways in which the priorities and procedures of Parliament might be changed to make serving in Parliament a more positive personal experience for members and their families.

The second measure is to recruit and train a new kind of politician for the twenty-first century, whose mission is to change the federal political system itself rather than to conform to it. The bottom line is to provide better government and better service for the electors of Canada, to make Canada a model democracy in an age in which genuine democracy is becoming the ideal of a growing number of countries, while enhancing rather than depleting the lives of those who choose to serve in the Parliament of Canada.

Question 6: *What kind of people is the Reform Party looking for to carry its banner in the next federal election?*

My short answer is that the Reform Party is looking for men and women who are trustworthy, reform-oriented, and able. If we could find such people, we are convinced that they would also be electable.

Trustworthy People

At public meetings, Reformers frequently hear people say, "We don't trust anyone in the current Parliament." The next question is usually, "And why should we trust these Reformers? They may mean well, but in the end will they be any more trustworthy?" It is a legitimate question. So we have been asking voters, "Whom *do* you trust? Whom would you trust to renegotiate your constitution? Whom would you trust to lower government spending to the point where it results in tax relief? Whom would you trust to make Parliament work better? There must be *someone* in your community, in your businesses or your unions or your community associations whom you would be prepared to entrust with the management of your public affairs. Tell us whom you are prepared to trust and we will try to recruit such people into public life at the federal level on the Reform ticket."

But finding good candidates should not be left entirely to us or any other party. There are hundreds of Canadian communities that have given more thought to hiring their rink manager than they have to electing their member of Parliament. Most Canadians take no interest whatsoever in the process whereby names get on the ballot prior to a federal election. And then we all complain about the limited selection and wish there was a box on the ballot where we could vote "None of the Above."

Finding candidates for election to the federal Parliament whom Canadians are prepared to trust also requires us to look at personal motivation. The objective should be to find candidates whose primary motivation is public service rather than the satisfaction of personal ambition.

One of the most insightful statements on this subject was made long ago by Jesus Christ, when he said to the most ambitious members of his small band of followers, "He who would be chief among you, let him be the servant of all." He was careful not to quench their ambition; he did not directly criticize their desire to be chief; but he tried to channel that ambition by insisting that the way to the top was through service to others.

Reform-Oriented People

The Reform Party of Canada is looking for people who are committed to more than protest. We are looking for people who are committed to constructive change and who actually practise the political values they preach. We wish to avoid candidates such as certain traditional Liberals who loudly proclaim their personal commitment to freedom of conscience and belief, and then attack other politicians for expressing opinions based on their most deeply held values.

The Reform Party is looking for spokespersons and candidates who don't just talk about fiscal responsibility, but who practise it in the place where they are now—in their own homes, businesses, unions, or community organizations. We are looking for people who don't just talk about social concern, but demonstrate a concern for the young, the old, the sick, and the poor in the place they are now. We are looking for people who don't just talk about the value of the common sense of the common people on a political platform, but who seek to find and listen to that voice in the place where they are now.

My personal experience is that if men or women practise a principle or pursue a policy in their home life or workplace or business, you may be able to count on them to continue to do so if you elect them to a council or legislature or parliament. This is why traditional Conservatives of the reactionary variety, who spend most of their lives resisting change, are usually the wrong people to reform constitutions or tax laws or institutions. If Canadians really want to reform the constitution, or the spending habits of the federal government, or the parliament, we should recruit and elect genuine Reformers to do the job.

Knowledgeable and Able People

The Reform Party is looking for candidates who are equipped with the necessary knowledge and skills to serve effectively in the next Parliament of Canada. We have provided all our constituency associations with a "job description" for a member of Parliament, listing the principal functions that an MP must be able to perform and the basic knowledge requirements of a parliamentary caucus. Our list gives highest priority to representing, legislating, administering, and communicating. Our knowledge list includes the major subjects and issues that are the focus of departmental and parliamentary attention.

We are not, at this stage, so much looking for grand visionaries with a thousand brilliant ideas on every public policy issue involved in building the New Canada. Rather, we are looking for a hard-working group of political tradespeople who can tackle the unglamorous but absolutely essential job of fixing the foundations, the plumbing, and the lights of our broken-down constitutional, fiscal, and parliamentary houses.

Electable People

If we can find candidates who are trusted by the people in their ridings, who personify the demand for change that is coursing through this country, and who have the skills and knowledge necessary to perform in a modern parliament, we will have come a long way towards finding candidates who are electable. The Reform Party does not, however, equate "high profile" with electability. Recycled politicians from traditional parties who jump on the Reform bandwagon may have high profile, but our preference would be to go with less well-known people, even younger people short on experience but long on potential, if they possess these other characteristics of trustworthiness, Reform orientation, and ability.

Question 7: *How are you going to protect the Reform Party from influence or takeover by extremists or single-issue people who are often attracted to new political parties?*

The membership and candidate recruitment programs of the Reform Party of Canada are designed to attract balanced individuals who are constructively committed to the principles and policies of the party and our vision of a New Canada. However, new political parties, especially if they are populist and "open" at the bottom end, are vulnerable to influence by extremists or single-minded people. As my father used to say, "A bright light will attract a few bugs."

As leader of the Reform Party, I intend to do everything within my power to protect the party from this danger. This intention is shared by the party's executive council and administrative personnel, and the vast majority of our constituency executives and members. But we need your help.

I frequently meet people who say, "You seem to be reasonable and sincere, and I agree with your Reform program. But I'm afraid that some of your supporters are extreme and eccentric, so I hesitate to join you."

May I respectfully ask, "Why do you hesitate? Why should a few extremists and eccentrics have more influence with you than I do? Why should they have more influence than the large numbers of Reformers who are neither extreme nor eccentric?" Is it not this tendency of so many Canadians to withdraw when confronted with extremism or aggressiveness that makes so many of our institutions and organizations vulnerable to influence by tiny minorities who do not represent the broader community?

If you believe that Canada needs constitutional, economic, and political reform, and if you recognize the vulnerability of a Reform movement to negative influences, you are right. But please react by joining with us to ensure that the Reform movement is not hijacked by unrepresentative minorities, rather than withdrawing and increasing the probability of such a result.

Question 8: *How is the Reform Party handling the recruitment of candidates for the next federal election?*

In addressing the challenge of candidate recruitment and training, the Reform Party's constituency associations and their nominating committees have been asked to "cast their net as widely as possible" by advertising the search for a Reform candidate all over the riding and consulting as widely as possible with the people in the riding about potential candidates.

Our constituency associations are supported by the executive council of the party and an administrative staff organized into four departments. These are: Finance and Administration, responsible for membership services, fund raising through Reform Fund Canada, and head office administration; Policy, Strategy, and Communications, responsible for policy research, development of issue statements, advertising, media relations, election planning, and election materials; Special Projects, responsible for expansion planning and the pre-election Assembly; and Constituency Development and Election Readiness, with direct responsibilities for support of candidate recruitment and managing the election campaign.

People who have been led to believe that the Reform Party of Canada is a one-man band with the organizational sophistication of a pink lemonade society are mistaken. People are welcome to contact members of our executive council or these various departments directly, care of the head office in Calgary, for information or assistance in knowing how to participate in the growth and development of the Reform option. As the election approaches, however, those who wish to actively support the Reform option can make their greatest contribution by contacting and assisting our constituency associations.

I deeply appreciate the efforts of people who write to me personally with policy advice, organizational proposals, and suggestions for candidates. But in the months ahead I will be telling an increasing number of these people, "If you really want to help the Reform cause, get involved with the Reform association in your federal riding. This is where the candidate recruitment will be done; this is where the election will be won or lost; this is where we need the strength and support of the best people we can find. We are not a hierarchical party; getting close to the leader or the administration is not as conducive to influencing our future course as you may suppose. You are not yet fully participating in Reform politics if you are not involved in some way at the constituency level."

Potential candidates for Reform Party nominations will be provided with the Reform Party's Candidate Questionnaire. They will then submit it to the constituency association's nominating committee, with instructions concerning how much of this information, if any, can be released to party members and to the public at large before the nominating meeting.

The questionnaire is not an "exam" that potential candidates must "pass" in order to secure a nomination. It is designed to help candidates and their families assess whether they should seek a Reform Party nomination and to enable nominating committees and participants in nominating meetings to assess potential candidates. Completion of the questionnaire is voluntary, and any Reform Party member in good standing can seek a nomination.

Besides asking for a personal résumé of the candidate, the questionnaire seeks information on the following matters: values and motivation (Why did you become a Reformer? Why do you want to run for Parliament? What are your most deeply held values?); attitudes toward Reform Party principles and policies (With which points do you agree, disagree, seek clarification or modification?); knowledge, experience, and skills that the candidate would bring to a Reform caucus; income projections (If you were elected to Parliament, would your family income and standard of living increase, decrease, or remain the same? If your income would increase, how would you defend yourself against the charge that you are running for public office for financial gain only? If your income would decrease, how would you handle the effect on your family? If your income as an MP would be supplemented by income from other sources, how would you avoid conflict of interest?); electability and acceptability to constituents, including familiarity with riding and associations with interest groups (Have you ever been identified with organizations that promote separatism or discrimination against people on the basis of race, language, colour, religion, or culture?); health and fitness; and political vulnerability (Have you ever been involved with personal or business bankruptcy, lawsuits, criminal charges, unfair labour practices, bonding, tax disputes? Would you consent to allow the Reform Party to conduct a credit check, criminal record check, and security check on you?).

The Reform Party's Candidate Questionnaire includes a lengthy section on conflict of interest, asking questions about shareholdings, employment positions, contracts, and other dealings with the government of Canada that could lead to a conflict of interest situation. This section specifically asks each potential candidate:

> Do you understand that no member of the House of Commons is to agree to receive any compensation, directly or indirectly, for services to any person in relation to any bill, proceeding, contract, claim, controversy, charge, accusation, arrest or other matter before the Senate or House of Commons or any committee of either House or in order to attempt to influence any member of either House and that the punishment for accepting such prohibited fees is a fine, ineligibility thereafter to hold any office in the public service of Canada, and disqualification as a member of the House of Commons for five years after conviction?

The questionnaire also asks, "Has your partner (if applicable) reviewed the above questions and does he or she concur with the answers given?" A line is then provided for signed acknowledgment by the spouse.

At the end of each section, the potential candidate is asked whether there is anything the Reform Party or its resource people can do to help remedy a deficiency (for example, in knowledge, skills, or experience), or to overcome a disability, or to provide help in resolving a problem (such as a potential conflict of interest, or potential financial problems occasioned by election or participation in a campaign).

The Reform Party created this questionnaire because we want the voters of Canada to trust our candidates, and this requires full disclosure. We also want the candidates to know exactly what they are getting into and to think through the implications of their decision. In particular, they should realize that any of the questions on the form might be asked by a constituent or a journalist or a political opponent during an election campaign. The questionnaire identifies potential problems and allows the Reform Party to help candidates solve them before they become political liabilities.

Canadians interested in seeing a sample of a completed Reform Party candidate questionnaire may write to our Department of Constituency Development and Election Readiness and ask for a copy of the questionnaire that I completed before being nominated as the Reform Party candidate in Calgary Southwest on March 22, 1991. In asking potential Reform Party candidates to complete this questionnaire, and to make the results public, I am not asking anyone to do something I would not be prepared to do myself.

The sceptic will say, of course, that a dishonest candidate could easily falsify the information on the questionnaire or make sure it is biased in his or her favour. This is true, but the more that information is made public, the more it will be subjected to scrutiny by others, and the more likely the truth is to emerge.

CHAPTER NINETEEN

The Road to a Healthy Economy

If you ask a broad cross-section of Canadians—young and old, skilled and unskilled—what ought to be the distinguishing feature of the New Canada, many will say, "It must be a place where I can find and hold a good job with a good income."

If you ask savers and investors what ought to be the distinguishing feature of the New Canada, they will tell you, "It must be a place that provides solid investment opportunities enabling me to earn a good rate of return."

If you ask economists and economic forecasters what ought to be the distinguishing feature of the New Canada, they will tell you, "It must be a country willing and able to take its place in a new world economic order dominated by three huge trading blocs—the European community (expanded to include the eastern European economies), the Asia-Pacific economic community, and the North American free trade area (expanded to include various Central and South American economies)."

If you ask forward-looking wealth-producers (business and labour leaders) what should be the distinguishing characteristic of a country trying to take its place in this new economic order, many will tell you, "It must be a country whose businesses and industries are financially viable, environmentally sound, and internationally competitive."

Synthesizing these responses, Reformers therefore say that New Canada must be a place where there are good jobs with good incomes, and good investment opportunities with good rates of return. And these must be generated by financially viable, environmentally sound, and internationally competitive businesses and industries and a supportive service sector.

The party's economic policy development has thus been focused—by popular demand and expert opinion—on a search for public policies that would move us toward this destination.

Many of the basic prescriptions for a healthier and more competitive Canadian economy are well known. The task of the Reform Party is to translate some of the most fundamental prescriptions for a healthier Canadian economy into terms which the man and woman on the street can understand; to present these prescriptions to as broad a cross-section of Canadians as possible, as part of the election platform of the Reform Party; and to secure the public support required to implement such measures and move this country into the economy of the twenty-first century.

Question 1: *What do you consider the single most important and immediate step toward strengthening the Canadian economy?*

I believe that reducing federal spending to the point at which it results in a lower tax burden on Canadians and reduces both the cost of living and the cost of doing business in this country, is the single most important step toward getting Canada's economic house in order.

At one time it might have been argued that "reducing public spending to the point at which taxes could be lowered" was only a concern of businesspeople. Today it is rapidly becoming a concern of all Canadians, including union members, consumers who rebel against the high tax component embedded in the price of Canadian goods and services, and even Canadians living below the poverty line.

During the last federal election, for example, I spoke at a public meeting in Port Alberni, a pulp and paper community on the west coast of Vancouver Island. A plant worker, who was also a union member, stood up during the discussion period and said, "I no longer think of payday as payday. I think of it as tax day. I am more conscious of what the government is taking out of my paycheque than I am of what's left for me and my family." For this man and thousands of workers like him, New Canada must be a place where payday is payday again.

In December 1990 I received a letter from a young woman who had moved from Atlantic Canada to central Alberta. The letter read in part:

> I am writing to you because I want you to know how much some
> of us little people need your Reform movement; and to assure you
> that your supporters are not all business people, wealthy ex-
> Conservatives, professionals, or political opportunists. You really
> are getting the support of the "grass roots" in this part of the
> country. I am twenty-five, married, the mother of one. As a
> teenager, my family moved from Newfoundland to Saskatchewan

in search of work and a better economy. Now, a decade later, my own small family must again move west in search of the same.

My husband works in——and I and my daughter live in—— ... where I am attending college. My husband earns $9.50 per hour and with that we struggle to pay rent, day care, tuition, bills, and groceries. We share a seventeen-year-old vehicle on which we both do all the repairs; we wear second-hand clothes; we use cloth diapers; we hang our clothes to dry; we make our own baby food; and we do not go out when we cannot afford it. We are well below what the current government is calling the "poverty line," but we are pretty well off compared to people fifty and sixty years ago. We have never, ever accepted any kind of welfare or government subsidy. *We live within our means and we demand as young, broke Canadians that our governments live within theirs.* [italics mine]

We work very hard, and we just want to live in a country where hard work can mean something, and a person can "make it" without government handouts, unfair taxation, supporting a pregnant bureaucracy, unreasonable interest rates, and an inequitable federal system where the concerns of my region are ignored.

The consciousness of government overspending and over-taxation reflected in comments and letters like these can be backed up with statistics on government spending, debt, and taxation.

In 1984, when the Conservatives came to power, the net federal debt was $199.1 billion, or 44.8 percent of Gross Domestic Product (GDP). By the end of 1991-92, the debt is projected to be $419.0 billion, or 59.9 percent of GDP. That is $16,000 of debt for every man, woman, and child in the country. And the primary instrument used by the Mulroney government to cope with the federal government's fiscal problem is increased taxation.

In citing these statistics, I am not saying, nor is the Reform Party saying, that the present Conservative administration is entirely responsible for the present fiscal situation of the federal government, or that it has made no effort to reduce spending. Credit should be given where credit is due. But the bottom line is that federal spending, federal debt, federal interest payments on that debt, and revenue from federal taxes will be higher next year than they were last year—and this statement has been true for many years. The federal Conservatives may not have started Canada down the Spend and Tax road, and they may honestly have tried to slow the pace, but they have not got us off that road.

Where does this road lead? It leads to ever greater restrictions on the ability of the federal government to meet the needs of Canadians. Right now, more than one-third of federal revenues must be used merely to service the debt, thereby restricting Canada's ability to provide essential services and meet new challenges, such as the cost of environmental conservation. It also leads to greater dependence on foreign capital as the national government sops up more and more of the savings of Canadians, forcing provincial governments and private borrowers to borrow outside the country. And it leads to ever-increasing taxation, reducing the competitiveness of Canadian business and inducing Canadian consumers to engage in cross-border shopping and black-market activities, or even to leave the country.

The existence of a large debt and deficit presents a standing temptation for the federal government to "inflate" its way out of the situation through unwise expansion of the money supply. This is the road to financial disaster, as various Third World countries have discovered.

The union man, the young woman living below the poverty line, and the thousands of other Canadians who have contacted the Reform Party on this issue are all saying the same thing. They are saying that if the intention is to create a New Canada, as far as they are concerned, one of its distinguishing characteristics must be "governments that live within their means." They rightly ask, "If we must live within our means, is it unreasonable to request that our governments do the same?"

Question 2: *What precisely is meant by "getting the federal government to a position where it is living within its means"?*

To the Reform Party this means balancing federal revenues and expenditures within three years of being given the opportunity to manage the government of Canada. For example, if a fiscally responsible government was elected in the fall of 1992, its first budget would be for fiscal year 1993-94, for which the government now projects a deficit of $16.6 billion on revenues of $150.5 billion. The primary objective would be to cut spending by 11 percent in three years.

In the longer term, the goal would be not only to achieve balance but also to attain sizeable surpluses, say about 3 percent of revenue. The priorities would then be first of all to apply such surpluses to reducing the national debt, and secondly to cope with "spending emergencies" such as that represented by the *en masse* retirement of baby boomers, which will begin around the year 2010.

Question 3: *What specific measures does the Reform Party propose, in order to bring the federal government to the point of living within its means?*

To achieve this objective, the Reform Party advocates "leadership by example" at the top of the government, the elimination of certain federal programs, a general downsizing of the federal bureaucracy, targeted social spending, and constitutional reforms to reinforce fiscal responsibility.

Leadership at the Top by Example
Whoever forms the government of Canada in 1992-93 should declare a state of fiscal emergency that would last until a modest surplus had been reached. This declaration should be accompanied by an immediate and clear demonstration of spending restraint at the top of the government. It should include highly visible cuts to the "three Ps" (pay, pensions, and perquisites) of cabinet ministers, deputy ministers, senators, and members of the House of Commons. The establishment of an independent commission to regulate compensation and benefits to members of Parliament, senators, deputy ministers, and cabinet ministers should be part of this process. Guidelines should include a requirement to bring benefit packages more in line with those of the private sector.

Spending restraint at the top should also include 15 percent reductions in the budgets of the House of Commons, Senate, Privy Council Office, Prime Minister's Office, and Governor General's Office. These cuts are important, not so much for the dollars they save as for the signals they send to the civil service and the public that the new leadership means business on spending restraint.

Finally, leadership from the top must include the establishment and enforcement of a clear set of federal government spending priorities. Following a suggestion from the C.D. Howe Institute,[1] I would group the federal spending priorities as follows:

1. Provision of public goods, services, and decision-making processes that are national in scope, for example, currency and money supply, defence, foreign affairs, criminal law, infrastructure.
2. Financial support of public goods and services that are best administered provincially but have important ramifications across provincial boundaries—for example, health care, advanced education, social assistance.
3. Income support (such as pensions) to guarantee a minimum standard of living.

1. Irene K. Ip, "Strong Medicine: Budgeting for Recession and Recovery," *Commentary* (C.D. Howe Institute), no. 27 (January 1991), pp. 13-14.

A Reform government would emphasize programs that fit comfortably into these categories while deleting or trimming back those that do not. If they do not fit into this list, they may still be essential activities, but they should be carried out by someone other than the federal government.

Elimination of Certain Federal Programs
Bringing the federal government to a position of living within its means will involve elimination of certain departments and programs altogether. The most obvious targets for a fiscally responsible government would be grants to special interest groups; subsidies to business, especially through regional development; subsidies to Crown corporations; federal expenditures on multiculturalism; and unnecessary bilingualism in the civil service.

Elimination of grants, handouts, and tax concessions to businesses is a big-ticket item. The following quotes from Donald Savoie's *The Politics of Public Spending* illustrate just how big:

> Especially since the early 1960s, governments have put in place a variety of incentive programs for the private sector. We have now reached the point where, in certain areas of the country at least, there is a government subsidy available for virtually every type of commercial activity. The federal government supports the private sector in numerous ways. It gives cash grants, funds federal-provincial agreements designed solely to assist the private sector, and makes tax incentives available. Other federal measures include special grants to support firms facing economic difficulties and to organizations and groups established to promote the views of the private sector.
>
> ... the federal government does commit well over $25 billion annually to the business community through cash grants, tax incentives, and a host of schemes under federal-provincial agreements. ...
>
> A former federal deputy minister of finance recently wrote: "Present expenditures in loans, grants, and subsidies, together with corporate income and sales tax expenditures, greatly exceed collections from the corporate income tax."[2]

General Downsizing of Federal Bureaucracy
Downsizing the federal government must also involve imposing a moderate across-the-board cut on *all* departments and activities of the

---

2. Donald J. Savoie, *The Politics of Public Spending in Canada* (Toronto: University of Toronto Press, 1990), pp. 290, 300, 304, 345.

federal government. This will involve reducing the thick layers of middle and upper management that characterize the federal government bureaucracy. The government of Canada currently includes about forty ministries and departments organized in a hierarchical fashion, with eight or more managerial layers in each. Excessive layering not only adds to direct costs of programs but also indirectly increases the overall cost of government by clogging decision making, eroding morale, discouraging efficiency, and diffusing accountability.

A management consultant once asked his audience to consider what might happen if the federal government took over McDonald's. McDonald's is one of the most efficient service organizations in the world—distinguished by its pancake organizational chart, which ensures that there is a relatively short distance between the person that makes the hamburger and a senior decision maker in the organization. If the federal government took over McDonald's, however, and organized it the way it organizes most federal government departments, it would no doubt appoint a deputy minister of fast foods, an assistant deputy minister for chicken burgers, an assistant deputy for fish burgers, an assistant deputy for hamburgers, a director general for mayonnaise, a director general for ketchup, a director general for chips, and so forth. Ronald McDonald would have an entire department to himself in both official languages; and while you would still get a hamburger, it would probably cost you $6.75 and take two weeks to deliver.

Since at least 60 percent of federal program spending is tied up directly or indirectly in medical care, pensions, welfare, unemployment insurance, family allowances, advanced education, and myriad smaller social programs, it is not possible to make significant cuts in federal spending without affecting those programs. The most important issue here should be to see that social spending is targeted to those who need it most and not absorbed by excessive administration or widely dissipated by providing unnecessary safety nets for those who are perfectly capable of taking care of themselves.

Fiscal Responsibility through Constitutional Reform
Reformers would also advocate a constitutional limit on unbalanced budgeting (by requiring the federal government to attain a balanced budget over a period of time or resign), provided that Canadians are prepared to adopt the requirement that "governments live within their means" as a national objective.

We propose that the Canadian constitution establish a clearer and more enforceable division of responsibility between the federal and provincial governments in social spending and the delivery of social services, and that the federal government focus on income transfers to individuals and no-strings-attached transfer payments to provinces to bring a minimum standard of social services within the financial reach of every citizen in every province. Reformers further propose that provincial governments be given wide powers to organize and administer the delivery of social services in accordance with the needs of their people.

Question 4: *Is the Reform Party going to slash pensions, medicare, veterans' allowances? How can you bring about "targeted social spending" without hurting the most vulnerable members of society?*

Social spending consumes 60 percent of the federal government's budget. Any increase in the percentage of federal spending on interest payments on the national debt will correspondingly reduce its ability to sustain these programs. The greatest threat to Canada's social service safety network (health care, pensions, and social assistance) is not attacks on these programs by fiscal conservatives; it is uncontrolled federal spending, the ever-increasing national debt, and rising interest payments, which leave fewer dollars available for the provision of essential services.

Those of us who depend in one way or another on Canada's social service safety network are like the passengers on the *Titanic*. We were guaranteed complete safety on the voyage across the sea. But as we sail merrily along, entrusting everything to the captain and the crew, we are headed toward an iceberg. The tip of the iceberg is the national deficit ($30 billion per year), the rest of it is the huge national debt in excess of $400 billion. If the *Titanic* hits that iceberg, it will tear a hole in her hull and send her to the bottom.

Reformers propose the establishment of SOS ("Save Our Safety-net") Commissions similar to the Forget Commission on unemployment insurance, which held a number of public consultations, commissioned various background studies, and produced a report for the government in 1986. The Forget Commission studied UIC, not in order to destroy the program, but to focus it more effectively on its primary function— providing short-term financial support to temporarily unemployed workers. Forget's recommendations were aimed at making UIC an insurance-based system, rather than a second-rate welfare system, and saving $3 billion per year in the process by improving its efficiency.

Similar commissions should be established to look at the funding of medicare, pensions, social assistance, family allowance, and similar social programs in order to preserve the essence of these programs and target the resources available for social spending to those who need it most. These SOS Commissions should complement efforts to downsize federal government departments and agencies.

Some public opinion surveys indicate that Canadians are most committed to conserving the universality of two social programs—medicare and the Canada Pension Plan. If this is in fact the case, then it may be that Canadians are prepared to accept major organizational changes and even deeper cuts in other social spending areas, in order to conserve the universality of higher priority programs. Such preference could be incorporated into the terms of reference of the appropriate SOS commissions.

If, however, the *Titanic* hits the iceberg, the most vulnerable among us— those who have no alternative safety nets whatsoever—must be helped into the life jackets and the lifeboats first. The social security of the crew (the administrators of social programs) must not be the first priority, and the crew must not be allowed to hijack the lifeboats, as often happens in attempts to downsize social service bureaucracies.

Question 5: *What encouragement or incentive can Reformers provide to Canadians to induce them to support control of federal spending?*

If Canadians are to support the painful efforts necessary to get the federal government's fiscal house in order and to reverse the spiral toward ever-increasing spending and taxation, there must be some visible and tangible reward at the end of the tunnel. That reward should be a lowering of personal and business tax levels, and the tax component of prices charged on goods and services, as well as a generally stronger, more competitive economy offering good jobs with good incomes.

Question 6: *Won't your proposals to downsize the federal bureaucracy involve throwing thousands of civil servants onto the streets or welfare rolls? How can you possibly expect to secure civil service cooperation, or cooperation from organized labour generally, for such a policy?*

In cutting back on bureaucracy, our first approach will be to appeal to federal civil servants who recognize the need for these measures to identify themselves early, to participate in the exercise, and to help us develop transition programs to move public-sector workers to more productive employment in the non-governmental sector.

The Reform Party has already received many letters from present and retired federal civil servants providing examples of waste and mismanagement in the public sector, but more importantly, providing suggestions for improvement in services and the use of taxpayers' dollars. Many conscientious public servants are just as frustrated by administrative overburden and the waste of taxpayers' dollars as you are. These people are part of the solution, not part of the problem, and they must be identified and listened to.

Canada needs large-scale transition programs to help civil servants move from underemployment in the public sector to more productive employment in the non-governmental sector. Agreements among industry, labour, and government will be needed to refinance, retool, retrain, and relocate workers and capital from one sector to another. Federal public servants are being asked to pioneer the type of adjustment agreements required to move Canadian workers from insecure positions in the economy of Old Canada to more productive positions in the economy of New Canada.

Downsizing the federal government so that it can live within its means will involve recruiting a significant number of key people from the non-governmental sector. I have asked my own contacts in the non-governmental sector to identify at least one hundred large organizations in Canada that have undergone downsizings of over 15 percent in the last ten years, and to provide the names of key executives, consultants, and union people involved in those exercises.

Over the next year and a half, my staff and I will contact these people, encourage them to study equivalent units within the federal government, and ask them to consider coming to Ottawa at some future date as part of a fiscal emergency team to implement spending control and downsizing measures. The difference between this team and the Nielsen Program Review Task Force established by the Mulroney government in 1984 is that it will be asked not simply to suggest spending controls and downsizing proposals, but also to help implement them.

Question 7: *How will the Reform Party help non-government workers adjust to the economy of New Canada?*

Canada requires broadly based labour force adjustment mechanisms to help move workers and capital from one industrial sector to another in response to changing market conditions and the effects of trade liberalization.

The position of the Canadian worker at the end of the twentieth century is like that of the old voyageurs who travelled the rivers of Canada. When they encountered waterfalls and stretches of rough water they sometimes had to make *les petits portages*—to haul the canoes from the river, carry them around the obstacle, and then refloat the canoes farther downstream on the same river. Unemployment insurance helps workers make *les petits portages* by getting them around relatively small and temporary disturbances in the labour market that do not require them to make a fundamental or long-term change in direction.

Sometimes, however, it was necessary for the voyageurs to make *le grand portage* in order to move from one river system to a completely different one. A voyageur travelling across the prairies on the Saskatche-wan River system who wanted to go north to the Mackenzie Delta had to haul the canoes out of the water east of Fort Edmonton and pack them down a rough trail over ninety miles to the Athabasca River, and then continue the journey. There are Canadian workers who will be forced by circumstances beyond the control of Canada to make *le grand portage* if they are to get to the New Canada—public service workers who will need to shift to the non-governmental sector to find more productive employ-ment; and private-sector workers who will have to shift from one type of employment to another as the forces of international competition and trade render old activities and jobs uncompetitive.

The training of workers in Canada currently takes place in many different ways: formal education in schools and universities, apprentice-ship programs in industry, informal job experience, formal instruction on the job, and formal training programs sponsored by government. Apprenticeship and job experience are controlled by the private sector, while schools and universities are under provincial jurisdiction. The role for the federal government in all of this is quite restricted. It is chiefly to fund job training and retraining programs that are usually provided by provincial schools and community colleges.

Although the Canadian university system has its problems, it is proba-bly second only to the American university system as a source of highly qualified, adaptable human resources for a free-market economy. In this respect, it is unquestionably superior to the British, German, French, and Italian university systems, all of which are burdened with an ancient tradition of training government officials, rather than productive entre-preneurs and employees.

Our job-training system, in contrast, is one of the worst among highly developed nations—sixteenth out of twenty-three, according to one recent study.[3] Countries such as Switzerland and Germany, which are renowned for efficient job training, train every young person aged fifteen to eighteen who is not enrolled in school or university. Our approach is often remedial. We tend to let young people drop out of school, wander around the labour market developing bad habits, and then try to retrain them after they have become chronically unemployed. Moreover, too much of Canadian job training takes place in educational institutions and not enough in the workplace. The money spent in this way becomes an important source of revenue for the institutions, thus promoting a climate of bureaucratic conservatism. Not surprisingly, students often end up in training for occupations for which there are no jobs.[4]

Solving these problems will entail a much greater and more direct role for business and labour and an expanded role for the federal government in job training and economic education, particularly in arranging for the support of workers in transition.

Question 8: *How can you expect business to support a program to reduce federal spending if that involves "elimination of grants, handouts, and tax concessions" to private corporations?*

The choice for private-sector decision makers is this: either accept continual increases in federal spending, debt, and taxation, or support spending reductions, including drastic reductions in federal grants and tax concessions to business, which will help lower taxation levels.

From my past experience and extensive contacts with private-sector decision makers, I believe that the majority would support the latter course, if they were convinced that reductions in federal grants and tax concessions to business would be made across the board—without exceptions that would give one sector or company an unfair advantage over another.

Most private-sector decision makers know that some sector that is currently a heavy-duty recipient of federal spending must take the lead in "taking less" from the federal government. Unless business leaders agree to accept major reductions in federal grants, handouts, and tax

3. IMD, *World Competitiveness Report,* 1990, cited in "Competitiveness and Productivity," *Economic Analysis of British Columbia,* July 25, 1991.

4. *Report of the Commission of Inquiry on Unemployment Insurance* (Forget Commission Report) (Ottawa: Ministry of Supply and Services, 1986), p. 141.

concessions to private corporations, there is not a ghost of a chance of getting Canadians to agree to a reform of federal spending on other big-ticket items such as social spending.

Question 9: *How do you propose to prevent reductions in federal spending and a downsizing of the federal government from inadvertently plunging the country into a politically manufactured recession?*

Fiscal policy must be coordinated with monetary policy. Under the Conservative administration, with its irresponsible fiscal policy, inflationary tendencies have been countered by a restrictive monetary policy enforced by the Bank of Canada. As ten of Canada's most prominent economists pointed out in 1984, this mix can be reversed. The deflationary effects of a transition to balanced budgets can be offset by a more expansionist monetary policy.[5] Lower interest rates would also reduce the burden of the deficit on federal revenues. However, this initiative must be undertaken with care. Overexpansion of the money supply could lead to inflation, which would push interest rates up again after a short lag, and the burden of the deficit would be worse than ever.

In 1988, when the Mulroney government began to realign Canada's trade policy in the Canada-United States free trade agreement, it failed to realign the corresponding monetary and fiscal policies. In the critical early stages of the free trade agreement, the Bank of Canada pursued an interest rate policy that put our interest rates up to five percentage points higher than those of our American competitors. We started to realign our tax policy by replacing the federal Manufacturers' Sales Tax with the unnecessarily complicated and expensive Goods and Services Tax, but we did not realign our spending policy, so that the overall tax burden falling on the Canadian manufacturer and producer is still much higher than the tax burden carried by many of our competitors.

The main focus of the Reform Party's platform is on measures to reduce federal spending and taxation in absolute terms, and on proposals for regionally sensitizing national policies through Senate and parliamentary reform. With respect to monetary policy, Reformers support a truly national policy, characterized by a slow but steady growth in the money supply. The Reform Party supports the proposition that a principal policy objective of the Bank of Canada should be the control of inflation, although it questions the practicality of immediately embracing zero

---

5. Peter Dungan and Thomas Wilson, "Altering the Fiscal-Monetary Policy Mix: Credible Policies to Reduce the Federal Deficit," *Canadian Tax Journal* 33 (1985), pp. 309-18.

inflation as a national goal. Lower, more competitive interest and exchange rates should be the product of sound fiscal policy, not money printing.

In spite of the populist heritage of the Reform Party, it does not support policies of easy money, repudiation of public debts, or deliberate inflation.

Question 10: *You have been quoted as saying, "Canadians are not going to win economically, on the road or anywhere else, unless we begin to pull together at home." What do you mean by this statement?*

In 1971, Hockey Canada negotiated an agreement between Canada and the Soviet Union to enable Canada's best professional hockey players to compete against the Soviets' best in an eight-game series. Most Canadians welcomed the agreement, confident that Team Canada could beat the Soviets as long as the rules were fair. In September 1972, however, that confidence was badly shaken when the Soviets won the first game in Montreal. Team Canada won the second in Toronto, but the game in Winnipeg was tied, and the Soviets triumphed decisively in Vancouver. The remaining games were to be played in Moscow.

I was at that game in Vancouver, at which frustrated fans booed a frustrated Team Canada almost constantly toward the end of the game. In his book *Home Game*, Team Canada's goalie, Ken Dryden, described the national reaction:

> Hockey had always been a symbol for Canadians of what we wanted to be. Now it seemed just another symbol of what we really were. Our hockey, built on natural resources—cold and ice—and exported south beyond our control, after a decades-long head start, had been caught by those who had added human resources, science, and system, to make something more advanced. All the stereotypes others held of us, and we held of ourselves, were confirmed. A spasm of self-hatred shook the country.

After the Vancouver game, Phil Esposito, the captain of Team Canada, was interviewed on national television. He spoke about disappointment, about what it takes to win on the road, and about the importance of pulling together at home. Ken Dryden vividly describes the scene:

> He was sad and weary and hurt and angry and every bit of every one of those emotions was there on his face and in his voice.

He was standing before millions of people who in their living rooms had been booing him and his team just as loudly as the fans had done in Vancouver, who were furious that their team, their high-paid superstars, in a series that mattered so much to them, were not trying and did not care. . . .

It was an incredible visual moment. He pleaded, he explained, he lectured, he seemed never less than fair. But it was that sad-eyed, washed-out face, bathed with the sweat of the world, that penetrated those millions of living rooms and hit like a bomb. Anger and disappointment remained, but now there was guilt as well. *It was time to pull together.* [italics mine][6]

The story, as every Canadian knows, had a happy ending. Somehow Team Canada pulled itself together, went over to Moscow, and won three out of four games, with the winning goal scored by Paul Henderson in the last game with less than one minute to play.

What caused the turnaround? There are many explanations, but Ken Dryden traces it back to that "speech" given by captain Phil Esposito after the disastrous Vancouver game, which said, in essence: "Canadians are not going to win on the road, or anywhere else, until they learn to pull together at home."

This basic lesson applies to Canada's economic performance. Many Canadians seem to think that our business teams (composed of investors, managers, workers, and contractors) can't win in the new free trade league. They see plant closures and job loss (much of it resulting from the recession and not the Free Trade Agreement) and assume that since we've lost the first game, we're going to lose the series. They argue that we should go back to the good old days of tariffs and government protection for Canadian business and industry—that there should be one set of rules for the home team and another set of rules for the visiting team. But that system won't work anymore (if it ever did) because as a trading nation we need trading partners, and they won't accept protectionist rules any longer.

Canada must stop penalizing its economic players at home. More than five hundred interprovincial barriers to trade—barriers that we have erected ourselves—cost Canadian taxpayers and consumers more than $6 billion annually,[7] further reducing our international competitiveness.

6. Ken Dryden and Roy MacGregor, *Home Game: Hockey and Life in Canada* (Toronto: McClelland & Stewart Inc., 1989), pp. 206-7.
7. *Canada in 1993: A Plan for the Creation of a Single Market in Canada,* Canadian Manufacturers' Association, April 1991.

The Canadian trucking industry, for example, is saddled with such barriers as different licensing requirements in different provinces, variations in safety restrictions, and punitive fuel and sales taxes.

Obsolete practices in labour-management relations, education, and manpower training make it more difficult rather than easier for Canadian business and labour to adjust to trade liberalization. Constitutional and political uncertainties of our own making repel rather than attract needed investment capital. And excessive public spending has resulted in tax and price levels that render our businesses uncompetitive, driving both businesses and shoppers across the Canada-United States border by the thousands.

Reformers are realists. Common sense—the common sense of the common people—tells us there is no magic policy fix that will automatically make the Canadian economy more productive and competitive, or ensure that we will continue to have one of the highest standards of living in the world.

But if we could start to pull together at home—reforming public spending so that governments live within their means, removing internal barriers to trade and labour-force transition, reforming our constitutional arrangements and political institutions to reduce domestic uncertainty—Reformers believe New Canada will be internationally competitive and able to "win on the road."

CHAPTER TWENTY

Will You Make
New Canada Your Home?

As leader of the Reform Party of Canada, I want to challenge Canadians, to challenge you, to leave Old Canada for New Canada—to start down the road that leads away from the Old and towards the New.

Canadians should be as well equipped as any people on earth to accept this challenge. In the background of virtually every one of us there is someone—an ancestor, a relative, a friend—who had to make exactly that decision once before: the decision to leave the old country with all its ties and all its liabilities, to emigrate to the new world with all its uncertainties and all its potential for a better life. There are already among us people whom we call, and who often call themselves, "new Canadians"— landed immigrants and citizens who have recently come to this country.

It is useful, in constructing our definition of New Canada, to ask these new Canadians, for whom Canada is already a "new land," what it is they thought they were coming to when they decided to leave the "old country" for this one. I have never yet heard a new Canadian say, "I came here to get in on the French-English partnership," despite the fact that this is the government of Canada's official definition of Canada. New Canadians say that they came here to get a fresh start, for economic and educational opportunities, and for freedoms for themselves and their children that were often denied them in the lands from which they came.

A Canadian is by definition someone whose heritage includes an acceptance of the challenge to leave an old country for a new one. Even among our aboriginal peoples there is the legend of the "long journey" when they too came here from somewhere else. And our generation must make a similar decision—whether to remain in Old Canada, which we can do by doing nothing, or to set our feet firmly on the road that leads to New Canada.

Demographic studies of the people who have so far joined the Reform movement in Canada indicate that many of them are self-employed— farmers, small businesspeople, professionals—people with pioneering backgrounds and instincts who are willing to become political pioneers as well. These studies also indicate that many Reformers are seniors who, when asked why at their ages they would leave their traditional party homes for a new one, say, "To provide a better economic and political future for our children and our grandchildren."

To elect Reformers to the House of Commons in sufficient numbers to lay the constitutional, fiscal, and parliamentary foundations of New Canada, the Reform Party must continue to broaden its base. This means broadening our appeal to youth, women, members of ethnic minorities, and the large numbers of Canadians across the entire demographic spectrum who have "opted out" of federal political involvement altogether.

Because I am the father of five children now ranging in ages from twelve to twenty-three, I tend to relate to younger people in much the same way that I would to my own children. Sandra and I do not try to tell our own children how to live their lives, although we share our values and visions with them, more by example than by explicit instruction. We feel that our primary responsibility toward them is to provide them with acceptance, roots, and wings. This is precisely what a new political movement must provide to the younger generation of Canadians.

Therefore, I sincerely invite younger people to become Reformers. In eastern European countries and in China, the schools and universities are the strongholds of the democratic reform movements. Reformers say to younger Canadians that the party's mission in the 1990s will be to "fix the foundations"—a deficient constitution, a deficient parliament, and a deficit approach to public spending, which, if uncorrected, will leave your generation with a crushing load of debt and taxation. If we do get the chance to fix the foundations, then it is your generation of Reformers who will be able to stretch your wings and truly build the New Canada of the twenty-first century.

To women, many of whom are seeking a new and more active role in politics, Reform offers the same opportunities as the old Progressive movement offered to Agnes Campbell Macphail, the first female member of Parliament, and to many other pioneers of the women's movement in Canada. It wasn't because the Progressives' platform was "feminist" that the party helped so many women break into politics. It was simply because it was new. It needed good people to fill its committees, task forces, constituency organizations, and candidate lists—and if people were willing and able, and had the interest and talents to do the job, there were few questions asked about ethnicity, gender, or experience.

If there is common ground between the Reform movement and the mainstream of the women's movement in Canada, it is on the issue of "fairness." The Reform movement also faces the same danger as the women's movement, namely that of being hijacked by fringe groups who would discredit it, just as feminist extremists would hijack the women's movement and discredit it with the rest of the population. The Reform Party of Canada is a potential political home for women with traditional values and for those who want more fairness in male-female relations, but not for those who carry any of these values and concerns to extremes.

To members of ethnic minorities, I have acknowledged that you are already New Canadians in the sense of having left an old country for a new, and I urge you to share the nature, emotion, and importance of that decision with others. To those of you who are of neither French nor English extraction, I especially say, "You are not only welcome in the Reform Party, your presence and support is essential to 'tip the balance' in Canada toward a new constitutional and political order."

The leaders and spokespersons of the traditional federal parties will tell you that the Reform Party is racist, that it stands for an all-white or English-only Canada, and that it is anti-immigrant and anti-immigration. All of these statements are lies.

What those parties want to keep you from discovering is that *the Reform Party of Canada is the only federal party that stands for abandoning the definition of Canada as an "equal partnership between the French and the English"—a definition that relegates you to the status of second-class citizens—* and moving to a definition of Canada as a federation of equals, regardless of race, language, and culture.

What the federal Conservatives, Liberals, and New Democrats fear is that if the twelve million Canadians of neither French nor English extraction ever discover the essence of the Reform Party's constitutional, cultural, and immigration policies—and vote for that option in large numbers in the next federal election—the French-English model, and the special status that it confers upon its political guardians, will be gone forever.

Finally, to those who have opted out of involvement in federal politics altogether, I offer you a positive and a negative incentive to reinvolve yourselves. The positive incentive is the existence of a fresh political vehicle, to be represented by trustworthy, able, and reform-oriented candidates seeking your active support. The negative incentive is simply to remind you of that iron law of politics the world over, that those who fail to involve themselves in the politics of their country are destined to be governed by those who do.

From what I know and have experienced of our Canadian psyche, there are at least three psychological obstacles to overcome if we are truly to set foot on the road to New Canada. One is represented by the fears and insecurities of our political adolescence. The second is the tendency toward narrowness and pettiness of political vision which plagues so much of our politics. And the third is the negative influence of those who say, "It cannot be done."

In order to leave Old Canada it will be necessary for Canadians—Quebeckers, English-speaking Canadians, even Reformers—to abandon the fears and insecurities of our political adolescence.

In the case of the Québécois, this will mean leaving behind the notion that Quebec has been and continues to be victimized by English Canada, and that only special status or independence or some other formula for cultural salvation will transform it from victim to victor. There was a time when Quebec had good reason to fear the English, but that was during Quebec's political childhood and adolescence. Surely the time has come to put away the fears of the past. We are told these days that the Québécois have developed a new self-confidence and optimism, and I earnestly hope that is true. The New Quebec will never emerge as a secure and prosperous part of New Canada if it continues to carry that old cross.

Lest we think that the fears and insecurities of political adolescence present a problem only in Quebec, let us frankly acknowledge that the rest of Canada has suffered from a similar syndrome. Only in our case, it is the Americans that we have been told to fear. If our economy isn't working, it's the Americans who have ruined it. If our culture is anaemic, it's the Americans who are to blame. If our constitutional arrangements fall apart, it's the Americans who will get us in the end.

Anyone who watches CBC TV or listens to Mel Hurtig or Audrey McLaughlin or Bob White knows what I am talking about. There is a whole school of Canadian academics, media personalities, and politicians whose definition of a Canadian is a North American who fears or dislikes the United States. This is largely a hangup left over from our political adolescence, and unless we grow out of it, we'll never make it to New Canada.

Even within the Reform Party itself, we have people who display some of the fears and insecurities of political immaturity. Some of us still give the impression that we resent any kind of constituted authority, even the constituted authority of grassroots democracy, and we challenge any decision by the duly elected officers of our constituency or party as top-down interference. Some of us still apparently feel threatened by the influx of new members and supporters with new ideas and talents sometimes greater than our own. We're afraid that growth may dilute our own influence, or threaten our chances to get that executive position or candidacy that we had our eye on. Some of us see these signs and problems in our constituencies, but rather than step forward and remedy them by bold and direct democratic action, we shrink back and do nothing, or we ask the leader's office to fix them.

All of these fears and difficulties are understandable, and are part of the growing pains of any new political party. But they are also the hallmarks of political childhood and adolescence. How can we ask our fellow Canadians to leave their political fears and insecurities behind if we still cling to our own?

The second psychological barrier to be overcome on the road to New Canada is narrowness and pettiness of political vision. F.W.G. Haultain, the last premier of the old North West Territories and a statesman with a vision as vast as the West itself, used two simple phrases to describe the different perspectives that he found among the people and the politicians of his day. This was before 1905, when westerners were debating whether the prairies should remain one big province to counterbalance Ontario and Quebec, or whether the prairie region should allow itself to be divided into three provinces as some of the politicians wanted to do. Haultain was in favour of one big province, and he coined the phrases "Big Westerners" and "Little Westerners" to describe the two perspectives on this issue.

Little Westerners, he said, were inward-looking. Their vision was narrow and parochial. They wanted the West carved into smaller pieces so there would be more government positions and patronage to go around. They were provincialists and even potential secessionists, for whom province was more important than country, and for whom their position in the politics of the day was more important than the place of the West in confederation or the place of Canada in the world. Big Westerners, on the other hand, took a broader, more long-range view. They were just as devoted to the West as the Little Westerners, but they saw the solutions to the West's problems in a fairer, stronger federal system, not in division and balkanization. They were even prepared to sacrifice their own positions in the political system to secure a better long-term deal for the West in confederation.

Haultain was years ahead of his time. His prediction that a divided West would be a politically impotent West came true. And his demand that westerners distinguish between Big Westerners and Little Westerners in their political leadership is still relevant today.

There are, today, federal and provincial politicians in the West who are essentially Little Westerners. They want to take advantage of the current troubles in confederation to strengthen their own power bases. Their only response to Quebec's demands for more powers is to say, "We want the same." If Quebec secedes, Little Westerners will recommend that the West follow suit. If their voices are heeded and their leadership accepted, we'll never get to New Canada. Old Canada will be succeeded, not by New Canada, but by disintegration into provincial fragments that will eventually be drawn into the American orbit.

Narrowness and pettiness of political vision is not, of course, confined to western Canada. There are little Ontarians, *les petits Québécois*, Little Maritimers, Little Newfoundlanders, and Little Canadians. The Little Canadians include those whose vision of Canada cannot transcend the old Upper-Lower Canada model of an equal partnership between the French and the English. Their constitutional mindset was born on the Plains of Abraham and will be buried there. The Little Canadians include people whose vision of Canada is defined in terms of "not American," or who have brought themselves to believe that the essence of Canadianism is government enterprise and a Social Insurance Number. If we look to such people for leadership in the hour of Canada's constitutional crisis, we will never get to New Canada. We might as well just curl up in the snow and let the chill winds of constitutional deadlock, negative nationalism, and executive federalism freeze us to death.

Canada needs leadership which can transcend this narrowness and pettiness of vision. Genuine Reformers, especially constitutional Reformers, must be drawn from the ranks of Big Westerners, Big Ontarians, *les grands Québécois*, Big Newfoundlanders, and Big Maritimers—the Big Canadians capable of envisioning, creating, and sustaining the New Canada.

Finally, there are the obstacles put up by those who will say, "You can't get to New Canada from Old Canada; it cannot be done." A dozen countries in eastern Europe may be writing new constitutions and reorganizing their economies, but these people say it can't be done in

Canada. The Berlin wall can be torn down, but these people say we'll never be able to tear down the walls that separate Quebec from the rest of Canada or that separate region from region. Other countries can reform their constitutions through constitutional conventions, democratize autocratic institutions, and replace tired old political parties with new ones, but that's not the Canadian way and it can't be done here. To get to New Canada, the first barrier we need to overcome is this type of negative thinking.

The carriers of this psychological virus are not new to the Canadian scene. These are the same type of people who said to Cartier and Champlain, "You'll never get to the New World, you'll fall off the edge." They said to the first French and English settlers, "You'll never survive; you won't last the first winter." They said to Alexander Mackenzie, "You'll never get to the Pacific or the Arctic, you'll drown or freeze to death or turn back." They said to Sir John A. Macdonald, "You can't build a railway across the continent, you can't get across the Canadian Shield, and you'll never get through the Rockies." They said, "You can't grow grain on the Canadian prairies, the season's too short," or, "You can't get oil out of tar sand, it simply can't be done."

Old Canada was built in defiance of those who said it couldn't be done, and New Canada will be built in defiance of the same voices, no matter how loud they are or what positions they hold.

I close, therefore, by asking you the questions that I intend to ask every Canadian who will listen over the next two years:

- Can we define a New Canada to replace the Old Canada that is dying? Are you personally willing to participate in this process?
- Can we leap the psychological barriers of childish fears, narrow vision, and negativism, and for once in our lives conduct ourselves like Big Canadians worthy of this vast land we call our home?
- Can we get on the road to New Canada by the next federal election, by electing Big Canadians to the next Parliament? Are you willing to support the Reform option and a Reform candidate?

If enough Canadians show the resolve and enthusiasm that has energized the Reform Party of Canada to date—if enough of our fellow Canadians will not only say, "Yes we can!" but "Yes we will!"—then New Canada is much closer than we imagine.

Invitation to Communicate

To correspond with Preston Manning or to get more information on the principles, platform, and personnel of the Reform Party of Canada, please contact:

Reform Party of Canada
#600, 833—4th Avenue S.W.
Calgary, Alberta T2P 0K5
phone (403) 269-1990
fax (403) 269-4077

Appendix I

Reform Party of Canada Statement of Principles[1]

1. We affirm the need to establish a Triple-E Senate in the Parliament of Canada—that is to say, a Senate which is Elected by the people, with Equal representation from each Province, and which is fully Effective in safeguarding regional interests.

2. We affirm that political parties should be guided by stated values and principles which are shared by their members and rooted in the political beliefs of Canadians.

3. We believe in dynamic and constructive change—in a renewal of the "reform tradition" of Canadian politics.

4. We believe that Canada's identity and vision for the future should be rooted in and inspired by a fresh appreciation of "our land" and the supreme importance to our well-being of exploring, developing, renewing, and conserving our natural resources and physical environment.

5. We believe that the people of Canada are this country's most valuable resource, and that the nurture and development of human knowledge, skills, and relationships are the keys to full participation in the knowledge-based service economy of the twenty-first century.

6. We affirm the value and dignity of the individual person and the importance of strengthening and protecting the family unit as essential to the well-being of individuals and society.

7. We believe that every individual, group, province, and region in Canada is entitled to fundamental justice, and that fundamental justice entitles the people of each region to benefit equally, without discrimination, from participation in Confederation and from the programs and expenditures of the Government of Canada.

8. We believe in the value of enterprise and initiative, and that governments have a responsibility to foster and protect an environment in which initiative and enterprise can be exercised by individuals and groups.

9. We believe that the creation of wealth and productive jobs for Canadians is best achieved through the operations of a responsible, broadly based, free-enterprise economy in which private property, freedom of contract, and the operations of free markets are encouraged and respected.

---

1. *Reform Party of Canada Principles and Policies 1991*, pp. 1-4.

10. We believe that Canadians have a personal and collective responsibility to care and provide for the basic needs of people who are unable to care and provide for themselves.

11. We believe in freedom of conscience and religion, and the right of Canadians to advocate, without fear of intimidation or suppression, public policies which reflect their most deeply held values.

12. We believe that public policy in democratic societies should reflect the will of the majority of the citizens as determined by free and fair elections, referendums, and the decisions of legally constituted and representative Parliaments and Assemblies elected by the people.

13. We believe that the interest of minorities and the people of the underpopulated regions of Canada should be safeguarded by constitutional guarantees and parliamentary institutions which effectively balance representation by population with regional representation.

14. We believe in the common sense of the common people, their right to be consulted on public policy matters before major decisions are made, their right to choose their own leaders and to govern themselves through truly representative and responsible institutions, and their right to directly initiate legislation for which substantial public support is demonstrated.

15. We believe in accountability of elected representatives to the people who elect them, and that the duty of elected members to their constituents should supersede their obligations to their political parties.

16. We believe that the legitimate role of government is to do for people whatever they need to have done, but cannot do at all—or do as well—for themselves individually or through non-governmental organizations.

17. We believe in public service—that governments, civil servants, politicians, and political parties exist to serve the people, and that they should demonstrate this service commitment at all times.

18. We believe that public money should be regarded by governments as "funds held in trust," and that governments should practise fiscal responsibility—in particular, the responsibility to balance expenditures and revenues.

19. We affirm our commitment to the rule of the law, and to the concept that governments and law-makers are not above the law.

20. We believe that Canada's conduct in international as well as domestic affairs should be consistent with the above principles.

21. We believe that Canadians should seek to maximize the benefits of our unique geographic and economic relationship with the United States, and that the establishment of more positive relations with the United States need not in any way impair Canada's national sovereignty or cultural identity.

APPENDIX II

Reform Candidates in the 1988 Federal General Election

British Columbia

(candidates in 30 of 32 ridings)

Burnaby-Kingsway—John Soanes
Capilano-Howe Sound—Neil Thompson
Cariboo-Chilcotin—Diane Johnson
Comox-Alberni—Gary Hein
Delta—John Cummins
Esquimalt-Juan de Fuca—William Cronkhite
Fraser Valley East—Ray Renwick
Fraser Valley West—John Russell Walsh
Kamloops—Ted Maskell
Kootenay East—Minnie Pearl Wilder
Mission-Coquitlam—Donald Sherling
Nanaimo-Cowichan—George Richard Wrean
New Westminster-Burnaby—Bill Anderson
North Island-Powell River—Dodd Pellant
North Vancouver—Ron Gamble
Okanagan Centre—Werner Schmidt
Okanagan-Shuswap—Donald McDonnell
Okanagan-Similkameen-Merritt—Ron Amos
Port Moody-Coquitlam—Bligh Stockwell
Prince George-Bulkley Valley—Svend Serup
Prince George-Peace River—Jay Hill
Richmond—Stuart Gilbertson
Saanich-Gulf Islands—Bob Slavik
Skeena—Don Buckland
Surrey North—Ray Herd
Surrey-White Rock—Val Meredith
Vancouver Centre—Paula Folkard
Vancouver Quadra—J. R. (Jack) Ford
Vancouver South—Don Evans
Victoria—Terry Volb

Alberta

(candidates in 26 of 26 ridings)

Athabasca—Betty Lebsack
Beaver River—Deborah Grey
Calgary Centre—John A. Hamilton
Calgary North—Murray Smith
Calgary Northeast—Stewart Larsen
Calgary Southeast—Gerry Maloney
Calgary Southwest—Janet Jessop
Calgary West—Steve Harper
Crowfoot—Jack Ramsay
Edmonton East—Elaine Sim
Edmonton North—Erich Bier
Edmonton Northwest—Paul Sherstan
Edmonton Southeast—Wes McLeod
Edmonton Southwest—Chuck Cripps
Edmonton-Strathcona—Doug Main
Elk Island—Dennis Tindall
Lethbridge—Phil Connolly
Macleod—Ken Copithorne
Medicine Hat—Larry Samcoe
Peace River—Daniel H. Fletcher
Red Deer—Michael Roth
St. Albert—Ken Allred
Vegreville—Sam Herman
Wetaskiwin—Jim Henderson
Wild Rose—Dal Brown
Yellowhead—Preston Manning

Saskatchewan

(candidates in 4 of 14 ridings)

The Battlefords-Meadow Lake—Ted Quist
Kindersley-Lloydminster—Elwin Hermanson
Mackenzie—John Froese
Prince Albert-Churchill River—Ken Suitor

Manitoba

(candidates in 12 of 14 ridings)

Brandon-Souris—Henry Carroll
Dauphin-Swan River—Peter J. Neufeld
Lisgar-Marquette—Roy McLaren
Portage-Interlake—Alan Beachell
Provencher—Lawrence A. Feilberg
St. Boniface—Gordon G. Duncan
Selkirk—Terrance Petty
Winnipeg North—Ritchie W. Gural
Winnipeg North Centre—Dennis Atamanchuk
Winnipeg St. James—Lloyd E. Kirkham
Winnipeg South—Gary Cummings
Winnipeg South Centre—Ross Malabar

Agricultural Policy[1]

A. The Reform Party seeks an agricultural policy that is frank and honest in facing up to the economic realities confronting Canadian agriculture, namely:
   - that the consumer interest in safe, affordable, secure food supplies will eventually guide and shape agricultural policy;
   - that there is increasing need, both internationally and domestically, to reduce rather than increase government subsidization of agriculture, due to the inability of governments and the community at large to finance such subsidization in the long run; and
   - that there is a need for transitional support to protect agricultural producers against policies over which they have no control, including international subsidies that increase supplies and depress prices.

B. The Reform Party believes that the Canadian agricultural producer should offer the rest of the world and the rest of the country a deal leading to a step-by-step reduction of government agricultural support at home and abroad if other economic sectors and our trading partners will do the same. This would result in a general improvement in export prices and a general lowering of the cost of doing business for primary producers.

C. The Reform Party supports a Trade Distortion Adjustment Program to compensate for the adverse effect of subsidies by other countries. The fund would be activated on the total volume of Canadian commodities that have historically relied on the export market. This fund could be subject to a sunset provision.

D. In the event that international trade liberalization cannot be achieved in agriculture, the Reform Party supports No-Proof-of-Injury Countervailing Duties on any subsidized competing product coming into the Canadian market. The countervail would be extended to include secondary products that are manufactured or derived from a subsidized primary product.

E. The Reform Party supports the establishment of a voluntary self-funded and self-administered Income Averaging Fund for all agricultural producers. This safety-net plan would operate in a way similar to an RRSP, but with appropriate guidelines and restrictions.

F. The Reform Party supports vigorous measures to ensure competition and to severely penalize price collusion in the markets in which farmers buy and sell.

G. The Reform Party supports an agricultural policy based on market mechanisms with the objective of meeting the needs of consumers for safe, affordable, and secure supplies of food. Where circumstances allow, this would mean a shift from a government-supported agricultural industry to an industry shaped by the free operation of comparative advantage between regions and commodities, free entry into all sectors of production and marketing, and free trade on a global basis.

H. If other domestic sectors and countries will do the same, the Reform Party supports the phased reduction and elimination of all subsidies, support programs, and trade restrictions, and the reform of supply/price controls in domestic and international agriculture. This would apply to the production and marketing of both agricultural commodities and agricultural inputs.

I. The Reform Party supports the phased reduction of the subsidy on grain and oilseeds in the Western Grain Transportation Act (Crow subsidy) and the Feed Freight Assistance Program, with the marketplace eventually paying all of the transportation costs.

1. *Reform Party of Canada Principles and Policies 1991*, pp. 15-17.

INDEX